Soccer
FAQ

Soccer
FAQ

All That's Left to Know About the Clubs, the Players, and the Rivalries

Dave Thompson

Backbeat
Books

An Imprint of Hal Leonard Corporation

Published in 2015 by Backbeat Books
An Imprint of Hal Leonard Corporation
7777 West Bluemound Road
Milwaukee, WI 53213

Trade Book Division Editorial Offices
33 Plymouth St., Montclair, NJ 07042

All images are from the author's collection except where noted.
Images on pages 2, 260, 264, 296, and 301 are from Getty Images.

The FAQ series was conceived by Robert Rodriguez and developed with Stuart Shea.

Printed in the United States of America

Book design adapted by John J. Flannery

Library of Congress Cataloging-in-Publication Data is available upon request.

ISBN 978-1-61713-598-9

www.backbeatbooks.com

To Louis Burgess—student, statistician,
and all-round devotee of the game at every level

Contents

Author's Note
Some Words on Usage

Soccer is an international sport, possessed of an international language. Yet there are many words that, meaning one thing to an American reader, will mean another to a British one. And something else, perhaps, to a Canadian or an Australian.

In the interests of clarity, the vocabulary in this book errs on the side of American English, but will inevitably lapse into Transatlantica.

The game, for the most part, is referred to as "soccer"—a Victorian English word dating from the sport's earliest days, when it was coined as an abbreviation of the game's full appellation "Association Football." Since that time, it has been most popularly grasped in those English-speaking nations where other forms of football (rugby, Gaelic, Australian Rules, American, etc.) have staked a prior claim upon the term "football" itself. Ironically, what should be regarded as one of English slang's most successful exports is now ignorantly despised by many English people, who condemn the word as a coarse Americanism.

The term "football" cannot help but creep in, however, particularly when discussing organizations, associations, magazines, and clubs who have the word in their names and titles—the universally familiar FC, after all, stands for "football club." To keep things simple, then, reference to other forms of non-Association Football (see above) will be prefaced by the appropriate cultural or geographical qualifier.

Elsewhere, the American term "fields" should be regarded as interchangeable with the English "pitches"; "stadia" are also "grounds"; and "spot kicks" frequently become "penalties." The period of play is usually a "game," but "match" and "tie" also creep in, and so long as we remember that a "tie" can also be a "draw," while a "draw" is also the process by which teams are paired together in cup competitions, then we should be okay.

For further details of these and many other terms, the reader is directed to the glossary that appears at the end of this volume.

Finally, financial details, fees—no matter where they originate—are initially given in their contemporary British pounds equivalent, followed by their modern-day equivalents in pounds and US dollars. (Figures accurate as of August 2014.) Keen-eyed readers discerning certain inconsistencies in these latter values are referred to sundry historical British currency devaluations.

Acknowledgments

Thanks to everybody who kicked something onto the field as I was writing, but most of all to Louis Burgess, for so many years of ceaseless enthusiasm, and to Dave Makin, for an equal amount of cynicism and rage. Between one example and the other, this book took shape.

To Amy, for letting me win at Subbuteo; to John Cerullo, Marybeth Keating, Wes Seeley, Bernadette Malavarca, John Flannery, and Gary Sunshine for bringing the project to life.

To Bideford, Gillingham, and Bournemouth and Boscombe Athletic, for being there when Saturday comes.

To *When Saturday Comes* for being there.

And finally, to all the people who, knowingly or otherwise, hoofed something strange into the stratosphere, even if it was just sympathetic glances in the direction of a teetering pile of cigarette cards, programs, and 1970 Esso World Cup coins: Karen and Todd; Linda and Larry; Betsy, Steve and family; Jo-Ann Greene, Sheelagh Crewe, Jen, Gaye and Tim, Oliver, Trevor, Toby, Barb East, Bateerz and family, the Gremlins who live in the heat pump, and to John the Superstar, the demon of the dry well.

Introduction
The Birth of the
Kicky-Round-Thing Game

For as long as man has had feet to kick with, he has kicked things. And that is really all we know about the origins of soccer. History and archaeology have unearthed countless supposed forefathers of the game, from ancient China to medieval Italy, from pre-Columbian America to Mesolithic Europe; and their discoveries have seen the modern ball preceded by everything from inflated animal bladders to the recently decapitated heads of enemies; from bundles of cloth rolled and tied into shape, to . . . well, you name it. If it's round (-ish), light (-ish) and bouncy (-ish), the chances are that somebody kicked it to somebody else, at some point in the distant past, and "Eureka! I have just invented soccer."

Certainly soccer is the most instinctual sport that we have today, and the most simplistic, too. See ball, chase ball, kick ball. And if you don't have a ball, then you can use a stone, a can, or yes, a skull. With the exception of those activities that are purely athletic (running, jumping, hopping), soccer is the most basic and uncomplicated sport there is, requiring the minimum of equipment.

The face of football, 1890-style. The players wear hats, the goals have no nets . . . It'll never catch on. *Sergey Goryachev/Shutterstock.com*

Other sports demand sporty stuff. Sticks, bats, rackets, clubs, nets, poles, hammers, spears, correctly proportioned egg-shaped projectiles. Even swimming insists upon water. Soccer demands something to kick and something to kick with, and that's it. No matter how much other "kit" is available to the discerning acolyte, from fancy shirts that do your breathing for you, to lighter-than-air cleated booties that make you run, kick, and dive like a pro, and onto training regimes and dietary schedules that claim they can transform you into a Marc Overmars overnight, in truth they are little more than window dressing. You need something to kick and something to kick with.

You don't even need someone else to play with. Soccer is one of the very few team sports that don't require a team. George Best, one of that select bevy of players who lived up to his last name in a good way (cue a host of infantile jokes about Kaka, Fanni, Fuckal, Quim, and Dickov), spent much of his youth perfecting his skills by volleying a tennis ball against a wall without another soul in sight.

Pelé used to do much the same. So did Diego Maradona, so did Stanley Matthews, so did Gerd Müller.

Modern coaching is full of Youth Academies, Centers of Excellence, Gulags of Greatness and so forth, all of them dedicated to transforming the youth of today into the soccer stars of tomorrow. Whether or not they will succeed in these aims appears to be a question that every successive generation puts off having to answer, insisting that we wait until the next crop of promising youngsters comes along.

One thing, however, does seem peculiar. No matter how magnificent the latest, "greatest" player to grace the game might be, we only ever hear of him being the "next" Pelé, the "modern" Maradona, the "best thing since" Best. A potential equal to the princes of the past. But rarely their successor and never their superior.

And why is that? Because even the future seems willing to admit that the past had something that modernity has found is irreplaceable. It's called history, it's called tradition. It's called acknowledging that sometimes, science does not have all the answers. Sometimes, primal instinct and unschooled skill are far more instructive mistresses.

Not that education should be despised. Indeed, without it . . . or, at least, without the grand establishments wherein education is disseminated . . . we might not even have a game to play.

For centuries, the glorious rough and tumble that would one day grow up to be soccer was a game played by veritable armies of uncoached, untutored, and utterly unrestrained peasants, madly rushing across hill and dale, bashing brains and breaking bones in their pursuit of a ball that could be five miles away at the time. Like the villagers massed with torches and pitchforks to march upon Baron Frankenstein's castle, a medieval soccer team probably looked more like a lynch mob than a bevy of sports enthusiasts, and generally it behaved like one, too.

What we would today regard as the playing field, the "pitch," was measured across however many acres the participants agreed was the appropriate dimension, with its boundaries marked not by neatly painted white lines, but by whatever natural features happened to be there—a raging river, a prickly hedge, a dreadful precipice, whatever.

The goal was whatever they said it should be, but it was rarely a scientifically measured and designed netted frame. It was far more likely to be another local landmark—"first to hit the lightning tree wins." And the participants were numbered according to however many people wanted to risk life and limb for the sake of a few hours (sometimes extending into a few days) spent playing the game.

"Mob football," as sniffy histories now refer to it, enjoyed a sticky relationship with officialdom. In 1365, insists tradition, the English king Edward III outlawed the game because it interfered with his military ambitions. Quite simply (and perhaps understandably), his troops preferred playing soccer to training for warfare.

Of course the prohibition did not, and could not, last, and the game quickly returned to the landscape; to the streets of London, where young apprentices played riotous street games on Cheapside, the Strand, and Covent Garden; and to the fields and bogs of the countryside, where Shrove Tuesday (the day before the commencement of Lent) was just one of many excuses to celebrate with a wild game of football.

Laws were enacted to restrict the game, sermons were preached against it in church. Landowners prohibited it, employers outlawed it. But deep into the nineteenth century, the game of football continued more akin to mindless thuggery than sport, as the sports historian Joseph Strutt, writing in 1801, makes clear. True, some semblance of order was creeping into the game, but the "equal number of competitors," to whom he refers, and the "goals placed at the distance of eighty or a hundred yards the one from the other" were but niceties that scarcely related to the game itself.

"The ball which is commonly made of a blown bladder, and cased with leather, is delivered in the midst of the ground, and the object of each party is to drive it through the goal of their antagonists, which being achieved, the game is won. The abilities of the performers are best displayed in attacking and defending the goals; and hence the pastime was more frequently called a goal at football than a game at football. When the exercise becomes exceeding violent, the players kick each other's shins without the least ceremony, and some are overthrown at the hazard of their limbs."

All of which sounds considerably more diverting than the often-anodyne displays served up to us in the guise of the modern game, but there, that's progress for you.

It was within the confines of the great British universities that the game developed along the somewhat more gentlemanly lines that we would recognize today. At Oxford, Cambridge, Eton, Charterhouse, Rugby, and so many more, the glorious game of football was refined and revised, reworked and redacted, and slowly . . . very slowly . . . the first sets of rules were devised and then distributed.

Different schools promulgated different sets of regulations, but within the multitude of variations that sprung up, "Association Football" was born and, in

1863, a Football Association was created by those members who agreed on one basic set of rules.

Other associations arose for those souls who preferred to play by other regulations, in England—where rugby became the preserve of those who believed *foot*ball was incomplete without hands; in Australia, in America, in Ireland; and for all the progress those games have made from their original violent prototype, somewhere deep in their DNA there lurks a few threads of the original game's primal joy. See ball, kick ball. Okay, and pick it up and throw ball too. If you must.

It was the absence of hands that separated Association Football from its peers. Indeed, the feet-only footballers frowned so darkly upon the wriggly things at the end of each arm that many early players took the field with coins clutched tightly in their fists, insurance against the devil ever tempting them to handle the sphere.

So that's what this book is about. Association Football in all of its glory and manifold beauties. What it isn't about, on the other hand, is a lot of the pomp and paraphernalia with which the game sometimes likes to bedeck itself.

It isn't about winners and losers, facts and figures, statistics and tables. It isn't about whose sheikh is richest, whose oligarch is oddest, whose multinational parent company has the most dubious ties to environmental carnage, child labor, and war. It isn't about which teams show up in the headlines the most often. And it certainly isn't about further tooting the trumpets of those clubs that currently consider themselves the greatest. Because, even for the clubs at the very top of the tree, success is not guaranteed.

If it was, the 2013 champions of Europe, FC Bayern München, would not have succumbed to a 5–0 mauling as they tried to defend their title the following year; just as the reigning champions of the world, Spain, would not have crumbled to a 5–1 hammering when it came, that same summer of 2014, to live up to their billing. Nor would Manchester United have finished with their worst points tally in almost twenty-five years; nor would Brazil have crumbled to their worst defeat in close to a century; and so on.

No matter how successful you believe the team that you follow is (we're talking here, of course, to the people who do support a successful team; the rest of us should go put the kettle on), and no matter how gloriously gold-plated their history may be, still they are just one game away from throwing it all away. One season away from abject self-destruction; one bad decision away from absolute dissolution.

An example.

In January 2011, potash mogul Suleyman Abusaidovich Kerimov took control of FC Anzhi Makhachkala, a modestly successful, but more-or-less unremarkable club that had just won promotion to the Russian Premier League. And life in that tiny outpost of Russian sporting aspiration, the capital city of Dagestan, changed overnight.

In a region where the average wage was around $265 a month, and the soccer team's own aspirations were scarcely any grander, Kerimov presented the club with an annual budget that fell just short of $200 million, and essentially challenged them to spend it all on success.

Which, of course, they did. Bugattis all round, and salaries so grandiose that not one of the newly assembled team (spearheaded by Cameroonian international, and former Barcelona and Inter striker Samuel Eto'o) thought twice about signing for them. Especially after they discovered that they could all live and train in Moscow, and only make the 800-mile journey to Makhachkala when they had to play a home game.

It was an audacious experiment, but it seemed to be paying off. With a team stuffed with more stars than the town had ever dreamed of meeting, Anzhi finished fifth in that first season, 2011–2012, and third in their second. The Europa League beckoned, and manager Guus Hiddink, himself fresh from stints with PSV, Chelsea, and the Turkish and Russian national teams, could have been excused for dreaming ever greater things.

Then the bottom fell out of potash.

Reeling from his business losses, Keimov slashed Anzhi's budget by more than half, and placed the entire playing staff on the transfer list. Eto'o and another star, the Brazilian Willian Borges da Silva, headed for Chelsea. Lacina Traoré moved to AS Monaco; others joined clubs around the Russian league. Manager Hiddink departed; his assistant, René Meulensteen, was briefly employed as his replacement but then sacked after just sixteen days.

The 2013–2014 Europa League campaign shuddered to a halt with just three victories to the straitened club's name, and the Premier League campaign collapsed around a similar statistic. Long before the season was over, it was clear that Anzhi was destined for relegation back to the First Division, and sundry doomsayers insisted that the team might well still have further to fall.

And all because someone with a lot of money happened to be passing by one day, and thought, "I think I'll buy myself a soccer team."

Soccer is a game played between two teams of eleven players, chasing a single ball around a field. It stands to reason, then, that the best soccer teams are those comprised of the best eleven players. Or, at least, the eleven players that best gel into a single cohesive force.

Sadly, reason is often not a key ingredient in the modern business plan. Not when it can be shouted down by so many other things. Wealthy sugar daddies, shady property developers, avaricious accountants, the tax man, politicians, even the courts, all have their role to play in the success or otherwise of a team, and often their contribution is more definitive than any the players themselves might make.

Would Scottish powerhouse Glasgow Rangers have been consigned to the depths of their nation's lowest league if their exploits on the playing field alone were what mattered?

Would Spanish giants Valencia have been saddled with two stadia, one they could not sell and one they couldn't afford to complete, had somebody—presumably *not* a member of the playing staff—recommended they get into the property market?

Would Parma have plunged down the Italian league had they not placed all their financial eggs into a basket being carried by a doomed and disgraced dairy company?

And that is before we even *begin* to consider several well-stocked leagues-worth of eastern European sides who were undone by their home countries' shift from Communism to capitalism, and the fact that it was no longer acceptable to win every game, just because you were the army's favorite side.

It's not all bad. The English Premier League's right to describe itself as the best in the world comes down to cash, as its own chief, Richard Scudamore, remarked at the official opening of the 2014–2015 season. "The fact of the matter is we have got the most competitive league. The way we distribute the TV rights to all the clubs, the way we make every club able to compete is very, very different to how they do it in other leagues—particularly in Spain." The result of that, he said, is "a league where we are talking about five, six, maybe seven teams that can possibly come and challenge to win the title. In Spain, it's not quite the same in terms of strength in depth."

He was right, too. Chelsea might never have established themselves as one of the most successful European teams of the twenty-first century, had they not been purchased by one of the wealthiest men in the world. Just as the French side, Paris St Germain, seemed destined to struggle through the 2000s until their fortunes came under the aegis of the Qatar Investment Authority. Money talks and, in these cases, money wins.

Indeed, there are times when the exploits of the players feel secondary *at best* to the wealth of their owners; and they are certainly immaterial when the shit hits the fan.

The team can win all the silverware in the world. But if the boss man fiddles the taxes, fills his office with goldfish, or sells off the stadium so that his shell company can build a parking lot on the ruins, it's rarely him that sinks out of sight. It's the team. He will just brush off the inconvenience, complain that the club still owes him a bucketful of cash, and then head off to work his murky magic some place else.

The impact of money is, of course, a detail (although some might call it a grouch) essential to any understanding of soccer, at least in terms of its role as the most popular game on the planet, and the sheer weight of coverage, cash, and competitiveness that it has assumed for itself.

But money is only one half of the equation. The other half is a somewhat less quantifiable kaleidoscope of opinions and obsessions, of admiration and antipathy, of never-ending love and undying hatred.

Soccer is about opinions and biases. It is about mad ambitions and crucifying disappointments, unimaginable highs and unfathomable lows. It is about joyless subservience to failure, and mindless adherence to the twisted but inescapable bondage that is loyalty to your team.

The Uruguayan journalist and author Eduardo Galeano famously declaimed, "In his life, a man can change wives, political parties, or religions but he cannot change his favorite soccer team." But he touches only a small part of the true, awful equation. Supporting a soccer team is like marrying a stranger when you're still wearing short trousers, and remaining with them for the rest of your life, no matter how atrociously they treat you. Because only one thing is guaranteed. They *will* treat you atrociously. And more than once, as well.

You may think you can leave them, and you may believe you have. But deep down inside, in a corner of your soul you may not even realize exists, there's a little bit of you that always looks out for your first love's results.

Soccer is about hoping, sometimes unreasonably, often fruitlessly, but always with a fervor that is tantamount to religious, that *this* will be the year when your team finally justifies the years, decades, and what seems like aeons that you have devoted to them, and wins . . . the League. The Cup. The derby. A game.

Pick your own target, but remember this. It is a sport in which the most fervently held beliefs can turn on the head of a pin; the most bitter, brutal prejudices can develop from less than zero; and the most deathless assertions can be harvested from next to nothing.

When I was ten, my mother established me as the envy of the schoolyard when four members of Brazil's 1970 World Cup squad signed the back of a Nana Mouskouri concert ticket for her. And not just any old four. Tostao! Brito! Fontana! Piazza! They didn't charge her for the privilege, either, or then recant grimly murmuring, "Better not. You might sell it on eBay later."

Simpler times. Happier times. And hopeful times, although Brazil's subsequent World Cup triumph only bore out what I already knew through the magic of those autographs. I had absolutely no doubt that any group of players who could squeeze their names onto one side of a two-by-two inch piece of paper would certainly be capable of performing miracles on a soccer pitch.

You may agree with this example. You may disagree with it. Perhaps you have four of the defeated Italian side's signatures on the reverse of a *Paint Your Wagon* ticket, and will go to your grave convinced that all four of the goals your heroes conceded that sunny Mexican afternoon were the result of dubious decisions and freak wind gusts.

Convinced, in the same manner that the viewing audience for the 1986 World Cup remains divided over whether or not Argentina would have won the entire competition had Diego Maradona not been possessed

Four Brazilians on the back of a 1970 Nana Mouskouri concert ticket.

by the spirit of a volleyball professional during the quarterfinal encounter with England; and that of the 1966 event still debate whether or not the third goal conceded by the West Germans really did cross the line.

They believe it in the same way that future author Nick Hornby and his friends once believed that if they purchased, and then bit the head off, a confectionary sugar mouse before a Cambridge United game, then threw the rest of the sweet into the path of an oncoming car, the U's would win. (It worked, too. "Thus protected," Hornby wrote in *Fever Pitch*, United "remained unbeaten at [home] for months.")

They believe it as fervently as Birmingham manager Barry Fry believed he could lift an old gypsy curse on the club's home stadium by urinating in all four corners of the pitch. As trustingly as Laurent Blanc believed that kissing his goalkeeper's bald head improved the French national side's hopes of victory at the 1998 World Cup (and that worked, too—they won the whole thing). Or Romanian striker Adrian Mutu believed that by wearing his underpants inside out, he stymied the evil curses that were regularly flung at him by jealous enemies.

All of these are very valid beliefs, and they demand our consideration. Because, unless you are staring at nothing more stimulating than an unadulterated list of results, there is very little about soccer history that has anything to do with reality, and not much more to do with what actually happened.

It is all about personal perceptions, which is how your favorite team could be relegated to the lowest level of park soccer and still be the greatest eleven ever to walk the turf, while the runaway champions of the Copa America are just a bunch of cheating expletives.

It is about rabbit feet and gypsy curses, lucky hats and muddy pitches.

It is about some sneering Billy Big Bananas stepping up to the spot to take the penalty that will send his club or country into triumphant ecstasy, and hoofing the ball into the stratosphere, while neutral viewers around the world howl with bladder-bursting laughter. Especially if he falls over as well. And extra-especially if he then bursts into tears.

It is about Norwich City going into the final game of the 2013–2014 season knowing, as the BBC website put it, that all they needed do to avoid relegation was to "beat Arsenal, hope West Brom lose against Stoke, and manage a seventeen-goal swing in the process." And the supporters who believed they could do it.

It is about a coach declaring "there are no easy games in football," when what he really means is "except for our next one, which will be a stroll in the park." And then coming a cropper as the penniless underdogs give his millionaire superstars a ninety-minute cookery lesson. On the menu tonight, humble pie.

It is about former Fulham owner Mohamed Al Fayed insisting that the side's relegation was all down to the removal of a statue of a pop singer named Michael Jackson. "I warned him," Al Fayed said of his iconoclastic successor. "I said 'You will pay with blood for that.' [And now] he's been relegated and if he wakes up [and] asks for Michael Jackson again and I'll say 'No way.'"

It is about the owner of Welsh giants Cardiff City changing the team's colors from blue to red because the latter is considered lucky in his native Asia; and Don Revie discarding Leeds United's blue and yellow for the all-white of Real Madrid, because he considered them the best team in Europe.

Which is interesting because, at the time of writing, fifty years on, Real Madrid still are the best team in the world. Leeds, on the other hand . . . not so much. Although they do still play in all-white. But Cardiff no longer play in red, after relegation proved that sometimes a lucky color isn't all it's cracked up to be. Particularly when the majority of your supporters, who didn't much fancy the change to begin with, were still wearing blue. In January 2015, Cardiff played their first game in traditional colors in almost three years—and they won, 1–0.

See? Soccer is a game of opinions, theories, postulations. Shot through with forthright erudition and swivel-eyed lunacy. Littered with dates and data, heroes and villains, fat cats and failures. And that's probably the best summation of this book's contents that one can come up with.

Soccer is a global game, and the text will reflect that, not only in the histories it tells, but in the examples it offers to illustrate wider points, and in the minutia mined to chart certain paths. As an Englishman writing in the United States, it is inevitable that those two countries will dominate the narrative, just as they probably, through a combination of environment and exposure, dominate the interests of the majority of readers. But even narrow-minded parochialism knows when to pull its nose out of its own belly button, and so we will meet some of the world's greatest players, and cheer on its greatest teams, although they may not always be the same players and teams that other authorities claim are the greatest.

We will visit stadia that possess the sanctity of cathedrals, and handle trophies worth their weight in gold, although again, they may not be the stadia or the trophies that transfix millions of viewers on satellite and the Internet.

In a modern world delineated by the demands of high finance, it is very easy to believe that the entire soccer universe comprises a mere handful of stunningly wealthy, sponsored leagues, a smattering of lucrative highly branded tournaments, and a dozen different clubs, all of them owned by an oligarch of some sort, and all playing at a stadium named either for a bank, an airline, or a law firm. First FAQ of the book: *Is that true?* No it isn't.

We will not be looking at the women's game because, quite frankly, it merits a book all to itself, just as long, opinionated, and detailed as this one; and to offer it anything less just seems rude.

But we will leaf through memorabilia, and browse through dusty record books. We will scrawl insults about a rival side on a bus-shelter wall in purple crayon, and we will get horribly drunk while extolling the virtues of the 1977 Cup–winning side. Any cup. Any side. It doesn't matter which one. Because, more than all those other things, we're going to have fun because I, for one, am sick to the back teeth of those soccer books that take everything so dreadfully seriously.

It's a game. Let's treat it like one.

Soccer

How Did It Get Here, and What Does It Want?

G rowing up a soccer fan in the English 1960s, there were certain so-called truths that were accepted as gospel, each of them as securely unquestioned as they were (we now realize) unproven.

The majority of them have since been forgotten, mercifully perhaps, but it was generally accepted that most "foreign" soccer players were cheats, most Latin players were dirty cheats, and any nation with which England had warred in the past century or so was still so hell-bent on revenge that you might as well start building the air raid shelters now. So that was Europe, Asia, and South America sorted, which just left the United States. Where did Uncle Sam's portrait hang on the wall of shame that was our global perspective?

Well, the fact of the matter was, it didn't. And why? Because Americans didn't play soccer. Never had, never would, and if you didn't believe the school-yard tattle, then there were plenty of adults who would tell you likewise. And the consequence, as another product of that same era, author Terry Pratchett, once put it, was simple. "I've never really liked the Yanks," he wrote in the novel *Good Omens*. "You can't trust people who pick up the ball all the time when they play football."

Things like that, you don't even need to think about them. You just file them away in that corner of the mind where you keep the most cement solid of convictions, and there they stay until . . .

Until the summer of 1972, when you're vacationing on the southern English coast, and a soccer match happens to catch your eye. You wander over to watch the game, and your ear suddenly detects a most unexpected accent. And not just one. Two or three. No, seven or eight . . . no! Ten or eleven. Eleven unexpected accents emanating from the pitch, and another few from the touchline, in what modern accounts would term "the technical area."

Americans. Americans playing soccer. Americans playing soccer in proper shirts, shorts (red and white), and boots, and not an ounce of padding or helmet in sight. They have the correctly shaped ball and the standard-shaped goals, and they clearly know enough about the rules to be conforming to the referee's directions, too.

I'm not going to say it was a life-changing moment, or claim that I would have been less surprised if Bigfoot had come riding a basilisk around the perimeter, to offer the players their halftime yeti-burger. But there was a moment's pause, and a moment's more confusion. And then the shy approach to the most approachable looking of the touchline tenants, to ask the only question that made any kind of sense. "Are you Canadians?"

No, they were not, although I wasn't, apparently, the first person to ask. I told you, we all believed this stuff back then, and Americans did not play soccer. Except, my newfound friends informed me, when they did.

The Wellesley Pilgrims. Aptly named for a band of teenagers (all were aged between sixteen and eighteen) spreading a gospel in overseas lands . . . the gospel that everything we English believed about American soccer was untrue.

Back home in Massachusetts, they were members of the Boston Area Youth Soccer League, a strapping young organization that began life in 1969 with nine members, and had added a full sixty more in the three years since then. It's still going strong today, operating leagues for players as young as nine, and probably none of its members think twice about going on tour anymore.

It was a big deal back then, though. Eight games were scheduled against youth sides from across southern England—Oxford, Brighton, Bognor, Kidlington. A couple of coaching sessions had been lined up at Chichester City FC, the nearest semiprofessional side to the visitors' base in Bracklesham Bay. They even had time to take in a play (Shakespeare's *Taming of the Shrew*), watch a cricket match and a couple of pro soccer contests, too. Proper sport and culture. The stereotypes were tumbling like ninepins.

Soccer? I'd Rather Play Horseshoes

All of which sounds really quaint today, relics of a distant past—we're talking forty-plus years ago. Things have changed a lot since then. But it took them a long time to do so, because little more than twenty years ago, Americans still didn't play soccer. Or watch it, or talk about it, or even acknowledge its existence as anything more than a barbaric European pastime at which large numbers of people seemed to get killed on a regular basis.

The triple punch disasters at Bradford, Heysel, and Hillsborough, close to two hundred deaths in three incidents just four years apart, were still relatively recent history. And, as the United States prepared to host the 1994 World Cup, some people . . . let's say a certain demographic, and leave it at that . . . were genuinely worried (or wanted to ensure that other people were genuinely worried) that the same things could happen here. That, the moment the first Alien Round Ball bounced on American soil, entire stadiums filled with innocents would either be torched or reduced to bloody rubble, while subhuman hooligans placed children's heads on spikes and chanted "we are the champions."

These people couldn't understand what soccer was doing even coming to the US. Apocrypha or not, a much-quoted poll of the country's favorite games found soccer lurking somewhere in the lower quarter of the Top 100, less loved even than horseshoes.

They came, they saw, they played really well. For Americans. The official team sheet and program for the Massachusetts tourists' summer '72 English tour. Fully autographed!

The sad thing is, that was probably about right. There was no Internet back then. No dedicated newsstand soccer magazines. *Soccer USA* was publishing, and so was *USA Soccer News*, but unless you already knew about them, or caught their occasional ads on the Prime Sports Network, you were never going to find a copy.

There was no Fox Soccer Channel, and network television ignored the game, with even the 1990 World Cup generally available only via the Spanish language broadcasters. Newspapers acknowledged soccer only when there was a juicy disaster or riot to drool over. Shortwave radio was the devoted European fan's best friend, the BBC World Service whipped on whatever winds there are that buffet radio signals in and out of earshot; and the soft tread of the mailman's once-a-month delivery of your extortionately priced (and usually grotesquely delayed) subscription to one of the overseas publications.

At best it was a girl's game. At worst it was un-American. And there was nothing to suggest this scenario might ever change.

American objections to the game were manifold and, if you regard them dispassionately, they were reasonable, too. How, for example, *could* a sport be considered exciting when so many contests were decided by scores of just a goal or two, and some, the much-derided 0–0 tie, were not even *that* eventful.

An audience raised on basketball (average score per team per game—sixty-eight), NFL (forty-five) and even hockey (five) was *never* going to get behind an encounter where the average score was zippity, as the economist Stephen Moore growled in the *National Review*.

"After watching my six-year-old son Justin's first two soccer games this spring I finally understand why Europeans riot at soccer matches. For the same reason that inmates riot in prisons: out of sheer boredom." Soccer, he decreed, "is about as scintillating as ninety minutes of Court TV" and "the least offensive-minded game ever invented."

The antipathy was, however, mutual. The United States's failure to embrace soccer had long baffled and bemused British observers, a point confirmed in 1986, when the magazine *When Saturday Comes* snarled, "their total failure to come to terms with soccer . . . [is] the thing that really condemns American society."

In fairness, that particular condemnation was delivered with tongue ever-so-slightly in cheek, but it encapsulated a lot of Europeans' beliefs all the same. As did certain British "experts'" much-bellowed aversion to the word "soccer," on account of it being a nasty American invention. Of course it wasn't; it was as English as black pudding, Marmite, and institutionalized xenophobia. But why let linguistics get in the way of a little local flag flying?

European suspicions were as firmly rooted in some form of reality as America's. Step outside of North America and it is very easy to wonder how a competition could call itself the World Series when it didn't actually involve the vast majority of the world. Step inside, on the other hand, and some Americans genuinely did ponder aloud how the World Cup could claim a similar title when the US had not the slightest interest in it.

Yet the fact is, even then, their country boasted one of the finest World Cup pedigrees of all. For, if statistics and final placings alone be our guide, the United States ranked high among the tournament's top twenty teams of all time. In fact, they still do. By virtue of finishing third in 1930, and regardless of what may or may not have happened since then, the United States find themselves level on World Cup honors with half a dozen nations whose soccer-playing heritage could never be decried.

Not bad for a country that didn't even know which end of a goalpost to swivel on.

Neither was that the end to the glory. Even then, back in the early 1990s, an admittedly sparse, but nevertheless impressive roster of other achievements had been racked up by American soccer players over the years.

The first ever hat trick in World Cup history was scored by an American, Bert Patenaude, of Fall River, Massachusetts, in the United States' 1930 encounter with Paraguay.

The United States were the first non-British team ever to defeat England in a competitive, as opposed to friendly, international tie at the 1950 World Cup; and only the tenth *ever* to achieve that feat under any circumstances whatsoever (victories for Spain, France, Hungary, Czechoslovakia, Austria, Belgium, Switzerland twice, Yugoslavia, and Sweden were all achieved at friendlies).

The US men's soccer team achieved Olympic qualification in every competition bar one between 1924 and 1956, making the last sixteen on one occasion (1920—where, though, they were beaten 3–0 by eventual gold medalists Uruguay, they nevertheless escaped the ignominious defeats inflicted by the free-scoring South Americans on Yugoslavia and France).

And the US were gloriously triumphant in the first ever FIFA Women's World Cup in 1991, where stars such as Michelle Akers and Carin Jennings helped inspire the team to a final victory over much-fancied Norway.

The history was there if anybody cared to look for it. Sadly, at the time, few did.

Today, the game is everywhere. At a grassroots level, over 13 million people are estimated to play soccer on a regular basis in the United States. There is a professional league (the MLS—Major League Soccer) whose nineteen teams attract, on a weekly basis, the third highest attendance of any sport in the country (only NFL and baseball are ahead). And both the men's and women's national teams have contested every World Cup competition since 1990, with often spectacular results. Spectacular, that is, when one considers the social, media, and cultural obstacles that the game needed to overcome before even horseshoes could be put in the shade.

Perhaps it would be ambitious to describe the United States as a soccer powerhouse waiting to be born; just as it would be hyperbole to describe its viewing public as a ravenous beast waiting to be fed. But in October 2012, NBC paid $250 million for the rights to screen the English Premier League for the next three years, and when viewing figures were tallied a little over a year later, over 12 million people were found to be regularly tuning in.

Leagues from across the world, and not just our Central and North American neighbors, have their own vast armies of devoted American-based followers; and a host of European and Latin American magazines are regularly available alongside a raft of domestic publications on magazine racks across the land. Bookstores have dedicated soccer sections in their sports shelves, local news broadcasts cover local soccer action, and when the US met Belgium in the 2014 World Cup knockout phase, 18 million Americans tuned in despite the match falling in the middle of the work day. The following morning's news headlines included the fact that great swathes of the country ground to a halt for the duration of the game.

Little more than a month later, a US record 109,318 people turned out to witness Real Madrid and Manchester United clash at the invitational Guinness International Champions Cup, at the Michigan Stadium in Ann Arbor. (The previous record attendance for a soccer game in the United States was 101,799 for the 1984 Olympic final, France vs. Brazil 2–0 at the Rose Bowl in California. But that was the Olympics. People will watch *anything* there. This was for a fairly

World Cup Role of Honor 1930–2014

Brazil—winners (5); runners-up (2); third (2); fourth (2)
Germany—winners (4); runners-up (4); third (4); fourth (1)
Italy—winners (4); runners-up (2); third (1); fourth (1)
Argentina—winners (3); runners-up (3)
Uruguay—winners (2); fourth (3)
France—winners (1); runners-up (1); third (2); fourth (1)
Spain—winners (1); fourth (1)
England—winners (1); fourth (1)
Netherlands—runners-up (3); third (1); fourth (1)
Czechoslovakia—runners-up (2)
Hungary—runners-up (2)
Sweden—runners-up (1); third (2); fourth (1)
Portugal—third (1); fourth (1)
Austria—third (1); fourth (1)
United States—third (1)
Chile—third (1)
Croatia—third (1)
Poland—third (2)
Turkey—third (1)
Belgium—fourth (1)
Bulgaria—fourth (1)
South Korea (fourth)
Soviet Union—fourth (1)
Yugoslavia—fourth (2)

meaningless friendly.) Scant days after that, an MLS All Star team in which every starting player was substituted at least once, won 2–1 against what amounted to a full-strength Bayern Munich side, four World Cup winners included, in a friendly in Portland. Fittingly, the winning goal was scored by Landon Donovan, himself a Bayern old boy.

And it all kicked off on November 19, 1989, with the thirty-first minute Paul Caliguiri goal that sent the United States triumphantly into the 1990 World Cup finals, the twenty-fourth and final nation to qualify.

The Shot Heard Around the World

That's how footage of the wonder strike on YouTube describes it, and while that epithet *may* be considered slightly hyperbolic, nevertheless it was a significant moment, and not only for the World Cup. Statisticians, too, delighted in what became the first US goal scored in 238 minutes of World Cup soccer, and the most crucial in forty years worth of fruitless striving.

Costa Rica had already qualified for the finals, to be staged in Italy that year. One other nation would join them—the United States, if they won this final game; Trinidad and Tobago, if they won it. It was victory or nothing, nothing else would suffice, and pregame, the omens seemed to be favoring Trinidad and Tobago.

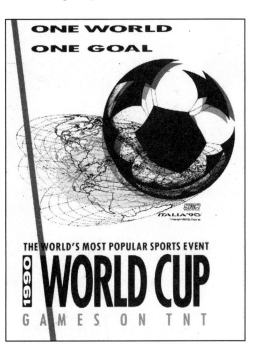

The 1990 World Cup unfolds on a printed schedule the size of the average business card.

The US had scarcely impressed so far. Their qualification campaign opened with a make-or-break preliminary qualifier against Jamaica in July 1988, two full years before the World Cup itself, and a 0–0 draw in Kingston did not bode well for the future. Neither did the opening hour of the second leg at St. Louis Soccer Park in Fenton, Missouri. Less than thirty minutes remained and the score was 1–1, a single Brian Bliss goal all that Team USA had to show for their efforts.

But then a penalty in the sixty-eighth minute was cooly converted by the magnificent Hugo Perez, and at last the flood gates could open. A third goal from Paul Krumpe, a pair from Frank Klopas—the US ran out 5–1 victors,

Landon Donovan in the cool colors of the LA Galaxy, up against Chivas USA in April 2014. *Photo Works/Shutterstock.com*

and suddenly people started believing in them. Their own federation, the United States Soccer Federation (USSF), began believing in them.

Incredibly, prior to the Jamaican game, no fewer than five of the players on the US team did not even have club affiliation. Now, the USSF swooped to tie as much of the squad as it could to itself; to make Team USA their number one employer, and then loan them out to other clubs when the occasion demanded. It was an audacious move—elsewhere around the world players are contracted to clubs and then loaned to their country, not vice versa. But that is a system that has arisen over decades of play and experience. The US did not have decades. It had eighteen months.

Coach Lothar Osiander, a part-timer who divided his time between his coaching duties and a job as a waiter, was let go, and replaced by the national team's first full-time boss, Bob Gansler. Philadelphia soccer legend Walt Chyzowych became the USSF's first-ever national director of coaching.

The round-robin phase of the tournament saw the US drawn against Trinidad and Tobago, Guatemala, El Salvador, and favorites Costa Rica—who they would meet in their first two matches in April 1989, a 1–0 defeat in San José and a 1–0 win in Fenton. A fortunate 1–0 win, conjured only by two disallowed Costa Rican goals and a heroic eighty-eighth minute penalty save by goalkeeper David Vanole. Any sense of home advantage that Team USA may have felt, incidentally, was completely underwhelmed by the Costa Rican support, so vociferous that the PA announcer was reduced to begging any Americans in the stadium to remind the players which country they were actually playing in.

On May 13, the US met Trinidad and Tobago for the first time, on a recently vandalized, and inadvertently mismarked Murdock Stadium pitch in Torrance, CA. Steve Trittschuh gave the US the lead and, for a long time, they looked like keeping it. But with two minutes left on the clock, the visitors equalized and that was that.

A 2–1 victory over Guatemala, eased by an own goal to complement Bruce Murray's strike, saw the US reach the halfway mark in third place with five points. But a run of friendlies through the summer of 1989 was hardly designed to instill confidence. In June, the US lost to Colombia. At the Marlboro Cup in August, South Korea and Italian club side Juventus both came out on top.

A Northern Irish representative side was beaten 1–0, and the visiting Soviets of Dnipro Dnipropetrovsk too. And a single goal was sufficient to push past El Salvador when qualifying resumed in September. Which was fortunate because the next two games, away to Guatemala and home to El Salvador, both ended in goalless draws, results that left even the most optimistic US followers staring grimly at the possibility of elimination. Only Bob Gansler seemed unfazed. He had predicted long before that the issue would not be settled until the very last kick of the very last game.

Nobody doubted the significance of the return match with Trinidad and Tobago. For the United States, it was their final opportunity to make a mark on the international stage before the World Cup arrived in the US itself. For their opponents, on the other hand, it was said that an entire nation's happiness rode upon this result. The national stadium in Port of Spain was sold out weeks in advance, the government declared a public holiday for the day after the match, and as the ground began filling up some six and a half hours before kickoff, the sea of black and red Trinidadian colors swiftly overwhelmed the handful of American supporters who had made the trip down.

In political terms, it was a veritable David and Goliath confrontation, the fourth largest country in the world against one of the smallest. (In fact, had Trinidad and Tobago qualified, they would have become the smallest country ever to make the World Cup finals.)

In footballing terms, however, the two were very evenly matched; indeed, one *Soccer USA* magazine correspondent insisted that watching US's earlier World Cup games reminded him "less of the preliminary stage of the greatest international tournament in the world, and more of the similar qualifying phase of the English FA Cup," so meager was the standard of play.

And so it was against Trinidad and Tobago. One goal separated the teams, and the match could have gone either way.

But it didn't. The United States qualified for their first World Cup in forty years, and all they needed do now was ensure that they weren't there simply to make up the numbers.

The Sounders' Mauro Rosales (#10) in action against the Portland Timbers in June 2012.
Anatoliy Lukich/Shutterstock

Which wasn't as easy as it sounded, although it wasn't as difficult as it might have been, either. Thrashed 5–1 in their opening World Cup match with Czechoslovakia, the US regrouped and kept their next two margins of defeat, against Italy and Austria, down to one goal apiece. Ultimately, only the United Arab Emirates went home with a worse record than the Americans, a goal difference of minus nine compared to the US's minus six. But still there were foundations to build upon and, while 1994 inched closer with the prophets of gloom still high on the hog, more people seemed willing to wager that the Cassandras would soon be tumbling down.

Soccer did have a place in the United States.

Get a Kick Out of Pasuchuakohowog

We have no firm record of when what would become soccer arrived in what would become the United States, although that's hardly surprising. We have no firm records about a lot of aspects of the continent's history and heritage, many of which could conceivably be considered far more important than a simple ball game.

However, anthropologists speak of a pastime that was apparently popular among the Powhatan and Algonquin tribes of the eastern continent. It was called pasuckuakohowog ("kicking ball sport") and, to all purposes, it sounds very similar to the mob football of old England. Which itself would certainly have been in the hand luggage of the waves of English settlers who peopled these shores during the sixteenth and seventeenth centuries. Very romantically, we can just imagine the surprise that the townspeople of Jamestown would have felt, the first time they came across their Powhatan neighbors playing pasuckua-kohowog. Who knows, but the first-ever international soccer match might have duly followed that discovery.

However the game arrived on American shores, and however it may have been perpetuated, by the 1820s "football" was firmly established in the collegiate system and in 1827, influenced by similar developments in the great public schools of England, Harvard inaugurated its first intramural contest.

By 1862, the game was sufficiently entrenched for a group of well-to-do enthusiasts, led by one Gerrit Smith Miller, to launch the legendary Oneida club in Boston. Drawing its playing staff from such establishments as the English High School of Boston, Boston Latin School, and Dixwell, Oneida became the powerhouse of the sport, not only proceeding to win every game it played, but allegedly never even conceding a goal.

It was a period of growth. Four years after Oneida came into being, and despite the privations of the Civil War, football fever had spread sufficiently for the New York publishing house of Beadle & Co. to publish the country's first rule book, covering both Association Football and rugby and, by the early 1870s, Yale, Cornell, and Columbia had all leaped aboard the bandwagon.

But stormy waters were ahead as the game found itself facing the same kind of schism as that which rent its English counterpart, advocates of a purely foot-oriented football coming into conflict with those who thought hands should also be a part of the game. And this time, the purists found themselves winding up on the losing side. While Association Football . . . soccer . . . continued to be played in working-class and immigrant communities within the major urban sprawls, it was American Football that rose to ascendancy in the colleges and schools; American Football that became the national pastime.

The American Football Association, Which Has Nothing to Do with American Football

Still, soccer flourished at the grassroots and in 1884, the first attempt at creating a national governing body was made, with the birth of the American Football Association (AFA), and the creation of what was only the second sports league ever launched in the US, following on from Major League Baseball (launched in 1876).

Until this point, soccer still existed within a welter of varying rules and notions. The AFA standardized them along the lines of the English model, and in 1884 the organization launched the American Cup, a knockout competition for its members—at this time drawn from in and around New Jersey and New York, but subsequently expanding into Pennsylvania and Massachusetts.

The new trophy was promptly won, three times in succession, by Clark ONT (Our New Thread)—a works team sponsored by the Clark Thread Company, a

Scottish-owned company based in Newark, New Jersey, and destined to become one of the giants not only of American soccer history, but local sport in general. Not content with establishing their supremacy on the soccer field, Clark also competed at cricket and baseball and, in 1885, added the latter's Essex League championship to their second American Cup triumph.

It was through the auspices of Clark ONT that the first-ever international match between the United States and Canada was played, in 1885. In fact, not only were five Clark ONT players included in the US side, the club also provided both the referee and the ground. Only the result, a goal to nil in favor of the visitors, did not go according to the threadmakers' script.

Having dominated the first three seasons of the American Cup, Clark ONT very surprisingly fell in the second round of the competition in 1888, the first indication that a new regional behemoth had entered the scene. Fall River, Massachusetts, was one of the fastest growing industrial regions in the northeast, its fortune founded on linen, and its population on work-hungry migrants from two of British soccer's most fertile regions, Lancashire in northern England and Glasgow in Scotland.

Swiftly these new arrivals formed themselves into soccer teams, including the Fall River Rovers (winners of the 1888 and 1889 American Cups), Fall River Olympics (who took the 1890 title), and Fall River East Ends (who won in 1891 and 1892). And so it continued, with the Cup and, indeed, the game itself, dominated either by works teams, or at least by sides built upon the industrial fortunes of their immediate locale: Pawtucket's Free Wanderers and Olympics, the Paterson True Blues, Kearny Arlington and, finally breaking the far north's stranglehold, Philadelphia Manz, Cup winners in 1897.

Their victory marked the end of an era, however. The following year was the last in which the American Cup would be staged until well into the next decade. Soccer had boomed; now it was crashing, its popularity partially eroded by the emergence of more "American" pastimes, but more dramatically by the continued preponderance of alternate rules and playing styles.

The AFA fought gallantly to maintain a single code, but in vain. Whereas other countries had settled upon a single set of rules and stuck to them, establishing the framework for what would become an internationally recognized sport, America's entrepreneurial spirit refused to allow a single game to thrive. Every year, from every direction, new and improved variations on the game were thrust forward, each trailing its own constellation of followers, each convinced that the rest of the soccer-playing world had got it wrong, and this new way was the only way forward for the game.

Not until 1906 was any kind of consensus arrived at, the warring forces finally acknowledging that, in the final analysis, the rest of the world probably *had* got it right. FIFA was up and running by now, the Fédération Internationale de Football Association, founded with seven members (Belgium, Denmark, France, the Netherlands, Sweden, Switzerland, and, in lieu of a national Spanish association, Madrid) in 1904, and gently expanding every year.

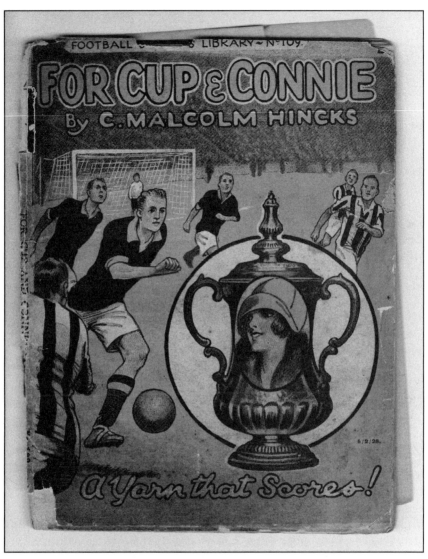

FOOTBALL ... LIBRARY ~ N° 109.

FOR CUP & CONNIE
By C. MALCOLM HINCKS

5/2/28.

A Yarn that Scores!

Canada had already make plain its intention to join, and the United States wanted to, too. First, however, its enthusiasts needed to establish a truly national association to oversee the development and execution of the sport throughout the United States as a whole.

A yarn that scores! A true love tale for soccer romantics everywhere.

By virtue of its age and experience, the AFA confidently expected to become that body, with the resumption of its premier tournament, the American Cup, a key element in proving their intentions were serious.

But their dreams, it swiftly transpired, were in vain. While the American Cup remained the preserve of the old northeastern industrial giants (the 1907 trophy was even reclaimed by its first-ever winners from the Clark Thread Company), a new organization, the American Amateur Football Association (AAFA), arose in October 1911, and swiftly made inroads into the remainder of the country.

True, its initial winners were drawn from the same old northeastern hotspots . . . Brooklyn Celtic took the AAFA's inaugural Cup in 1912, beating Newark FC 3–0 in the final; Yonkers won the 1913 event, defeating the deceptively named Hollywood Inn FC . . . deceptive, because it too was based in Yonkers. But they would expand, and do so faster, and more convincingly, than the old AFA.

A list of the entrants to the inaugural American Amateur Football Association Cup paints a vivid picture of the nature of the game, or at least of its players, in the 1910s. Outfits rejoicing beneath such exotic, and culturally distinct names as Arcadia Thistle, Clan MacDonald, Clan MacKenzie, Clan Gordon, and Clan McDuff spoke loudly of a heavy Scottish influence; the Anglo Saxons, St. George, and the Baltimore Sons of St. George remarked upon the English contingents.

Italians, Irish, Greeks, and Germans likewise seized upon distinctly national-ist names for their teams, fostering loyalties between club and neighborhood that were intrinsic to their hopes of success, and delineating some astonishingly lethal power bases. Unfortunately, the same nomenclatural segregation would also become a stick with which the anti-soccer-because-it's anti-American lobby could beat the game, and possibly with good reason. Early twentieth- century America was frequently described, and saw itself, too, as a melting pot. In so resolutely retaining identities that belonged to the "old country," soccer seemed to be one ingredient that refused to melt.

In 1912, the AFA's international ambitions were finally shattered as a host of its member associations suddenly and unexpectedly defected to the AAFA. With victory now assured, the AAFA reorganized itself as the United States Football Association (USFA) on April 5, 1913, and, soon after, was officially recognized by FIFA.

If its officers believed the war was over, however, they would soon learn the error of their ways. The USFA's domestic supremacy would continue to be chal-lenged by the AFA for another decade, with the American Cup running merrily alongside the official organization's newly instituted National Challenge Cup, and throwing up some mighty rivals to the USFA's finest, as well.

2

Belo Horizonte and All That

What Was So Special About 1950?

O
f all the teams that flourished in the United States throughout the first decades of the twentieth century, the greatest was Bethlehem Steel, based out of the steelworks in Bethlehem, PA—another city with a proud, if not lengthy, association with the game.

For close to two decades, the Steel dominated American soccer, even taking their talents overseas for a Scandinavian tour in 1919, and receiving invitations to travel elsewhere, too. But no matter what advances the Steel, or any other team, might make toward establishing an international profile, the temperamental nature of the game's domestic administrators was always against them, petty rivalries, private egos, and regional power plays ensuring that nothing of lasting value ever got accomplished.

Many reasons have been advanced to explain soccer's historical failure to grasp the national stage in America, not least of all the insurmountable challenges mounted by other, more "American" pastimes. Equally damaging, however, particularly at this point in the game's local history, was its own tendency toward internecine squabbling, that constant drive to "improve" things by messing with something that didn't need impoving in the first place. In fact, no sooner had the old AFA finally been filed away among the USFA's vanquished foes, than another rival, the American Soccer League (ASL), raised itself to a similar challenge by encouraging its membership to boycott the National Cup in 1925 as an opening shot across the USFA's bows.

The ASL played hard and loose with the laws, both local and international. As early as 1927, FIFA found itself forced to become involved after the ASL was accused of trying to lure away players who were already contracted to European clubs . . . at the same time as the home front was facing growing discontent from supporters questioning why there were not more American-born players in the game. The modern debate over whether there are "too many" foreign imports in the game, to the exclusion of homegrown talent, is by no means a new one.

Politics, cash, greed, asset-stripping vampires, fat-cat businessmen, avaricious local politicians, bleed-'em-dry bankers, breakaway threats . . . exactly the same ills that afflict the worldwide game today were making their presence felt just as brutally eighty years ago.

England captain Tom Finney rising between USA defenders Charlie Colombo and Walter Bahr, that fateful afternoon in Belo Horizonte.

Sanctions and suspensions flew back and forth; accusation and counterclaim; and as if the sheer chaos in the game's back rooms was not a sufficiently unedifying sight for the average supporter, the Great Depression was just around the corner, meaning most people could no longer even afford to watch a soccer match, let alone care about the so-called Soccer Wars raging between the clubs and their governors.

The USFA pulled together a side to compete at the 1930 World Cup, and stunned many people (maybe even themselves) by advancing to the semifinals and, ultimately, a third place finish. But the ASL collapsed in 1932, the National Cup faded into irrelevance, and even mighty Bethlehem Steel went belly up. By the time the country reemerged from those dark days . . . just in time to become embroiled in World War Two . . . soccer in America was in terminal decline.

Even the national side's appearance at the 1950 World Cup passed by without attracting any attention of note, at least at home. Indeed, the lack of excitement surrounding the USA's 1–0 defeat of England was almost as remarkable as the result itself, at least in the eyes of the rest of the world. But that's how it was, an icy indifference that stood in absolutely polar opposition to the shockwaves that radiated across the rest of the globe.

It was a strong England side that filed out to meet the upstarts that afternoon. The maestro Stanley Matthews was rested, but his absence scarcely dented a side that also included Wilf Mannion, Tom Finney, Alf Ramsey, Stan Mortenson and Jimmy Dickinson. And the postgame stats justify England's confidence. Four times they hit the woodwork. A goal was almost certainly unjustly disallowed when it was sent clear from a yard *behind* the American goal line; another clear goal scoring opportunity was lost when Mortenson was rugby-tackled by Charley Columbo. At the other end of the field, England keeper Bert Williams did not touch the ball once throughout the second half of the game.

But thirty-eight minutes in, the US scored. And that was all she wrote.

Elevated almost to household-name status in Britain, where *nobody* could believe what they had accomplished, the American players returned to their own homeland to no fanfare, no headlines, no nothing.

Inside-right John Souza was elected onto the World Cup All-Star team by the Brazilian newspaper *Mundo Esportivo*. Nobody noticed.

Goalkeeper Frank Borghi had kept out everything the English could throw at him. Nobody cared.

Walter Bahr sent in the assist that so bedazzled the English defense. Nobody heard.

And Joe Gaetjens scored the goal that broke the English hearts, and not only did nobody care about that, they didn't notice when he disappeared, either. Haitian born, Gaetjens returned to his homeland (he actually played for the Haiti national side in a World Cup qualifier against Mexico in 1953) where he was murdered by one of Papa Doc's death squads in 1964.

It was a tragic end to a life that had touched the very apex of legend—for as long as soccer is played in England, his goal and that defeat will remain a defining moment in its history, the day the English realized that the rest of the world played their game as well.

Yet, with cruel irony, it might also be seen as somewhat fitting. For just as its greatest-ever hero died brutally, forgotten, and a long way from the scene of his biggest triumphs, so did the game he played. In 1954, the United States' World Cup qualification campaign was effectively ended by a 4–0 mauling at the hands of Mexico; in 1958, the US finished bottom of their three-team qualifying group, played four, lost four, scored five, conceded twenty-one. Mexico beat them 6–0 in Mexico, 7–1 in Long Beach. Canada whipped them 5–1 in Toronto.

The US did make the finals of the 1956 Olympics soccer tournament, but only because Mexico withdrew from the qualifiers. Then they advanced to the quarter-finals—but only because so many other nations had pulled out of the games that their first-round match with Yugoslavia was postponed to that later stage. The Slavs then thrashed them 9–0. But perhaps the most decisive moment came when the United States faced off against England once more, and a decade that began with a single US goal sending the English home heartbroken ended, miraculously, with another single US goal. This time, however, the English scored eight.

And so it was that soccer faced the sixties from deep within the doldrums, a state of affairs in which a growing number of pessimists believed it might dwell forever more. But that was because they didn't know of a certain William Cox, a businessman whose past interests included ownership of the Philadelphia Phillies baseball team, but whose new dreams revolved around a very different ballgame altogether.

Cox was not the first person to look at the popularity and success of soccer elsewhere around the world, and wonder why it did not translate to American shores. Nor was he the first to cast around the current state of the American game and realize that the country's own sides offered little to appeal to a thrill-hungry domestic sports audience.

He was, however, the first to actively set about doing something about it. The International Soccer League, he declared, would be an invitation-only event bringing the very cream of European and South American soccer to the United States for a series of competitive, meaningful, and (of course) highly remunerative games.

Touring sides were already a familiar part of the off-season landscape, particularly in the northeast and California; as far back as the 1900s, European sides had been visiting—sometimes the giants, like Manchester United, sometimes minnows, like the Pilgrims amateur club. Representative sides drawing on the cream of an individual FA's membership had been visiting since the 1920s; in 1921, the Scottish side Third Lanark even put together its own "best of Scotland" for a stateside visit.

Headlines were occasionally wrought. When the German side Hamburger SV was invited over in 1950, at a time when Germany itself was still enduring its post–World War Two ostracism from FIFA, an attempt to introduce the players to New York City from the steps of City Hall ended when onlookers produced a hail of tomatoes.

Generally, however, the tours trailed around in more or less obscurity, entrancing to the handfuls who were aware that they were happening, and irrelevant to everybody else. Cox's target audience was that "everybody else."

The USFA had changed since the days when it was a deeply conservative, darkly suspicious organization, almost paranoically opposed to any suggestion that might rock the very stable (if more or less submerged) boat that it had spent the years since the Soccer Wars constructing. It had a new name, for a start; it was now the USSFA, the US Soccer Football Association. Apart from that, though, it remained less than enthusiastic by any prospective change to the landscape, which was a major obstacle for Cox. Charged as it was with overseeing soccer in the US, no new league, not even one for foreign sides, could be initiated without USSFA approval, as several decades' worth of past dented dreams could testify.

Cox made his initial approach through the American Soccer League, the most influential of the USSFA affiliates, portraying his International Soccer League as an adjunct to the ASL's own competition. And with their approval swiftly forthcoming, plans were laid for the ISL to kick off in 1960.

Invitations were sent out to, and accepted by, eleven clubs from around the world: Bangu Atlético Clube of Brazil, FC Bayern München (Germany), Burnley (England), Glenavon (Northern Ireland), Kilmarnock (Scotland), OGC Nice Côte d'Azur (France), IFK Norrköping (Sweden), SK Rapid Wien (Austria), Crvena Zvezda—better known in the West as Red Star Belgrade (Yugoslavia), UC Sampdoria (Italy) and Sporting Clube de Portugal (Portugal), with the field completed by an all-star side representing American interests named for New York—the host city for the first year's competition.

With local television pitching in, and a healthy advertising budget drawing curious crowds to ensure that every game at least drew some attention (and, of course, money), the 1960 season—won by the Brazilians—was successful enough that Cox immediately began preparing for the following year's event. The ASL, itself enthused by the popularity of the ISL, agreed to schedule as few of its own league games as possible against ISL attractions, and Cox entered into discussions to expand the ISL's base to other major cities, including Chicago, Boston, Los Angeles, and Detroit.

The 1961 tournament boasted an even broader field than its predecessor: defending champions Bangu Atlético Clube and the returning Rapid, Red Star, and Kilmarnock were joined by Beşiktaş JK (Turkey), Dinamo Bucureşti (Romania), RCD Espanyol (Spain), Everton (England), Hapoel Petah Tikva (Israel), Karlsruher SC (West Germany), AS Monaco (France), Montreal Concordia (Canada) and Shamrock Rovers (Ireland), together with the team destined to sweep all before them, FK Dukla Praha of Czechoslovakia.

The competition's third season, 1962, brought a new innovation, the American Challenge Cup, to be played out between the defending champions, Dukla, and the new season's victors. That would be Rio de Janeiro's America RJ, emerging triumphant from a powerful pack that also featured CF Os Belenenses (Portugal), Dundee (Scotland), IF Elfsborg (Sweden),

With collisions like this, there was no need to dive! Hungary and Austria offer up the face of world soccer, 1962.

Club Deportivo Guadalajara (Mexico), HNK Hajduk Split (Yugoslavia), MTK Budapest (Hungary), US Città di Palermo (Italy), Panathinaikos (Greece), Real Oviedo (Spain), SSV Reutlingen 05 (West Germany) and Wiener AC (Austria).

Dukla won, setting up a remarkable run of success for the Czech side. Future Challenge Cup battles were to be played between the current league champion and the previous season's Cup winner, a device that allowed Dukla to compete the next four finals, and win three of them. Only in 1965 was their dominance shattered, when they were defeated by the Polish side Polonia Bytom.

Meanwhile, the league continued going from strength to strength. In 1963, it was competed for by the returning Belenenses, Wiener AC, and Kilmarnock, with fresh blood provided by Club Deportivo Oro (Mexico), GNK Dinamo Zagreb (Yugoslavia), Górnik Zabrze (Poland), Hälsingborgs IF (Sweden), Mantova (Italy), SC Preußen Münster (West Germany), Real Valladolid (Spain), Sport Club do Recife (Brazil), Újpest Dózsa (Hungary), Valenciennes (France), and West Ham United (England), with the latter poised, though none could have known it, on the eve of one of the most successful spells in their history.

By the end of the upcoming season, 1963–1964, the Hammers would have won the English FA Cup; the year after, they would take the European Cup Winners Cup, and in 1966, West Ham would provide the backbone of England's World Cup winning team. The ISL was the foundation stone for each of those future triumphs, as West Ham swept to the 1963 championship.

1964 brought appearances from AEK Athens (Greece), Esporte Clube Bahia (Brazil), Blackburn Rovers (England), Heart of Midlothian (Scotland), Vicenza Calcio (Italy), Schwechater SC (Switzerland), Vitória de Guimarães (Portugal), SV Werder Bremen (West Germany), the returning Red Star Belgrade, and the ultimate champions, Zagłębie Sosnowiec of Poland, and again, in terms of crowds and reaction, all seemed to be going well.

However, the 1965 season was to be the ISL's last. Dukla, Kilmarnock, West Ham, Ferencvárosi TC (Hungary), Portuguesa (Brazil), TSV 1860 München (West Germany), AS Varese 1910 (Italy) and West Bromwich Albion (England) all competed in a tight contest whose ultimate victor was Poland's Polonia Bytom. Unfortunately, other forces were moving against the league.

Financially the ISL was doing a lot better than many people had expected, or predicted. Across the six seasons to date, Cox had lost around $100,000, which was substantially less money than most US soccer leagues of the time were hemorrhaging. And maybe that was what bothered the powers that be, the fact that somebody else, a complete outsider, had walked into their comfortable little universe and proved that soccer could actually make money. Or maybe not. Maybe they were just annoyed that Cox continually refused to allow the USSFA to play any part in the organization and management of his baby.

Either way, at the conclusion of the 1965 games, the USSFA informed Cox that it was withdrawing its support for the tournament, meaning that any future games would effectively be outlaws not only in domestic eyes, but also those of

FIFA. Competing players could be banned from plying their trade anywhere in the world; competing teams could have their membership of both their own domestic league, and FIFA itself, suspended.

No matter that fans, teams, and sponsors alike howled "foul" at the USSFA. Cox had no alternative but to pull the plug on the ISL and, while he did eventually win an antitrust suit against the USSFA, the dream was over.

For now.

The Los Angeles Wolves and Other Passing Hybrids

On July 30, 1966, more than eight million Americans calmly put to one side whatever else they intended doing that Sunday evening, and settled down instead to watch what, for many of them, was a unique televisual event: the live broadcast, on the ABC television network, of the World Cup final from London, England.

And in boardrooms and think tanks all across the United States, brows furrowed in concentration, and eyes narrowed in thought. If eight million people were willing to watch a soccer game on television, how many would be prepared to watch it in real life?

Of course, there were a lot of people who could have answered that question without any resort to market research or fancy graphs and spreadsheets. A few thousand on a regular basis, a few more on a casual level, and a modicum of passersby who may or may not last the course.

But the people doing the market research, and commissioning the graphs and spreadsheets, didn't want to hear that. They wanted to hear numbers that hung round the stratosphere somewhere, numbers that soared and reached for the stars. Numbers that would make rich men out of them all.

The USSFA had heard it all before, of course. Even after the ISL got underway, and before it was closed down, there was always someone coming along with a foolproof scheme to make soccer big, and the USSFA had shot every one of them down. Usually with very good reason.

Even ABC, astonished though they were by the size of the World Cup audience, was sensibly admitting that it was the novelty of the event (the first World Cup final ever screened live in the US) and the perceived gravity of the situation (England vs. West Germany) that pulled eight million viewers away from their yardwork. It would be a long time before you ever saw figures like that for a soccer game again.

But the USSFA was always willing to listen to new ideas, just in case one of them had something going for it. And also, because in order to even be listened to in the first place, would-be suitors were asked to stump up a franchise fee of $25,000 per competing team, plus a guaranteed slice of gate receipts and television income.

It was amazing how quickly the field thinned out after that.

The USSFA ultimately placed its support behind the USA (United Soccer

Association), essentially a rerun of the ISL in that it involved a dozen European and South American clubs being invited to the US, to play out a competition. The big difference was, each of the twelve would be renamed for the occasion, to represent a different American city.

Ireland's Shamrock Rovers became Boston Shamrock Rovers; the Italian side Cagliari Calcio were redrafted as the Chicago Mustangs; England's Stoke City were sent to become the Cleveland Stokers, Sunderland journeyed to Canada to become the Vancouver Royal Canadians, and Wolverhampton Wanderers became the Los Angeles Wolves.

Scotland's Dundee United and Hibernian were reborn as the Dallas Tornado and Toronto City respectively; while a third Scottish team, Aberdeen, was rebranded the Washington Whips. Glentoran of Northern Ireland were the Detroit Cougars; ISL veterans Bangu of Brazil glittered as the Houston Stars; Uruguay's Cerro Largo became the impressively named New York Skyliners; and ADO Den Haag of the Netherlands, the correspondingly dreadfully dubbed San Francisco Golden Gate Gales.

The clubs' owners were just as cosmopolitan. The Skyliners were owned by the Madison Square Garden Corporation, the Gales by George Fleharty of the Ice Follies, the Whips by lawyer Earl Foreman, Toronto by businessman Steve Stavro.

It was an audacious exercise, and one that grabbed attention no matter what you thought of its actual mechanics. But could it keep that attention? Six games were played on the inaugural Saturday, May 28, and the results were as drab as any of soccer's most brutal critics could have dreamed.

Whips vs. Stokers, 1–2. Stars vs. Wolves, 1–1. Rovers vs. Cougars, 1–1. Skyliners vs. Toronto, 1–1. Mustangs vs. Tornado, 0–1. Only in the city on the bay did soccer sound as exciting as its cheerleaders insisted, as the Gales blew the Royal Canadians all the way back to Wearside, a 6–1 victory that set the standard for the remainder of Sunderland's stateside sojourn, but might have flattered the Dutchmen.

At the end of the twelve-game season, the LA Wolves topped the western division with five wins and only two defeats to their name; across the continent, the Whips had an identical record, to set up what has been described—with considerable justification—as the greatest soccer final ever played in the United States.

Eleven goals whipped into the nets, a 6–5 Wolves win so breathlessly battled that even reading the press reports leaves the heart pounding. And then the imports all went home.

Meanwhile, a rival National Professional Soccer League had also sprung up, marked out from the USA by its refusal to pay the franchise fees and, therefore, its wholly outlaw status in the eyes of soccer's administrators.

The NPSL didn't care. With the entire operation largely financed by a CBS television contract, players recruited to the league from overseas tended to be those whose careers had already ended, or had never got off the ground to begin with—those for whom an immediate payday in the United States represented either a last chance at banking some money from the game, or an only chance.

The anti-soccer lobby always complained that the game did not appeal to Americans. The NPSL listened to their complaints and addressed them. In league competitions elsewhere around the world, teams received two points for a win, one for a tie, and it didn't matter whether one goal was scored or one hundred. The tally remained the same. NPSL awarded six points for a win, three for a tie, and then sweetened the deal by adding on a bonus point for each of the first three goals scored by either team.

So, win 1–0 and you'd get seven points. Draw 3–3 and you'd get six. Win 5–3 and you'd get all nine. And it has to be admitted that, of all the myriad schemes that have been cooked up over the years to encourage attacking soccer, and to keep the goals a-flowing, it would be difficult to top that one.

Yet neither of these experiments, the USA's importing of thrilling foreign talent or the NPSL's invoking of wild award systems, proved especially successful. Playing standards, while not exactly poor, never really raised themselves beyond the level of a preseason friendly kickabout, which of course is all the USA league was; and over in the NPSL, attendances were minuscule, TV figures low, and the lack of any real star power among either players or teams left the floating neutrals completely nonplussed. Why should it matter how many points a team gets, if you haven't actually heard of them?

Because that is what it all boiled down to. Where soccer was going wrong now—had, in fact, been going wrong since the Soccer Wars first introduced franchising to the sport—was in its refusal to comprehend perhaps the single most powerful element in the European and South American game's popularity. The fact that it is not enough simply to plop a team into a town and expect a grateful populace to rise up and support it. A team needs to develop organically, to represent its home base with something a lot more tangible than a mere name.

Even more than the instant turn-the-TV-off effect of the over-enthusiastic experts who would (and, all these years later, sadly still do) pop up periodically to "explain" the game to viewers, ignoring the fact that being shouted at by a swivel-eyed nerd tends not to put the average couch potato at its ease . . . yes, even more than that, the failure to understand the game's appeal at the grassroots level was a serious error, and one that was committed by administrators and owners alike.

One cannot, of course, fault the businessmen who believed otherwise. Every other major American team sport is all but founded upon franchising. Why should soccer be any different?

Why indeed. A game whose very foundations are built on a business principle can reasonably expect to thrive upon it. But soccer's core audience in the United States at this time (and for some decades to come) was drawn either from immigrant communities or from supporters knowledgeable of how things were done elsewhere. In order to succeed, then, it needed to be seen to develop in an overseas manner. Meaning, a team that could thrive without the ever-present danger of its owner whisking it away to the other side of the country at the first sign of falling attendances. Or send it back to another country entirely, the moment the season is over, as was the case with the USA league.

When Is a Franchise Not a Franchise?

It's strange how certain truths take root in the soccer psyche, and stranger still that that is one of the most deeply anchored. In reality, not even the most established foreign soccer teams can claim to have remained geographically static their entire lives. One of England's most storied sides, Arsenal, started life in Woolwich, in south London, before relocating to Highbury in the north of the city; while the 1920s saw the South Shields club, founder members of the Third Division North, shift to a different (albeit still local) town altogether, Gateshead.

The Scottish side Meadowbank Thistle relocated from Edinburgh to Livingston in 1995, and changed its name accordingly. Wimbledon FC was sold to a consortium of businessmen in 2003, and relocated ninety minutes away in Milton Keynes. Not every move has been popular, not every one has been successful. More than a decade on from the birth of the Milton Keynes Dons, there remain English soccer fans who refuse to call them anything other than Franchise FC, while the magazine *When Saturday Comes* still effectively refuses to even acknowledge their existence.

A traditional soccer club is more than a name. It is an accumulation of traditions and heritage, and a healthy serving of local culture. Features, the clubs' supporters sadly sigh, that apparently have little place in the modern business-run world, and which do in fact look increasingly archaic as

Program for the St. Louis Stars's August 1971 encounter with the Dallas Tornado.

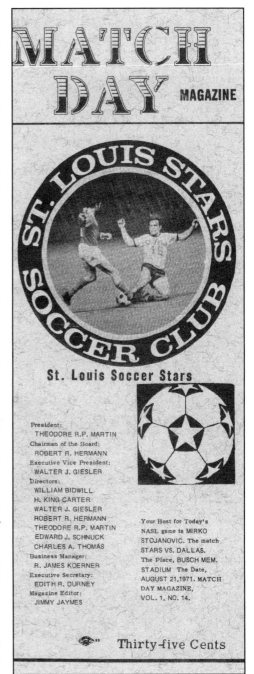

St. Louis Soccer Stars

President:
  THEODORE R.P. MARTIN
Chairman of the Board:
  ROBERT R. HERMANN
Executive Vice President:
  WALTER J. GIESLER
Directors:
  WILLIAM BIDWILL
  H. KING CARTER
  WALTER J. GIESLER
  ROBERT R. HERMANN
  THEODORE R.P. MARTIN
  EDWARD J. SCHNUCK
  CHARLES A. THOMAS
Business Manager:
  R. JAMES KOERNER
Executive Secretary:
  EDITH R. DURNEY
Magazine Editor:
  JIMMY JAYMES

Your Host for Today's NASL game is MIRKO STOJANOVIC. The match STARS VS. DALLAS. The Place, BUSCH MEM. STADIUM The Date, AUGUST 21, 1971. MATCH DAY MAGAZINE, VOL. 1, NO. 14.

Thirty-five Cents

A special edition of the NASL's *Kick* magazine, geared toward the Surf's 1981 encounter with San Jose.

organized club soccer expands its global reach into new territories that have no century-old tradition of the game.

There . . . in Japan, in Australia, in China and, yes, in the United States . . . there is no alternative but to launch a club anew. And if the businessmen who launch them want to protect their investment by knowing they can shift, or even sell the club to another businessman in another city, then naturally they are going to demand a league setup that allows them to do so.

The North American Soccer League

The USSFA certainly had no alternative but to accept franchising as the way forward, and in December 1967, with both the USA and the NPSL chastened by the failure of operations to date, the USSFA oversaw their merger into an entirely new tournament, the North American Soccer League (NASL).

Eight of its competitors were drawn from the NPSL: the Atlanta Chiefs, the Baltimore Bays, the Kansas City Spurs, the New York Generals, the Oakland Clippers, the St. Louis Stars, the San Diego Toros (hailing from from Los Angeles), and the Toronto Falcons; nine hailed from the USA: the Boston Beacons, the Chicago Mustangs, the Cleveland Stokers, the Dallas Tornado, the Detroit Cougars, the Houston Stars, the Los Angeles Wolves, the Vancouver Royals, and the Washington Whips.

Again, foreign clubs were to provide the majority of the playing talent, and again it proved a less than successful enterprise. Supporters buying into the existence of the clubs nevertheless remained unconvinced by the imports, while local pride itself found little to connect with. Across the entire seventeen-club league, no more than thirty North American–born players were involved that first season.

Even more alarming, however, and the root of much of the suspicion with which the rest of the world would eye American soccer, was the welter of new and exciting rule changes that were implemented in an attempt to bring the game to the masses.

The wild distribution of points had been accepted by all but the most tiresome traditionalists—the same people who would be equally aggrieved when the notion of *three* points for a win was introduced elsewhere round the world beginning in the late 1970s. But nobody, and that means *nobody*, could comprehend what came next.

As a part of its pact with the television network, the NPSL had introduced breaks during the two halves of the game so that paid commercials might be run on schedule. It was an unheard of interference, but the tinkering had only just begun.

Elsewhere around the world, soccer matches begin with the clock at zero and count up to ninety minutes. The NASL was to follow other American sporting traditions by counting down.

Elsewhere, halftime was a fifteen-minute break during which supporters could get a pie and a cup of tea, read the program, and moan about the game. The NASL introduced cheerleaders, fireworks, clowns, and jugglers.

Elsewhere, offside was a law, almost as old as the game themselves, designed to prevent players from spending the entire game standing on their opponent's goal line, and knocking the ball in every time it comes close—"goal hanging," as it is known. The NASL decided it got in the way.

They could not just scrap it altogether, not if they wanted to remain members of FIFA. But they could maybe modify it, and so the game's American administrators (who included a couple of Englishmen, former Aston Villa striker Phil Woosnam, and one-time Scunthorpe coach Fred Goodwin) set about doing so.

A new thirty-five meter "blue line" was drawn across the pitch. In other lands, a player could be caught offside anywhere within his opponent's half of the field. In the NASL, he had to travel beyond the blue line, shaving fifteen meters off the old zone, and it did the trick. Goals did come easier, offside calls did become less frequent . . . and FIFA did take a long hard look at it and demand its immediate abandonment.

The NASL's furthest reaching revision, however, is still with us today. Any fan, any place in the world, who loathes the penalty shootout as a means of deciding a tied game . . . blame the NASL.

In the eyes of their perpetrators, each of these changes was justified as a means of drawing American sports fans into the game. Few, however, succumbed to the temptation, and the NASL's first season alone depicted it as one vast money pit.

No team owned its own ground, so other stadia had to be rented, an extravagant cost that was in no way recouped via attendances. Television was no more than vaguely interested. And four separate mini-leagues, divided between the Eastern Conference (Atlantic and Lakes divisions) and the Western Conference (Gulf and Pacific divisions) demanded a lot of attention, cash, and care.

They received none. The first season was played through, with the Atlanta Chiefs, the Cleveland Stokers, the San Diego Toros, and the Kansas City Spurs marching to the Conference finals, and the Chiefs winning the tournament outright, 3–0 over two games with the Toros. But no sooner did the NASL crown its first champions, than it was also facing its first crisis. Just five of the teams involved in the 1968 campaign showed any interest in returning for the following year's competition: the Atlanta Chiefs, the Baltimore Bays, the Dallas Tornado, the Kansas City Spurs and the St. Louis Stars. If soccer was a growing sport, it had a very strange way of demonstrating that.

But the NASL persevered. For its second season, the domestic club campaign was augmented with a second, shorter series of games rejoicing beneath the title of the International Cup, and inviting a handful of British clubs to masquerade as their hosts. Aston Villa were quartered in Atlanta, where they became the Chiefs for the duration of the tournament. The Bays were represented by West Ham, the Tornado by Dundee United, the Spurs (confusingly) by Wolves, and the St Louis Stars by Kilmarnock. And with glorious symmetry, the Spurs won both the International Cup and the regular season title, too.

Slowly, the NASL was placing its tentative beginnings behind it. The following season, 1970, brought the Rochester Lancers into the fold, with the Washington Darts replacing the Baltimore Bays, and the two new sides immediately established themselves by winning the divisional titles and thus competing in the final—won 4–3 by the Lancers.

The following year, the loss of the Spurs was readily mitigated by the addition of Montreal Olympique and the Toronto Metros, bringing Canadian interests firmly into the league; while behind the scenes, Phil Woosnam was busying himself creating the team that was destined to carry the NASL's name around the world, and which remained the best-known American club side of all time, long after the club itself became extinct.

The New York Cosmos were coming.

3

That Was Then, What About Now?

The Cosmos and the Birth of Modern Soccer

The New York Cosmos was the brainchild of Phil Woosnam, the afore-mentioned Englishman abroad. One of several British players recruited to the Atlanta Chiefs setup in 1966 (his Aston Villa teammates Vic Crowe and Peter McParland accompanied him), it was Woosnam who engi-neered that club's rise up first, the NPSL and then the inaugural NASL. Which was followed by his own ascent from head coach at the Chiefs to commissioner of the league itself.

Of all the manifold drawbacks that the NASL faced, its failure to maintain a solid presence in New York City was perhaps its most obvious, at least from a public relations point of view. What kind of sport is it, after all, if it doesn't even have a standing in the largest city in America? In 1970, then, Woosnam set about remedying the situation by entering into negotiations for the Warner Communications media conglomerate to launch its own soccer team in the Big Apple. And so persuasive were his arguments that when the 1971 season kicked off, the Cosmos were ready to go.

Once the naming rights had been decided, of course. General Manager Clive Toye, another Englishman and a former sports writer who had occupied a lofty role at the Baltimore Bays, had always wanted to call the new team the Cosmos, short for Cosmopolitan, in a bid to outdo the baseball side, the *Metr*opolitan*s*.

Ahmet and Nesuhi Ertegun, top executives at Warners, however, preferred the New York Blues—a reference to their own heritage at the greatest R&B and blues record label in America, Atlantic. In the end, the decision was thrown open to a public competition, and it seemed that other people were thinking along the same lines as Toye. The Cosmos it was.

The pieces fell into place. Player-coach Gordon Bradley was another Englishman, one who spent the majority of his playing career at such footballing outposts as Workington Town and Carlisle United before moving to Canada at the age of thirty and continuing his career there. Now he was a coach in the German American Soccer League, but he came to Woosnam's attention and was duly installed at the Cosmos.

The playing staff was just as cosmopolitan, but the Cosmos made an immediate splash. Playing their home games at Yankee Stadium, they finished second in their division in 1971, behind the Rochester Lancers. The following year, based now at Hofstra Stadium, they took the NASL Championship, losing just three of their sixteen games as they marched to the title, with their star player, Bermuda-born Randy Horton, rounding out the season as both the league's top scorer (nine of the Cosmos's thirty-one goals were his) and MVP.

But 1973 saw the Cosmos slip, finishing second in the Eastern Division to the newly formed Philadelphia Atoms, and then tumbling out of the play-offs with an uncharacteristic semifinal defeat to Dallas Tornado. The Atoms took the championship and the Cosmos sat back to contemplate their future. They shifted home once again, this time to Downing Stadium, and went into the 1974 season with understandably high hopes.

The NASL had expanded again, to sixteen clubs. Atlanta and Montreal had dropped out, but no fewer than eight new teams had pitched in: the Baltimore Comets, the Boston Minutemen, the Denver Dynamos, the Los Angeles Aztecs, the San José Earthquakes, the Seattle Sounders, the Vancouver Whitecaps, and the Washington Diplomats; and, as so often happens, it was the new blood that triumphed.

Sharing the Northern Division with the Toronto Metros, the Rochester Lancers, and the suddenly hapless Cosmos, the Boston Minutemen swept all before them as they galloped into the play-offs—where they were promptly unhorsed by the eventual champions, the similarly newborn LA Aztecs. The Cosmos, on the other hand, finished bottom of their division. It was time for a change. And what a change it would be.

Bendier Than Beckham—the Pelé Effect

Both Randy Horton, the Cosmos's top scorer in every season so far, and coach Bradley departed New York at the end of the 1974 season. And, in their stead, there came Pelé, the most famous soccer player in the world.

It is impossible to capture today the sheer enormity of Pelé's recruitment. In 2007, people treated David Beckham's arrival in Los Angeles as big news, and so it was. Ronaldo's transfer to Real Madrid. Luis Suarez's every move. In the world of cheap thrills and even cheaper filler that today's celebrities are forced to inhabit, all of these things deserved the headlines with which they were greeted.

But Pelé coming to the Cosmos was bigger.

At a time when most Europeans seemed to believe that anybody with a spare parking lot and a hamper full of soccer shirts could call themselves an American soccer team, Pelé's arrival showed that the NASL meant business. At a time when a lot of Americans still thought soccer was a joke, it proved that some people took it very seriously indeed. Even the most soccer-hating media personality, if they hadn't already heard of Pelé, was at least willing to buy into the notion that he was a seriously enormous acquisition. And, while some would (and did)

Official matchday program for the New Jersey Eagles's July 1989 friendly with Polish tourists Ruch Chorzów.

point out that the great man was already several years past his best, and that the Cosmos's proffered riches was simply one final mega payday, still they were going to turn out to see him perform his magic.

Even without Pelé, NASL attendances had finally started moving toward respectability, with several of the newly added West Coast teams averaging over 10,000 supporters per game. Now, numbers were about to explode, and the vaguest predictions of the Pelé effect set fresh chain reactions in motion.

No fewer than five new clubs joined the league, surely encouraged at least in part by its sudden wild visibility, and suddenly Pelé was no longer the only incoming superstar. The NASL was big news worldwide now, and a host of players—many, like Pelé, nearing the end of their top-level careers in other lands—flocked to the United States.

Portuguese hero Eusebio joined the Boston Minutemen (and would later turn out for Toronto and Las Vegas Quicksilvers); and others would follow: Manchester United's George Best, Ajax Amsterdam's Johan Cruyff; FC Bayern München's Franz Beckenbauer, marquee attractions one and all, players whose very name on a team sheet, it was widely believed, would add thousands to the attendance at the same time as striking fear into the hearts of the opposition.

Certainly television audiences were impressed. On June 15, 1975, the largest-ever domestic television audience for a soccer game, ten million, tuned in to watch the highest paid soccer player on the planet (he was receiving $1.4 million per year) make his Cosmos debut against the Dallas Tornado.

No expense was spared. According to legend, the club's groundsman even spray-painted the pitch green, to disguise how little grass was actually growing on it. Anything to give a good impression, and he was probably right to do so. Twenty-two other countries received a live feed of the match, and the NASL was under no impression of how the rest of the world viewed American soccer . . . that is, as an overpaid, jumped-up little upstart who didn't even play by the same rules as everyone else. This was the game's opportunity to strike back.

Pelémania hit. Not only was he contracted as a soccer player, a number of other enterprises also bore his name, including, incredibly, a recording contract with Atlantic Records. Few (if any) of these extracurricular opportunities were expected to be acted upon; rather, wily accountants inserted them into the deal to ensure Pelé paid as little tax as possible. Their promise, however, made the media and just stirred up fresh excitement. At their peak (which means, at Pelé's peak), the Cosmos were regularly attracting crowds of 40,000, and that despite ending the superstar's inaugural season in an utterly unexpected third place.

They would not remain there for long. Another Englishman, Ken Furphy, was coaching the side now, and the decision to pair Pelé with another import, the Italian Giorgio Chinaglia, swiftly paid dividends. Vastly improving on the previous season, when it seemed that many of Pelé's teammates were as over-awed by his presence as their opponents, the Cosmos at least reached the 1976 play-offs, only to stumble to the Tampa Bay Rowdies, whose own frontline was bolstered by yet another legend of the game, the Englishman Rodney Marsh.

And what a legend he was.

It is strange, but it is also, perhaps, human nature, that many times a soccer player is best remembered *not* for what he accomplished on the pitch, but for what he may have said, or had said to him, off it. Not Pelé—his goal-scoring exploits will doubtless be remembered long after we have completely forgotten his role as a television spokesman for Viagra.

But no discussion of George Best is complete without recalling the hotel worker who, delivering room service to the by-then fallen star, could not help but ask, plaintively, "George. Where did it all go wrong?" And Best looked at the Miss World stretched out beside him on the bed, and the wad of cash that they had, for some reason, strewn across the mattress; at the champagne that had just been deposited in his room . . . and, for the first time in his career, he was probably speechless. Where did it all go wrong indeed.

For Rodney Marsh, the *bon mot* that remains so many people's favorite reminder of his maverick genius and playboy insouciance was delivered before his first-ever appearance in an England shirt.

Widely regarded as a brilliant but erratic player, one who was as likely to win you the game as cost you a championship, Marsh was the epitome of the fast-thinking, sharp-talking, wisecracking Cockney geezer so beloved of American visions of English life. England manager Alf Ramsey, on the other hand, was a straitlaced, straight-faced man whose upper class aspirations were so pronounced that he even took speech therapy lessons to try to dampen his natural (common) accent. Chalk and cheese even before they met, Marsh ensured that he and Ramsey would never see eye to eye, with more or less the first words out of his mouth.

"I'll be watching you for the first forty-five minutes," Ramsey warned Marsh, "and if you don't work harder, I'll pull you off at halftime."

"Crikey," Marsh replied. "We usually just get an orange and a cup of tea."

America, too, would witness the iconic comic side of the mercurial Marsh. Arriving in Tampa Bay, he learned that his new chairman had recently described him as "the white Pelé." Marsh was quick to correct him. "Pelé is the black Rodney Marsh." And there were moments, particularly in his prime at Queens Park Rangers, but also during his years with the Rowdies, when both comments were correct.

With his unconquerable Cosmos undone by Tampa's rowdy Rodney, Ken Furphy did not remain Cosmos coach for long. Preparing for the 1977 season, with the previous year's "failure" an all-pervading cloud, the club turned back to Bob Bradley, reinstating him first as coach and then shifting him upstairs to become vice-president of player personnel, while ex-Italy international Eddie Firmani moved into the hot seat.

Franz Beckenbauer and another Brazilian legend, Carlos Alberto, wore the Cosmos colors now, and the cumulative impact of these changes was decisive. The Cosmos took the NASL championship in 1977, and even though Pelé retired at the end of that season, they would repeat the feat in 1978 and 1980. The Cosmos' dream of becoming the number one soccer team in America had finally been realized.

Before a shockingly empty Hinchcliffe Stadium in July 1989, the New Jersey Eagles launch an attack on the Ruch Chorzów goal. *Photo by Dave Thompson*

The Empty Stadium

There was just one tiny problem. Nobody was watching. No matter how high a caliber Pelé's teammates and successors may have been, no matter how great their legend in the annals of the round ball game, all were at one major disadvantage. They were not Pelé.

In terms of media coverage and crowd recognition, the most famous soccer player in the world had broken down the most tautly erected barriers. But they were erected again the moment his back was turned. Without Pelé, what were the Cosmos or, indeed, any other NASL side, but a bunch of elderly foreigners and wet-behind-the-ears local lads, chasing a ball around a field?

The larger crowds vanished, the smaller ones shrunk. Television found other things to ogle. Even the most successful franchises were losing money, and the rest were on the verge of collapse.

In 1978, Detroit Express launched under the co-ownership of the oddly bearded Jimmy Hill, the latest in a long line of British sports and media personalities to see a future fortune spooling out of the NASL's seemingly bottomless coffers. Two years later, the Express were no more and today, their dream home, the Pontiac Silverdome, stands (completely coincidentally, but atmospherically all the same) as a testament to the maniacal avarice and ambition that ultimately brought the entire NASL crashing down.

Still standing at the time of writing, but surely an imminent candidate for demolition and redevelopment, the Silverdome in 2014 is a wind-wracked, weed-infested bowl, a ruin whose Teflon-coated roof was long ago stripped away by the elements; whose playing surface, on which the likes of Trevor Francis, Alan Brazil, Pato Margetic, and Ted MacDougall once bossed the field with such imperious ease, is either underwater or split by impudent saplings. Wildlife

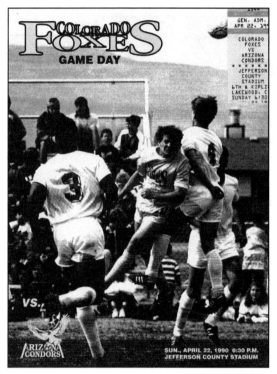

The Colorado Foxes make their bow against the Arizona Condors at Jefferson County Stadium in Denver, on April 22, 1990.

inhabits the seating, mold murals the walls. Recent years have seen a major upsurge of interest in disused and decaying soccer grounds in Britain and beyond. The Silverdome is as tragically atmospheric as any of them.

That is today. But even back then, at the end of the 1970s, everywhere one looked during those final years of the NASL, disaster grinned back.

Wages were the chief culprit, each team offering greater and greater sums to lesser and lesser foreign stars in the hope of even a soupçon of Pelé-shaped lightning striking back. In 1980, the Portland Timbers literally *tripled* their previous season's wage bill, simply to stay abreast of the sums being splashed about elsewhere, while the Cosmos were blowing a staggering 70% of their operating budget on players' pay.

The NASL was wallowing within a deficit that approached $30 million, and the teams were not far behind. When the Washington Diplomats closed up shop in November 1980, it was because their owners had just watched $5 million disappear into the black hole that was American soccer. Tulsa saw $8 million vanish between 1980 and 1983, the appallingly named San Diego Sockers managed to misplace $10 million between 1978 and 1983.

Expensive, experienced foreigners fell from fashion; untried local youngsters filled their boots, but this time, not only for financial reasons. An increasingly popular criticism of the NASL, and perhaps a reason for its own fans losing interest, was that it was simply a showcase for overpaid imports, a foreign-filled circus that had nothing to do with American sporting aspirations. In came a new rule, then, insisting that each side field at least two US- or Canadian- born players in every game, with a minimum of six homegrown souls in the overall squad.

Of course it didn't help, and neither did another change in 1980, raising the quotient to three players per game. The problem went beyond who wore the shirt and what accent they spoke when they shouted for the ball. Soccer simply wasn't engaging people. Crowds and cash continued to gush away.

At least outdoors, they did. Soccer in America was dead, but only conventional soccer. Almost exactly mirroring the decline of the NASL, the late 1970s saw the emergence of the NISL, the National Indoor Soccer League, a peculiar sport that resembled, to the traditional soccer-playing outsider, nothing so much as a vast game of human pinball, the ball ricocheting off walls as two tiny teams of six ran pell-mell to catch it.

Games lasted just an hour, divided into four fifteen-minute quarters. The pitch was tiny, the goals were closets, the entire affair had no more in common with soccer than cricket does with baseball. And people loved it. Or they certainly loved it more than they did the outdoor, full-size game. It had a lot more cash to flash, as well. Soon, budding US soccer players were being lured into the indoor game without a glance at the NASL, and while the outdoorsmen did launch their own indoor league in 1979, it was never more than a fitful, desperate response.

As was everything else that the NASL tried.

In 1984, the NASL introduced a salary cap as one last gallant stab at staving off the inevitable. It worked to an extent, in that it allowed one final season to be played out, but it also painted the competition's doom in vast, neon-lit letters. In a culture where sporting success and fabulous wealth were two sides of the same coin, the idea that there was one sport that effectively promised even its greatest stars nothing but impecunious obscurity only broadened the divide between soccer and America.

By the end of the 1984 season—or, more accurately, by the time the NASL should have started preparing for the 1985 season—the league comprised just two teams, the Minnesota Strikers and the Toronto Blizzard. Every single one of their compatriots had either gone to the wall, or was now bouncing off one—the Chicago Sting, the Minnesota Strikers, the San Diego Strikers, and even the Cosmos were all fervent adherents of the indoor game.

The season was cancelled and, though the NASL heroically pledged that it would return in 1986, it was fooling nobody. Not even FIFA who, with a sense of timing that would have been comical if it didn't seem so suicidal, waited just two years more before announcing that the 1994 World Cup would be staged in the United States—a country, groaned the rest of the world, that not only had no national soccer league, it scarcely knew what soccer was.

A Major Soccer Conundrum

To the administrators entrusted with the organization of the 1994 World Cup, the timing of the announcement meant they had six years in which to bring the American game up to a level that *might* prove to the world they knew what they were doing.

To their detractors, on the other hand, it meant there were six years in which to joke, laugh, and generally make fun of the entire affair.

Everything was ripe for roasting. A sports journalist might point out that some of the American stadiums had retractable roofs, immediately sparking rumors that the tournament would be played indoors, to indoor rules.

American football's love affair with commercial breaks was invoked, promptly arousing fears that soccer games, too, would be interrupted to bring you this important commercial message.

The NASL's old penchant for tinkering with the rules saw fresh specters emerge; wider goals, smaller fields, bigger balls, chestier cheerleaders. If the notion of deciding drawn games with penalty kicks hadn't already been introduced to the World Cup back in 1978, no doubt that calumny, too, would have been added to the doomsday scenario.

And all the while, at their modest headquarters in Colorado Springs, the United States Soccer Federation (as the game's national governing body was now known) simply got on with their work. No rule changes, no costume changes, no silliness of any description. Just a successful World Cup, staged in a successful soccer-playing environment. There. That wasn't too much to hope for, was it?

Among the manifold conditions and guarantees demanded by FIFA prior to awarding the 1994 World Cup to the United States, perhaps the most insistent was that, at some point within the next eight years, either this side of the World Cup or in the two years immediately following it, the USSF would launch a new national league competition. And that this time, they make it work.

Ultimately, it was 1993 before the MLS was founded, and 1996 before it actually got underway, with the success of the 1994 World Cup a definite component within its own development. But having got underway, and overcome some initial teething troubles, it was to prove a remarkably sturdy child.

There were no surprises in the constitution of the competition. While there were, and are, many people who would welcome the creation of a truly national league that featured clubs that have already established roots and history in their individual communities, the new tournament would again be organized along strictly business-like lines. Ten initial franchises were split between the traditional Western and Eastern Conferences: Tampa Bay Mutiny, DC United, the Metrostars, Dallas Burn, Kansas City Wizards, Colorado Rapids, San José Clash, Los Angeles Galaxy, New England Revolution, and Columbus Crew. A full season of games would then climax with the two divisional champions, DC and the Galaxy in this inaugural season, meeting to complete the MLS Cup final—at which, first time around, a crowd of 34,643 gathered to watch a United triumph.

Which was not too shabby an attendance.

Past mistakes were heeded. Each newly constituted side would draw its sixteen-man squad from the MLS Inaugural Player Draft; and each would be restricted to just four so-called marquee players—names that were already regarded as stars within the universes of college and international soccer, and who could therefore earn a bit more than their teammates. Eric Wynalda, who proved his worth by scoring the first-ever MLS goal during the Clash's opening day clash with DC United; the distinctively bearded and grunge-styled Alexi Lalas

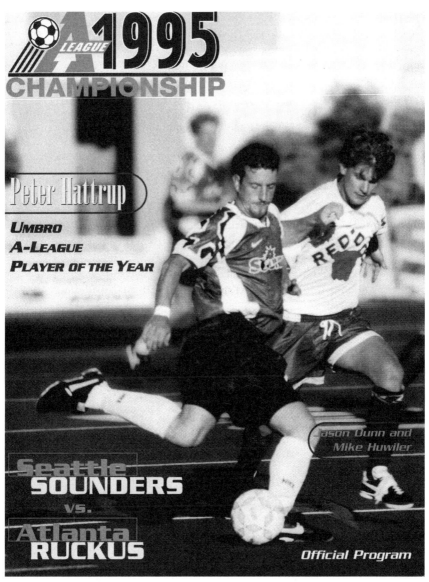

1995 A-LEAGUE CHAMPIONSHIP

Peter Hattrup

UMBRO
A-LEAGUE
PLAYER OF THE YEAR

Jason Dunn and
Mike Huwiler

Seattle
SOUNDERS
VS.
Atlanta
RUCKUS

Official Program

at the Revolution, Brian McBride at the Crew, and so forth.

The reigning A-League champions Seattle Sounders defending their title against the Atlanta Ruckus.

Such temperance and caution proved invaluable. The league's early seasons were difficult, with crowds small and interest fleeting. Several times, the MLS's imminent demise was rumored, but slowly it gathered ground, with the national team's growing presence on the world stage reflecting back on the homeland. Team USA's glorious advance to the World Cup quarterfinals in 2002 definitely gave the domestic game a shot in the arm, and that season's MLS Cup, between New England Revolution and Los Angeles Galaxy, drew a record 61,316 spectators to the Foxborough Stadium in Massachusetts. Indeed, over the next half-decade, rising crowds even saw a number of teams finally vacate the American Football stadiums they had hitherto called home, and develop their own soccer specific grounds.

The league expanded, too, with Chivas USA and Real Salt Lake joining in 2005 (the first new blood to enter the MLS since 1998); the San José Earthquakes uprooting to become Houston Dynamo (a new San José team was formed in 2008); and Toronto FC becoming the first Canadian competitors in 2007.

The much ballyhooed arrival of Englishman David Beckham to play out the twilight of his career in Los Angeles in 2007 added to the excitement, while the league also finally acknowledged two cities that might reasonably claim to rank among the country's most fertile hotbeds of soccer, with the arrival of the Seattle Sounders in 2009, and the Philadelphia Union the following year. It has expanded even further since then.

The MLS will celebrate its twentieth anniversary in 2016, and it is already firmly entrenched within the American sporting landscape. And things are only going to get better.

4

Let's Call It a League

How Did Soccer Kick Off
in the First Place?

Early in 1888, a Scottish gentleman living in Birmingham, England, was seized by a quite remarkable notion. Sixteen years after the birth of the country's first national soccer competition, the FA Cup, twenty-five years after the launch of the governing Football Association itself, England's soccer teams were still little more than a gaggle of disconnected entities, scrabbling week in, week out, to arrange fixtures with which to amuse themselves and entertain their public.

There was little organization, and even less accountability. A team might travel miles for a prearranged game, only to arrive and discover their opponents had forgotten, and were about to play another side entirely. Days and times could be confused, teams might even fold without anybody bothering to notify the clubs they were scheduled to play.

Any number, and any manner of pitfalls awaited every soccer team that ventured out to play another under the then-prevalent banner of self-sufficiency. What they needed, what they cried out for, was some form of central organization . . . and one of national organization, too. How many supporters, after all, were driven away when they perused their local team's fixture list and saw it

A philatelic cover produced to mark the 1988 centenary of England's Football League.

CLARKE'S
Football Series No. 1.

G. O. Smith.
Photo by Thiele, London.

One of the undisputed giants of the Victorian game, the effervescent G. O. Smith.

yawn ahead with countless matches against the same handful of near-neighbors? A competitive sport needs competitive fixtures, else it will simply shrivel up and blow away upon the breeze of public apathy.

William McGregor saw all this, knew all this, and solved all this. He himself had seen the deprecations caused by the current system by virtue of his role as a director of Aston Villa Football Club. On March 2, 1888, he put pen to official Aston Villa notepaper, writing to five of the country's top soccer clubs to suggest that they, and a select band of others to be decided upon, organize a national championship among themselves.

All five letters received positive responses, not only from the addressees, but also from various other club secretaries who learned of McGregor's scheme. By the end of March, no fewer than twenty clubs around England had made it known that they wished to partake in this new league championship and McGregor, rather than having to canvas for support, now found himself forced to turn teams away

He chose to begin his league with a dozen teams and it is, perhaps, a symbol of his sagacity that more than 125 years later, all but one of the original twelve remains a member of either the Premier League or the Football League (teams comprising the former broke away from the latter in 1992, although they remain umbilically linked), and even the twelfth still has representation in the league.

Aston Villa, Preston North End, West Bromwich Albion, Blackburn Rovers, and Notts County, McGregor's original addressees, were joined by Bolton Wanderers, Burnley, Derby County, Stoke City, Everton, Wolverhampton Wanderers, and, last but not least, Accrington, a Lancashire-based side that had in recent years proven itself among the most powerful clubs in a region that boiled over with soccer talent and enthusiasm.

Accrington Without the Stanley

Over the previous two seasons, 1886–1887 and 1887–1888, Accrington had scored a staggering 259 goals across eighty-two games, while meting out some positive humiliations to many of the sides luckless enough to encounter them.

Lower Darwen were thrashed 20–1 in a Lancashire Cup match; Rossendale were dispatched 11–0 in the FA Cup; Thornliebank were beaten 10–0, Church were whipped by 10–2. In the light of all that a capricious future was to deal out to Accrington, their inclusion within the charmed twelve may seem strange. Tumbling, penniless, out of the league and into oblivion in 1892, Accrington returned with a new team, Accrington Stanley, thirty years later, only for that club, too, to be forced by finance to resign in 1962 (the current Accrington Stanley side, again holding their own in the lower reaches of the English League, was formed in 1968).

Back in 1888, however, nobody doubted Accrington's right to be ranked among the top twelve teams in the land and on the morning of September 8, 1888, the sports correspondent of the *Accrington Observer*—like his counterparts at newspapers the length and breadth of the land—had only one thing on his mind: the birth of this exciting new Football League tournament.

"This season will be more important than any that have yet been experienced in the records of the favourite winter game," he wrote that morning. "The constitution of the Football League [has] greatly enhanced interest and if football doesn't prove profitable and attractive this season, it never will. Thanks to the Football League, the good folk of Accrington will be enabled to witness on their own ground matches with the very cream of English clubs, and that the Reds [the club's nickname] may come out of the encounters with credit to themselves and the town they represent is a prayer to which all my readers will most devoutly say 'Amen.'"

In fact, Accrington made their Football League bow away from home, in front of ten thousand supporters packed inside Everton's Anfield Road ground, and a goalless first half could do nothing to dampen the crowd's enthusiasm. While the goals were flying in elsewhere in that first ever Super Saturday (Bolton's Kenny Davenport is generally credited with scoring the Football League's first-ever goal, two minutes into his side's match with Derby County), Everton and Accrington seemed destined to deliver the competition's first-ever goalless draw.

But then Everton broke the deadlock, Waugh's cross to Farmer finding Fleming, who effortlessly headed home, and suddenly the visitors were galvanized into action. "From the restart," declared the *Accrington Observer*'s report, "Accrington spurted up and the most exciting scuffle followed in front of the home goal, Accrington experiencing very hard lines. Fleming and Waugh then dribbled along the right, Waugh centered and Chadwick shot in hard. [Accrington goalkeeper] Horne rushed out, hit the ball clear, but in doing so came into contact with Lewis. [He] fell heavily on Lewis's foot and unfortunately fractured a rib. He was assisted off the field."

The Football League had claimed its first injury.

There were no substitutes in those days; there would not, in fact, be any for another eighty years. Accrington were down to ten men for the remainder of the game, and with defender McLellan taking up position between the posts, the team gallantly tried to get back on even terms. But, almost immediately after the restart, Fleming notched up Everton's second, and while the visitors did finally get on the scoresheet, as Holden sent the ball soaring past Everton keeper Smalley, it was too late. Everton had recorded the first of what would become many victories; Accrington the first in many defeats.

Supplement to " THE DAILY CITIZEN."

1913   GLOSSOP FOOTBALL CLUB   1914

Copyright Photo.   A. Willes, 46, Legge Street, West Bromwich.
BARNETT. MONTGOMERY. LITTLEWORTH. HAMPTON. STAPLEY. DEARNLEY. BERWICK. CAUSER. MR. MACEWEN. CARNEY.
                                                          (Trainer)   (Manager)
        TURNELL.   BOWDEN.   DONCASTER.   BAMFORD.   KNIGHT.

THE "DAILY CITIZEN" IS ALWAYS WELL INFORMED ON SPORTS-TOPICS.

Glossop, hailing from the smallest English town to have enjoyed First Division soccer, photographed on the eve of their finest hour, drawing over 10,000 spectators to a Cup game with Preston.

They did not know that at the time, of course. The following week, away to Blackburn, Accrington matched their hosts goal for goal, and the resultant 5–5 draw was the first game in Football League history to amount to double figures. Another week, another draw, this time at Derby; the competition would be into its fourth week before Accrington finally knocked up a victory, 4–2 at Stoke City, and it would be week five before the Reds at last played their first Football League match in their hometown, facing off against the Wolverhampton Wanderers. They lost.

And so it went on, establishing in that very first season of national soccer league competition anywhere in the world the truths by which such contests have been judged ever since.

There will be the winners—on this occasion, Preston North End, who marched through the entire season unbeaten and justly earned themselves the title of "the Invincibles." There will be the losers, a role that Accrington slipped into without even trying. And there will be the rest, that great mass of teams in between, jockeying for position on the table every week, but never really having much more to play for than pride and the chance of pulling of a surprise.

Oh, and the opportunity to make some money.

Money, Money, Money

Soccer was never the world's most remunerative sport, at least throughout its first century or so of life. As late as the 1970s, more than a decade after the FA's insistence on a maximum wage for players had finally been lifted, you could still raise a bitter laugh by remarking, "The only money you'll find playing soccer is Richard." Richard Money, head coach at the time of writing of Cambridge United, was a neat defender at Scunthorpe and Fulham (and later, Liverpool and Luton). Money—the other sort, cash money—did circulate in the game. But it stayed very close to the boardroom, just as it always had.

From the moment professionalism was legalized in the English game, and even before that, money greased the wheels of soccer as effectively, and imperatively, as it does any other business. For, at the end of the day, and despite all the emotional and cultural components that comprise a club, soccer is a business, and at the end of this inaugural season of league soccer, Accrington published their accounts in the local paper. They make interesting reading today.

Having commenced the season with a princely £154, fourteen shillings and one penny in the bank (the equivalent today of around £14,000 or $24,000), the club's income (in English pounds) was:

Home gate receipts—£795.2/2d (£72,244 or $121,932)
Share of away gates—£165.17/4d (£14,994 or $25,306)
League guarantees—£132 (£11,995 or $20,245)
Subscriptions, etc.—£57.16/- (£5,270 or $8,894)

Expenses were:
Gate keepers'/bag carriers' wages—£57.7/2d (£5,179 or $8,741)
Players wages—£433.12/- (£39,348 or $66,410)
Materials and furnishings—£41.0/7d (£3,725 or $6,287)
Printing/advertising—£32.11/ (£2,907 or $4,906)
Rent—£48 (£4,361 or $7,360)
Gate receipts to visiting clubs—£257.7/10d (£23,354 or $39,416)
Train and bus fares—£98.3/10d (£8,905 or $15,029)
Hotels—£14/4d (£75 or $126)
Umpire and referee wages—£33.5/1d (£2,998 or $5,059)
Repairs to ground—£73.4/2d (£6,633 or $11,195)
Second team expenses—£15 (£1,363 or $2,300)

After a full season of Football League soccer, the club was left with a balance of £104.7/8d (£9,451/$15,951)), representing a *loss* of over £54 (£4,907/$8,281) on the previous season. In years to come, however, the Accrington officials were to look back on this inaugural campaign with considerable affection. Despite concluding the next campaign in a respectable sixth place, the club's losses only mounted up, with the greatest expenses—unsurprisingly—being those that, today, still take the greatest bite out of a club's accounts. Players' wages.

In five years, players' wages at Accrington had skyrocketed from the aforementioned £433.12/- to a staggering £1,372.13/9d, or around £123,261 ($208,038) in modern money. That said, and to illustrate the old canard that you really don't know what you've got until it's gone, the amount that Accrington paid their entire squad in one season is roughly equivalent to the *monthly* wage paid out to a single Premiership player today.

Accrington were lucky in a way. Their lowly status ensured that they never attracted any of the day's superstar players. If they had, then their expenses might have soared even higher. In 1888, Everton allegedly lured twenty-five-year-old Nick Ross from Preston with the promise of a staggering £10 a week (£908/$1,532) for his services—staggering, because the average shopworker of the same age earned not much more than double that, £25 (£2,271/ $3,833), in an entire year.

It was a harsh divide, and one that eventually prompted the English game's authorities to set a maximum wage for players. As recently as 1961, even the greatest player in the land could be paid no more than £20 a week (the equivalent today of around £400/$700), a sum that kept them at least roughly in the same financial bracket as the people they lived among. The moment the system was scrapped, Fulham placed their star Johnny Haynes on £100—$3,500, or $5,907 in modern terms, or not much less than the average second-tier player receives in England in the present day.

By then, however, it was too late for Accrington. They went to the wall, the first of many Football League clubs to collapse, resign, or be removed from the competition, and almost every one of them could point to cold cash as being their single most efficient assassin. Which is why the FA did try to keep a lid on things. They just didn't succeed very well.

Attempts were also made to rein in transfer fees—the amount of money one club could pay to another to secure the services of a player. In 1893, there was something of a public outcry when Aston Villa paid neighboring West Bromwich Albion £100 (£8,984/$15,163) for Scottish striker Willie Groves, and in 1899, the English FA established the first in a series of maximum allowable payments. Of course, nobody paid attention to it, which is why the league kept having to raise it. It had reached £350 (£29,437/$49,531) in 1908, before being scrapped altogether.

These fees, unlike players' wages, did excite public comment, all the more so since the system was so rife with loopholes that few deals ever went through according to the intention, as opposed to an interpretation, of the law. By which time, Middlesbrough had already paid a breathtaking £1,000 (£85,010/$143,478) for Sunderland's Alf Common, and that was only the beginning of the madness.

By the mid-1920s, the world transfer record stood at £6,500 (£276,284/$466,307) paid out when Bob Kelly moved from Burnley to Sunderland; and in 1928 it took another great leap as Arsenal established David Jack as the first-ever five-figure player. A staggering £10,890 (£483,687/$816,359) changed hands to effect his move from Bolton Wanderers, yet the purchasing manager, Herbert Chapman, considered he had landed a bargain. Bolton had originally asked for £13,000 (£577,404/$974,533), a sum that the wily Chapman reduced by surreptitiously arranging for the Bolton negotiators to be rendered very, very drunk.

In 1932, the world transfer record departed England for the first time, as Argentinean powerhouse River Plate forked out no less than £23,000 (£1,122,456/$1,894,464) for Bernabé Ferreyra, a twenty-three-year-old striker of such strength and accuracy that one national newspaper, *Crítica*, even offered a prize to any goalkeeper who could prevent him from scoring in a match. It was seldom claimed; throughout a career that ended with retirement in 1939, "La Fiera" (the Fierce) played in 185 games, and scored 187 goals.

His transfer fee, too, seemed unlikely to be challenged. It would be seventeen years, 1949, before Derby County raised the ceiling with a £24,000 (£592,950/$1,000,772) fee for Manchester United's Johnny Morris. (Note for the attentive reader: the British economy's recent, massive devaluation accounts for the vast discrepancy in relative modern values between these figures and those quoted for the 1932 transfer.)

Now the genie was truly out of the bottle. In Italy in 1952, Napoli more than doubled Morris's sum by spending £52,000 (£1,046,086/$1,765,568) on Atalanta's Swedish star Hans Jeppson; and two years later, Uruguayan Juan Schiaffino moved from Club Atlético Peñarol to AC Milan for an eye-watering £72,000 (£1,378,285/$2,326,248), a deal that firmly established the Italian game as the undisputed moneybags of world soccer.

Indeed, over the next thirty-five years, Italian clubs would smash the world record on no fewer than nine occasions, with fees rising from the £93,000 (£1,567,714/$2,645,964) that brought Enrique Omar Sívori from River Plate to Juventus in 1957, to the cool million pounds (£5,864,985/$9,898,833) that changed hands in 1975 when Giuseppe Savoldi crossed from Bologna to Napoli; while Diego Maradona chalked up no less than eight million in combined European transfer fees, first when he moved from Boca Juniors, in Uruguay, to Spain's Barcelona for £3 million (£7,402,621/$12,494,032) in 1982, then when they sold him on to Napoli for £5 million (£11,236,498/$18,964,792) two years later. And today, we might as well be talking about Monopoly money for all the sense that transfer fees make, with the record being routinely smashed not because a player is actually worth the money, but because that's what records are for. To be smashed.

With no disrespect intended whatsoever to the Hungarian Lajos Détári, it seems most unlikely that the Greek side Olympiacos Piraeus felt they truly got their money's worth when they paid an unprecedented £7 million (£13,123,547/$22,149,725) for his transfer in 1988; and for all the success that he has achieved since his move to Real Madrid, it still seems strange to consider Gareth Bale to be the world's most expensive player purely on his footballing merit, as opposed to one more chapter in Real Madrid's continued quest to spend more money on fewer players than any other team in world history.

Real Madrid's Welsh international Gareth Bale cost around £80 million. Roughly equivalent to one helluva lot of Alf Commons. *Maxisport/Shutterstock.com*

Especially as it could be argued that the most genuinely valuable players in the world, those who one might even be considered priceless, are those who were never put up for sale during their prime, who remained at one club more-or-less their entire career long, and for whom bids might well have proven stratospheric, had anybody ever been delusional enough to tender one.

In recent years, in the world of the English Premier League, Manchester United's Ryan Giggs, Liverpool's Steve Gerrard, Southampton's Matt Le Tissier, Chelsea's John Terry, and Wolves's Steve Bull might all fall into that category. Others may have scored more goals, dribbled more flamboyantly, tackled more dramatically, or dived, their face contorted in agony, more theatrically. But, as old-fashioned as it might sound, loyalty is also a valuable quality in a player, and selflessness, too. For without those qualities, what is a club really buying beyond a mercenary who will kiss his badge this week, then be off to smooch with someone else's the moment the next transfer window opens.

In the decade and a half since Luis Figo moved from Barcelona for around $60 million in 2000, Real Madrid has demolished the world transfer record on five occasions, dropping some $500 million in the process: on Zinedane Zidane, Kaká, Cristiano Ronaldo, and Bale (at $145 million, the most expensive player in the world at the time of writing).

In that same period of time, the club has won five La Liga titles, two Copa del Reys, four Spanish Supercups, and one Champions League trophy. By comparison, Real Madrid's fiercest national rivals Barcelona (who have not spent anything approaching that much money) have topped the *Galacticos'* tally in almost every department.

Of course, the notion that on-the-field success is simply another commodity to be bought (and sold—Tottenham certainly became a poorer team following the departure of Bale) is not a new one. As far back as the 1900s, when Alf Common was sold for that thousand smackeroonies, Sunderland were widely known, and derided, as the Bank of England club, and the effects of cold, hard coinage register throughout the history of the sport.

It feels like small potatoes now, but when Blackburn Rovers splashed the cash to the tune of £27 million (£37,548,284/$63,373,430) in the mid-1990s, and won the English Premier League in 1994–1995, even their own supporters agreed that they had bought the title. Yes, £27 million. On the international market of today, you could scarcely buy an out-of-shape, past-his-prime, two-left-footed clogger for that.

Fanfare for the Common Man

Transfer fees may, then, have been the source of some controversy. But still soccer retained its reputation as the workingman's sport. It was workingmen— sailors, railroad laborers, builders, navvies—who were responsible for taking the game overseas, and workingmen who were responsible for forming many of the world's greatest clubs.

The game's rules evolved with its lengthening reach. In 1890, penalty kicks were introduced, and it became an offense to push, kick, or otherwise batter the opposition goalkeeper to prevent him from reaching the ball. Henceforth, he needed to be in possession of the sphere before he could be legitimately bundled into the net—a crude device that nevertheless led to the scoring of a great many goals over the years, including the one that ultimately paved the way for the practice to be outlawed altogether. In the 1958 English FA Cup final, Manchester United's goalkeeper Harry Gregg was bowled so decisively into the net by Bolton Wanderers' Nat Lofthouse that many observers marveled that he was even fit to play on. The goal stood, but it would be one of the last to be registered in this fashion.

Rule changes notwithstanding, it was soccer's simplicity that allowed it to spread around the world, and spread it did, gaining rapid popularity wherever it landed. The early 1890s saw the game take root as far afield as Finland, Greece,

New Zealand, and Brazil, with the first-named promptly introducing a new dimension to what had hitherto been considered a strictly winter pastime. The Finnish winter is so bitterly cold and impenetrably dark that the game's local adherents had no alternative but to run their season through the summer months.

The British navy was probably soccer's most vocal cheerleader. Even France, Britain's nearest neighbor beyond its own island grouping, was only introduced to the game by English sailors who took advantage of some shore leave to have a kickabout in Le Havre in 1872. Likewise, author John Foot's masterful study of Italian soccer, *Winning at All Costs*, opens with the absolutely unequivocal "in the beginning there were the English"—more sailors having more kickabouts, this time in Palermo and Naples, Genoa or Livorno, before a textile worker from Turin, Edoardo Bosio, employed (of course) by a British company, returned home from a trip to England with a soccer ball.

Moneyed and titled characters lent their enthusiasm, too. The Lipton Cup, competed for by Argentina and Uruguay between 1902 and 1992, was the gift of the Scottish tea magnate Sir Thomas Lipton, while he also sponsored an Italian-based competition that many people regard as a precursor of the World Cup.

But Bethlehem Steel was originally formed by laborers at a steelworks; Coventry City by the employees of the Singer sewing machine factory (hence the side's original name of Singer FC); Bayer 04 Leverkusen by the staff of the Bayer pharmaceutical company, PSV Eindhoven by workers at the Philips electronics company.

In an age when entertainment was largely considered something that you supplied for yourself, before radio and television (let alone the Internet) took up residence in people's homes, playing sport, or at least watching it, was a leisure activity that almost anybody could afford.

It is only in recent years that the cost of loyally following a topflight soccer team in many countries has become comparable to spending a night at the opera every week. For season 2014–2015, single match tickets at Arsenal, for example, were between £26 ($44) and £127 ($216); single performance tickets for *Rigoletto* at the Royal Opera House ranged between £7 ($12) and £145 ($247). The Royal Opera House, incidentally, also permits standing. Nor can the Premier League alone be singled out. In the MLS, tickets for the Philadelphia Union are priced between $25 and $150 a game. The last time Neil Young played Philly, the cheapest tickets were in the $150 region too. But he plays for longer than ninety minutes, and he doesn't expect to see you back again week after week.

For much of the twentieth century, admission prices were pegged at sums that made even a trip to the movies seem extravagant by comparison. (In 1989, Arsenal's cheapest tickets were £5, or under $15 in today's money) and that too appealed to what sociologists might term the "working classes." Let the namby-pamby idle rich have their Henley regattas and Wimbledon tennis. Real people went to watch real sports.

It was a social divide that would, of course, cause ruptures of its own, although not always through any politicization of the game itself. Sometimes, the mere popularity of soccer with the working classes was all a passing politician needed to scent, in order to be leaping aboard the bandwagon. What other aspect of society, after all, can be said to unite such vast numbers of people behind a common interest, regardless of creed, color, or political conviction? Soccer is society's hopes and dreams in microcosmic form, and in those lands where it really matters, it would be a foolish leader who overlooked that.

In Uganda in the early 1970s, the dictator Idi Amin passionately encouraged his people to become involved in following the game, in the knowledge that large numbers of excitable men united behind the national team could easily be translated into a form of patriotism that would withstand any political iniquity in which he might feel disposed to indulge. And, for many years, he was correct.

In Libya, President Gaddafi; in Iraq, Saddam Hussein; and in Argentina, General Galtieri all used "the people's sport" as a carrot; indeed, by hosting the 1978 World Cup, Galtieri's regime succeeded not only in winning the tournament, but also in organizing the most successfully propagandist sporting event since the Olympics pitched up in Adolf Hitler's Berlin in 1936, to become the biggest bucket of political whitewash in history.

Three years before he led the German nation into World War Two, Hitler saw the Olympics as the opportunity to respond to, and "disprove," all the unsettling allegations creeping out regarding the Nazi government's treatment of the Jews and other minorities. In Argentina, four years before he dragged his country into the Falklands War, Galtieri employed the World Cup as camouflage for the excesses of his brutal military regime.

Even Italy, such a shining light in the history and development of the game (periodic match-fixing scandals notwithstanding, of course), saw soccer utilized as a political weapon, in the 1920s as the Fascist Benito Mussolini rose to power.

The local game had already distanced itself somewhat from its English origins; in a youthful nation brimming with youthful nationalism, it simply wouldn't do to merely translate "football" into the native tongue, as so many other countries had done. An Italian sport (how quickly history can be rewritten) needed an Italian name—*calcio*, to illustrate its direct descent from *calcio fiorentino*, a game popular in Renaissance Florence, and whose deployment of both a ball and a pitch apparently established it as the indisputable parent of the new game.

In fact, beyond standing as a Mediterranean take on what the rest of us call "mob football," *calcio fiorentino* had very little to do with what we would recognize as soccer. But Mussolini took this gentle revision very seriously indeed. Under his aegis, the original game was reintroduced to Florence, and guidebooks were rewritten to specifically describe the so-called "invention" of soccer as nothing more than a case of the English borrowing an Italian brainwave. Nothing could be permitted to stand in the way of this new article of national pride, and today, soccer is still better known as *calcio* in Italian circles.

Mussolini was also very fortunate that his years in power coincided very smartly with the Italian soccer . . . sorry, *calcio* . . . team coming into its own period of pomp, victorious in both the 1934 and 1938 World Cups, while Italy itself made as fine a job of hosting the latter as Mussolini's pal Hitler did the Berlin Olympics.

Perhaps that is why the last of the twentieth century's truly divisive right-wing leaders, Britain's Margaret Thatcher, made such a show of taking the opposite tack entirely, and loathing soccer with a passion. Because far from proving an all-conquering behemoth, all four of the national teams that fell under her rule, England, Scotland, Wales, and Northern Ireland, were essentially rubbish (or, at best, nondescript) through the decade that she spent in power, 1979–1990.

Far from fostering the kind of nationalist glory that Thatcher herself deemed so vital to national pride, in fact, English soccer in general, with its hooligan following and death-dealing reputation, actually appeared diametrically opposed to all that she represented, and wanted for her people.

Indeed, the latter part of her governance saw English clubs banned outright from European competition following years of hooligan-related problems—culminating in the deaths of thirty-nine Juventus supporters at the 1985 European Cup final. Just fourteen Liverpool supporters were later found guilty of manslaughter, but UEFA had had enough. An indefinite ban was placed on all English clubs (it was lifted in 1990), with Liverpool receiving an extra three years in the cold (later reduced to one), and Thatcher responded accordingly.

Far from harnessing soccer for her own political ends, Thatcher believed her purposes would be better served by outlawing it altogether. That would ultimately prove a bridge too far even for a woman of her self-belief, although it sometimes felt like a close-run thing. Caging fans, compulsory ID schemes, Draconian banning orders, and increasing police presence to proportions normally associated with outbreaks of major civil disorder were all seriously considered (and in some instances, acted upon) by her government, and it took the carnage of the 1989 Hillsborough disaster to bring home to her the sheer misguidedness of her policies.

Like those leaders before (and, sadly, since) she was neither alone nor unique in her total misunderstanding of the nature of the sport, but at least she was honest about her opinion of it. Which is a lot more than can be said for those would-be political goliaths who have attempted to jump onto the soccer bandwagon in the years since she proved that an anti-soccer platform can only end in tears.

Attempts that often include such schoolboyish lies and misrepresentations that even the most sympathetic newspaper reporter eventually starts picking apart the story, while wondering whether he (it's always a he) was just making the right noises in the hope of winning votes.

Thankfully, that is seldom the case. After all, how could we ever be expected to trust, or even believe, a politician who would place blatant populism before his true intentions, in the hope of blindsiding the electorate?

The Christmas Truce

It was for political reasons, in 1914, that the English authorities initially decided *against* closing down the Football League following the outbreak of World War One. The idea that a semblance of normalcy should be allowed to persist on the home front is not, sadly, one that modern governments tend to entertain, but a century ago the belief that people should at least be given the *option* of whether or not to carry on as usual was deeply seated in the English psyche.

As it turned out, the public did *not* want to carry on as usual. The league survived just one season under wartime conditions, scorned and even occasionally boycotted by people who believed that sportsmen should be signing up to the military and heading off to fight, the same as everybody else.

In fact, many already had, and others would continue to do so. Two Football League players even received the Victoria Cross, the country's highest military honor, for the part they played in winning the war: Bernard Vann, who turned out for Burton United and Derby County before being ordained a priest: and Bradford Park Avenue's Donald Simpson Bell, honored (albeit posthumously) for singlehandedly destroying an enemy machine-gun nest. Bell's medals are now on display at Egland's National Football Museum in Manchester. A third VC was awarded to Willie Angus of the Scottish side Glasgow Celtic, for a rescue mission in which he received over forty wounds, including the loss of an eye and permanent damage to one foot.

The game would survive on the homefront, in the form of regional leagues set up around the country, the teams staffed by on-leave players, and military police checkpoints established at the entry gates to demand every supporter's credentials—there would be no soccer for draft dodgers or deserters, and none for would-be saboteurs and Fifth Columnists either. There was even a Footballers Battalion established, the 1,350 strong 17th Service Battalion of the Middlesex Regiment, headquartered at Richmond Athletic Ground and permitted a day's leave every Saturday afternoon so that they might play for their respective clubs.

Soccer would also take a significant role in the war's mythology. In July 1916, with the East Surreys regiment playing their part in the so-called Great Advance, a soccer ball was produced and the troops charged across No Man's Land in pursuit of it, and into the German trenches.

Other balls bounced in other battles; and regardless of whether or not the events actually transpired as the history books and mythologies insist, the first Christmas of the war in 1914 was marked by what remains one of the most famous soccer games in history. Played out not between famous clubs or storied sportsmen, but between English and German soldiers emerging from their trenches, to put a halt to the war for one special day.

It was late on Christmas Eve when the soldiers of the British Expeditionary Force first heard the sound of Christmas carols rising from the enemy trenches on the other side of No Man's Land, and saw the first lanterns being lit, and decorations being hung. Maybe they feared a trick at first—both sides had been growing increasingly wily as the conflict dragged on. But soon, seasonal messages and greetings were being shouted between the trenches and the following morning, when light broke and no shots were fired, the first British and German soldiers raised their heads above the trenches, then clambered out and advanced, unarmed, across No Man's Land toward one another.

Some exchanged gifts, cigarettes, and food. Others took photographs, or shared pictures of their families. Casualties were buried and repair work was carried out on the trenches and dugouts. And somebody produced a soccer ball from somewhere, and a game kicked off. Not just one game, either. Up and down the lines, hostilities ceased and Christmas was celebrated with, among so many other creature comforts, soccer. And the following day, the two sides went back to shooting at one another.

The story of the Christmas truce is one that is irrevocably woven into the history of the Great War. No matter that sundry revisionist historians have done their damnedest to deny that it ever happened, or at least deny that it happened like the myths make out; no matter, too, that the British and German high commands were outraged that their war machines should have ceased for even a few hours R&R.

A century on, in 2014, Prince William spoke for many when he said, "We all grew up with the story of soldiers from both sides putting down their arms on Christmas Day, and it remains wholly relevant today as a message of hope over adversity, even in the bleakest of times."

And it's true. It does.

The Inter-Allied Games

Different nations approached the question of soccer in wartime in different ways. In Scotland, the league program continued on much as it had before. In general, however, it was 1919, with the fighting finally over, before anything approaching normalcy returned to the majority of the combative nations, with the resumption of a full sporting calendar celebrated by the organization of the Inter-Allied Games.

A vast, Olympic-style tournament, the Inter-Allied Games (as their name suggests) were to be competed for by representatives of each of the victorious militaries so recently embroiled in war. With the games sponsored by the United States, and staged in the newly refurbished Pershing Stadium in Paris, twenty-nine nations in total were invited to participate, of whom a little more than half accepted: Canada, Newfoundland, Guatemala, Brazil, France, the newly formed Czecho-Slovakian Republic, Italy, Greece, Belgium, Serbia, Portugal, Romania, Australia, New Zealand, China, and Hedjaz (within the modern Saudi Arabia).

Conspicuous by their absence, for a variety of reasons, were Great Britain, Russia, Japan, and South Africa, while many of the smaller nations—Haiti, Cuba, Nicaragua, and Siam (modern Thailand) among them—simply didn't have the wherewithal to offer up a competing team. Indeed, Hedjaz was represented only with an exhibition team, while Guatemala fielded just one sportsman, a 100 meters sprinter. Still, close to 1,500 athletes, the majority of whom were either active or recently discharged servicemen, gathered in Paris to compete in a full program of sporting events.

Sprawling across a full fourteen days, June 22 through July 6, 1919, the Inter-Allied Games hosted a wealth of disciplines: conventional sports such as baseball, boxing, rowing, rifle shooting, fencing, tug of war, water polo, and golf, together with multitudinous athletic and equestrian events. But there was room for some *un*conventional activities, too, to remind competitors and spectators alike of the game's awful origins—things like the hand grenade throwing contest.

Eight nations fielded soccer teams, which the organizers divided into two groups of four, each of whom would play one another once. In Group A, France rapidly established their superiority, defeating Romania 4–0, Greece 11–0, and Italy 2–0, to qualify for the final with a 100% record; Italy finished second, having thrashed Romania 7–1 and Greece 9–0; and the Greeks, whose one victory was a tight 3–2 triumph over the hapless Romanians, finished third.

Group B, meanwhile, saw the Czecho-Slovakian Republic represented by an eleven who had hitherto played for one of the strongest club sides on the prewar central European scene, Dukla Praha of Prague. Coached by Scotsman Johnnie Madden, instantly recognizable by his omnipresent cob pipe, the Czechs effortlessly maintained their superiority in Paris.

First Belgium, by 4–1; then the United States, 8–2, and finally Canada 3–2, perished before them; while Belgium, in finishing second, easily put both North American nations to the sword, defeating Canada 5–2, and the US by 7–0. Perhaps the most exciting game, though, and certainly the most evenly matched, was the nine-goal thriller fought out between the US and Canada, a 5–4 victory for the United States which guaranteed them third place in the group.

The final, played between the French and the Czechs, took place on Sunday, June 29. The stadium was packed, and the many locals among the crowd were initially delighted by the ease with which France seemed to be controlling the game. For reasons unknown, the Czechs had opted to play their finest striker, Janda, in defense, with a new face, Cerveny, taking over for him in the forward line.

It was a surprising tactic, and it was a total failure. France's halftime lead of 2–1 was deceptive; they could have had far more. But the resumption of play saw Janda return to his customary position, and now the game was all the Czechs'. Twice in that final forty-five minutes, the brilliant French goalkeeper Chayriguès was powerless to prevent the Czechs from scoring, first to equalize and then to snatch victory, with Janda and teammate Pilat widely regarded not simply as the men of the match, but ranked among the most popular sportsmen of the entire tournament.

Even the watching American soldiers were impressed: according to the official history of the games, "there were no more ardent fans than the American soldiers and at the conclusion of the game, they carried Janda . . . from the field on their shoulders."

Oddly all but forgotten by sporting histories today, the Inter-Allied Games were a vital component in world sport's passage back into the normalcy of peacetime; and, like the rest of the world, soccer entered the new postwar era with high hopes.

In England, where the original twelve-team league had already expanded to incorporate a second division, the competition was now poised to more than double in size with the addition of two regional third divisions, one catering for northern sides, the other for southern.

A Brief Diversion—When Is a Third Division not a Third Division?

This format, with the four divisions very sensibly named One, Two, and Three (or First, Second, and Third—the terms were utterly interchangeable) was to persist unchanged until the late 1950s saw the regionalization scrapped and a new Fourth Division created; and then survive again until 1992 brought the wholesale revamp and rebranding that created the Premier League, and left the other three divisions to fend for themselves, nomenclaturally at least.

Over the years since then, a variety of changes have seen the old Second Division become the new First, before it became the Championship and the old Third Division was in turn rebranded the First, while the Fourth went from Third to Second. Meaning, a lowly team that has spent its entire career at the fourth and lowest level of the Football League can now claim to be vying for promotion to what, until the early 1990s, was regarded as the highest.

All of which makes life hell for statisticians and historians, which is why this book, in common with many others published since the early 1990s, prefers to refer to the divisions as tiers or levels: the Premier League is the first, the Championship the second, the First is the third, and the Second is the fourth. Just as they have always been. The fifth, incidentally, is the Conference Premier which, also under a variety of names, has enjoyed automatic promotion and relegation to the fourth tier of the Football League since 1987; and which, as of the end of the 2013–2014 season, was home to no fewer than fourteen former Football League clubs, out of a total twenty-four.

Several of these—Luton Town, Southport, Grimsby Town, Wrexham, Lincoln City, and Halifax—were among the founding members of the two newly minted Third Divisions back in the early 1920s; with one of that same number, Luton Town, competing in the old First Division as recently as 1991–1992. In taking the Conference Championship at the end of 2013–2104, perhaps the Hatters, as they are known, are finally on the way back there.

Perhaps.

5

The Global Game

Are All Leagues the Same?

Wherever soccer is played, there is a soccer league.

When Nelson Mandela was imprisoned in South Africa, he joined with fellow inmates to create a league within their prison. When a handful of British players, playing or coaching at clubs in Germany, found themselves rounded up at the outbreak of World War One, and interned at Ruhleben prison camp . . . a former stables, still being hastily converted as the first inmates arrived . . . they formed a league.

When the former Soviet Union broke up at the end of the 1980s, independent soccer leagues were among the first things that each of the newly constituted nations created.

And a century previous, even before England's national Football League was launched in 1888, local organizations had been forming their own competitions for years already, weeks-long tournaments within which teams battled for positions on an ever-shifting table, playing regular matches against a largely unchanging roster of others.

William McGregor, the superbly bearded founder of the Football League, spoke of these local competitions as predecessors of his own grand scheme,

Once among the most picturesque villages in Kent, England, Hoo also boasted, in the 1920s, one of its doughtiest non-league teams.

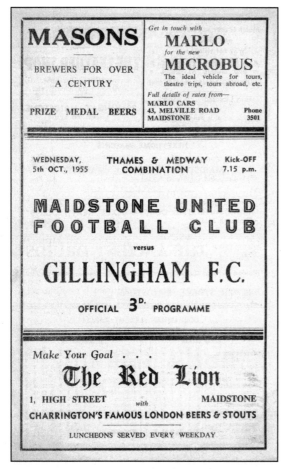

A headline conflict from the old Thames & Medway Combination. Gillingham already had a team playing in the Football League; three decades later, Maidstone would join them there. They'd been rehearsing for the ensuing derby for a long time.

and within a year of the Football League getting underway, the near-national Football Alliance and the self-explanatory Northern League had launched.

Further enterprises swiftly followed, ranging in size from the similarly far-reaching Southern League (formed in 1894 at the suggestion of Arsenal), to exclusively local ventures—the county-wide Lancashire Combination (1891), the almost neighborly Thames & Medway Combination (1896), and many more.

Scotland's national league launched in 1890; and again was swiftly followed by others, again along similar geographical lines—the Scottish Alliance and the Ayrshire League both launched in 1891, the Highland League in 1893, the Central League in 1896. And the rest of the world was right behind them.

The Welsh Premier League— A Thoroughly Modern Tournament

Established in 1876—that is, thirteen years after its English counterpart, and three after its Scottish—the Football Association of Wales is the third-oldest organization of its type in the world. Its own national soccer league, however, is one of the youngest, albeit with deeply embedded roots.

The North Wales Coast Football League was up and running by 1893, and while a so-called Welsh National League launched in 1919, it was largely a southern affair, with its titular veracity further challenged by the fact that most major Welsh clubs preferred to compete in England, at best fielding reserve sides in their own national competition.

Cardiff City, Swansea Town (later City), Newport County, Wrexham, and, briefly in the 1920s, Aberdare Athletic and Merthyr Town, all played in the *English* Football League; other Welsh sides competed in the Southern and Northern Leagues, and so forth. (Cardiff remain the only non-English side to have won the FA Cup, in 1927; Swansea have a similar claim on the League Cup.)

A burst of reconstruction in the early 1980s saw the formation of a Welsh National Division, but still there was no sense that it could in any way be compared with the national leagues in operation elsewhere around the world. This sense was further compounded by UEFA's outright refusal to allocate a European Cup place to the so-called Welsh league champions, even though Welsh *Cup* winners had been welcomed into the European Cup Winners Cup since its launch. Not until 1991 did this century-long oddity finally come to an end, although it was political, rather than sporting reasons that hastened the change.

Historically, the four British Football Associations, England, Scotland, Wales and Northern Ireland, have always been regarded as separate entities by FIFA, despite the fact that, in political and geographical terms, they simply represent different regions within the overall United Kingdom.

No other nation has ever been afforded this privilege—it was granted to the British nations as acknowledgement of their role in inventing the sport in the first place. But for how long should one expect gratitude to last? Many fellow FIFA members fiercely resented what they regarded as the Brits' preferential treatment, and it wasn't too difficult to see their point.

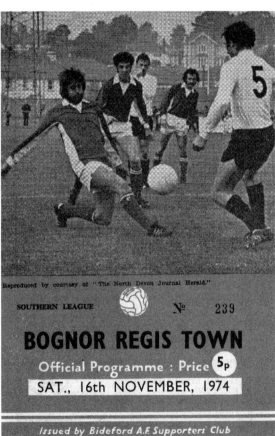

Reproduced by courtesy of "The North Devon Journal Herald."

SOUTHERN LEAGUE   № 239

BOGNOR REGIS TOWN

Official Programme : Price 5p

SAT., 16th NOVEMBER, 1974

Issued by Bideford A.F. Supporters Club

More than twelve decades after its birth, the Southern League today remains one of the most fiercely contested "minor" leagues in the world. This clash, from 1974–1975, epitomizes its appeal.

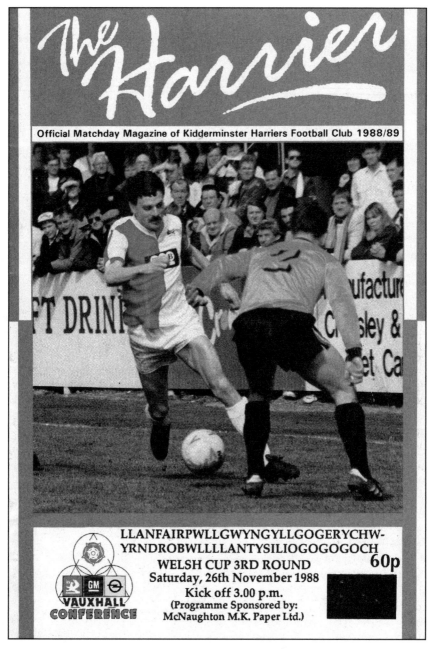

If trophies were awarded for magnificent names, Welsh village side Llanfairpwllgwyngyll-gogerychwyrndrobwllllantysiliogogogoch would take some beating.

The existence of very separate national leagues within three of the four associations was one of the vehicles with which the British organizations justified their separate existence, meaning that Wales's failure to follow suit was often regarded as a weak link in the chain. In 1991, therefore, the Welsh FA resolved to finally put a hundred years of internecine squabbling, greed, and stubbornness behind it, and at last realize a genuine national league.

It would not be easy. Even with UEFA guaranteeing a Champions League berth for the champions, those sides that remained members of the Football League, or who held out hope of becoming one, were swift to refuse to join. A number of other clubs raised objections of their own, with the FAW forced to resort to coercion and worse in order to change minds.

Nonparticipating clubs were barred from the Welsh Cup, and five of the refuseniks, Barry Town, Caernarfon Town, Colwyn Bay, Merthyr Tydfil (successors to the old Merthyr Town), and Newport County were even exiled, forced to play their home games on grounds beyond the Welsh border, unless they joined the new league. Ultimately, the courts would force that particular sanction to be lifted, although by that time, Barry had already given in, and Caernarfon were about to.

But the English league contingent would continue (and remain) absent from the Welsh Cup, and while they doubtless continue to look down their noses at the competition, the Welsh Premier League (as the League of Wales was renamed in 2002) went from strength to strength.

Today it comprises a dozen clubs, operates a system of promotion and relegation with the pyramid of smaller leagues beneath it, and furnishes European competition with no fewer than four clubs. The league champions enter the qualifying stages of the Champions League, and Europa League berths awaiting the Welsh Cup winners, the league runners-up and the winners of a play-off between the sides placed between third and seventh.

Around the World in Eighty Leagues

The mania for league soccer spread rapidly across the globe. By the end of the nineteenth century, national competitions had been established as far afield as Denmark and the Netherlands (1889), Argentina (1891),

From Scotland in the mid-1930s, the Aberdeen Shop Assistants Union side.

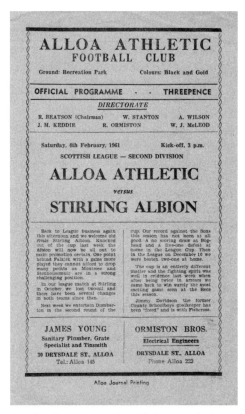

Another day, another Scottish League clash.

Belgium, Switzerland, and Gibraltar (1895), Sweden (1896), Italy 1898), and Uruguay (1900).

Many more competitions arose in the period ahead of World War One; and more still in its immediate aftermath, as the European map in particular was redrawn to give birth to fresh nations—Poland and Estonia (1921), Latvia and Lithuania (1922), Czechoslovakia (1925). The decolonization of Africa and Asia saw national leagues spring up almost before the independent governments were in place, and everywhere the game took root, a neighboring nation would peer over the border and launch a league of its own.

Not all of these leagues would survive. Present in the first European Cup, and the qualifying competition for the 1954 World Cup, Saarland was a briefly independent territory on the Franco-German border, absorbed into Germany following a plebiscite in 1955.

Other competitions, whether through financial, political, or other developments, stuttered through a false start or two before emerging in the form by which they are known today. Others still would gestate through decades of amateur competition before emerging as full-fledged professional setups. Without exception, however, all speak to the phenomenal popularity and growth of the game, the only sport in history that can claim, within fifty years of its inception, to have conquered more-or-less the entire globe.

The First Latin Leagues

As the first league to form in Latin America, the Argentinean contest is widely regarded among the grandfathers of world soccer in general. It sprang, of course, from the presence of the British in the country, in this case a community in the capital Buenos Aires that numbered some 40,000 people and amounted almost to a city within a city.

The British banked at their own banks, shopped at their own stores, sent their children to their own schools, and devised their own entertainments—one of which, from around the mid-1880s, was a soccer championship played out between the English High School, under the tutelage of a Scot, Alexander Watson Hutton, and various other similar establishments.

In 1891, these schools organized themselves into a league championship, arranged along the lines of the English model, and in 1893, again with Hutton at the helm, they formed the Argentine Association Football League.

The contest grew rapidly, both within and without the English population. By the turn of the century, the AAFL was administering four divisions in Buenos Aires alone, peopled by such sides as St. Andrews (the first AAFA champions, in 1891), Lomas Athletic (perennial champions between 1893 and 1898), Belgrano AC (1899, 1904, and 1908 league title holders), the English High School (winners in 1900), Alumni (champions through the remainder of the 1900s), Quilmes Rovers (the last English winners of the league, in 1912), CA Banfield, and the magificently named Club de Gimnasia y Esgrima La Plata.

More followed, in the form of future legends CA River Plate (founded 1901), Ferro Carril Oeste (1904), CA Estudiantes , CA Platense, CA Independiente, and CA Boca Juniors (all formed in 1905). Beyond the city, Lobos Athletic were operating as early as 1892, while Newell's Old Boys and Rosario Central became primal powers in Argentina's second city, Rosario.

Hutton remained President of the AAFA for three years, before giving way, in succession, to fellow Britons A. P. Boyd, Charles Wibberley and F. C. Boutell. In 1906, however, Argentine Florencio Martínez de Hoz stood for election and won. The last vestiges of the old Anglo order were dispensed with, just as the last remnants of immigrant power, too, were swept away; annually, Argentinos met Británicos in a friendly match in Buenos Aires, and the visitors usually won.

But not any longer. A 5–1 crushing saw the boot firmly on the Argentinean foot, and in 1913, Racing Club became the first local side ever to win the championship—and they continued to win it, year after year, until finally, Boca Juniors snatched the title away in 1919, and proceeded to divide it between themselves and Huracán for the remainder of the decade.

This original league was amateurs-only, and was not the only game in town; short-lived rival competitions flourished on either side of the First World War, before all were consolidated into a professional league in 1931. The giants of the Argentine game were consolidated, too, with River Plate joining Boca Juniors, Racing Club, and Independiente in what amounted to an exclusion zone erected around the top of the league table.

Other sides might briefly emerge to challenge their supremacy but, between 1931 and 1966, only San Lorenzo were capable of shattering the Big Four's monopoly on the league championship. River Plate won twelve titles, Boca Juniors took ten, Racing Club six, Independiente five. San Lorenzo won three.

As the game developed in Argentina, so it also picked up speed across the River Plate in neighboring Uruguay. Tradition insists that the first soccer matches there were staged between visiting British sailors and Montevideo's own British community, and in 1886, one William Pool established the country's first team, Albion FC.

Echoing developments across the river, the game's early development was wholly in the hands of immigrants. A league formed in 1900, in tandem with the Uruguayan FA, but only four clubs competed it—Albion, the Uruguay Athletic Club, the German Deutsche Fussbal Klub, and the extraordinarily named Central Uruguayan Railways Cricket Club, all of them ex-pat concerns based in Montevideo.

The locomotive cricketers were the local game's first giants. Internationally renowned today as Peñarol (named for the Montevideo neighborhood in which the club was based), they took the first two championships. Nacional, the first non-immigrant-run club in both country and continent, arose to take the next two and, with the exception of even fewer interlopers than Argentinean honors have permitted, that is how it has been ever since.

Gambling on the Football Pools

The speed with which league football spread around the world, and the ease with which it took root in so many national psyches, can be misleading, however. Not every nation necessarily welcomed either the competition or the game itself.

The United States was famously a very tough egg for the game's supporters to crack, but even within the realms of the British Empire, Canada, India, South Africa, and New Zealand all found other sports more appealing.

Cricket, among certain British colonies; baseball, within the American sphere of influence; hockey, rugby, and hurling can all claim to have fought off soccer's bid to become the most popular sport in various corners of the world, while Australia had incredible difficulty taking soccer seriously, so deeply entrenched were the (admittedly unassailable) delights of Aussie Rules. Indeed, it is ironic that Australian soccer had a far greater following, and meaning, in England than it ever did in Australia, at least until the 1990s.

The reason for this was not, however, some deep English appreciation for sporting skills that the Aussies simply didn't understand. It was because, when the English soccer season ended, Australian results would fill the empty space on the back page of the newspapers, and on the "Pools" coupons.

Gambling on the outcome of soccer matches is almost as old as soccer matches themselves, and the Pools are the grandaddy of it all.

As far back as 1892, the game's English administrators were already so concerned with the "evil effects" of organized gambling that they banned players and club officials from taking part. In 1910, when an investigation discovered soccer betting to be rife throughout the army, the penalty for contravening the ban amounted to nothing less than a lifetime suspension from playing the game.

Football lotteries, however, remained commonplace. Many publicans operated them, while in factories and mills, popular workers were sought out by enterprising outsiders, and offered eye-opening commissions to organize "pools"—weekly competitions in which gamblers bet not on the winners and losers of specific games, but on the likelihood of them *drawing* a match. The gambler's stake dictated how many guesses he or she could have; and the more correct guesses on a single coupon, the greater the chance of winning.

The press got involved, some as willing advocates of the Pools, others as their most devout foes. Early in the 1920s, an editorial in the *South Shields Football Gazette* proclaimed, "I am quite sure that the football-loving public of this country will be emphatic and unanimous in their condemnation of the pernicious practice of betting on the outcome of football matches, and in the best interests of the game, it is hoped that the FA will do everything in its power to suppress this evil."

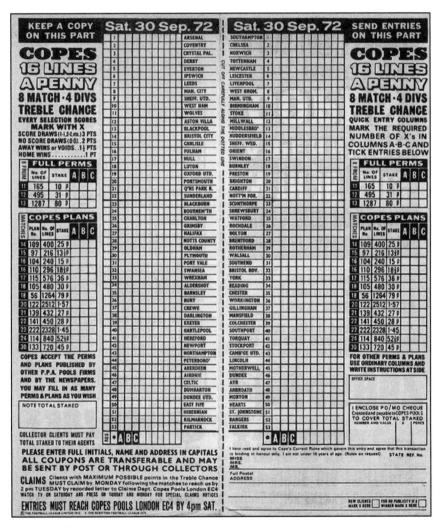

A "typical" English pools coupon from 1972. Hard to believe such an innocent piece of paper once started a war!

Around the same time, no personage less than the vice president of the Football League addressed a meeting at Third Division North side Nelson FC, there to describe "organized gambling" as "a menace to the game and a danger to the country."

The Football League came down hard on clubs seen to be encouraging the vice, no matter how innocently. When Clapham Orient attempted to organize a sweepstake as a benefit for a former player, the League banned it. When Crystal Palace allowed a Pools coupon company to advertise in their ground in 1922, they were censured. Five years later, Newport County received a similar rebuke after allowing a similar concern to advertise in their matchday program.

But really, how could the authorities truly stem the tide? Particularly after the 1933 Royal Commission on Lotteries and Betting overlooked the existence of the "Football Pools" altogether.

There was but one solution. War.

By 1934, it was estimated that the various pools companies were raking in some £9 million (£45 million/$76 million) a year. By 1936, the total had risen to more than twice that. It was alleged that more than sixteen times as many people gambled on the outcome of games as actually watched them being played, and with all this in mind, a Liverpool accountant named Watson Hartley approached the Football League with a suggestion that would divert some of this revenue into the game's own coffers.

The pools, he explained, represented a massive copyright infringement. Every time a pools company reprinted the next week's fixtures without having first sought permission from the Football League authorities (who devised those fixtures in the first place), it was technically breaching the League's copyright.

Throughout December 1935 and early 1936, the League—both management and representatives of the clubs—was embroiled in discussion with its legal advisors. So was the Pools Promoters Association, the umbrella body to which all legitimate pools companies belonged.

Offers were made, counteroffers delivered. According to John Moores, founder of the largest pools company of them all, Littlewoods, the League was demanding the sum of £100,000 (£4,972,327/$8,392,218 in modern terms) for the use of its fixtures. Small beans compared to the sums that the pools companies were raking in, but far more than the mere honorarium payment they intended offering.

Other considerations arose and became complications. The government levied taxes on the pools companies. The Post Office received income from so many millions of people mailing in their forms every week. The pools companies' own employees had to be considered. For both sides, but perhaps most of all for the League authorities, any legal tussle was set to bristle with problems.

So the League decided to take another route entirely. On February 20, 1936, a meeting of eighty-five clubs decided, with only eight dissidents and eleven abstentions, to scrap the fixture list altogether. Clubs would be notified of their next match no earlier than was absolutely necessary for them to make any required arrangements. How, the League celebrated, could the pools companies print a coupon if they didn't know what the matches were going to be?

Well, they could always use the Scottish fixtures, which continued to be published. Or the Irish ones. Or non-league ones. All the pools companies required was a set of fixtures that could be gambled upon. They didn't care who, or where, the fixtures were.

The media, too, gazed aghast at the League's notion, raising more pitfalls and obstacles than could ever have been considered at the original meeting. But the League was unabashed.

The scheduled fixtures for the following Saturday, February 29, were cancelled, and on Thursday, February 27, the League hierarchy set about the onerous task of completely rearranging the program, and notifying the affected clubs. Needless to say, the information was revealed on a strictly "need-to-know" basis. And equally needless to say, by noon the following day, the entire country seemed to know that Saturday's fixtures would be those previously scheduled for March 14 in Division One, and April 11 in Division Two. By midafternoon, coupons for the rearranged games were on the streets, and life for the pools companies went on as normal.

Less so for the clubs. The League itself liked to blame bad weather for the fact that just 193,000 people turned out for that Saturday afternoon's worth of games, close to half the number of those attending games on the corresponding Saturday twelve months before.

But the clubs themselves knew the truth, and when the League announced that the charade would continue the following week, many of them were in open revolt. On the evening of March 5, seven clubs were cabled with detail of their weekend fixtures. By the morning of March 6, the entire League program for the following day had been calculated, and published. Three days later, the League surrendered.

Relations between League and pool companies would, ultimately, be settled to both sides' satisfaction; John Moores, of Littlewoods, even ended up owning a League team, Liverpool; while the pools companies also wound up sponsoring a European club competition, the Inter Toto Cup—*toto* being the popular name for the pools across continental Europe.

Payment would eventually be demanded and paid, but it was indeed an honorarium. In 1988/89, permission to reprint the entire season's fixtures for whatever purpose cost £1,500 (£2,812/$4,746). In the meantime, fortunes were made, riches were won. In 1957, a Ms. Nellie McGrail won £205,235 (£3,459,675/$5,839,187) on the pools. In 1972, Mr. Cyril Grimes scooped £512, 683 (£4,729,605/$7,982,556); in 1979, Ms. Irene Powell won £882,000 (£3,119,951/$5,265,806) and, in 1986, the first million-pound jackpot was paid out (equivalent to £2,048,717/$3,457,793 today).

The pools' first double millionaire soon followed and, while the popularity of the pools was seriously dented when the British government introduced its own national Lottery, still they remain a much-loved part of the national sporting life. Even in the summertime, when the absence of British games was simply supplanted with a coupon filled with Australian fixtures.

Balls Down Under

The needs of the English gambler notwithstanding, soccer in Australia really was not taken seriously by Australia at large until the 1990s, or even later. The country's participation in the 1974 World Cup passed many locals by, in the same way as the United States's appearance in the 1950 tournament was overlooked by many Americans, and when soccer did hit the headlines, it was usually for the wrong reasons—growing discomfort, for example, that so many clubs were named for, and still regarded as synonymous with, the immigrant communities from which they arose.

Slowly, however, a combination of publicity for the right reasons; further successes for the Socceroos national side, and the growing influence of Australian players in other countries' leagues, began to raise public awareness. So, in 2005, did the launch of a ten-team A-League, featuring nine Australian sides and one from New Zealand, and sensibly playing out as a winter attraction. Aussie Rules remains the undisputed summer game, and now that soccer has accepted its supremacy, so Australia has accepted soccer.

Building the Bundesliga

Even among the game's traditional superpowers, sports historians can point to considerable local resistance to the game before it finally hit the big time.

In nineteenth- and early twentieth-century Germany, for example, soccer was simply a minority pursuit that was tolerated, but scarcely encouraged, by both the political and sporting authorities. Athletics were far more to their taste, a legacy of the stoic Prussian attitudes that had, after all, bound the separate German states into a single nation in the first place. The church disapproved of the game, many schools outlawed it, and the armed forces banned it until as late as 1911.

Those soccer clubs that did form—Hertha BSC Berlin in 1892, VfB Stuttgart in 1893, Karlsruher FV in 1894, Fortuna Düsseldorf in 1895, Dresdner FC in 1898 and Werder Bremen in 1899 were among the pacemakers—often did so under the auspices either of an existing athletics club, or a factory; nobody could imagine forging a stand-alone soccer club at that time.

Nor did the game's administrators help. The German FA, the Deutscher Fussball-Bund, was formed in 1900, and took such a ferocious stance against professionalism that several sides were banned from competing in FA-sponsored competitions because their players were employed by the company that formed the club. It mattered not that they might work, and be paid, as miners or laborers. The fact that they received payment from the same source as the club was sufficient to enflame the authorities' amateur bile.

The first national German championship arose from what we would term as play-off matches between various regional league champions—in 1898, the winners of leagues in southern Germany and Berlin met in one such contest; and by 1902, other local competitions offered up their victors, too.

A 1992–1993 season program for Bundesliga mainstays Kaiserslautern.

The first champions of what can truly be called a national competition were VfB Leipzig, representing the Verbandes Leipziger Ballspiel-Vereine (VLBV) against the champions of Saxony, Saxony-Anhalt, and Thuringia. It was a journey that began, for Leipzig, with a 4–0 victory over Dresdner SC VfB. This then qualified them for the first round of the DFB Cup, where victories over Britannia Berlin 92 (3–1) and Altona 93 (6–3) placed them in the final, to meet the Bohemian (now Czech Republic) side DFC Prague at the end of May.

It should have been a contest. Instead it was a slaughter. A few weeks before the game, Leipzig's much-loved coach Theodor Schöffler passed away. Playing the game of their lives, the players admitted, in memory of their lost leader, Vfb Leipzig swept to a 7-2 victory.

Unlike other nations, where the early champions of the national league tended to become the undisputed giants of the game (Rangers and Celtic in Scotland, Real Madrid and Barcelona in Spain, and so forth), the German championship was never to prove predictable.

VfB Leipzig won a second title in 1906, and a third in 1913. But around them, a dizzying array of fellow champions swirled: Union 92 Berlin, SC Freiburg, Phoenix Karlsruhe, Karlsruher FV, Holstein Kiel, SpVgg Fürth, and Viktoria Berlin (twice). Not until the league regrouped following the First World War did a single side emerge as a constant power, as FC Nürnberg took the title in 1920, 1921, 1924, 1925, and 1927.

The 1930s were the era of FC Schalke 04, while the following decade saw the championship trophy leave the country for the first and only time, following the incorporation of Austrian teams into the competition following their land's absorption into "greater Germany." Rapid Wien won the 1941 championship, and no matter how loudly the Nazi authorities tried to pretend there was nothing untoward about that, traditional supporters knew otherwise.

Despite increasingly straitened circumstances, and mounting wartime difficulties, the league remained in play until 1944; that is, the year before Nazi Germany finally fell to the Allies. Peacetime, and the division of the country into separate nations, the democratic West and the communist East Germany, then saw the entire league restructured.

The newly formed East German league (to be fought along conventional season-long league lines) would survive throughout the life of its parent nation—that is, until 1991. Despite constant calls for reform, however, the West German league would continue under the old amateur format until 1963. Not even the fillip of a shock 1954 World Cup victory could shake old beliefs; indeed, it probably had the opposite effect, allowing the old authorities to point to the world championship as irrefutable evidence of their wisdom.

The World Cup was, however, a fluke. In 1958, West Germany were knocked out in the semifinals by host nation Sweden; in 1962, they fell at the quarterfinal phase to Yugoslavia. The country's international team was at its worst ebb, the country's best players were looking to move overseas to play. Not even Germany's growing success in the European Cup, with Eintracht Frankfurt even making the final of the 1959–1960 tournament (there to be positively destroyed by Real Madrid) could paper over the cracks.

When delegates gathered at the DFB Convention at the Westfalenhallen in Dortmund, on July 28 1962, just weeks after that second World Cup exit, there were two primary orders of business. The first was to elect a new DFB president, Hermann Gösmann; and the second was to completely redesign German soccer.

Out went the five Oberligen (Premier Leagues) that had hitherto engrossed the country's North, South, West, Southwest, and Berlin. In came a new single national league, its sixteen founder members winnowed down from no fewer than forty-six applications.

Eintracht Braunschweig, Werder Bremen, and Hamburger SV were accepted from Oberliga Nord; Borussia Dortmund, 1. FC Köln, Meidericher SV (now MSV Duisburg), Preußen Münster, and Schalke 04 from Oberliga West; 1. FC Kaiserslautern, and 1. FC Saarbrücken graduated from Oberliga Südwest; Eintracht Frankfurt, Karlsruher SC, 1. FC Nürnberg, TSV 1860 München, and VfB Stuttgart from Oberliga Süd; and, finally, Hertha BSC from Oberliga Berlin.

Seven of these clubs remain in today's eighteen strong Bundesliga, but subsequent soccer history highlights one very peculiar omission. FC Bayern München, surely the most successful German club of all time, were not rated worthy of inclusion in the initial Bundesliga.

The first weekend of Bundesliga matches got underway on August 23, 1963. Fifty years later, celebrating its anniversary in 2013, the Bundesliga was established not only as the most popular soccer league in the world, with an average attendance of 45,116 per game, but also as the planet's second most popular sporting contest. And that is just the most pronounced of the manifold facts and figures that make the Bundesliga the envy of Europe's other major leagues.

It boasts, for instance, some of the cheapest ticket prices on the continent (with free rail vouchers often included in the purchase). The pestilence of season tickets and waiting lists that clogs other country's club soccer scene is nowhere in sight; the Bundesliga actively encourages open admission and impulse visitors.

Likewise, the English Premier League's insistence on all-seater stadia, born out of the disorder and disasters of the 1980s, is ferociously contradicted by the Bundesliga's encouragement of standing fans. Indeed, Borussia Dortmund's Westfalenstadion has standing room for 27,000 supporters, and never ceases to pack it out—a figure higher than the average attendance at no fewer than *seven* Premier League teams during 2013–2014 (Norwich, Stoke, WBA, Fulham, Hull, Crystal Palace, and Swansea).

Not for nothing do Bundesliga officials and supporters look askance at the Premier League's claim to be the world's most exciting/popular/etc. soccer league!

Of course, the Bundesliga has not escaped the pan-European fascination with a so-called Big Two/Three/Four. FC Bayern München collected their twenty-third Bundesliga title in 2013–2014, and their eighth since 2000. Runners up Borussia Dortmund, champions in 2010–2011 and 2011–2012, are their main competitors today, as was proven when the two giants went head-to-head in the 2012–2013 Champions League final, the first all-German final in the tournament's history.

Don't You Get Sick of Winning the League Every Season?

The Bundesliga is not, however, the stultifying procession of the same names jostling for the top three or four spots every season. Schalke 04, Bayer 04 Leverkeusen, VfB Stuttgart, Werder Bremen, VfL Wolfsburg, and Hamburger SV have all been there-or-thereabouts this century, with five different clubs claiming the championship trophy in that time.

Compare that to Italy, where just three sides (Internazionale, AC Milan, and Juventus) have won Serie A since 2001; to Portugal, where Porto and SL Benfica have won every title since 2002–2003; to Scotland, where that hasn't been a non-Rangers or Celtic champion since Aberdeen in 1984–1985; and to England, where Manchester United, Chelsea, and Arsenal won nineteen of the first twenty-two Premier League titles.

And spare a thought for Greek supporters, who must look back to 1987–1988 for the last occasion upon which their national title was not bound for either AEK Athens, Panathinaikos, or Olympiacos. In fact, only three clubs outside of that trinity, PAOK, Larissa, and Aris, have *ever* won the Greek championship since its formation in 1927–1928, with Aris's last title coming in 1945–1946, at a time when (like Germany) the championship was still decided on a play-off basis between regional victors.

Such monopolies are not, of course, a product of the modern age—as Greece proves. The true giants of Spain, Italy, and Scotland, as we have already seen, were established long ago, and the teams that dominate Uruguayan soccer today, Club Atlético Peñarol and Nacional, are the same as those that dominated it back in 1932.

In Argentina, River Plate, Boca Juniors, and Independiente were powers then and they are powers still; and so forth. Other clubs may rise to challenge the traditional giants and even, for a time, surpass them—through the 1970s, for example, América and Guadalajara's hold on the Mexican title was torn away by Cruz Azul, who indeed cruised to seven titles between 1969 and 1980.

But they are rare, and they require remarkable circumstances. In France, where the traditional powerhouses are Marseille and Saint-Étienne, a hitherto title-less, but suddenly very flush Olympique Lyonnais (Lyon) rose up in the early 2000s to claim seven successive championships (2002–2008). More recently, Paris Saint-Germain have likewise emerged as a major challenger, thanks to their acquisition by the Qatar Investment Authority. Successive title victories in 2013 and 2014 suggest that—at least for as long as the investors keep investing—they will remain such.

Excising the influence of cash from any discussion of modern soccer, at least in those countries considered to be at the forefront of the game, is a fraught exercise. Yet it doesn't always make a difference. Or, to put it more cynically, it doesn't always make the difference that its owners expect.

It is certainly possible to try to buy success, but it is not always so easy to actually succeed; many more clubs around the world have thrown quite absurd amounts of money at the problem, assembling star-studded squads full of world-renowned internationals, only to find that eleven great players do not necessarily equate to one great team.

Egos clash, playing styles differ and, while a good coach should be able to paper over those problems, that is all he can ever do. Nothing saps a center-forward's confidence and enthusiasm faster, or more effectively, than being played hopelessly out of position in order to accommodate the coach's latest tactical brainwave, particularly if success is not immediate.

Similarly, nothing makes a banker more nervous than investing in a club with the assurance that glory is just around the corner than the discovery that the corner is still a few blocks away.

How to Keep Things Interesting

Depressing, but salutary, is the story of England's Leeds United, whose entire future was mortgaged on the dream (and rewards) of immediate Champions League qualification, and whose failure to attain it on schedule precipitated a dive that saw the club drop two divisions in four seasons.

Yet that is also the essence of league football. The fact that no club, however powerful it considers itself to be, should be immune from "the drop." Manchester United were the European of Europe in 1968. Six seasons later, they weren't even numbered among the top twenty clubs in England, and were promptly relegated to the second tier.

Neither was it a fluke. In 1982, Aston Villa won the European Cup. Five years later, they too were in the second division.

It wasn't money that did it for either of them, though. It was, quite simply, the fact that they were no longer good enough to mix it with the big boys. Of course they would be back—both United and Villa bounced up again the following season, and both have remained members of the top division ever since. But they are the exceptions, not the rule. Of the twenty-two clubs that contested the first-ever English Premier League season in 1992–1993, just seven have never been relegated—Villa and United are joined by Arsenal, Chelsea, Everton, Liverpool, and Tottenham; and several of those have clung to that record only by the skin of their teeth.

Forty-six clubs, meanwhile, have contested the competition since its inception, including one—Wimbledon—that effectively disappeared altogether, before clambering its way back into the fourth tier; six more who spent 2013–2014 in the third tier and one, Portsmouth, who are also currently in the fourth.

Traveling the other direction, meanwhile, current Premier Leaguers Swansea City were in the third tier in 1992–1993; and Hull City were on their way there.

The Football Federation Islamic Republic of Iran was founded in 1946. The first league competitions were regional, before 1973 birthed the Takht Jamshid Cup—a league, despite its name. Today, the Iran Premier League is the nation's leading contest, and of course the country enjoys a buoyant soccer media.

For supporters of both, darker days could scarcely have been imagined. Today, it is hard to see them getting much brighter.

This experience of such dreadful lows and such brilliant highs is the essence of league football. Of course there are those supporters who have never known relegation (Arsenal have been in the top flight since some dubious dealings in the aftermath of World War One saw them parachuted in for no reason at all; Everton since the mid-1950s; Liverpool since the early 1960s), and for whom a mid-table finish would be tantamount to disaster. But they are thoroughly outnumbered and, some would say, outclassed too, by those supporters who have truly ridden the swings and roundabouts of promotion and relegation.

Five times, Crystal Palace have risen to the Premier League; four times, they have slipped out of it again. West Bromwich Albion spent the first decade of this century practically yo-yoing between first and second tiers; and then there are those sides who have spent one season, and one season alone dining alongside soccer aristocracy, before slipping back below the salt—Barnsley, Swindon Town, Blackpool, Cardiff City.

Neither are the aristocracy really as high-born as some people like to paint them. Again, forty-six clubs have enjoyed membership of the Premier League since its formation. Yet there are only ninety-two clubs in the entire four-division setup that tops the English system—twenty in the Premier League, seventy-two in the Football League. Meaning, a full 50 percent of the present competition has played top-flight soccer at some point in the past quarter century, and a competition that is often accused of being a tightly barricaded meritocracy is, at least on paper, as democratic as it possibly could be. Certainly when compared to those leagues elsewhere around the world that operate either a closed shop utterly devoid of promotion and relegation, or which have so weighted the process that an established side has more chance of reaching the moon than it does of slipping a rung, no matter how richly their actual performances may deserve it.

Perhaps the same two or three teams do win the Premier League title every season; perhaps the same four or five clubs will forever be fighting for the European qualification places below that. But still there is a glory and a pride to be taken from maintaining a place in such a competitive competition—and, because money cannot be excised from the equation, a financial incentive as well. Thanks to the Premier League's latest television deal, Cardiff City received more money for finishing bottom of the table in 2013–2014 than Manchester United did for finishing top the year before, a total of £62.1m/$104,642,000 compared to £60.8m ($102,954,885).

Such riches (and they are by no means confined to England, or even Europe) are sufficient to ensure soccer clubs and competitions rank as high in the estimation of the world's top financiers and bankers as any more traditional asset.

Yet there remains vast tracts of the planet where soccer is played for the love of it, and where leagues operate for the sake of competition only; where the winning side receive a possibly silver pot and their name in the local history books; and where the losers . . . well, they don't get anything anymore. But there was a time, sometime before the First World War, when the eighteenth-century Cambridge University tradition of presenting the losing side with an actual wooden spoon was still in fashion. And it ought to make a comeback.

The term, if not the presentation, has survived in rugby union and Australian Rules football, and it is frequently encountered in early twentieth-century soccer reportage, too. Perhaps today, we are way too sensitive regarding other people's feelings to publicly humiliate them with the awarding of any kind of trophy (or anti-trophy) as a memorial to their finishing last.

But perhaps we need to stop taking such things so seriously. Yes, you finished ignominiously bottom. Yes, you have now been saddled with a wooden spoon with your name engraved upon it. Maybe it will encourage you to do a little better next year? And if not in the league . . . well, there's always the Cup.

6

The Greatest Competition in the World

We're Going to Win the Cup . . . Aren't We?

T he Cup" is the oldest soccer tournament in the world. Years before the first national leagues were put into place, pitting teams to play one another on a season-long schedule that could be compared to a marathon, the Cup was the short sprint that got in there first, a straightforward knock-out competition that placed rich against poor, big against small, good against bad, and simply let them get on with it.

Rarely is "the Cup" a country's sole cup. Rival trophies come and go, rising and falling at the whim of sundry benefactors, organizers, sponsors, and more. In any given season in England over the past forty years, the supporter could pick his way through a bewildering selection of tournaments, all of which appended their name with those same three letters, or words to similar effect. The Full Members *Cup*. The Football League *Cup*. The Anglo-Italian *Cup*. The Milk *Cup*, the Littlewoods *Cup*, the Zenith Data Systems *Cup*, and it is the same all over the world. Anywhere that soccer is played, there will be Cups to win, trophies to clutch. All have their supporters, all have their stories, and all apparently have their purpose.

But, in every land, there is only one trophy that can truly be called *the* Cup.

It is usually the oldest, it is certainly the most established. It is generally the most prestigious and it is probably the best looking. And, for the most part, it is presented by the one organization in the local game of which it can truly be said . . . "without whom": the national Football Association, whose affiliation to the world governing body FIFA establishes them, with almost Biblical potency, as the one true authority in the land.

In England, they even call it the FA Cup. But, more often, they call it "the Cup."

It is immutable. No matter how many teams may think they can win it, everything comes down to just one in the end. There may be eight competitors, there may be 800. But week by week, round by round, the field is ruthlessly pruned. Sixty-four teams in one round becomes thirty-two in the next; sixteen in the one

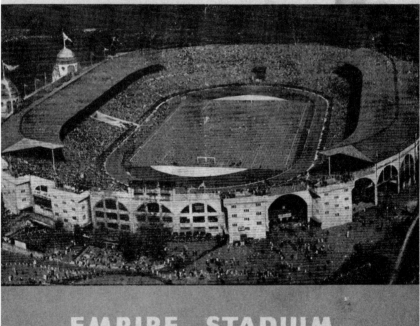

THE FOOTBALL ASSOCIATION CHALLENGE CUP COMPETITION

FINAL TIE

ASTON VILLA

v

MANCHESTER UNITED

SATURDAY, MAY 4th, 1957   KICK-OFF 3 pm

EMPIRE STADIUM

WEMBLEY

OFFICIAL PROGRAMME   -   ONE SHILLING

The biggest day in the footballing calendar—the FA Cup Final, here contested by Aston Villa and Manchester United's legendary Busby Babes. Villa won, 2–1.

after that. Eight are destined to fight out the quarterfinal, the four survivors will meet in the semifinal. And then the last two standing come together in the final, and the Cup is what awaits the eventual victor.

Those other cups might ape the format; might hold themselves up as somehow equal. They might offer grander cash rewards, or a shinier, more silvery trophy. But that is all they will ever be. "Other cups." They can never be *the* Cup.

You Can Stop Scoring Now—I Think You've Won

The Cup is utterly unpredictable. On the right day, under the right conditions, any team is capable of defeating any other. On paper, in 2012–2013, what chance did Luton Town (English level five) possibly have when they were drawn to play against Norwich City (level one) in the Cup? None whatsoever. But it was Luton who marched into the next round, and Norwich who were left to lick their wounds.

Sutton United (non-league) vs. Coventry City (top division) in 1989. Harlow Town vs. Leicester City in 1980. Wimbledon vs. Burnley in 1975. Hereford United vs. Newcastle United in 1972. Yeovil Town vs. Sunderland in 1949. New Brompton vs. Sunderland in 1907–1908 (yes, New Brompton. They hadn't even become the mighty Gills yet!). In every instance, the first name was simply a guileless lamb to the slaughter. And in every instance, the lamb rewrote the script at the last minute.

Or sometimes, they didn't. First Division Preston North End vs. the part-timers of Hyde in 1887. The final score of 26–0 to Preston remains the highest ever registered in an English FA Cup match . . . and still falls short of the 36–0 victory with which Arbroath saw off Bon Accord in a Scottish Cup tie two seasons earlier.

Nottingham Forest 14, Clapton 0 in 1891. Swindon Town 10, Farnham United Breweries 1 in 1925. Gillingham 10, Gorleston 1 in 1957–1958. Bournemouth & Boscombe Athletic 11, Margate 0 in 1971. Shrewsbury 11, Marine 2 in 1995. Colchester United 9, Leamington 1 in 2005.

On occasions like these. the phrase "fish in a barrel" comes cruelly to mind. But these, and the giant-killing corollaries of which every minnow dreams, are the extremes. In reality, and across the course of most Cup competitions, the scoring stays in single figures, and the two teams' relative standings in the league usually have some bearing on the final score. Usually.

Those other occasions? They are flukes perhaps, master classes rarely. When Colchester United beat Leeds United in the FA Cup in 1971, it was because the third-tier tiddlers scored more goals on the day than the first-division behemoths. On any other day, Leeds might have started scoring when the opening whistle blew, and never stopped until the last second of stoppage time had passed.

But not today. Which meant it was not the Colchester supporters who filed away from Layer Road with their bottom lips dragging on the sidewalk, and

PLAYER'S CIGARETTES

ALDRIDGE GREEN

ROBERTS

HORTON TIMMINS

PERRY

BASSETT PEARSON

BAYLISS

WOODHALL WILSON

ASSOCIATION CUP WINNERS
WEST BROMWICH ALBION. 1888

FA Cup winners have always fascinated the public. From 1930, a popular brand of cigarettes enticed purchasers with images of the past fifty years worth of victors.

their scarves stuffed deep inside their pockets for fear of inviting further ridicule. It was not the Colchester supporters who averted their eyes from one another on the trains that took them back to their hometown, and who avoided the following day's newspapers, because they knew what all the headlines would say.

And it was not the Colchester supporters who had to console themselves with the eternal chorus of the vanquished Cup campaigner. "We can concentrate on the League instead." If history books could laugh, they would still be chuckling over that one. Instead they file it under "the magic of the Cup." Because that's what it was.

A Nice Cup of English

As the oldest national Cup competition of them all, the English FA Cup also serves as the archetype for almost all of those that developed in its wake. Of which there are today almost as many as there are countries playing soccer. The Scottish Cup was the first to follow the English lead in 1874, Wales in 1877. Ireland, united under British rule until 1921, launched its knock-out trophy in 1881; the Netherlands in 1899, when RAP Amsterdam promptly did the league and Cup double and then vanished from view.

Into the twentieth century, and Europe caught Cup Fever. Norway and Spain commenced their competitions in 1902. Hungary (1910), Belgium (1912), France and the newly birthed nation of Czechsolovakia (1918), Austria (1919), Italy (1922), Poland (1926), Cup followed Cup followed Cup.

The first Greek Cup final, an eight-goal thriller between AEK Athens and Aris Salonica, was contested in 1932. Romania joined the Cup club in 1934. Germany was surprisingly slow, not launching its Cup until 1935, the same year as little Malta, and the vast lands of Russia were forced to wait until 1936 brought a railroad network that was far-reaching enough to allow a truly national competition to get underway. Although, having done so, the capital city's concern for the provinces did not extend so far as to allow them to actually win anything. With the exception of one quick visit to Leningrad, it was 1963 before the Cup was won by any team bar a Muscovite.

Portugal's trophy was even later in arriving, kicking off in 1939. Sweden, members of FIFA since 1904, did not inaugurate the Swedish Cup until 1941. The Yugoslavian Cup was first fought for in 1947. The Danes got off the mark in 1955, in the same year that Haka Valkeakoski won the inaugural Finnish Cup. The Turkish Cup set off in 1963, and was won for four years straight by Galatasaray.

But the FA Cup out-glamours them all.

The tournament begins in the summer, while most of the top clubs are still enjoying their preseason break, or else topping up the coffers with lucrative international tours and invitational competitions.

It is not the largest competition of its kind. The French Cup, the Coupe de France, regularly attracts some 7,500 entrants, from the uppermost echelons of the league, to the lowliest parks and recreation grounds. Thanks to a rule that cuts competitors off at the tenth tier of the English game, the English tournament draws around one-tenth as many clubs. In 2014–2015, there was 736 entrants, "seeded" according to their relative status within those ten levels, and, in the very earliest

Another Player's cigarette card, depicting 1891 FA Cup winners Blackburn Rovers.

stages, by location—financing is always a concern at this level, so travel is kept to a regional minimum.

Those two criteria satisfied, the lowliest 368 clubs met in the Extra Preliminary Round, with the 184 winners then moving into the Preliminary Round, to be joined by a fresh intake of 136 further clubs. And so it continues; the winners of one round, and another batch of debutantes marching through a further four qualifying rounds, until the First Round Proper sees a mere thirty-two non-league survivors pitted against the forty-eight members of the lowest two divisions of the Football League.

Eighty clubs become forty in the Second Round Proper; the twenty survivors of that conflict are then matched with the forty-four clubs that represent the Premier League and the top division of the Football League. And now the winnowing begins in earnest.

There is no further seeding. The French model, again, offers home advantage to any side two or more levels below its opponent. England relies wholly on the luck of the draw. A club from the uppermost echelons of the Premier League is as likely to be drawn away against its most potent rival in the title race as it is to be entertaining a doughty survivor of the earliest rounds. In 2013–2014, three teams who entered the competition in the Fourth Qualifying Round were still involved in the Third Round Proper, with one of their number, Kidderminster Harriers, pulling off a giant-killing act by disposing of third-tier Peterborough, and marching into round four.

There they were narrowly eliminated by Sunderland; who went on to beat Southampton in the Fifth Round Proper before being knocked out in the quarterfinal by Hull. And Hull would ultimately reach the final, but only after overcoming a side that had made its own FA Cup entry way back in the First Round Proper, third-tier Sheffield United—whose own progress to the semifinal saw them knock out no fewer than four clubs from higher levels than they. Four clubs who might reasonably be excused for having gone into the tie thinking, "Well, this should be easy. . . ."

That, too, is the magic of the FA Cup; that, for the casual supporter, is its appeal. There is no form book to rely upon, no special formula with which the game's administration can ensure, to a more-or-less flawless level of certainty, that the two clubs left in the showpiece final will be the two richest, grandest, best supported sides in the land. In Grand Slam tennis, it's a shock if the top two seeds don't meet in the final. In Cup soccer, it's a surprise if they do.

Of course, it has happened. Chelsea vs. Manchester United in 2007 and, before that, in 1994. Arsenal vs. Manchester United in 2005. Arsenal vs. Chelsea in 2002, Arsenal vs. Liverpool in 2001, Manchester United vs. Liverpool in 1996. As of the 2014–2015 season, out of the twenty-two FA Cup finals competed since the birth of the English Premier League, Liverpool have been involved four times, Manchester United six, Arsenal seven, Chelsea eight. A mere four sides account for more than half of the total number of FA Cup finalists since 1992–1993.

The FA Cup's reputation for pairing Davids with Goliaths needs no further illustration than this 1953 tussle between Manchester United and Walthamstow Avenue.

But what of all the others? Hull City. Wigan Athletic. Stoke City. Portsmouth. Southampton. Middlesbrough. West Ham United. Newcastle United. Sheffield Wednesday. Aston Villa. All Premier League sides at the time of their appearance, but scarcely numbered among the *crème de la crème.*

Other finalists, Cardiff City and Millwall, weren't even that; both were languishing in the second tier when they marched into the Cup final, and even their achievements (both were beaten by Premier League opposition) pale when compared to the more distant past, the years when West Ham United (1980), Southampton (1976), and Sunderland (1973) rose from similar depths to win the Cup. Or, reaching back to the dawn of the last century, Tottenham Hotspur who were not even *in* the Football League when they won the Cup in 1901. A non-league team, in other words, although as members of the then very powerful Southern League, they entered the competition at the same time as the big kids whom they would be so blithely dispatching as they advanced.

The Butcher, the Baker, the Candlestick Maker, and That's Just Their Midfield

The fascination with non-league teams in the FA Cup—and in every other, similarly organized competition—is not difficult to understand. Part of it is the novelty value of seeing new names marching forward; or the novelty of those names themselves, and that itself is a never-ending source of wonder. A selection of the club sides competing in the opening rounds of the 2013–2014 FA Cup would include the likes of Darlington Railway Athletic, Glasshoughton Welfare, Jarrow Roofing Boldon Community Association, Pontefract Collieries, West Allotment Celtic, Sunderland Ryhope Community Association, West Didsbury & Chorlton, and Cray Valley Paper Mills.

All exist in the very lowest reaches of the English pyramid, the ninth and tenth levels where the league names themselves feel like survivors from a different age—the Wessex League, the Hellenic League, the Kent Invicta League, the South West Peninsula League, wholly localized contests where attendances may not register higher than double figures, and every one of the players, and the staff as well, have full-time occupations far from the "glamour" of professional or even semiprofessional soccer. Bankers, builders, postmen, shop clerks, factory workers, miners, whatever.

For a team in level ten, five promotions are required before the Football League is even in sight, although one does not have to travel too far down there to encounter some familiar names. Nelson were members of the Football League until 1931; Northwich 1874 are the modern successors to a club playing in the Second Division in the early 1890s. Today, both ply their trade in division one of the North West Counties Football League, one tier down from Glossop North End, a Football League First Division side in 1899–1900.

The traffic is not all one-way, either. Fleetwood Town, promoted to the Football League's First Division in 2013–2014, were playing at the same league as Glossop, Nelson, and Northwich as recently as 2004–2005, their record of six promotions in ten seasons standing as an inspiration to every side they have passed along the way.

For the majority of the teams down here, though, it is the FA Cup that offers the fastest and most likely route to glory, whether that be making it all the way to the Third Round Proper, and the chance to take on one of the true giants; or simply holding on for as long as possible, just to see what happened.

In 2010–2011, Hythe Town of the Kent League (now the Southern Counties East Football League) were among the 402 sides that kicked off the entire tournament in mid-August, in the Extra Preliminary Round. They beat Bookham Town 4–0, and probably didn't raise an eyebrow by doing so. Nor when they defeated Deal 4–2 in the Preliminary Round, or Epsom & Ewell in the First Qualifying Round. It was still early days; let the little ones play.

Come November, however, and the arrival of the first Football League sides, little Hythe were still in there, a ninth-tier side whose usual matchday fare saw them battle the likes of Faversham and Herne Bay, but who were now in the draw with Sheffield Wednesday and Southampton . . . and Hereford, whose 5–1 triumph not only brought the seaside town part-timers back to earth with a bump, it also ended another dream. The dream of emulating the legendary Chasetown, an eighth-tier team (from the British Gas Business Southern League Midland Division) who reached the Third Round Proper in 2007–08.

Again, their initial progress was unremarkable. They entered the competition at the Preliminary Round stage, and a 4–1 win over Oadby Town was played out in front of just 321 spectators. Chasetown only really caught the eye in the Fourth Qualifying Round, when they knocked out Nuneaton Borough, by which time the attendance at their Scholars Ground had soared to almost 1,500.

Team Bath were their next victims, themselves something of an FA Cup Legend after becoming (in 2002–2003) the first University team to reach the First Round Proper since 1880. A 2–0 victory in Bath set Chasetown up for a second-round meeting with third-tier Port Vale and, following a 1–1 draw at the league club's ground, Chasetown took them home and nearly 2,000 people roared the minnows to a 1–0 win in the replay.

The tradition for any non-league side making it to the third round is to dream of who they might be paired with, and Chasetown were no different. Liverpool, Chelsea, Arsenal . . . all the usual suspects would have flitted through the Chasetown daydreams, which means second-tier Cardiff City probably came as something of a disappointment.

But still, 135 places separated the two teams on the pyramid, and Chasetown coach Charlie Blakemore—by day, a supply manager for British Aerospace—spoke for every tiddler who has ever progressed in the Cup when he said, "I am the proudest man in the world at what they have achieved. It's been an absolute dream, the whole journey."

Close to 2,500 people crammed into the Scholars Ground for the Welsh side's visit, and for almost forty-five minutes, the impossible seemed to be within reach, as a Kevin McNaughton own goal placed Chasetown ahead. But, from the moment Cardiff equalized, shortly before halftime, it was clear that there would be no shocks today.

Yet the fairy tale was not quite over. For, with a run of results that, in its own way, was as shocking as Chasetown's progress, Cardiff were that year destined for the FA Cup final. They would ultimately stumble at that last hurdle, but still theirs was a journey that none would have predicted when it began. Much like Chasetown's.

The Robin's Tale

The approach to drawn games in the FA Cup is as prosaic as it is blunt. Tied teams have one further shot at breaking the deadlock; a single replay to be staged at the original visitor's home ground. If that, too, is tied, the result is decided on penalties.

It is not a satisfactory way of deciding a tie. Whether it's the World Cup final, or the first round of a minor domestic tournament, the very notion that a full game's worth of effort and expertise should be nullified for a few minutes of decisive spot kicks is patently absurd. All the more so since "PKs" (as American TV once tried to rename them) were only ever introduced in a bid to brighten up soccer for American audiences. "Look ma, no ties."

Slowly, however, they encroached. First they replaced the second replay. In some tournaments they replace the first replay—and nobody watching the 2014–2015 English League Cup match between Dagenham & Redbridge and Brentford, a dynamic 6–6 tie at the end of extra time, could ever have agreed that a shootout was just reward for either side. (Brentford won, incidentally.) This was a contest that should have been played out to the death. Instead, penalty kicks.

Soon, they will probably replace the match itself, on those occasions when the clubs agree that the full ninety minutes would be boring, and the local police admit they'd rather not have the overtime, and the supporters agree they'd like to get home at a reasonable hour. Full teams would not even need to travel. Just send along the goalie to one another's ground, set up the cameras, and do the whole thing online.

Soccer—the Final Evolution.

This was not always the case. Once, a game would simply be replayed and replayed until a legitimate victor was decided, no matter how long it took to do so. As non-league Alvechurch and Oxford City discovered in the Fourth Qualifying Round of the 1971–1972 FA Cup. A 2–2 draw in the original game was followed by two 1–1 ties and two 0–0 stalemates before Alvechurch finally scraped through with a 1–0 win at the *sixth* time of asking. No less than eleven hours of play had been required to decide the match, and after all that, the plucky heroes went out 4–2 to Aldershot in the first round.

Even Alvechurch's endurance pales, however, against that displayed by Bideford two seasons later.

The pride of North Devon—and the kings of endurance, too.

Based on the northern coast of Devon, in the English southwest, the Robins are one of the unsung treasures of the English non-league scene. Formed in 1945, they started life in the Exeter & East Devon League, before joining the region-wide Western League in 1949. They were accepted into that tournament's newly formed (and very short-lived) Third Division; won that at a canter, and two seasons later, topped Division Two as well, a season of memorable victories crowned by a positively merciless 16–1 demolition of Soundell FC.

Division One beckoned, a league staffed not only by various other regional giants, but also by a number of well-heeled reserve teams; Weymouth, Yeovil, Torquay, and Bristol City, the latter pair Football League sides, all had a presence in the division. Nevertheless, Bideford took the title in 1963–1964, were runners-up the following year, and they were there-or-thereabouts for the remainder of the decade.

The Kent County Football Association

CENTENARY CELEBRATION

FACIT KENT SENIOR CUP FINAL

Sponsored by FACIT

1889   1989

100 YEARS

Maidstone United F.C.

versus

Welling United F.C.

MONDAY, 1st MAY, 1989, Kick Off 3.00 p.m.

PRIESTFIELD STADIUM, GILLINGHAM

OFFICIAL PROGRAMME 50p

FACIT

Celebrating the centenary of the English county of Kent's own Cup, a special program for the Maidstone United vs. Welling United final in 1989.

It was during the early 1970s, however, that Bideford truly took control. Western League Champions in both 1970–1971 and 1971–1972, the following season they were elected to the Southern League, at that time the joint-highest level of non-league soccer in England, and in 1973–1974, an FA Cup adventure unfolded, one that was to be of record-breaking proportions.

Entering the fray in the First Qualifying Round, Bideford had no problem disposing of Penzance, 4–1 at the Sports Ground. The next round saw them again drawn at home, and this time Newquay were vanquished 6–1. It was in the Third Qualifying Round that things got tough, when Bideford came up against Falmouth Town, South Western League champions elect and destined, over the next few years, to dominate the Western League as well.

The first game, at Falmouth's Cornish home, ended in a thrilling 3–3 tie. The first replay, back in Bideford, finished 1–1; and it followed by two 2–2 stalemates. The two teams were into the *fourth* replay before Bideford finally crept through by the odd goal in three. And they then came close to repeating the entire exercise all over again in the Fourth Qualifying Round. In the first match, Southern League rivals Trowbridge Town kept honors even with a 2–2 draw; and followed up with a pair of 1–1s before, in the third replay, Bideford squeaked a 3–2 win.

After all that, after *eleven* games shoehorned in around their usual Southern League responsibilities, simply to advance them two rounds in the FA Cup, Bideford received their reward, a home tie with high-flying Bristol Rovers. And there, the gulf in league status, probably coupled with a good dose of exhaustion, saw the plucky Robins dismissed by 2–0. But still they achieved one thing: a place in the record books for the most FA Cup games ever played in a single season, and one that the abandonment of second replays has ensured will probably never be beaten.

If the qualifying rounds of the FA Cup fascinate from the aspect of unlikely antics and sheer derring-do, the latter stages can weave their own magical spell over even the most disinterested neutral. The world's oldest Cup competition is also its most viewed, with recent finals watched by an estimated half a billion viewers in over a hundred different countries. No other domestic soccer tournament, and that includes the German, Italian, and Spanish Cup final, command such an audience; indeed, it is often said that in many lands, the FA Cup final has a larger following than the country's own domestic trophy.

The Final Conflict

Tradition plays a major part in this, of course. Even before the television age, there were certain English players, and certain English clubs, whose names seemed to be known in the most unlikely places. Apocryphal though some may be, there is no shortage whatsoever of travel journals or news reports in which a visitor escapes from a potentially dangerous situation by naming Stanley Matthews or Bobby Charlton, Gordon Banks or George Best, and transforming a mob of murderous locals into a gaggle of widely grinning acolytes.

Where the teams' names go, their honors follow, and with the FA Cup final's traditional home at Wembley Stadium being almost as famous as the teams that have played there, glory by association was probably inevitable.

But of course there is more to it than that. Legendary FA Cup finals dot the history books. Prior to 1923, the Cup final had never had a home; rather, it wandered around different grounds and even different cities. The 1923 event was the first to be staged at the newly built, suitably grandiose Wembley Stadium, and such was the anticipation surrounding the event that no fewer than 126,000 people attended that game—and possibly more; some reports claim up to 200,000 were present, once the barriers broke and the crowds surged in.

The game itself, Bolton Wanderers vs. West Ham United, may or may not have been memorable. But history has never forgotten the image of the police officer riding a white horse around the perimeter of the field, keeping the crowds in order.

There was the 1953 final, when the entire British Isles, it was said, was willing Stanley Matthews' Blackpool team to victory, simply out of love and admiration for one of the finest players ever seen on an English field. They were rewarded with a seven-goal thriller, and Blackpool triumphing over (again) Bolton Wanderers.

Bolton, ironically, were on the sticky end of another massive wave of national sentiment just five years later, when they pitched up to play Manchester United, so recently devastated by the Munich Air Disaster, in the 1958 final. This time,

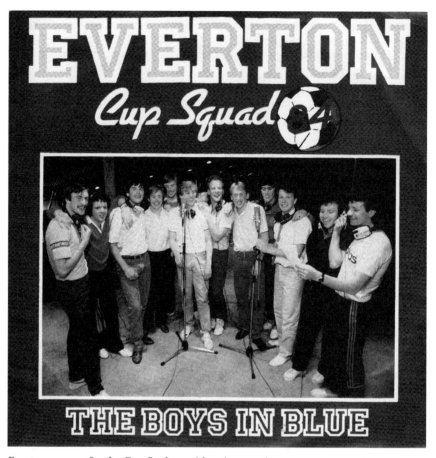

Everton prepare for the Cup final . . . with a sing-song!

however, Bolton were in no mood to be swayed by public sentiment. Indeed, not only did they win 2–0, but (as we saw in chapter four) one of their goals was so ruthlessly designed, and caused so much outrage, that the rules of the game were changed almost immediately afterward. Never again would an attacking forward be permitted to score a goal by bundling both the ball, and the goalkeeper who was holding it, into the net.

There was the 1973 final, when one of the aforementioned second-tier sides, Sunderland, beat Leeds United 1–0, with manager Bob Stokoe's gleeful victory jig at the end of the game preserved now in a statue that stands outside Sunderland's stadium. And the 1979 event, when a ruthless Arsenal swept to a 2–0 lead against Manchester United, only for the northerners to hit back with two goals inside two minutes, when the game itself had just four minutes to run. Arsenal would ultimately prevail, with a very last minute strike sinking United's dreams of one of the greatest comebacks ever, but it is unlikely that the whistle will ever be blown on memories of the so-called Five Minute Final.

Sometimes it is not entire games, but mere incidents within them, or anecdotes around them, that consign a Final to legendary status. The passage of play, in the dying moments of the 1983 clash between Manchester United and Brighton, which culminated with an excited television commentator insisting "and Smith must score..."—only for Brighton striker Smith *not* to score, and his side's chance of victory reduced to a replay instead.

The 1987 final when Coventry City not only shocked much-fancied Spurs to take the trophy home with them, they also finally removed themselves from the punchline to one of Monty Python's Flying Circus's most venerable routines, that moment in the Communist Quiz when Che Guevara is asked the fateful question, "In what year did Coventry City last win the FA Cup?"

The answer—which neither Che, nor fellow competitors Mao Tse Tung, Lenin, and Karl Marx could supply—was "Coventry City have never won the FA Cup. It was a trick question." Not any longer. Although there was certainly a Pythonesque surrealism to the side's defense of the trophy the following season. They were bundled out in the third round by non-league Sutton United.

We remember the 1988 game, when all-conquering Liverpool faced unfancied Wimbledon, and not only lost 1–0, but also earned the ignominious title of becoming the first team ever to have a penalty saved in a Wembley final. Moments like these, and a hundred more besides, are what long ago established the FA Cup final among the most fondly remembered, and hungrily anticipated dates in the entire soccer calendar, in countries all over the world.

Sometimes, the game itself is appalling, ninety minutes of such turgid negativity that even the participants probably have difficulty remembering it in later years . . . the 1996 final, for example, is better recalled for the absolute tastelessness of the losing Liverpool's prematch outfits (matching cream suits, ghastly striped ties, and white Gucci shoes) than for anything that transpired on the pitch.

Other times, the game is so one-sided that it might as well have been a friendly. Manchester United's 4–0 victory over Chelsea in 1994 marked the highest margin of victory ever recorded in a Wembley final, and the most net-stretchingly one-sided final since Bury beat Derby 6–0 in the 1903 event.

None of this matters. The FA Cup final is the FA Cup final, the culmination of nine months, and almost 800 clubs' worth of dreams and despair, hope and hubris, agony and ecstasy. It is the greatest day in the soccer calendar, at the end of the greatest tournament in all of sport, and in every other country where a similar tournament thrives today, the same wild sentiment holds equally true.

Particularly in those lands where (as is the case across Europe) it offers a route into continental competition that is still wide open to any club in the country, as opposed to the usual clutch of multimillionaires who have carved the League Championship up between them.

7

Okay, There's a Lot Riding on This Game . . .

But Is It Really a Matter of Life and Death?

I t was not only the game's popularity that expanded as the twentieth century grew older. The game's problems, too, appeared to be multiplying, not least of all being what the authorities like to term "soccer violence."

Crowd disorder had been a part of the game since its birth. Indeed, reflecting back on mob football, it might even be said to have been one of the modern game's own parents, or at least the attending midwife. Early reports of even the organized game are rife with incidents that the average reader might read with mounting horror.

There was the Glasgow Celtic player who, on the eve of an important game in the late nineteenth century, received an anonymous letter warning him of what would happen if the team let their supporters down. Attached to the letter were the decapitated corpses of eleven mice.

There were the antagonistic crowds that would gather outside the different grounds that dotted 1890s Buenos Aires, all but barricading them against the afternoon's opposition even entering the premises, let alone getting onto the playing field.

And there was the English FA Cup tie between Darwen and Bootle in 1891, during which a string of refereeing decisions pushed the partisan Bootle crowd to the very precipice of what might have been organized soccer's first full-fledged riot.

A hail of snowballs and, according to the *Darwen Post* newspaper, "other potent missiles" rained down upon the unfortunate referee, and as the crowd spilled over onto the playing surface, police and club officials were forced to rush to the hapless official's defense.

Neither were the players safe. Again in the words of the local paper, Darwen defender McEvoy wasn't simply set upon by a Bootle supporter. He was also "kicked in the nasty leg."

It was in Italy, however, that supporter violence seemed set to become a way of life, at least for some people. Pitch invasions and stone throwing were both tried and trusted means by which crowds made their dissatisfaction known, and referees were frequent targets. In December 1913, one offending official was actually chased off the pitch and out of the ground by an incensed crowd after one questionable call too many, while a month later, shots were allegedly fired in the referee's general direction during a Livorno vs. Pisa game.

As in so many other lands, Italian soccer paused while World War One ran its course, and then returned in 1920, eager to pick up where it had left off . . . with even more stone throwing, gunfire, and mob violence. Only now, the events of a simple soccer game were less the *cause* of the violence, and more of an excuse. Mussolini's aforementioned rise to power was not a peaceable operation; Italy was rent by political discord and violence as it struggled to come to terms with the new world that had dawned across postwar Europe—inflation was rife among winners and losers alike, and far-right organizations were growing increasingly powerful as the embattled populace looked for answers. Or for somebody to blame.

In April 1920, in the Tuscan town of Lucca, a derby match with neighboring Sporting Club Viareggio boiled over into something approaching . . . but not quite reaching . . . violence. On that occasion, the authorities were able to quell the fervor. They would not, however, be so fortunate when the two clubs met again the following month, or so vowed the aggrieved Viareggio supporters.

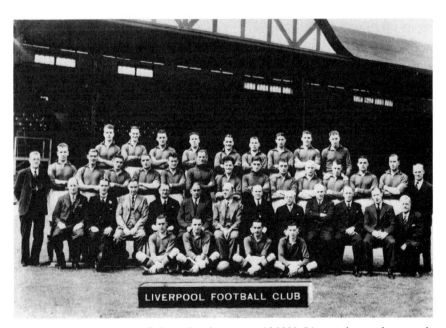

Proof that soccer was never all about the players—a mid-1930s Liverpool team shot rounds up all the backroom, management, and directorial faces, too.

Their threats were taken seriously, too. In the days leading up to the game, warnings went out to Lucca supporters suggesting that they give the game a wide berth, and many appear to have heeded the advice. Certainly the crowd was surprisingly meek as the game got underway.

Unfortunately, there was one Lucca resident who had been quite incapable of staying away. Incredibly, the game was to be refereed not by an obvious impartial, but by a Luccan, and if the crowd had been prepared to give him the benefit of the doubt as SC Viareggio charged imperiously into a 2–0 lead, they were less prone to sympathy and understanding when the visitors swept back into contention. Suddenly the two teams were on equal terms once again, and the crowd did not like it.

Neither did one of the linesmen, a Viareggio native named Augusto Morganti. As the game moved into its final minutes, Morganti fell into a bitter argument with one of the Lucca players; so bitter that the referee was forced to end the game early. At which point, first the pitch and then the remainder of the stadium became the scene of a pitched battle, into which a small band of military police was forced to wade to save the Lucca players from the mob, while simultaneously forcing that mob out of the ground.

More police were called for, arriving to find the ground in a veritable state of siege. At which point one policeman, under the impression that he had just been threatened by the raging Morganti, pulled out his gun and shot the man in the neck at more or less point-blank range.

The linesman fell to the ground, dead, and the watching crowd exploded. The police were chased away (in the confusion, the Lucca players were able to effect their own escape), but the mob followed them to their barracks, and demanded that Morganti's killer be surrendered to them.

That was not going to happen, but the enraged crowd was not going away. Barricades were raised, and all communications with the outside world were cut off—a relatively easy thing to do in those days when there'd be just the one telephone line in and out. The mob ruled the streets, their numbers and organization swollen by the arrival of anarchists from other surrounding towns, and it would take no fewer than two days, and the intervention of *three* military columns, before the authorities were able to regain control of the town.

Naturally, it did not take much longer for Italy's burgeoning Fascist movement to paint the events of the weekend as a chilling portent of how life would be all across Italy if the Reds—Communists, anarchists, socialists, all were beasts of much the same hue in right-wing eyes— were allowed to take control of the country. And similar conclusions, by similar sensationalists, have been drawn for political ends ever since.

Of course, isolating any one country, or any single circumstance, as somehow indicative of the nature, and spread, of "soccer hooliganism" is ultimately a pointless exercise. Human beings in general are both fiercely opinionated, and ferociously defensive of those opinions, and soccer rivalries are no more or less destructive than those that exist in any other forum that demands the partisan involvement of a crowd. Witness the passions that run riot every day in Internet chat rooms or comment pages, and then imagine what would transpire were those same puce-faced pugilists to be having an identical debate in person.

Besides, the violence that afflicted the Italian game during the early 1920s, and which also sparked elsewhere in central Europe during that decade, was largely divorced from the sport itself. It was a manifestation of a far wider, far deeper discontent, and one that a simple game of soccer was never going to solve.

Much the same can be said of the clashes that sparked in England in the late 1970s, as unemployment soared, homelessness boomed, poverty rocketed, and already discontent soccer crowds became a popular recruiting ground for members of the ultra-right-leaning National Front party. And to draw a parallel that history insists can never be overworked, for the circumstances surrounding an international match played between England and Germany some forty years before that, in Berlin in 1938. The game itself passed without any violence whatsoever, much as one would expect in a Nazi-run authoritarian state. But beneath the surface, tensions approached a boiling point.

It has been said that sport is often a simple substitute for warfare, an opportunity for lifelong belligerents to tackle the might of their foes without resorting to actual armed violence. On this occasion, a lot of people felt it was simply a dress rehearsal.

The Little World War

On May 14, 1938, England's national soccer team traveled into the heart of Hitler's Germany and, in front of almost every Nazi dignitary in town, whipped the Master Race by six goals to three.

The game was the first of the three matches England were scheduled to play that month. Switzerland and that year's World Cup hosts France were also on the agenda and, while all three games were billed as friendlies, nobody was taking them at all lightly.

Having withdrawn from soccer's international governing body FIFA a decade previous, England were, without doubt, the most significant absentees from the World Cup tournament. In forty-six officially recognized internationals against European opposition, dating back to 1908, England had lost just six times. And of their six conquerors, only one, the French, had the temerity to defeat them by more than a single goal. No Continental team had ever bettered them on their home turf, while England's defeat of FIFA's own World Champions Italy ensured that, regardless of their "official" status, England were truly the masters of the game.

In Berlin, however, Hitler had other ideas. While the 1936 Olympic Games in Germany had not panned out exactly as he had planned them, Nazi Germany had proved itself a force to be reckoned with in world sports.

German athletes won thirty-three gold, twenty-six silver and thirty bronze medals, and established new Olympic records in the shot and hammer events.

A postage stamp issued by Nazi Germany to commemorate the 1936 Berlin Olympics.

Germany's Olympic soccer hopes had taken a very early bath, but so had Great Britain's (the four United Kingdom nations at that time pooled their resources for Olympic competition). Both sides had been confident of taking the gold; both had tumbled in the second round; Britain to Poland, Germany to unfancied Norway.

But Hitler had no doubts that this time, his Master Race would not only beat the English, they would annihilate them, erasing in the process German soccer's previous miserable record against them.

Soccer-playing relations had never been good between the two countries. Early, amateur-level encounters ended in almost uniform humiliation for the Germans: in Berlin in 1908, England won by 5–1; in Oxford the following year the English came through by 9–0; and while 1911 brought a 2–2 draw in Berlin, 1913 saw a visiting England notch up a fine 3–0 win.

Neither would matters improve after the Great War. In fact, in 1919, England were one of several nations (Scotland, Wales, Ireland, France, Belgium and Luxembourg included) who refused to remain members of any organization—FIFA included—in which Germany, Hungary, and Austria, defeated in the conflict, were also involved. It would take until the end of the decade before Britain's relations with the three wartime aggressors at last began to take on a semblance of conviviality.

Scotland were the first of the four United Kingdom nations to play Germany at full International level, leaving Berlin in June 1929 with a very credible 1–1 tie. The following May, England were held to a 3–3 draw, again in Berlin, and in May 1935 Germany won their first, and thus far only, victory over a team from the British Isles, 3–1 against the Republic of Ireland in Dortmund.

Other results steadfastly put the Germans in the shade. That December, England defeated a visiting German team 3–0 in London; the following October, a second German tour saw the Irish romp home by 5–2 in Dublin, while Scotland triumphed 2–0 in Glasgow.

The match with England in 1938, then, was more than a simple game of soccer. For Germany in general, and Hitler in particular, it was a matter of national pride.

For England, on the other hand, the game came at the end of a particularly tiring season. The annual British Home International Championship had been even closer than usual, with Scotland snatching their first Wembley win in ten years. The domestic season, too, had taken a harsh toll on the England squad, drawn as it was from the cream of England's soccer elite.

Eddie Hapgood and Cliff Bastin, veterans of the Arsenal club, were both exhausted from their team's dramatic last-minute run for the Championship.

Aston Villa's Frank Broome—like Charlton Athletic's Don Welsh, set to make his first-ever appearance in an England shirt—was similarly drained after his team's triumph at the top of the Second Division. Other England regulars, Stan Cullis of Wolves and Arsenal's Wilf Copping included, were not even expected to play.

Huddersfield's Ken Willingham and Alf Young, the latter fresh from the disappointment of giving away the penalty which ensured his side's defeat in the FA Cup final, could also have been excused had they felt a little short of their best. And the greatest English player of them all, Stanley Matthews, was still recovering from Stoke City's so-narrow escape from relegation. The English squad radiated exhaustion, disappointment, and disillusion, and that is what German strategists were relying upon.

Six members of the England side that had fallen to Scotland, but only three of those who had battled to a fine 5–4 win over Czechoslovakia in the match before that, were chosen to meet the Germans, with the final eleven lining up as: Woodley (goalkeeper with the Chelsea club); Sproston (Leeds United); Hapgood (Arsenal); Willingham and Young (Huddersfield); Welsh (Charlton); Matthews (Stoke); Robinson (Sheffield Wednesday); Broome (Aston Villa); Len Goulden (West Ham), and Bastin (Arsenal).

Against them was pitted a German side selected not only from within the country's traditional borders, but also from Austria, annexed to Greater Germany just two months previous. Indeed, the side was coached by an Austrian, Josef Pesser, who had master-minded so many of his home nation's past soccer triumphs. All of Germany expected him to weave similar magic for the Fatherland.

Elsewhere in the team, Jakob was amongst the most formidable goalkeep-ers in Europe. Muenzenberg had already proven his worth against England when his control of Stanley Matthews had all but snuffed the player out of the game in 1936, while his partner in defense, Paul Janes, and the gallant attacker, Josef Gauchel, would surely have ranked in any All-Europe XI.

But they were an aging side, overflow-ing with names that had been familiar to German audiences even at the time of the 1934 World Cup (a tournament, incidentally, in which Germany's victory over Austria in the Third Place Play-Offs

S. CULLIS
WOLVERHAMPTON WANDERERS

One of the stars of the 1930s England national team, Stan Cullis was also a member of the great Wolverhampton Wanderers side.

remained the apex of the country's soccer success). Any doubts as to England's sharpness had surely to be offset against that factor.

There were deeper currents running below the surface, however. In England itself, the decision to even play Germany in the first place was widely regarded as a strange one.

Under the nervously watchful eye of all Europe, Hitler had completely revitalized Germany, flying in the face of every one of the treaties agreed at the end of the Great War as he did so. The absorption of Austria notwithstanding, his policy of *Lebensraum* had already seen German boundaries increase far beyond those proscribed in 1919, and while the process had been bloodless so far, few people throughout Europe's corridors of power doubted that there would come a time when armed might would replace propaganda and appeasement in the growth of Greater Germany.

The match also had a variety of political implications. At the 1936 Olympic Games, a number of athletes had refused to offer Hitler the traditional Nazi salute, infuriating the Führer and sending further, nervous palpitations throughout Europe. In both London and Berlin, worried diplomats were adamant that a repetition of that incident could never be permitted to happen.

At the same time, however, would not the sight of English soccer players saluting Hitler be seen by the rest of the world as an endorsement of Hitler's policies?

Certainly Josef Goebbels, Hitler's wily Minister of Propaganda, would have no hesitation about portraying it as such. The England team were literally the chosen ambassadors of their nation; how they conducted themselves would automatically be seen as an indication of their own government's sentiments.

Many of the England players themselves were far from happy about giving the salute. While Hitler's Germany was still more than a year away from attaining the devilish status with which it is today remembered, still it, and the politics that controlled it, left many people feeling distinctly uneasy.

Countering those emotions were ranged those men whose belief was that the salute should be given, not as a sign of approval but simply as a matter of courtesy. International soccer had long since developed the tradition of playing, and respecting, both competing nations' national anthem, during which both teams would stand rigidly to attention. In Germany, the Nazi salute had, for better or worse, become an intrinsic part of that ritual. Failure to comply would be nothing short of insulting.

Against this argument, against the voices of FA Secretary Stanley Rous, committee member Charles Wreford-Brown, and Britain's ambassador to Berlin, Sir Nevile Henderson, the dissidents were powerless to resist. The England team would offer the salute, and Eddie Hapgood later admitted, albeit with words heavily colored by postwar sentiment, that giving that salute was "the worst moment of my life." That afternoon at Berlin's Olympic Stadium, however, his right arm was as straight as any other as the band struck up "Deutschland Uber Alles." So were those of the rest of the team, of their opponents, and of their audience.

The watching Nazi officials (Hitler alone of the party's upper hierarchy chose not to attend, sending deputy Hess, Goering, Goebbels, and von Ribbontrop along in his stead) were in seventh heaven. But they were not to remain there for long. From the moment play commenced, England were in control, and just twelve minutes into the game, Matthews shrugged off Muenzenberg and launched the ball toward Goulden.

Jakob, in goal, barely got a fist to the ball, but the rebound went only as far as Bastin, who gratefully slotted the ball home. First blood to England.

Within minutes the Germans were level, capitalizing on England's celebrations to hammer home a goal that a more aware defense would never have let past. But it was England's last significant mistake. Suddenly galvanized, a through ball from Bastin was clinically slammed into the German goal by Robinson. Welsh sent his fellow debutante, Broome, through for England's third, and as halftime loomed, Matthews weaved an incredible journey through the German defense, beat four defenders, then unleashed a shot that gave Jakob no chance.

Virtually the last shot of the half gave Gauchel the gratefully accepted opportunity to pull one back for the Germans, but still England's lead seemed unassailable. Certainly the watching thousands thought so. Where once there had waved a seething mass of red-and-black banners, now only the infuriated Goering's face retained the colors of the Nazi flag. The constant roar that had welcomed both teams onto the pitch forty-five minutes previous was gone too, to be replaced by a discontented muttering and predictions that in this mood, England were unstoppable.

And it seemed as though they were. The second half had barely commenced before Robinson punched in his second, and England's fifth goal of the game. Again the Germans rallied, Pesser hitting home a fabulous goal, but still the yawning gulf between the two teams could not be bridged. Instead, Goulden increased it, collecting Matthews's perfect pass from twenty-five yards out and, with barely a pause, thundering the ball past Jakob and into the net.

Hitler was furious, more furious even than he had been following Germany's appalling performance in the Olympic soccer tournament. He berated the team, he berated their coach, he even berated Goering, Goebbels, Hess and von Ribbontrop, arguing that if only they had shown greater enthusiasm during the match, then both players and supporters would have rallied to the cause.

His temper was not improved by England's next result. Against Switzerland in Zurich, the visitors fell first to an easy goal from Aeby, equalized through Bastin, but ultimately lost by 2–1 against a team whose defense normally boasted more holes than a piece of their own country's cheese.

And while England went on to defeat France 4–2 in Paris, paving the way, perhaps, for the surprisingly early exit that awaited the host team when the World Cup got underway in Paris at the end of the month, for Nazi Germany the future was even grimmer.

They were dismissed from the World Cup at the very first hurdle, by Switzerland, and even as Hitler prepared the game plan that was to take so much of Europe by storm little more than a year later, the soccer team that he believed would first spread the word by more peaceful means lurched from disappointment to disgrace.

On May 23, 1939, in one of the last international soccer matches played before the lights finally went out across the continent, the little fancied Republic of Ireland traveled to Bremen, saluted the Führer, and went home with a 1–1 draw under their belts. Hitler should have realized there and then. Not even the small fry went down without a fight any longer.

8

We Are the Champions. Probably.

Who Are the Greatest Teams?

W hat's in a name?

Quite a lot, actually.

In 1972, Bournemouth & Boscombe Athletic, newly promoted from the fourth to the third tier of English football, announced that henceforth they should be known as AFC Bournemouth.

The Cherries. They were a terrific side to watch back then. You could switch on the TV and see the big names banging the ball around, the Manchester Uniteds, Arsenals, and Leeds, but seriously, there was nothing so bracing as marching up Petersfield Road on a Saturday afternoon, paying your pence at the Dean Court turnstile, grabbing a program and finding your roost, and then . . . you waited.

Waited for the team to emerge in the red-and-black stripes they'd picked up the previous season, à la the then-mighty AC Milan. Waited for that weekend's hapless victims to take their allotted places on the field, *for all the good it was going to do them*. Waited for the referee to blow the kickoff whistle. And waited for Ted MacDougall to start scoring.

MacDougall was a Scottish player who wound his way down to the English south coast via a year or so at Liverpool, where he never played a solitary senior game; and York, for whom he rattled in forty goals in two seasons, but who never squeaked out of the lowest reaches of the fourth division. When Mac moved to third-tier Bournemouth for £10,000 (£115,080/$194,095) in the summer of 1969, he felt like he was going up in the world. Unfortunately, he wasn't . . . Bournemouth were relegated to the fourth themselves, and manager Freddie Cox was fired.

But the new boss, John Bond, engineered a hasty bounce back, and suddenly Mac was in the news. He scored six of Bournemouth's eight in an FA Cup tie with Oxford City, and forty-two of his side's goals across the promotion season. The following season, in November 1971, he banged nine past Margate in another Cup game. A cat with no ears could tell you that he would not be remaining at Bournemouth for much longer; that one of the top-tier giants now circling like predatory bats above our heads would come swooping in to buy him soon enough.

Wolves, West Ham, Crystal Palace, Coventry, all were said to be making offers. Aston Villa, whose own net had been ruthlessly stretched by SuperMac, were in there too. But it wasn't just football folk whose attention was captured. Bournemouth in general puffed its chest out a little. People you never imagined had ever glanced at a soccer match were holding forth on how much MacDougall should be sold for, or whether he should even be transferred at all.

Kids at school who had hitherto devoted all their energies to supporting some northern side they could barely place on a map (and if you're in Bournemouth, almost *every* team in Britain is northern) were suddenly singing the praises of the Cherries. And the little sports store that MacDougall had opened at the top end of the High Street was apparently doing a roaring trade, even if most of the people squeezing in and out seemed to be either newspapermen or autograph hunters.

The star shone in our midst for about another year. But in September 1972, the inevitable happened. Manchester United put in an offer of £200,000 (£1,845,040/$3,114,030), more than anyone had ever paid for a third-division player before, and SuperMac was off. But he left behind him a team for whom the only way, surely, was up. A team with a new strip, new respect (from the bank manager, if nobody else!), and now, a new name as well.

Or not.

The Football League's rules are very firm on the subject of club names. Essentially, if you're going to change one, you'd better have a very, very good reason, and throughout the game's first century or so, in Britain at least, name changes were rare.

There was a flurry of them in the very earliest years of the game, as wholly local sides moved onto a more national stage and opted to retitle themselves for the city in which they plied their trade, as opposed to a mere neighborhood. And so Small Heath became Birmingham City, Thames Ironworks FC (named for the manufactory whose workers originally formed the side) became West Ham United; New Brompton became Gillingham; and so forth. Bournemouth themselves had been plain old Boscombe until they became a Football League team in 1923, and renamed themselves for the district as a whole.

Other name changes have been engineered by circumstance. When the Welsh town of Swansea was granted City status in 1969, it only made sense for the local soccer team, Swansea Town, to follow suit. When the 1920s League club South Shields moved to a new stadium in nearby Gateshead, the team's name equally sensibly changed accordingly. Clapham Orient became Leyton Orient when they moved from one London suburb to another, and Woolwich Arsenal became plain old Arsenal when they left Woolwich.

But the League said "no" when Hull City's owner, in 2014, announced that he was going to change the club's name to the Hull Tigers, because "'City'

The forebears of the modern Arsenal, named for the military installation whose workers founded the club.

is common" and "Tigers" would somehow make the club more attractive to Asian supporters and investors. Those were not good enough reasons to abandon over a century's worth of tradition, history, and local pride. A soccer club is not a candy bar, and it is more than a business as well. It is, at least in those lands where the game can boast deep historical roots, a part of the fabric of local life.

The reasons behind Bournemouth's proposed name change were manifold, but scarcely pressing. From a supporter's point of view, there was something to be said for streamlining a name that, as the longest in the Football League, was an absolute beast to daub across the cover of your schoolbooks. The club was also thinking of the alphabetical listing of League clubs with which every new season's League table was born. AFC Bournemouth would top the division at least once every season, and they'd be firmly atop any other A–Z that a football fan could conceive of. True, the pessimists pointed to the fate that befell the last club to sit at the head of the alphabetical table . . . Accrington Stanley resigned penniless from the League a decade previous . . . but it hadn't hurt the side that replaced them there. Arsenal won the FA Cup and League double in 1971.

In fact, it was an academic exercise. The Football League announced that Bournemouth began with the letter *B*, no matter how many initials it might be preceded by, and refused to sanction any change in the club's original registration. In the eyes of the authorities, they remained Bournemouth and Boscombe Athletic, the name they'd rejoiced beneath since 1923, and it is still officially their name today.

Plus, their stadium is actually in Boscombe.

What Else Is in a Name?

What indeed.

Loyalty to a neighborhood. Loyalty to tradition and history. Support for the supporters. Money, trophies, success, and headlines all play their part in a soccer club's sustainability, but when you physically delve into the soul of the however-many thousands, hundreds, or dozens of loyal souls that constitute a team's core support, it is the intangibles that matter the most.

Which is why so many of the "ten greatest clubs" lists that are most frequently reprinted, recalibrated, and regurgitated in the media mean so little to the majority of supporters. We don't care who the ten richest teams in the world might be. The ten best supported. The ten most successful. It doesn't matter. Tell us the ten most traditional. The ten most honest. The ten most true to their history. The ten least corrupted by cash and commerce.

You can't, can you? Because those things in turn are intangible. Mostly, anyway.

Believe the modern media and, apparently, it really *does* matter that some shady eastern European oligarch has pumped more money into *your* club than a dubious Middle Eastern arms and oil salesman has pumped into mine. It is of vital import that your center forward's wife has larger breasts than my goalkeeper's girlfriend. And the future of the entire planet might indeed hang on whether your club's official birdseed manufacturer (stop sniggering—it's only a matter of time) is floated on the Dow before my club's official provider of cheese-flavored soda.

The problem is, stuff like this is really boring. The biggest stadium, the biggest parking lot, the biggest Hadron Collider, the biggest yawn. In fact the only real wonder is, how it took so long for the corporate mega-giants of the world to realize where they'd been going wrong all these years. They used to pay money, good money as well, to splash their names and logos in our faces via newspaper adverts, television commercials, billboards and the like.

Now there's *xx* million dedicated supporters who happily, gratefully, and desperately drop $80, $100 a pop for a shirt emblazoned with the exact same company name and logo. *We* pay *them* for the right to be that advert, that commercial, that billboard. Brilliant. Even more brilliant than (although nowhere near as subversive as) the guy who buys old soccer jerseys on eBay, for the express purpose of publicly associating modern clubs with defunct brand names. It makes absolutely no difference to anybody on this entire planet. But you just know that somewhere, there's a corporate busybody preparing to spend several million bucks, hiring consultants to help combat the menace.

Several Names That Certain Teams Probably Don't Want to Remember Having Once Had Emblazoned Across Their Fronts

We, as supporters, wear club jerseys to show our support. The players wear them because they have to, and we should remember that no matter how much fun it is to poke fun at a grown man with "Virgin" splashed across his chest, the players themselves have no say whatsoever in whatever it is they are advertising. As Newcastle United's Papiss Cissé discovered when he objected, as a devout Muslim, to wearing a shirt advertising a payday loan company. His objections were overruled.

For example . . .

Scotland's Clydebank might have the most impeccable musical taste imaginable, but when Wet Wet Wet sponsored their shirts, the Anthrax, Slits, and Dead Kennedys tees would swiftly have been wardrobed away.

Atlético Madrid rolling out, back in 2003–2004, in shirts emblazoned with whatever movie title Columbia Pictures told them to—although, in truth, some of the resultant outfits were considerably more eye-catching than the branded doodles preferred by more traditional strip designers. Especially the *Spider-Man 2* one.

Portsmouth, running around for a few years bearing the exact same label as your Beanie Baby collection. (Okay, maybe not *yours*. But it's in your house all the same.) Manchester United, the richest club in the world, branded by AIG, poster children of the late 2000s recession; 1. FC Nürnberg doing their best to look tough through the season when their shirts bore the bold words "Mister Lady"; Getafe CF looking healthy and buff in tops declaring their love for Burger King.

Students of irony in advertising enjoy unearthing ads from the 1940s and 1950s in which a vim-and-vigor-packed soccer player suggests his supporters should smoke a certain brand of cigarette. (It's okay; doctors used to do the same thing.) Future followers of the same pursuit will scarcely know where to begin with twenty-first-century soccer strips. Maybe we should make a list for them.

Or not. Because there's another reason why soccer fans hate reading lists. Hate them, in fact, almost as much as they enjoy compiling them. They are always wrong.

Soccer is not unique in being so eminently listable. Name a sport, hobby, pastime, or pursuit that does not involve making lists, and you must be a bundle

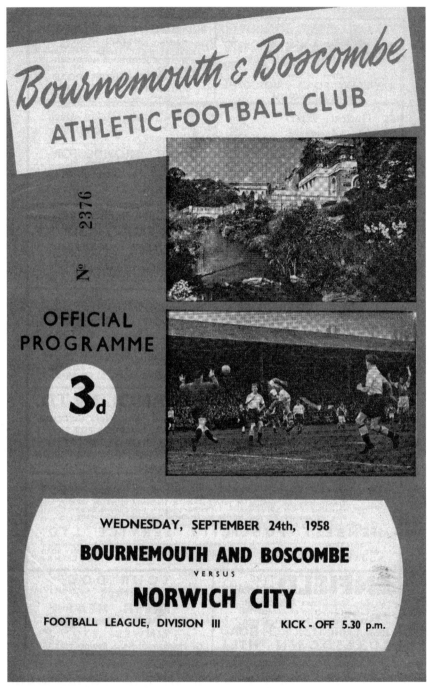

Even in the late 1950s, space concerns prompted Bournemouth and Boscombe Athletic to abbreviate their name occasionally.

of laughs in the grocery store. A stamp collector's catalog is a list. A train schedule. A comics price guide. An itemized receipt. An electrician's estimate. All of these things are lists, and so is the soccer league table. Indeed, it might well be the most immutable and incorruptible list of them all. Which is why it is also the most contentious. For there can be few people reading this who have not, at some point, glanced at the current standings and known in their soul that the league table is in error. That, if [inset your team] had won that game; if the bent ref hadn't stopped them from winning that one too; and if they'd only scored a few more goals when they met up with so-and-so, they wouldn't be in this predicament.

Despite our personal reservations about their overall honesty, however, the league standings are, sadly, unimpeachable. Occasionally, a team will be denied promotion, or consigned to relegation regardless of what the league table says, but it tends to be for off-the-field misdemeanors or on-the-field misbehavior, points deductions and things like that. What the league table says, the league table means. A list that cannot be argued with.

Others lists, however, are more debatable, as the staff of the world's soccer magazines could tell you, every time they decide to fill a few pages with a feature purporting to present the "best players," the "greatest teams," the "most earth-shatteringly orgasmic goal celebrations," and so on, of all time.

List one hundred players, and the readership will point out a thousand more who should have been included. Rank a thousand games, and there will be ten thousand that were omitted. In a table of the world's greatest clubs, you could list, in strict alphabetical order, every soccer team that has ever existed in the history of the world, and the complaints and omissions would still come rolling in.

A reckoning of the world's richest clubs will automatically be panned because it omits the one with a boatload of hitherto undisclosed cash stashed beneath the chairman's bed.

A recounting of the world's best supported sides will always say more about the kind of questions asked, than the rabidity of the actual support ("given the choice, which would you prefer: to attend a Boca Juniors game, or be eaten by piranhas in your bathtub?").

Any list of the world's greatest players is going to start blathering on about transfer fees sooner rather than later; and even a list of the Top Ten World Soccer Clubs That I Just This Moment Invented will promptly ignite a furious debate over the inclusion (or otherwise) of Real Gone Cosmos United.

What follows, then, is less a list of the world's best/worst/costliest/win-ningest/whiniest/*whatever*-est clubs, than it is a wholly random sampling of sides whom some people (although not necessarily you, or I, for that matter) might say deserve to be mentioned in a list of some description.

Perhaps they are more popular than others of their peers. Perhaps they have won more seasonal silverware than many of their competitors. Perhaps they are so obscenely wealthy that even the ground staff have money leaking out of the lace holes in their fabulously sponsored rainbow-colored boots. It doesn't matter. The fact is, they are all so much a part of the game's fabric that it would be difficult to imagine life, or at least their league, without them.

Which, one hastens to add, is a very dangerous prediction to make, as supporters of Scottish Premier League perennials Glasgow Rangers discovered in 2012. Their story, however, must wait for a later chapter, for history, and the Scottish game itself, could argue in favor of a far greater influence than the Rangers on the development of the game. One that shone but briefly during the earliest years of Association Football, but which, while it did so, could easily have claimed to have been the greatest team in the world.

Remembering, of course, that in soccer-playing terms, the world didn't really extend much farther than England and Scotland.

Queen's Park—the Champions of Scotland, 1874–1884

Formed in 1867, Queen's Park are the oldest soccer club in Scotland and, beyond the borders of England and Wales, the oldest in the world. Largely comprising members of the local YMCA, the side's first battle was to choose a name, with the Northern, the Morayshire, and the Celts all being considered before a vote decided upon titling the team for its immediate locale, the Glasgow area of Queen's Park.

As the only team in town, not to mention the rest of the country, Queen's Park were naturally instrumental in spreading the gospel, in search of opponents if nothing else. Many of their earliest games, then, were against so-called scratch sides—unaffiliated players who simply came together to play the club, although 1868 saw a rival Glaswegian outfit, the Thistle, emerge. The two teams clashed for the first time in August, with Queen's Park running out 1–0 winners.

Other occasions saw Queen's Park venture south of the border in search of opponents; and when, in November 1872, the notion of an international match was first raised, Scotland versus England, Queen's Park provided the entire Scottish side.

Their dedication to the sport was flawless. According to the club's official history, published to mark its Golden Jubilee in 1917, "The club . . . never neglected practice, and this practice was indulged in systematically. Sides were arranged— North vs. South of Eglinton Toll, Reds vs. Blues, Light vs. Heavy Weights, President's Team vs. J. Smith's Team (a series of six games), and Clerks vs. The Field, etc. In these games the dribbling and passing, which raised the Scottish game to the level of a fine art, were developed. Dribbling was a characteristic of English play, and it was not until very much later that the Southerners came to see that the principles laid down in the Queen's Park method of transference of the ball, accompanied by strong backing up, were those which got the most out of a team. Combination was the chief characteristic of the Queen's Park play."

In 1870, seeking the opportunity to pit their abilities against fresh opponents, Queen's Park joined the English Football Association and, two years later, they were among the entrants in the first-ever English FA Cup.

Luck (and geography) was certainly on their side. Their first round match with Donnington School was rescheduled for the second round, after it became apparent that there were insufficient entries to create a well-rounded competition, only for Donnington to then withdraw before the match was played. Their next match, too, was a bye; five clubs were left in the competition, four from southern England (Royal Engineers, Hampstead Heathens, Wanderers, and Crystal Palace), and Queen's Park. Given the cost, and the difficulty of travel, it was agreed that the Scots should be given free passage to the next round, thus placing Queen's Park in the FA Cup semifinal without them even having played a single game.

There the story ended, but not in defeat. Held to a 0–0 draw by Wanderers, and faced with the unaffordable expense of a return trip to London for the replay, Queen's Park withdrew gracefully from the competition, allowing Wanderers to advance unimpeded to the FA Cup final, which they duly won 1–0.

Queen's Park repeated their march to the semifinal the following year, 1872–1873. Again they advanced unopposed through the first four rounds before being drawn to meet Oxford University in the semifinal; and again, finances forced them to withdraw, this time without even playing a first game. In fact, while the side would enter several subsequent FA Cup tournaments, it would be 1883 before anything beyond a succession of byes and walkovers highlighted their involvement.

Meanwhile, the game was developing at a steady rate back home in Scotland. In early 1873, Queen's Park placed an advertisement in a local newspaper, detailing their intention to form a Scottish Football Association. Responses were received from eight other teams, of whom one, Kilmarnock, still exists at the highest level today. The remainder—Clydesdale, Vale of Leven, Dumbreck, Eastern, Granville, and Third Lanark, have all since fallen by the wayside, but they offered sterling competition at the time.

That same season, 1873–1874, also saw the launch of the Scottish FA Cup, and a first round match with Dumbreck saw Queen's Park inaugurate the stadium that is still their home, and that of Scottish football in general, Hampden Park. The side celebrated by adopting new colors, black-and-white hoops, and a new nickname, the Spiders (hitherto they had played in blue), and they won the game 7–0.

Queen's Park were on the march. They disposed of Eastern and Renton en route to the Cup final and, inevitably, they won it 2–0. Having dominated unorganized soccer in Scotland for the past five years, Queen's Park were now set to rule its organized successor, with individual stars like Billy and Angus MacKinnon, Robert Leckie, Thomas Highet, and the M'Neil brothers becoming Scotland's first soccer-playing household names.

Scottish Cup winners in both of the following seasons, a sense of Queen's Park's majesty can be gleaned from the fact that it would take until the 1874–1875 semifinal against Clydesdale before Queen's Park even conceded a competitive goal (they drew 2–2), and it was not until December 1876 that the Spiders actually lost a game, going down 2–1 to eventual Cup winners Vale of Leven in the fifth round.

The late 1870s saw Queen's Park experience what, by their standards, was a fallow patch. But they reclaimed the Scottish Cup in 1880, and clung on to it for three of the next four years (1881, 1882, and 1884), while enjoying further stirring adventures south of the border.

In 1883, having assured themselves of sufficient funding to this time play every game that they were due to, Queen's Park marched steadfastly into the English FA Cup final, while racking up some astonishing results en route. Crewe Alexandra perished 10–0 at their hands in the first round; Manchester went down 15–0 in the second; the Welsh club Oswestry were dispatched 7–1 in the third, Aston Villa 6–1 in the fourth. Old Westminsters put up sufficient fight in the quarterfinal to hold the Glaswegians back to a single goal, but the equally free-scoring Blackburn Olympic fell by 4–1 in the semifinal, before finally Queen's Park's progress was halted by another Blackburn side, the Rovers. The Englishmen won the final 2–1.

The following season, Queen's Park were back, and if their progress this season was a little less emphatic, still they were an almighty force. Stoke City withdrew before their first-round tie, and Crewe signposted their own improvement by holding the score down to a mere 2–1 defeat in the second. Leek, of Wales, fell 3–2; it took until the fourth round, and a match with the Old Wykehamists (a public schools team) before Queen's Park enjoyed one of their traditional goal feasts, as they romped home by 7–0.

In the next round, a battle of the historic giants saw the oldest club in Scotland meet one of the oldest in England, with Notts County holding Queens Park to a 2–2 draw before going down by the odd goal in three in the replay. Nottingham Forest were brushed aside 3–0 in the semifinal, and then it was time to renew hostilities with Blackburn Rovers in the final.

Once again, the English side was triumphant, and Queen's Park's interest in the FA Cup faltered now. They withdrew before the second round of the 1885–1886 tournament, and were defeated in the first round the following season. The Scottish FA—now operating independently of the club that founded it—then passed a new law banning clubs within its remit from entering the English competition, and Queen's Park's great adventure was over, both abroad and domestically.

When the Scottish League was founded in 1887, Queen's Park were conspicuous by their absence. Proudly amateur as they were, they wanted no part of a contest that was clearly designed with professionalism in mind. It would be 1900 before they recanted and entered the competition, by which time their glory years were over.

Neither have they returned in the century-plus since then. Four times in their first fifteen years of League competition, Queen's Park finished bottom of the table, while club honors in later years are restricted to just three Second Division titles, and one Third Division. However, Queen's Park's record of ten

Scottish Cup victories, all racked up between 1874 and 1893, has been surpassed only by Glaswegian neighbors Rangers and Celtic, while their continued amateur status has seen them dominate the Scottish Amateur Cup, too—the most recent of their twelve victories was in 2009.

Darwen—The Little Town That Could, 1873–1879

Mob football! Two teams of indeterminate numbers, seemingly concerned more with bloodletting than anything resembling sport, charging boisterously around a three mile pitch that stretched from Moulden Water to Cathshaw Bar. It was they who were responsible for bringing soccer to Darwen, a small town in the northern English county of Lancashire. And they who set in motion one of the infant game's most glorious adventures.

The games, an old Shrovetide tradition even at the turn of the eighteenth century, boasted more casualties than rules, a place where the simmering rivalry between the neighboring towns of Darwen and Blackburn could be given vent in a contest whose only real winner was the local physician.

Even after the Public Schools had done their utmost to regulate and sanitize what had hitherto been a most irregular and unsanitary sport, still it was not unusual for local sportsmen to return home ragged and bloody, and still pursued by a baying pack of bloodthirsty opponents. And while Darwen might not have been the only neighborhood to permit such barbaric practices into its sporting calendar, its players were renowned throughout the county for the ferocity of their tackling, the harshness of their demeanor and the sheer unmitigated joy with which an opposing player might be trampled face first into the mire.

Sundry historical skirmishes notwithstanding, Darwen's first chronicled game took place in 1873, when the town's team became the inaugural opponents of the nearby Turton club. The side had, however, already been in operation for some three years at this point, coming into being around the same time as the Darwen Cricket Club was formed in 1870. Their earliest opposition, it seems, was supplied by a side from Birmingham, the Brookhouse Lambs—although nobody would claim that they were aptly named.

By 1874, contests between Darwen and Turton were a regular highlight of the local calendar, while Darwen's own reputation was soon such that they put forth a challenge to one of the most renowned clubs in Scotland, Partick Thistle.

This historic meeting took place on January 1, 1876, and came about through the friendship between Darwen captain Entwistle, and his opposite number at Partick, WH Kirkham. Unfortunately for Darwen, that friendship did not extend to the soccer field. Partick ran out emphatic 7–0 victors, but Darwen were fast learners. By the end of the year, they had joined the Football Association, and were launching onto an era of absolute invulnerability.

Out of fourteen matches played during the 1876–1877 season, Darwen won ten and drew the remaining four, their opposition including Blackburn Rovers (who themselves had some pretensions towards greatness at the time), the neighboring towns and villages of Turton, Egerton, Eagley, Church and Witton, and Christ Church Bolton, the side that would eventually become mighty Bolton Wanderers. Darwen's reserve side, itself an innovation that few other clubs could boast, was even more impressive. Throughout a two year spell, the second eleven conceded just two goals, and those both came in a 2–1 defeat inflicted by the first eleven!

In 1877–1878, with their undefeated record still intact, Darwen became one of the first northern clubs to enter the English FA Cup, following in the recent footsteps of the Sheffield club, and the Scottish giants Queen's Park and Clydesdale.

It was a short lived venture; having dispatched fellow Cup novices Manchester in the first round, by 3–1, a hotly disputed goal gave Sheffield victory in the second round and Darwen went home smarting from a most unaccustomed sensation: "defeat."

Of course, they soon resumed business as usual. Darwen suffered just one further beating that season, when Patrick Thistle returned to put six past them; and the following year, it was again Patrick and the Cup alone that prevented Darwen from sweeping all before them. Local games certainly gave them no trouble whatsoever, as they crushed Bolton 8–0, Blackburn Olympic 8–2, Church 7–0, Turton 7–2, Manchester 6–2 and Accrington 6–0. Altogether, Darwen registered 101 goals throughout the 1878–1879 season, and conceded just forty, seven of which came via their annual drubbing by Partick.

In the Cup, Darwen's first round opponents, Birch (from Manchester) withdrew. Next up, Darwen saw off Eagley by "four goals and a disputed one to one." Locally, they were on the march; elsewhere, however, few folk paid any attention. For all their ferocity and skill, Darwen's fame had yet to reach England's southern climes and the Cup, in those days, was very much a southern affair. As Darwen would discover when the FA Cup draw determined that they were to travel south to Slough, to meet the Remnants, a side comprised entirely of various Public School old boys.

Nobody watching that afternoon believed it possible that the scruffy mill workers from the north should emerge victorious, by 3–1, from a match that one onlooker described as "the hardest struggle the players ever went through, a most stubborn game in which every inch of the ground was tenaciously fought over, and two hours of play [the regulation ninety, plus thirty more of extra time] was required."

But they did. Darwen were into the final eight.

In the early rounds of the Cup, home advantage was decided by the toss of a coin. The final rounds, from the quarterfinals on, however, could only be contested in or around London, testament to the south's hitherto unchallenged domination of the tournament.

It was a ruling that had already deprived Queen's Park of two semifinal appearances, the cost of the journey being too great for them to undertake. Darwen, having already been forced to travel south for the match with the

Remnants, were hard pressed to raise the fare for the return journey required by their quarterfinal confrontation with the Old Etonians.

Twice Cup finalists, the Etonians were regarded by many as the perfect footballing machine and by halftime, with the Darwen players already exhausted from their long journey, it seemed that the game was going according to form. The *Bootle Times* newspaper recorded, "the Old Etonians played for all they were worth during that first half, and had notched four goals to Darwen's none when time was called for a temporary cessation of hostilities. This lead was added to in the second half."

But Darwen refused to lie down. Five goals down with fifteen minutes to go, two blinding strikes suddenly reduced the deficit by almost half. And while a 5–2 deficit was scarcely one to either relish or take heart from, now there was no denying Darwen. Magnificently marshaled by captain Jem O'Bobs, Darwen completely overwhelmed the Etonians. Attack after attack shattered the home side's defense, and their composure swiftly followed. By the time the final whistle blew, Darwen had achieved the impossible. The scores stood at five goals apiece.

And now we learn the lie behind the nostalgic visions of soccer having, at any time, been a truly sporting contest, even in the heyday of the amateurs.

There was no way that the traveling Darwenites could afford yet another trip to London for a replay. They threw themselves on the mercy of their opponents, trusting that the Old Etonians, like the Remnants in the previous round, would do the honorable thing and agree to thirty minutes of extra time.

The toffs didn't even need to confer with one another. To a man, they recalled prior appointments that necessitated their immediate departure from the sporting arena. If Darwen wanted to play more football, they would have to come back next month for the replay.

Sadly, and perhaps even stunned (for they, too, believed that Public school-boys possessed a fair sense of play), Darwen returned to the north, prepared to forfeit their stake in the FA Cup . . . only to discover themselves local, regional, and even national heroes. Within a fortnight a public fund, the newspaper-led forerunner of modern crowdsourcing, had raised no less than £150 (over £13,000/$21,941 in modern terms) to enable Darwen to return to London to finish the Etonians off, with the FA contributing ten pounds, and the Etonians themselves ultimately shamed into throwing in five.

And so it was, twenty-three days after that first epic encounter, Darwen boarded once again the steam locomotive that would take them back to London. But again the battle proved inconclusive, and *again*, the Etonians refused to play extra time. A third game was called for, and even that would not be an end of it. For if they won, Darwen would have to return to London again for the semifinal, and maybe even yet again for the final.

The modern complaint that the game is all about money, that a single "top" player's monthly earnings could finance the running of a lower league club for a year, that both the laws of the game and the people who make those laws are blindly in favor of the wealthiest few, all of these things were as true 140 years ago

A later but equally heroic Darwen line-up—the 1891 Lancashire Cup Finalists: (from top row) J. and W. Marsden, J.W. Smith, W. McOwen, J. Haddow, J.R. Leach, R. Thornier, Jonty Entwistle, R. Smith, J. Nightingale, D. Owen, and secretary B.C. Jepson. Sadly, the side fell at the final hurdle against Bolton Wanderers.

as they are today. Indeed, even the "amateur" status of many players was often a sham, as a combination of legitimate "expenses" and less-discussed under-the-table fees saw them earning as much, if not more, than many professionals.

The Old Etonians epitomized these qualities. Desperate, Darwen even invited the amateurs to travel north for the replay, but the Etonians were unshakable in their desire to "play by the rules." Either the northerners returned to London once again, or they forfeit the match. And this time, there could be no doubting the outcome. The Etonians were already planning their semifinal entertainment before Darwen's letter of forfeiture dropped through the mailbox.

Unfortunately, however, they reckoned without one thing, and that was the general public's own sense that sometimes, fair play means more than the rules. On March 15, again funded by public donations, Darwen traveled down to London once again, and this time the fairy tale ended. With no money for an overnight stop, the side tumbled off the train and directly onto the pitch, there to be defeated by six goals to two.

But the men who turned out for Darwen that day were heroes nonetheless, and just as the Manchester Uniteds, Real Madrids, and Dynamo Kyivs of today have their legends, the names that represent a standard to which all subsequent recruits should feel duty-bound to aspire, so the Darwen side of 1879 was to live on long after the men themselves had hung up their playing boots.

Jack Duxbury, W Brindle, James Love and Fergus Suter, James Knowles, W. H. Moorhouse, Tom Marshall, Will Kirkham, Dr. Gledhill, R. Kirkham, T. Bury, and Billy McLachan, we salute you all.

Bethlehem Steel—There Should Have Been a Soccer World Series for Them, 1912–1920

According to an account published in 1925, the first soccer ball arrived in Bethlehem, Pennsylvania, in 1904, carried in the luggage of a newly arrived Scotsman. Perhaps a little period hyperbole adheres to the insistence that it caused "quite a lot of excitement among the athletically inclined," but life in a fast-growing steel town was certainly heading for a major change of pace. First, a soccer team came together; soon, regular matches were being arranged with a team from nearby Allentown.

Early games gave no hint of Bethlehem's future renown. In November 1907, a visit to Harrison, New Jersey, saw the side collapse by 11–2 against the then-powerful West Hudson; and when the same two sides met again shortly after, West Hudson racked up another nine-goal advantage, this time with no reply whatsoever from the visitors.

Nevertheless, the Bethlehemites persisted. According to the *Philadelphia Inquirer*, the side was largely composed of "Scotchmen, Englishmen and Welshmen employed hereabouts, some of whom were stars in the old country" (although there is no evidence of that latter claim), and in 1911, the amateur Bethlehem were founder members of the Eastern Pennsylvania League, comprising teams from Harrisburg, Reading, Summit Hill, Lancaster, and Lansford.

There they tasted glory. On May 4, 1912, unbeaten all season, Bethlehem met Cardington in the final of the Allied Amateur Cup competition.

They faced stiff opposition. Cardington, newly crowned champions of the Philadelphia and Suburban League, swept into a two-goal lead within thirteen minutes of kickoff, and scored a third on the edge of halftime. But the final score of 3–1 was to be Bethlehem's sole defeat of the entire campaign, and it proved the impetus for the club to scale greater heights in the years to come.

The following season, 1912–1913, saw Bethlehem FC sweep all before it in the Allied American Football Association league, itself one of no fewer than *seven* leagues operating in the Philadelphia area at that time. Again according to the *Inquirer*, "counting all the league and independent teams in this vicinity, there are nearly twice the number of clubs of any other city in the East without taking into account the Grammar School leagues, which will be organized later in the season."

Bethlehem were perched firmly at the top of the pile. Peabody were defeated 5–0, despite the game lasting just forty minutes, instead of the regulation ninety, after the luckless losers were late arriving in Bethlehem. West Philadelphia fell 7–0, Cardington 6–1, and as early as December, the *Inquirer* was predicting, "Bethlehem should top the Allied League first division with lots to spare, for there appears none of the teams able to hold them." Ultimately, it would be February 1913 before Bethlehem finally lost a game, exiting the Cup 4–1 at the hands of second division Tacony . . . a feat of giant killing comparable today to, for example, Colchester United beating Chelsea.

Hitherto, Bethlehem had been a stubbornly amateur concern, despite the team's activities (not to mention its players) all taking place under the auspices of the vast Bethlehem Steel works. In 1914, however, company owner Charles Schwab decided it was time for his team to embrace professionalism. The steelworks' fortune, already apparent in the team's magnificent home stadium, was made available to recruit and pay players' wages and, over the next eight years, Bethlehem Steel proved, indeed, to be made of steel.

The club won the American Cup five times (1914, 1916–1919), were losing finalists once (1920), and defeated semifinalists twice (1915, 1921). In four of those seasons, 1915, 1916, 1918, and 1919, they also claimed the National Challenge Cup (they were beaten finalists in 1917), while they routinely romped off with the championships of the regional leagues in which they played, the Allied American Football Association between 1913 and 1915, and the North American Football League between 1919–1921.

Perhaps most significantly of all, however, Bethlehem Steel also became the first-ever US club side ever to visit Europe, three years after the national team undertook its debut international tour, and two years after America's entry into World War One saw the Ben Millers of St. Louis forced to cancel their own groundbreaking journey across the ocean.

In fact, Bethlehem Steel had originally been approached to represent their homeland on the 1916 European sojourn, only for club officials to decline the offer for fear of the German submarines that had transformed the Atlantic into a virtual shooting gallery. Two Bethlehem Steel players, right halfback Thomas Murray and center halfback Neil G. Clarke, would make the journey, but the remainder of the national side was made up of players from elsewhere.

This time, however, there was to be no holding back. On April 22, 1919, with Bethlehem Steel having once again won virtually every prize that the American game could throw at them, the *Globe* reported, "Thomas W. Cahill, secretary of the United States Football Association, announced . . . that in recognition of the remarkable record complied during the season by the team it was definitely arranged that the Steel Workers tour Norway, Sweden and Denmark for a series of exhibition games."

Six days later, the *Inquirer* enthused, "you certainly have got to hand it to the players for the manner in which they keep in the game. What is more, they have more soccer in their think tanks than the average player, while they are also there with the combination stuff."

Other nations sat up and took notice. Although they ultimately came to naught, negotiations were underway for Bethlehem Steel to play a handful of friendlies in London, en route to Sweden; and then, upon their return, to visit Brazil. When it was discovered that both Chelsea and Tottenham Hotspur would be playing in Sweden at the same time as the Steel, matches were proposed with both of them.

As the *Globe* put it, "When challenges are received from different parts of the world for international soccer clashes with the United States champions, it fully indicates the widespread fame established by the team. The fact that the

Bethlehem team has won the national honors for the past four years and that the last season has been the 'greatest ever' since the club was established, has placed the team in great demand."

On July 22, 1919, Bethlehem Steel set off for New York, to board the Swedish-American liner *Stockholm*. Faced with a twelve-day voyage, the players had arrangements made for them to to train onboard ship; they would then have another week of training once they arrived in Sweden, before facing their first opponents, AIK, on August 10. A sold-out 20,000-seat stadium awaited them, with thousands more locked out, and rumors circulating of tickets exchanging hands for as much as 100 kroner.

Bethlehem did not necessarily distinguish themselves. A 2–2 draw was followed by a local match report, translated and reprinted by the *Inquirer*, that declared, "Some people say that they were disappointed in the American team. Why? Because they did not beat the AIK. It is true that they, in this their first match in Stockholm, did not play the Scotch play that was expected from them.

"The forward line did not hold together very well, and the halfbacks did not follow properly when they were pressed the hardest by the AIK. These combinations did sometimes not succeed and especially Ratican, the center, was for the day, indisposed. The speed was just the same, greater than what had been seen in [Stockholm] Stadium for many a day. Add to this that the Americans played their first match in a foreign country on a practically strange field and before a foreign crowd and for their own local team, partisan public. They were during the first half period nervous and this nervousness did not disappear during the second."

However, August 14 saw the tourists defeat the Stockholm Tigers 1–0, and three days later an All-Star Swedish XI was beaten 2–1. On August 17, the Steel faced an All-Star Swedish team in Stockholm, winning 2–1 and inspiring the *Globe* to proclaim that, based on the evidence so far, "the Steel Workers . . . will return with the greatest honors ever garnered by an American soccer eleven in the history of the game in this country. . . . A victory in this international series in a sport that is really still in its infancy in this country is another high tribute to the standard of athletics developed in America.

"The Bethlehem Steel team has won all the honors possible in the United States and to add to its glowing record was forced to invade foreign shores for still more glory. Prophets, who from time to time last season could not fully reconcile themselves to the fact that the team sporting the Bethlehem colors was the peer of all other soccer aggregations in the country and contributed many of the victories to games played on home grounds or some other ridiculous reason, are awakening to the fact that their contentions were all wrong and that the champions possess the ability to carry on their victorious stride on foreign soil as well as at home."

A few days later, the same paper insisted, "they will return home with the laurels of ranking with the greatest soccer elevens in Scotland and England."

Two further draws, with Djurgårdens and IFK Norrköping (both 1–1) preceded the Steel's next victory, a 4–0 trouncing of another all-star side in

Helsinburg. Then it was off to Denmark, for another 1–1 draw, this time against Boldklubben af 1893; before finally, the side suffered its maiden defeat, 3–2 to an All-Malmo team.

A second defeat, 3–1 to Göteborg Kamraterna, followed, but Bethlehem swiftly shrugged off the disappointment, remaining unbeaten for the remainder of the tour as they saw off Goteborg Orgryte 1–0; ran up two goals without reply in a rematch with IFK Norrköping; beat an All-Stockholm side 1–0, and an All-Sweden side 3–2. The final game of the tour, a 0–0 draw with Hammarby, might look tame, but to have played fourteen games in a foreign land and lost just two of them, was an accomplishment that any touring XI might aspire toward, no matter who they might be.

In the event, Bethlehem Steel did not make those other planned visits and journeys. Controversy surrounding their late arrival home from Scandinavia, and the delays caused to the start of the new National League season, conspired to leave a very sour taste in the Steel officials' mouths, and the Brazilian visit was placed on hold, while London was cancelled altogether.

The side's domestic supremacy continued unalloyed, however; in fact, so utterly dominant were they that the Steel's owners became convinced that their fortunes could only be increased if they broadened their catchment area. In 1921, as founder members (and prime instigators) of the newly established American Soccer League, Bethlehem Steel was removed lock, stock, and barrel to Philadelphia, and rebranded the Philadelphia Field Club.

It was a controversial move, abhorred by existing supporters and none too convincing to any new ones that the side hoped to attract. Although the side remained successful, taking the first ASL championship, the expected boom in finances went in the opposite direction entirely and, by the following season, the club was back in Bethlehem, and prepared to resume business as usual.

In 1924, Bethlehem Steel won the last-ever American Cup before the AFA finally conceded defeat to the USSF (see chapter one), and for the remainder of the 1920s, they remained a power in the land. But ill winds were buffeting American soccer now, and America itself as well. By 1930, Bethlehem Steel was no more.

They have not, however, been forgotten. Indeed, in 2013, MLS side Philadelphia Union announced a new third uniform designed wholly in tribute to their most illustrious predecessors.

Mohammedan Sporting Club— The Jewel in India's Crown, 1934–1940

Mention soccer in India, and it is generally better remembered for what it didn't do, in 1950, than for anything it might have accomplished in the decades on either side of that. For that was the year in which India withdrew from the first and only World Cup for which they had ever qualified, after learning of a FIFA ban on playing barefoot—the manner in which the national team traditionally disported itself.

Not once since then has India, or any other nation from southeast Asia, traveled so far; nor, for that matter, especially distinguished itself in Asian soccer in general. India is a cricketing hotbed, with soccer a popular but (even following the much-ballyhooed launch of its Premier League) scarcely wildly oversubscribed sport.

However, travel back eighty years, to a time when India, together with the modern nations of Pakistan and Bangladesh, were all considered one within the old British Empire, and there was one soccer team whose name was known throughout the region, and spoken of abroad as well. For, not only was the Mohammedan Sporting Club the finest "native" club in the land (to adopt the disgraceful parlance of the age), they were also as good as anything that the mother country could offer, too, as they proved in 1941.

Inevitably, soccer arrived in India via the country's vast English community, with the earliest reports of the game being played emanating from Calcutta (modern Kolkatta), where office clerks and military men used to relax with a game after work or at weekends. (Interestingly, the colonial Indian military had very little interest in soccer, much preferring to play field hockey.)

In 1877, the game spread into local schools when a student at the Hare School in North Calcutta, Nagendra Prasad Sarbadhikary, began knocking a ball around with his classmates. Of course the game exploded in popularity and, encouraged by their primarily European teachers, the boys first formed their own team, the Boys Club, and then began introducing soccer to friends at other schools and colleges.

More clubs followed, several of which were also founded by Nagendra Prasad, and in 1893 the Indian Football Association (IFA) was founded by, among other worthy gents, the immortally named former England international player, Elphinstone Jackson. Anecdotally, the side that became Mohammedan SC was already in action by this time, formed as the Jubilee Club by the local ruler Nawab Aminul Islam, in honor of Queen Victoria's fiftieth year on the throne, in 1887. Several name changes followed; it was the Crescent Club for a time, and the Hamidia Club, too, but by 1891 it had adopted the name with which it would one day conquer India.

One day. But not yet. The Mohammedan Sporting Club struggled for some time, eking out a career in poorly attended friendlies on a barely fit-for-purpose field on Sealadh Kaiser Street, itself in one of the poorer districts of town. Wealthy Moslems looked elsewhere for their sporting pleasures; Mohammedan SC were the the poor people's team and, by the end of the century their closest glimpse of glory had been defeat to Hastings in the now-barely remembered Trades Cup.

Slowly, however, things turned around. A wealthy benefactor, Sayeed Anees Hossain Khan, helped the club acquire their own ground, and three times during the first decade of the twentieth century, in 1902, 1906, and 1909, Mohammedan SC won the regional Coochbehar Cup.

Further fallow years followed, but in 1930, the giant began to stir. Under the management of one-time hockey star S. A. Aziz, that year saw Mohammedan SC join the Second Division East of the Calcutta Football League—a competition founded back in 1898, and absolutely dominated by the British ever since then.

The Calcutta Football Club, an offshoot of the already venerable Calcutta Cricket Club (founded by members of the British East India Company in 1792), won the first tournament, the first of eight championships won over the next three decades.

Other victors were drawn almost exclusively from representatives of the British army—the Royal Irish Rifles, the North Staffordshire regiment, the Gordon Light Infantry, the King's regiment, the Black Watch, and the Durham Light Infantry all rank among the competition's champions, with the latter side ushering in the 1930s with three successive championships. Nobody doubted that the new season, 1934, would end in much the same way.

Instead, it marked the absolute end of British supremacy in local soccer. Fourth in their first season in the league, Mohammedan SC had quietly but completely rebuilt their side. Kale Khan and Hafiz Rashid were brought in from local rivals Mohun Bagan. Aaqil Ahmed was recruited from Kalighat, Samad from Rail.

An entire new team was constructed around these earliest acquisitions: Aaqeel Ali, Anwar, Musha, and Mohiuddin. Rahamat, so silkily skilled that he was known far and wide as the Magician. The goalkeeper Osman; Jumma Khan, so imposing that his teammates nicknamed him the Great Wall of China; and two of the most lethal marksmen in the entire league, Rashi Khan (destined to score sixteen goals in the 1935 league season) and Rahim (who netted eighteen in 1938). Even the British teams acknowledged that Mohammedan SC had pieced together a formidable squad.

But Mohammedan SC had another trick up their sleeves. Like the other Indian sides, but unlike their military opponents, the side traditionally played barefoot. This season, however, they were booted, and that was where the difference lay. In the past, Indian players had been regarded as skillful and fast but, in the heat of competition, ultimately hamstrung by the absence of footwear. Placed on a level footing, literally, with their opponents, all of that skill and speed came into its own.

Effortlessly, Mohammedan SC swept not only to the 1934 championship, three points ahead of runners-up Dalhousie, but those of 1935, 1936, 1937 (six points clear of East Bengal), and 1938 as well. Mohun Bagan took the 1939 title as a dispute with the Indian FA over the creation of a Bengali FA saw Mohammedan SC sit that season out, but then Mohammedan bounced back for the 1940 and 1941 crowns as well, the last before war disrupted the competition altogether.

By which time, other honors had tumbled into their lap. In 1936, Mohammedan SC became only the second Indian side (after, again, Mohun Bagan) to win the IFA Cup, the Indian Football Association's national trophy, defeating Calcutta 2–1. The Rovers Cup was theirs in 1940.

But the real prize was the Durand Cup, the oldest soccer tournament in India, and the third-oldest surviving national cup competition in the entire world. First competed for in 1888, only the English and Scottish FA Cups predate it, yet it was also a symbol of just how utterly the British dominated everyday life in India at the time.

Named for its founder, Sir Mortimer Durand—India's Foreign Secretary at the time—the Cup was conceived as part of a drive to improve sporting excellence within the British community; indeed, for many years, it was purely a military affair, and when the British withdrew from India in the late 1940s, the Indian army continued to run the tournament until as late as 2006.

It opened up to nonmilitary and governmental sides a lot earlier than that, of course, although that really didn't matter. While civilian sides frequently acquitted themselves well enough, they could never shake the dominance of the British army teams.

Echoing the strength of Scottish players elsewhere around the world at the time, the Royal Scots Fusiliers won the inaugural Cup; the Highland Light Infantry took five of the next seven, and the King's Own Scottish Borderers the remaining pair. It was 1896 before an "English" side won the Cup, when the Somerset Lights beat the Black Watch; and while an Indian side, the 2nd Punjab Volunteer Rifle Corps, aka the Simla Rifles, twice competed the final, in 1889 (when the Highlanders crushed them 8–1) and 1897, there was no flood of further local talent to emerge in their wake. Like the Calcutta Football League, the Durant Cup was British territory.

Originally the Cup final was played in Simla, before moving to Dagshai. Now, it had moved again to New Delhi, but 1940 was not only marked by new surroundings. It was also the first year that a ground full of army

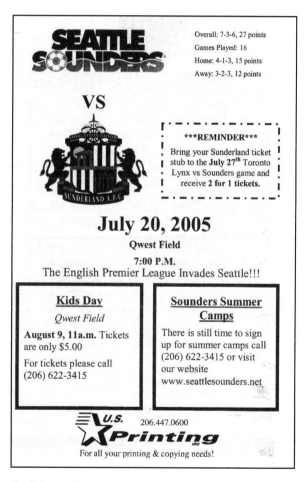

Overall: 7-3-6, 27 points
Games Played: 16
Home: 4-1-3, 15 points
Away: 3-2-3, 12 points

VS

REMINDER
Bring your Sunderland ticket stub to the July 27th Toronto Lynx vs Sounders game and receive 2 for 1 tickets.

July 20, 2005

Qwest Field

7:00 P.M.
The English Premier League Invades Seattle!!!

Kids Day

Qwest Field

August 9, 11a.m. Tickets are only $5.00

For tickets please call (206) 622-3415

Sounders Summer Camps

There is still time to sign up for summer camps call (206) 622-3415 or visit our website www.seattlesounders.net

206.447.0600

Printing inc
For all your printing & copying needs!

English Premier League side Sunderland visited the Emerald City on their 2005 summer tour.

green, there to witness what everybody expected would be a famous victory for the Warwickshire Regiment, was silenced. For the first time ever, an Indian team, Mohammedan SC, won the Cup, 2–1 victors over the runaway favorites.

In soccer-playing terms, it was a shock. In cultural terms, it was an earthquake. Indian independence was still a distant dream; and no matter how fervently the people wished for it, it was not going to come quickly or easily. Little victories alone marked time for them, blows against the empire that individually might seem insignificant, but cumulatively added up to something profound and meaningful. Knocking the English off the perch of their soccer-playing supremacy was one such blow.

Mohammedan SC did not follow up on their famous triumph. Their victory, perhaps fittingly, marked the last Durant Cup competition for almost a decade. First war, then independence and partition followed, and it would be 1950 before the tournament began again (when it was won by the Hyderabad City Police).

Neither did Mohammedan SC maintain their dominance elsewhere. Although they took the IFA Cup twice more, in 1941 and 1942, and occasional other trophies came their way in later years, it would be another seventy-three years before they lifted the famous old Durant trophy again, when goals for Anthony Soren and the Australian Tolgay Ozbey saw off the challenge of ONGC, again by 2–1, in the 2013 final.

The headlines that accompanied their triumph, however, proved that Indian soccer has never forgotten all that Mohammedan SC had accomplished in the past. Nor all that those accomplishments meant to the Indian people.

Torino—They Could Have Rewritten History, 1943–1949

The top level of Italian league football, Serie A, made it through World War Two surprisingly unscathed. Whereas many of the continent's other combatants saw their national league competitions cancelled for the full duration of the conflict, 1939–1945, Italy lost just two seasons, 1943–1944, and 1944–1945. For, just as the game had been vital to the prewar dictator Mussolini's vision of a Fascist Italy, so it was crucial to the postwar administration's as well. And just as Torino won the league and Cup double in the final season before the tournaments were suspended, so they were champions again in 1945–1946. It was, it seemed, business as usual.

Except Torino's back-to-back championships were anything but business as usual in terms of Italian soccer history. In fact, with the exception of Roma's championship in 1942, Serie A had hitherto been a procession of triumphs for just three sides: Ambrosiana-Inter, who took the first title in 1930 and a brace more since then; Bologna, with four championships between 1936 and 1941; and Juventus, the *other* team in Turin, whose five in a row, 1931–1935, was already being described as an unrepeatable feat.

Torino, like the rest of Italian soccer, were very much in the Juventus's shadow throughout this period. They won an Italian Cup in 1936, and 1938 saw them reach the final once again (there to be beaten by Juventus), and they had a couple of Serie A runners-up spots as well. But since the side was formed back in 1906 by workers from the Voigt brewery on Via Pietro Micca, Torino had never aspired to become much more than a stuttering power.

Their first season in the amateur championship that preceded the formation of Serie A, 1907, saw Torino finish runners-up, but a dispute with the authorities over the number of foreign-born players permitted in a side saw them absent themselves from the 1908 series, and very much sink into midtable anonymity for the two decades that followed.

Just once, in 1914–1915, did they resurface. With one game left to play in the season, Torino lay in second place in the table, two points behind Genoa (whom they had already defeated 6–1 that season) and with a superior goal difference. Victory in that final game, against Genoa themselves, would take the title to Turin at a time when Juventus, too, were still struggling to truly establish themselves.

Instead, Italy's entry into the Great War in April 1915, just days before the decisive match, saw the championship suspended, the final game cancelled, and the title awarded to Genoa.

Play resumed in 1920, and Torino began building for the future. A new club president, Count Enrico Marone Cinzano; a new home ground, the Stadio Filadelfia; and a new outlook on recruitment saw Torino build one of the most powerful sides of the era, constructed around a forward line that even their opponents described as the *trio delle meraviglie* (trio of wonders): Gino Rossetti, Julio Libonatti, and Adolfo Baloncieri.

They could, and should, have swept all before them. But the club was not above a little skullduggery either, and barely had Torino been acclaimed 1926–1927 champions than their title was rescinded after an illegal payment of 25,000 lire, paid to Juventus's Luigi Allemandi immediately prior to a derby match, came to light.

Somewhat wryly, and certainly adding insult to injury, the Torino official who paid the bribe, Dr. Nani, later professed *himself* to be the victim of the plot. Although Torino won the game in question, Allemandi's performance was scarcely that of a bribed player. Quite the opposite, in fact. Inevitably, Nani refused to pay the player the remainder of the proffered bribe, a further 25,000 lire, and the pair fell to arguing loudly and, carelessly, very publicly. A nearby journalist overheard their squabble, and the rest became despicable history.

One title was lost, but another was won. Torino took the 1927–1928 championship without controversy, and finished runners-up the following season, the last before the national competition was reorganized as the modern Serie A.

They sank back into the shadows after that, overwhelmed by the emergence of Juventus. But the Cup win in 1936 preceded a sequence of three successive top-three finishes in the league, the last of them under the new presidency of Ferrucio Novo, a former (if undistinguished) player who had since made his fortune in leather goods.

A new coaching and administrative staff was recruited, including several former players, and an aggressive new transfer policy was instituted, beginning with the arrival of eighteen-year-old Franco Ossola, purchased from Varese for 55,000 lire. He finished the 1939–1940 season as Torino's top scorer, even as the team slumped to seventh place. The following year then saw Valentino Mazzola, Ezio Loik, Petron, and Mezzadra arrive from Venezia in an audacious 1.4 million lire deal, one that was apparently arranged within just minutes of President Nova seeing the quartet play in a match against Torino.

A new playing system was adopted, a 3–2–2–3 formation borrowed from the Arsenal side of a decade previous, but unseen in Italy until now. It became Torino's trademark, an all but unstoppable force as they swept to second place in the 1941–1942 season, defeated just twice all season. And the following season they went all the way, becoming the first Italian side ever to win the Serie A league and Cup double.

The suspension of the league in 1944, as Italy found itself divided between the invading Allies and the defending Nazis, did not cause the end of organized soccer. Many clubs even succeeded in retaining both their administrative and playing staff, by the simple expedient of joining forces with sundry local "essential industries," and claiming their employees were vital cogs in those other enterprises.

Torino hooked up with the car and aircraft manufacturer Fiat, with players even posing for news photographs operating the company's machinery. In fact, for the most part, their footballing duties were left undisturbed, and when the league campaigns resumed in 1945, the heart of the side remained intact, while being bolstered by a slew of new arrivals—manager Luigi Ferrero, goalkeeeer Valerio Bacigalupo, Eusebio Castigliano, Aldo Ballarin, and more.

Torino were irresistible that season. Scoring goals for fun, successive games against Genoa and Ginnastica Sampierdarenese saw Torino's forwards stretch the net eleven times. Against AS Roma, Torino deluged their opponents with six goals in thirty minutes. Napoli fell 7–1, Pro Livorno 9–1. The championship was Torino's.

They repeated the feat the following year, scoring a staggering 104 goals in a season that included a sixteen-game undefeated run; and again in 1947–1948, when even the previous season's goal-scoring feats were wiped out of the record books as Torino netted an incredible 125 times—ten of them coming in the club's all-time record victory, the utter demolition of US Alessandria 1912.

Another game, against Lazio, saw Torino certainly cruising toward a rare defeat as the hosts raced to a 3–0 lead, and then turning it around to win 4–3, with all four goals coming within one hectic thirty-minute span. Roma fell 7–0, Lucchese 6–0, and Torino took the championship with sixteen points worth of daylight between themselves and second-placed AC Milan.

Unstoppable domestically, the Torino side also formed the backbone of the Italian national team, itself managed by a former Torino player and official, Vittorio Pozzo. When Italy met Hungary in a May 1947 international, only goalkeeper Lucidio Sentimenti was not a Torino player. He hailed from Juventus; and when the new campaign, 1948–1949, kicked off, it was in the knowledge that Torino was destined not only for another league title, but possibly for the World Cup as well. Pozzo made no secret of the fact that the squad he was now assembling for the forthcoming (1950) tournament in Brazil would again be based around the all-conquering Torino.

All of those plans were shattered on the afternoon of May 4, 1949. Returning to Turin after a friendly in Lisbon, Portugal, the three-engined plane that was transporting the entire Torino playing staff, plus coaches and officials, slammed into the church that surmounted Superga, the hill overlooking the town. There were no survivors.

Eighteen players perished: Valerio Bacigalupo, Aldo Ballarin, Dino Ballarin, Milo Bongiorni, Eusebio Castigliano, Rubens Fadini, Guglielmo Gabetto, Ruggero Grava, Giuseppe Grezar, Ezio Loik, Virgilio Maroso, Danilo Martelli, Valentino Mazzola, Romeo Menti, Piero Operto, Franco Ossola, Mario Rigamonti and Julius Schubert.

Italy was plunged into mourning, Turin was devastated.

The league season continued. Four games remained, and Torino gamely remained in the competition, despite having just three first-team players left alive. Instead, they fielded their youth side, Primavera, and it is an indication of just how deeply the disaster was felt elsewhere in the country that all four of their scheduled opponents, Genoa, Palermo, UC Sampdoria, and Fiorentina, sent their own youth sides out to meet them. Primavera won all four matches and so Torino claimed their fourth successive title, only the second team in Italian history (after Juventus) to do so.

That was the end of Torino as a major force. Manchester United, stricken by a similar disaster nine years later, famously went on to rebuild and, just ten years later they were crowned champions of Europe. Torino, on the other hand marked the tenth anniversary of the Superga disaster with relegation.

They returned to Serie A in 1960–1961, but it would be 1975–1976 before the side claimed another championship; since then, further relegations, scandal, and bankruptcy have all haunted the club. Tragedy, too, continued to stalk the side. In 1967, winger Luigi Meroni was killed in an automobile accident, at a time when his renown, his talent, and his public image were all shaping up to transform him into the Italian George Best.

But the club lives on regardless. The Europa League is an annual target, and the immediate future apparently includes a return to the team's spiritual home, the Stadio Filadelfia where they played until 1958. And, in the seething morass of Italian soccer loyalties, Torino are perennially regarded as the neutral's favorite team.

Which isn't a bad tag to live with.

AGF Aarhus—In the Middle of Aar-Street, 1955–1960

Or so the jokers sang in the mid-1980s, as the super-Danes stepped out to compete in the 1987–1988 European Cup, a new name for many continental onlookers. What the comics did not know, or had at least forgotten, was that there was a time, thirty years previous, when Aarhus Gymnastikforening were not simply champions of Denmark. They were a force of nature.

Three successive Danish league championships kicked off in 1955 (with a fourth following in 1960). Their record of nine Danish Cup victories has still to be surpassed, with three of those also counting toward a double triumph. Their European record is not so impressive—just two quarterfinal appearances, in the European Cup of 1960–1961 and the Cup Winners Cup in 1988–1989. But still, Danes of a certain age continue to remember that midfifties side with an affection that borders upon religious fervor.

Soccer was not a major sport in Denmark at the time, with the league still adamantly amateur. Nevertheless, it had deep roots. The Danish FA formed in 1889, and AGF Aarhus traced its soccer-playing roots back to 1902, when the gymnastics club that provided its full name first introduced the sport. They won their first soccer trophy, the Jutland County Championship, in 1908, and between 1921 and 1925, were habitual runners-up in the play-off style Danish Championship final.

A truly national Danish Football League commenced in 1929, with AGF elected to the second division. Champions the following year, they were promoted to the first division, although it cannot be said that they, or any other provincial side, was anything more than a makeweight in a league thoroughly dominated by teams from in and around the capital, Copenhagen.

KB København, B93 København, B1903 København and BK Frem København between them represented a cartel that none could penetrate. Akademisk Boldkub Gladsaxe, from the nearby town of Gladsaxe, was as close to an outsider as the honors had ever strayed and you could set your watch by the predictability of the league. Without fail, one of these five sides placed its name on the championship trophy every single season.

It was Køge BK, from the coastal town of Køge, who finally broke the monotony with a glorious triumph in 1954, having first served notice of their intentions with a second-place finish in 1952, But it was AGF Aarhus who were truly poised to take advantage of the capital city's confusion.

The second largest conurbation in Denmark, and the country's primary port, Aarhus had threatened greatness before, when AGF finished runners-up to Akademisk in 1945. The Copenhagen elite, however, simply saw it as a fluke. Provincial sides had finished second in the past (Fremad Amager had the temerity to do it twice!); they would do so again.

Køge's 1954 triumph, then, seriously upset the status quo. Now AGF were set to overturn it altogether.

The odds were stacked against AGF from the start. As recently as 1952, they had suffered the ignominy of relegation, and while they bounced immediately back up to the top table, the 1954 season ended with them in a very unthreatening seventh place. Behind the scenes, however, another story was unfolding.

Hungarian coach Géza Toldi was newly installed as club manager, following on from a couple of years at Odense Boldklub, and bringing with him not only the experience of a long career with Ferencvárosi, but also the discipline and determination that was a hallmark of the Hungarian national side of the age—the magical Magyars who had just beaten the hitherto invincible English on their own turf.

Goalkeeper Henry From was one of four team regulars who had starred in the national side's run to the 1952 Olympic quarterfinals: defender Per Knudsen, midfielder Jørgen Olesen, and forward Aage Rou Jensen were all at the peak of their game. (From would still be Denmark's first choice keeper eight years later, at the 1960 Olympics; while Jensen went on to make 410 appearances for AGF.) Hans Christian Nielsen, another future Olympian, was pushing into the side; other stars included Erik Bechmann Jensen, Svenning Pilgaard, Gunnar Kjeldberg, and Svend Thørgersen.

The new season, 1955, marked the inaugural year of the Danish Cup, a national challenge trophy that got underway across three initial rounds fought out between the country's lesser sides. The competition would be into its fourth round before the first division and the majority of second and third division sides entered, with AGF immediately facing a stiff challenge, drawn away to the defending league champions Køge.

AGF scraped a 1–0 victory in that match, but were far more assured in disposing of BK Frem 3–0 in round five. A quarterfinal tie with second division Randers Freja ended with a narrow 2–1 victory; OB were sent packing by 3–1 in the semis, and AGF were into the final, paired there with the runaway surprise side of the entire tournament, *third* division Aalborg Chang, whose own campaign had begun in the third round, and had seen them indulge in a remarkable feat of giant killing, too, as they dumped out B1909.

They were no match, however, for AGF. A 4–0 victory set AGF up for a truly historic league and Cup double, as the side finished the eighteen-game league season two points clear of AB, winning twelve and drawing one of their games. And that was enough to pitch them into the European Cup for the following season.

That particular campaign swiftly came unstuck (a 4–2 aggregate defeat to Stade de Reims), but domestically, AGF were invincible. Four points separated them from their nearest challengers in the 1956 league championship, and not even the loss of manager Toldi, moving on to coach the Belgian national side, could dampen their spirits. He was replaced by Peter Vesterbak, his predecessor in the job, and life went on.

In 1957, the decision was taken to extend the length of the Danish season, from eighteen games to twenty-seven, but AGF took it in their stride. Again they suffered another early exit from the European Cup, a 5–1 hammering by OGC Nice only marginally mitigated by a 1–1 draw in the return leg. But in the league, seventeen wins and five ties saw them power to their third title in as many years, while the 1957 Danish Cup held out further glory.

Non-league minnows Skjold Bikerød were crushed 6–0 in AGF's opening fourth round tie; third division Fremad Amager were brushed aside 5–1.

Imperiously, AGF swept past Vejle BK in the quarterfinals, while the semifinal paired them with BK Frem, the previous season's winners (and AGF's own conquerors in that year's semifinal). But a 4–1 victory for AGF left nobody in doubt that the boot was truly on the other foot now, and in the final, two unanswered goals saw off Esbjerg, the side that had run them close for the league title the previous season.

The balance of power shifted briefly after that. AGF finished sixth in the table in 1958, although they were arguably at lesat a little distracted by their third successive European campaign. Drawn against the Northern Irish minnows Glenavon in the qualifying round, a 0–0 draw at home was more than remedied by a 3–0 victory in the away leg, with two goals from Peder Kjaer and one from John Jensen. The next round then brought a famous 2–0 triumph over Spanish giants Sevilla, with Erik Bechmann Jensen netting both, and its just a shame that Danish dreams had already been crushed in the away leg, as the Spaniards romped home by 4–0. They were out of Europe once again.

The following season, AGF rallied slightly under new coach Austrian Walter Pfeiffer, to finish fifth in the league, and in 1960 they rang the curtain down on their most glorious era with one further league title, and one more stirring European adventure.

First, Poland's Legia Warszawa were dispatched, a 3–0 home win more than compensating for the 0–1 reverse in Warsaw. Norway's Fredrikstad FK were beaten both at home and away, the first time AGF had managed such a double;

Santos were never a one-man team, but Pelé epitomized them regardless.

and while they stood no hope whatsoever in their quarterfinal pairing with mighty SL Benfica of Portugal, the very act of scoring a goal in each leg, a 1–4 defeat at home, 1–3 away, was considered glory enough by many observers. SL Benfica, after all, were en route to the final, and a 3–2 victory over Barcelona. For AGF to score as many goals (through John Amdisen and a Germano own goal against them as the Spanish giants (albeit over twice as many games) was indeed a triumph.

AGF tumbled. In 1968, just a decade after their hours of greatest triumph, they were relegated, and though promotion followed in 1971, it was shortlived. It would be the 1980s before AGF again began threatening for top Danish honors, by which time their domestic feats had long been consigned to the history books. And they were best known now as a mispronounced lyric in a Madness song.

Santos—And a Man Named Pelé, 1957–1974

When sixteen-year-old Edson Arantes do Nascimento—Pelé—made his debut for Santos in September 1956, scoring one goal in the club's 7–1 rout of Corinthians, the club was already regarded as the best team in Brazil, reigning state champions and the home of Pinto, Pepe, Urubatão, and Tite.

Across the decade and a half that followed, however, they would amplify that billing many times over, to become the best-known team in Latin America and then, perhaps, the finest in the whole world. And while that escalation was not all down to the presence of Pelé, it has to be acknowledged: it helped.

Santos formed in 1912, shortly after two of the city's original teams, Atlético Internacional and Americano, respectively dissolved and relocated (to São Paulo). Early practice matches took the side through the summer of 1912; and in September the newly minted Santos played its first official match, a 2–1 victory over neighboring Santos Athletic.

The following year saw Santos join the Campeonato Paulista, their local state championship, where their first match ended in an 8–2 reverse to Germania. It would be the late 1920s before Santos made any kind of lasting mark on the Brazilian game, when *O ataque dos 100 gols* (the attackers of 100 goals) did indeed score a century in just sixteen games in 1927, an average of 6.25 goals per game.

Despite such a display, Santos could only finish second that season, and were to remain runners-up in both 1928 and 1929. But 1930 saw them registered for the first time on the international stage, when the French national team, visiting Brazil after the Uruguay World Cup, was thrashed 6–1—leading the French to suspect that they had been entertained by the Brazilian national team, and not just a local club. In terms of its European renown, the legend of Santos began there, when the French returned home to speak, still awestricken, of the phenomenon they had just witnessed.

Amateur up until now, Santos turned professional in 1933 and two years later, the club won its first championship, beating Corinthians 2–0 in the final. But the team broke up soon after and it would be the late 1940s before Santos again mounted a serious challenge for the title, and 1955 before a free-scoring side again claimed the championship.

Enter, then, Pelé, the undisputed star of Brazil's victory in the 1958 World Cup in Sweden and, back home, the inspiration behind Santos's third Campeonato Paulista title. He scored no fewer than fifty-eight goals, more than one-third of the side's own remarkable 140, yet Santos were never a one-man side. A 12–0 victory over Ponte Preta was achieved without Pelé in the side; teammate Coutinho simply stepped up a gear and scored five himself.

In 1960, Santos reclaimed the Campeonato Paulista, alongside the Taca Brasil, or the Brazilian Cup, but these triumphs were merely an appetizer for the 1962–1963 season, in which they won every competition they even glanced at.

At a time when Latin American soccer was largely a matter of hearsay in Europe, its existence acknowledged only by the World Cup every four years, Santos's achievements saw them become Europe's favorite Latin team by default. Yet, in truth, the near-immortal lineup of Gylmar, Lima, Mauro, Calvet, and Dalmo, Mengálvio and Zito, Dorval, Coutinho, Pelé, and Pepe really didn't win that much. In terms of major trophies, their dominance was largely restricted to half a dozen Brazilian titles. Only twice, in 1962 and 1963, did they collect the Copa Libertadores (the bulk of the titles went to Argentinean sides), with the attendant Intercontinental trophies following thereafter.

But that odd statistic must be balanced against the fact that Santos actually sat out the 1966, 1967, and 1969 Copa Libertadores tournaments, rather than risk injury to their players in the often seething cauldrons of their continental rivalries. The most prestigious title in Latin American soccer, the continental equivalent of the European Cup, was also the most ferociously contested, with many matches decided not by soccer skills, but by sheer brute force. Santos were not playing prima donnas when they opted not to place Pelé and his teammates in the line of fire; they genuinely did fear for the players' safety. It was not only their club that relied upon the players, after all. Santos players also formed the backbone of the Brazilian national side, with as many as eight appearing in the team at one time.

Not that the club's concerns were wholly altruistic. Santos might have absented themselves from South American competition, but the club happily furthered its global appeal (and, of course, bolstered the coffers) by undertaking a number of foreign tours and exhibition matches. There was never any shortage of takers.

Perhaps the greatest compliment to Santos, however, was delivered by the Portuguese player Antônio Simões, commenting after watching Brazil's 1970 World Cup win. They were one of the greatest sides he had ever seen, he said. Comparable only with the Santos team of 1962–1963.

Pelé himself added further honors to Santos's roll, of course, including his status as the best-known (and at one point, best-paid) sportsman in the world, and the greatest goal scorer of all time. He scored a record 541 league goals, mostly in Santos's colors (he continued, of course, as a member of the New York Cosmos prior to retirement in 1977), while his overall tally more than doubles to 1,281 if internationals, friendlies, and tour games are included.

His renown is furthered by the knowledge that Manchester United, Juventus, and Real Madrid all attempted to bring him to Europe in the early 1960s, only to have their offers rejected not only by Santos, but also by the Brazilian government. The man was a national treasure. He must stay with the nation.

Santos's success continued on into the 1970s, but an aging team—and an aging Pelé—inevitably saw them slow; and, hardly surprisingly, replacements for the outgoing brilliance were hard to find. Further Campeonata Paulista titles followed in 1978 and 1984, but it was not until the late 1990s that Santos truly reemerged as a domestic powerhouse.

Dukla Praha—Czech Out the Champions of the United States, 1960–1965

Of all the apparent, and alleged, iniquities that the Communist system visited upon the societies that it ruled, its subpoening of international sport into the machinations of government, in all of its manifold forms, was frequently regarded in the West as one of its most devilish. What chance, after all, did honest Western athletes have, with their amateur status and local training facilities, when placed up against the vastness of the Soviet machine, with its state-run sports clubs and state-sponsored training. As a probably apocryphal, and sadly anonymous, Western Olympian is once said to have remarked, "it was almost like they *wanted* to beat us."

That the system had worked without much complaint under other regimes—the colonial army's supremacy over Indian soccer, for example, was repeated throughout the old pre–World War Two British Empire—often tends to be overlooked during such conversations. As does the success of the militarily run, and favored, Royal Engineers club in the early days of organized English soccer. Like so many other of the issues that divided West and East throughout the Cold War years, it was less a matter of "do as we do" than "do as we say," and neither side ever truly struck an equitable balance between the two.

In Czechoslovakia, drawn into the Soviet sphere of influence in 1945, as the victorious Allies divided liberated Europe between them, ATK Praha was the army side, formed in 1948 alongside half a dozen other military sports clubs. It was a formidable outfit from the outset, as compulsory military service gave the club first pick of all the nation's most gifted players, although it took a few years for the side to truly make its mark.

When the Czechoslovakian League returned to action following the war, the first winners were the same as those that had monopolized the competition since its formation in 1925, AC Sparta Praha and SK Slavia Praha; between them, the pair accounted for every past championship but one, and every runners-up place but three, and they seemed set to maintain this proud record.

Now, however, a new era was dawning. While Czechoslovakia was firmly placed within Soviet Russia's domain by the Allied treaties of 1945, its people nevertheless continued to look to the West for inspiration and influence. In February 1948, then, the Kremlin organized a coup d'etat, fronted by the Communist Party of Czechoslovakia, to confirm the country's political, social, and cultural allegiance to Moscow.

Immediately, the authorities set about realigning the face of Czechoslovakian soccer, by stripping away the remnants of the past and proclaiming in their stead the glories of the new. The victorious old guard of local soccer certainly stood no chance, with SK Slavia Praha—historically the side of the old city liberal intelligentsia—simply torn to shreds.

Their players were compulsorily removed from their employ, and distributed elsewhere. Their supporters were routed toward other teams, with threats if necessary, with bribes if required. Even referees somehow, suddenly, seemed less likely to notice an infringement against SK, but were far more alert to infringements *by* them. Whether they actually took place or not.

It did not take long for the new regime to be felt in the trophy cabinets. For the first time, new names were destined to be engraved onto both the championship and the national Cup: NV Bratislava ran up a hat trick of league titles between 1949 and 1951; Sparta CKD Sokolova became champions in 1952; and in that same year, the army's ATK Praha won their own first trophy, the Czech Cup.

The following year, newly renamed UDA Praha, the army took the league title, and in 1956, following another name change, they were back again. Now they were Dukla Praha and, over the next few years, they were constantly there or thereabouts.

Cup finalists (and league runners-up) in 1955, champions again in 1958, runners-up in 1959, Dukla Praha were already being described by observers as destined to dominate Eastern European soccer for the foreseeable future. Few imagined how adroitly they would also challenge its Western counterpart as well.

Between 1961 and 1966, Dukla Praha took the Czech championship five years out of six (in 1965, archrivals Sparta snatched it). They won the Cup, and therefore the double, in 1961 and 1966; the Cup alone in 1965 and were beaten finalists in 1962. They also came close to effectively winning the 1962 World Cup, as no fewer than seven Dukla Praha players starred in the Czech side's run to the final, although it took until that final game, a 3–1 defeat to Brazil, before a Dukla player finally got onto the score sheet. Team captain Josef Masopust put the Czechs ahead on the fifteen-minute mark, only for Brazil to equalize within 120 seconds, before scoring twice more in the final twenty-one minutes.

Masopust made his mark on the European Cup, too. Indeed, when that grand old trophy was rebranded as the Champions League in 1992, and its predecessor's statistics were tallied for the final time, Dukla had played more matches in the tournament than any other Czech side (forty-five), and no fewer than five of their players topped the all-time appearances list: Masopust, strikers and fellow World Cup veterans Josef Vacenovský and Jozef Adamec, defender Jiří Čadek, and midfielder Dušan Kabát.

Dukla never won, or even reached the latter stages of the European Cup. But Masopust was elected European Footballer of the Year in 1962, while Dukla's activities did not go unnoticed across the ocean in the United States, either.

Clint Dempsey in action against the Galaxy, October 2014. *Photo Works/ Shutterstock.com*

The first half of the 1960s was the era of the International Soccer League, staged annually in the United States, and the Czechs all but owned it. In 1961, facing a field boasting crack sides from Turkey, Romania, Spain, Brazil, England, France, Yugoslavia, and more, Dukla were unstoppable. The following year, facing the 1962 champions America RJ of Brazil in a new trophy, the American Challenge Cup, Dukla added that to their silverware cabinet, winning 3–2 on aggregate over the two-legged final. In 1963, they defeated England's West Ham United by 2–1; 1964 saw them beat Poland's Zagłębie Sosnowiec by 4–2.

It would be another Polish side, Polonia Bytom, who finally snatched away Dukla's invincibility in the 1965 season; and domestically, too, their glory days were over. Pipped to the 1965 league title by Sparta Praha, chased to a close finish by the same side in 1966, Dukla slipped now. It would be 1977 before they again tasted league glory, a drought broken by just one Cup win in 1969. Further titles would follow, but no new dynasty of greatness was ever hatched and by 1987, Dukla were probably better known as the subject of a song by the British band Half Man Half Biscuit, than for any recent sporting accomplishments: "All

I Want for Christmas Is a Dukla Prague Away Kit"—an ode to the writer's search for a Subbuteo table football team painted in those desired colors.

In 1993, Dukla was relegated from the top division for the first time. The following year, the club and the army parted company, and a second relegation followed. The 1994–1995 campaign saw the once mighty Dukla playing in the Bohemian Football League, the third level of the Czech soccer pyramid, and in 1996, a merger with the second division side FC Portál Příbram saw the name disappear altogether. They even left Prague.

Old habits, however, die hard. With the original club's old home ground, the Juliska Stadium, standing tenantless, another local side, Dukla Dejvice, not only took up residence there, they also adopted Dukla Praha's old yellow-and-red strip. They played no higher than the Prague Championship at the time, but they were ambitious all the same and, in 2006, the club's management concluded a deal to buy out second division Jakubčovice Fotbal's league position.

It was a shortcut to glory that left even certain of their supporters feeling a little queasy; what, after all, is the point of *playing* the game, if you can just flash the cash and buy your way in instead? But in this case, Dukla proved their worth, growing increasingly more powerful as a second division side, and finally returning to the first division in 2011.

Floreat Athena—When Soccer Was All Greek to Australia in General, 1982–1986

In 1982, ten years after Ted MacDougall broke a thousand Bournemouth hearts by moving to Manchester United (and four years after he repaired them all by returning to the Cherries for one last grand hurrah), followers of Australian soccer found themselves doing something of a double-take.

For suddenly and, in truth, only fleetingly, that same familiar name was turning out in the blue-and-white stripes of Floreat Athena, a soccer team in Perth who had just celebrated promotion to the Football West State League Premier Division but who, at that time, were still rated relative unknowns in a sport that itself rated among Australia's most obscure outdoor pastimes. Indeed, in one of the most sports-mad nations on earth, soccer's reputation and support was even lower than it was in the United States. At least the US *tried* to make it work. Australia simply pretended it wasn't there.

MacDougall was no stranger to soccer's outposts by now. Earlier in the 1970s, he spent a summer playing in South Africa; and at decade's end, he was onboard the Detroit Express in the NASL. Back in England, however, he drifted into non-league soccer as his playing days neared their end, but his appetite for the game was undiminished.

The majority of Australian soccer action at this time emanated from within the various immigrant communities—the original Athena FC was launched on Wellington Street in 1951 by Perth's Greek Australian group, and by 1953 the side had won entry to the Western Australian State League's third division, alongside along the equally Eurocentric likes of East Fremantle Tricolore and Inglewood Kiev.

Slowly rising up the divisions, Athena reached the State Premier League in 1960, the same year that the club became a founder member of the Soccer Federation of Western Australia. Hopes of a challenge on top honors were bolstered by a couple of third-place finishes in 1963 and 1964, but 1966 brought relegation and, while Floreat would soon win promotion back, a second relegation swiftly followed. It would be 1973 before they returned to the Premier League.

Athena became Floreat Athena with the club's move to Perry Lakes Stadium in Floreat, and again a couple of third-place finishes followed (1975, 1976). In 1977, however, Floreat went all the way and topped the Premier League—only for infighting behind the scenes to force the departure of winning coach Bill Dumbbell. By 1980, Floreat were again on course for relegation.

The club at which Ted MacDougall arrived in 1982 was on the up once again though. While he would have moved on long before the glory days truly arrived, the foundations that he saw being laid were those that flowered so brilliantly later in the decade.

Another move, this time to the Lake Monger Velodrome (now the E & D Litis Stadium, because that really trips off the tongue) preceded another third-place finish behind Spearwood Dalmatinac and Stirling Macedonia in 1986, a feat that served notice of Floreat's intentions. The following season, they won the Western Australia Association Cup, the D'Orsogna Cup, for the first time; and in 1988, the side finally delivered on its slow-burning promise, sweeping to the Premiership and D'Orsogna Cup double.

Neither was it a one-off. Table-topping performances followed in 1989, 1990, and 1991 too, with 1989 delivering a third successive Cup win; and the 1990 season confirming Floreat Athena's place among the legends. In an eighteen-game season, they drew just once and lost not at all. Undefeated, they marched into the play-off final with local rivals Perth Italia as the most vibrant favorites in memory. Their ensuing defeat, then, was very hard to take.

But so were all three of Floreat's defeats, at the same stage, to the same rivals, in 1989, and again in 1991. Not because they were beaten, but because the games did not even need to be played. Those three seasons were the only ones in which the regular season was capped by a championship play-off. Prior to 1989, and from 1992 on, the team that topped the table was league champion. If anyone ever tells you that there was a conspiracy against Floreat at the end of the eighties and into the early nineties, that one statistic is the only evidence they require.

Floreat fell away a little after that. Another championship followed in 1997, with the club achieving a record treble of titles by adding the Night Series and Association Cup to the trophy cabinet; and they came within a breath of a second treble in 2001. Today, Floreat Athena compete in the Football West State Premier League. Their most recent league championship (and second undefeated season) fell in 2007.

Nagoya Grampus—J-League Juggernauts, 1993–1997

In terms of Asia's overall footballing history, soccer arrived in Japan comparatively early. The country's first club, the Kobe Regatta & Athletic Club, was founded in 1870 by, as usual, a group of British residents. As the club's name suggests, it was not wholly devoted to Association Football, but the game was on the curriculum, and a few other similar organizations also flourished within the immigrant community.

On a purely domestic level, Japanese histories tend to prefer 1917 as the starting date for the sport, with the formation, by Japanese enthusiasts, of Tokyo Shukyu-Dan. No matter who was first, however, interest was swift to develop. Regional football associations burgeoned across the country, while 1921 saw the foundation of both the national FA (at that time dubbed the Greater Japan Football Association, in accordance with the empire's expansionist vision) and the Emperor's Cup, a national, annual competition that fittingly was won in its first season by Tokyo Shukyu-Dan.

No single side was to dominate the early years of the tournament; Hiroshima's Rijo Shukyu won the Cup two years in succession in the mid-1920s; Kwangaku repeated the feat in 1929 and 1930. The mid-1930s, however, saw the emergence of Keio University, from Minato, Tokyo. Clubs representing Keio won the Emperor's Cup in 1932, 1936, 1937, 1939, and 1940, and were finalists in 1930 and 1938.

World War Two saw the tournament suspended until 1946, and then again during 1947 and early 1948 as Japan continued to normalize following the conflict. Finally, 1948 saw the launch of the country's first national league, the All Japan Works Football Championship—open, as its name suggests, only to company teams. The Inter-City Football Championship followed in 1955, and it would be a decade more before the Japanese Soccer League was launched.

Eight sides were involved, all representing major companies, and of the first seven championships, five were won by Toyo Industries; the remainder by Mitsubishi Motors; the runners-up during this same period included sides representing Yawata Steel, Furukawa Electric, and Yanmar Diesel.

But a Japanese side finished third in the 1968 Olympics soccer tournament, and the interest that precipitated swiftly convinced the league authorities to launch a second division, with the first professional players also being welcomed into the fold—all of them well-remunerated foreign imports. Domestic players, already being employed by the companies that sponsored their teams, were to remain resolutely amateur for some years to come.

Despite all of these strides, change was slow to come, with the authorities remaining sluggish even when confronted with the growing number of Japanese players who were moving abroad to play. And, of course, being well paid for doing so.

The first to go was Yasuhiko Okudera, departing Furukawa Electric in 1977 for the German Bundesliga side 1. FC Koln. The first Japanese player to compete at the highest level in Europe, he then became the first to win a national championship, as his new side topped the Bundesliga that season, and the first to score in a European Cup match, against Nottingham Forest in the 1980 semifinals.

Further interest in the international aspects of the game arose when Toyota became sponsors of the Intercontinental Cup, that bad-tempered annual slugfest between the reigning champions of Europe and Latin America. Dogged by controversy almost since its inception in 1960, the trophy had degenerated so far that European champions Liverpool, Nottingham Forest, and FC Bayern München all refused to even contest it when their turn came, and it seemed the trophy was destined for the dumper.

With the new sponsors, however, came a new birth. The old practice of playing two-legged finals, one in each competing continent, was scrapped; instead, the sides would meet for a single game in Tokyo beginning with the 1980 match between the Uruguayan side Nacional, and England's Nottingham Forest.

In 1993, a new professional Japanese league, the J-League, was inaugurated. Basing its membership on community-driven sides, as opposed to sponsored company outfits, and opening its doors to an influx of foreign talent, the J-League kicked off in 1993 with ten sides, JSL First division veterans Gamba Osaka, JEF United Ichihara, Nagoya Grampus Eight, Sanfrecce Hiroshima, Urawa Red Diamonds, Verdy Kawasaki, Yokohama Flügels, and Yokohama Marinos; the second division champions Kashima Antlers, and one new team, Shimizu S-Pulse.

Of these, Nagoya Grampus Eight were swift to grasp European attention, not only via their activities on the field, but also through the inspired recruitment of latter-day England legend Gary Linekar and the Serbian Dragan Stojković, to lead the playing side of things. Few people at the time even raised an eyebrow when the club also announced the arrival of a new manager, the little-known Frenchman Arsene Wenger, latterly of AS Monaco. Nevertheless, Japanese soccer had its first international super team.

The side had, in fact, already been around for over fifty years at this point, albeit under the colors of the Toyota car manufacturers. Toyoto Motor SC was founded in 1939, and in 1972 were founder members (and first champions) of the Japanese Soccer League's second division.

Relegated and promoted twice more over the next two decades, the revitalized Grampus gave early notice of their domestic intentions with a third-place finish in the 1995 J-League season, and a first-ever Emperor's Cup triumph. The following season they were runners-up in the league, but their greatest exploits were in the 1997 Asian Cup Winners Cup.

Wenger had departed by now, lured to England where he took over as manager of Arsenal; Linekar, too, was gone, hanging up his boots after a long and glorious career. A powerful crop of homegrown players formed the Grampus nucleus now, with the veteran Stojković (the J-League's MVP in 1995) the inspirational linchpin.

Given a bye in the Cup Winners Cup first round (one of four teams to receive such a respite), Grampus kicked off their campaign with the defeat of Vietnamese Cup holders Hai Phong, a tightly fought 1–1 draw away followed by a resounding 3–0 There are few jungles to be found around Seattle, but the 1982 Sounders squad apparently discovered one.

home victory. The quarterfinals saw Hong Kong's South China dispatched in a similar fashion; a 2–2 draw in Hong Kong and a 2–0 victory in Japan; but Grampus saved their finest performance for the semifinal, played (as would be the final) in Riyadh.

The South Korean Ulsan Hyundai were their opponents, themselves conquerors of Japan's other representatives in the competition that year, Bellmare Hiratsuka—the tournament's defending champions. With first-half goals from the Ivorian Donald-Olivier Sié and Tetsuo Nakanishi, and second-half strikes from Stojković, Shigeyoshi Mochizuki, and Kenji Fukuda, Grampus simply breezed into the final, there to meet the Saudi side Al Hillal.

And there, sadly, the story ended. Despite going in at the break on even terms, a Nakanishi goal equalizing the Saudi's early lead, two further Al Hillal goals in the final quarter-hour ended Grampus's dream. But only temporarily. Grampus remain one of Japan's, and Asia's, leading clubs. Emperor's Cup winners again in 1999, and finalists in 2009, J-League champions in 2010 and runners-up in 2011, they have also become regular competitors in the Asian Champions League, reaching the semifinals in 2009, and the round of sixteen on two occasions since then.

Stojković remains on board, too; hanging up his boots after seven seasons, he returned to the club as manager in 2010. And today, whenever casual conversation elsewhere in the world turns to the topic of favorite J-League figureheads, Grampus and Stojković alike remain many people's club and player of choice.

Not for the honors they have accumulated over the years, but for the vivid light that they shone on the Japanese game in the first place.

Seattle Sounders—Major League Sensations, 2007–

The story of the Sounders is one of US soccer's most storied. It is also one of the most episodic. While the name has remained the same for more than forty years, there have been no fewer than three Seattle Sounders plying their trade in the Pacific Northwest since the birth of the first in 1974. True, those enterprises were interrupted by the equally memorable lifespan of the Seattle Storm, but when major soccer success finally embraced the region in the mid-2000s, it was the Sounders whose name was inscribed on the trophies, an unbroken bond of affection that stretched back to the heyday of the NASL, and reminds us once again of what you are probably already tired of reading. A soccer team is more than a business. It is a cultural artifact.

The original Sounders were among the expansion teams added to the NASL for the 1974 season, as the league commenced its drive into the West, and while they would forever be overshadowed by the noisy neighbors from Los Angeles, still the side acquitted themselves admirably.

Third in the Western Conference during that inaugural season, the Sounders reached the play-offs in both 1975 and 1976, before 1977 took them to the culminating Soccer Bowl itself. There, however, awaited the all-conquering New York Cosmos, and despite the Sounders at least claiming a modicum of "home advantage"—the game was played in neighboring Portland—goals from Stephen Hunt and Giorgio Chinaglia were answered with but a solitary Tommy Ord strike, and the Sounders returned defeated up 1-5.

Unlike so many of their peers, the Sounders never truly relied upon imported superstars for their impact. Onetime Tottenham Hotspur great Mike England was a leading light in the side's mid-1970s heyday; but his teammates included players from considerably less glamorous surroundings: Barry Watling, on loan from Hartlepools United; John Rowlands, from Crewe Alexandra; Arfon Griffiths of Wrexham. Doughty, stouthearted team players whose application to the game of soccer, as opposed to the publicity circus that consumed so many other teams, somehow seemed suited to the dour, rainswept landscape of their adopted home town.

The Sounders did not build immediately upon their 1977 success, but poor showings in 1978 and 1979 preceded a rush to the play-off semifinals in 1980. Now the team was built around a newly arrived trio of Englishmen schooled in the crucible of Derby County, the first of the awesome seventies sides designed by the legendary Brian Clough.

Future Arsenal and Scotland manager Bruce Rioch, striker Roger Davies, and the distinctively permed and white-booted Alan Hinton were a magisterial presence throughout the Sounders organization, Rioch and Davies on the field, Hinton as a manager who explained, in a 1995 interview with *Total Soccer* magazine, why he believed even then that the US was destined one day to conquer the world game.

"The American athlete has the strongest upper body in the world. If we can get good coaching and good habits pushed into these American kids at an early age, eventually they'll beat the whole world. Whether they'll do it in my lifetime, I don't know. But they'll get there."

Hinton arrived in Seattle having wrapped up his playing career with a season apiece at the Dallas Tornado and the Vancouver Whitecaps. He spent another year coaching the Tulsa Roughnecks, but Seattle was where he was to make his home.

Those early years in the city were, by the standards he and his English teammates were accustomed to, very different from anything they had hitherto experienced. Encouraged to engage with the community at every opportunity, the Sounders found themselves becoming involved in all manner of extracurricular activities—speaking at schools, giving demonstrations for kids and, perhaps the strangest of all, teaming up with the local *Seattle Times* newspaper and the local fire department to deliver a series of "fire safety slogans" to the world.

"Don't play with matches and stay in the game," cautioned Roger Davies. "Fire is a bad roommate," continued Hinton; "Keep him off your team." They were wholly irreverent yet irresistible regardless. One cannot help but imagine the mighty Sounder warriors furrowing their brows over mounds of screwed-up paper, struggling deep into the night to come up with their slogans. Well, it's either that or acknowledge they were probably supplied to them by the firemen.

The Sounders lost their NASL franchise following a disappointing 1983 campaign (which itself followed a return to the Soccer Bowl, and another defeat at the hands of the Cosmos), and Hinton went back to the Whitecaps, a mere two-hour commute away. When the NASL itself went under, he turned to the indoor game, coaching the nearby Tacoma Stars. But when the Sounders regrouped in 1994, as members of the newly restructured A-League, Hinton was at the helm.

Seattle had not been wholly deprived of competitive soccer during the intervening decade. With Bruce Rioch overseeing the coaching, FC Seattle Storm launched in the mid-1980s, playing in the Western Soccer Alliance and finishing runners-up in both 1987 and in the inaugural year of its successor, the American Professional Soccer League, 1990.

From there, the side dropped down into the Pacific Coast Soccer League, but with Seattle bidding to host some of the games at the 1994 World Cup, and the city also vying for a berth in the inaugural season of the newly minted Major League Soccer tournament, interest in soccer remained pronounced, and nostalgia for the old glory days as well. It was only ever a matter of time before the old team name was relaunched from amid the mothballs.

Rejoining the APSL, Hinton's reborn Sounders were both league champions and play-off semifinalists in 1994. The following season, they wound up in second place on goal difference, but bulldozed their way all the way through the play-offs. Ultimately, it required a penalty shootout to decide the final, which pitched the

Sounders against the Atlanta Ruckus, but still they won in style. Goalkeeper Dusty Hudock netted the decisive goal!

News of the Sounders' triumph was quick to travel. Back in England, onlookers jaded by their own national team's continued lack of success, and the apparent inability of any homegrown manager to win any kind of trophy, celebrated Hinton's emergence as one of just two Englishmen to win a national professional league title since the birth of the Premier League in 1992. (Bobby Robson, leading the Portuguese side FC Porto to glory, was the other.)

Hinton himself was disarmingly modest about his accomplishments, although he never underestimated the job itself. "It is harder [in America], no question about it. The game's not settled. They've had tastes of it, but you've got different nationalities, you have a media that's very set in its ways, you have to work in the community to sell the sport, you have to go out coaching and promoting all the time. It's a full-time job. You're building a club, not simply managing a team."

A second championship trophy was won in 1996, and in 1997 the Sounders joined the United States League (USL), the second level in the national league pyramid (behind the MLS, of course). There, they remained comparable to a big fish in a small pond, and by the time Hinton retired, to be succeeded by Neil Megson, the Sounders had not once finished lower than third in the table; and were about to finish first again, in 2000.

By past standards, Megson's second season in charge was a disappointment, as the Sounders plunged to fifth in the table. But the arrival of a new coach, Brian Schmetzer, reestablished their supremacy, with the overall championship finally returning to Seattle in 2005, and again in 2007.

At which point, close to a decade and a half spent knocking on the MLS door finally came to an end, as Seattle was at last awarded a franchise, and finally fulfilled the prophesy made by Alan Hinton a full decade before. "Seattle . . . has the best soccer team in the country. We'll work something out in the end."

Much of the historical Sounders infrastructure was absorbed directly into the new MLS franchise, with the club's ambition further illustrated by the recruitment of coach Siegfried "Sigi" Schmid, a German-American whose own record in the American game was second to none. As coach of the UCLA Bruins during the 1980s and 1990s, he as good as devoured existing records for breakfast, while stints with the LA Galaxy and Columbus Crew proved that he could coach just as effortlessly at the highest level.

He received the MLS Coach of the Year award in 1999 and 2008, and when the Sounders launched their new life in 2009 by winning the US Open Cup, Schmid claimed another record, as the 2–1 defeat of FC Dallas cemented him with more MLS victories to his name than any other coach in history. It was his 125th victory, easing him past Bob Bradley (the former US national team coach, who then worked with the Chicago Fire, the Metrostars, and Chivas USA in the MLS).

Another page was written in the history books when the Sounders became the first MLS expansion team to make the play-offs since the Chicago Fire back in 1998, and the first to win a berth in the CONCACAF Champions League (as holders of the US Open Cup). They progressed no further than the opening salvos of both competitions, but still it was clear that Schmid was building something great.

The Sounders won their second successive US Open Cup victory (the first MLS team to successfully defend that particular title) in 2010, and that year made a second brief appearance in the play-offs. The following year, they repeated the feats yet again, this time marching into the knockout phase of the CONCACAF Champions League, while 2012 saw them go one step further in that latter competition and reach the quarterfinals before being dispatched by Santos Laguna of Mexico (the 7–3 aggregate speaks volumes for the quality of the encounter).

The Sounders' apparent ownership of the US Open Cup was finally broken by Sporting Kansas City; and further disappointment awaited in the Sounders' Western Conference final against the Galaxy. And as the 2013 season got under-way, it appeared that the Sounders were still laboring beneath a cloud of mis-fortune. Five games elapsed before the side even registered their first win of the regular season.

They were shockingly poor in their opening US Open Cup tie with the Tampa Bay Rowdies, and paid the price accordingly. The Champions League offered some respite, but Santos Laguna again awaited them in the semifinals, and sent them packing.

There was one golden moment, however, as the Sounders shattered the MLS transfer record by paying England's Tottenham Hotspur $9 million to bring US soccer legend Clint Dempsey back home. He made his debut on August 10, coming on as substitute in a 2–1 win over Toronto FC, played through the remainder of the season, and then returned to England on a two-month loan to Premier League side Fulham. But he was back in Seattle for the new MLS campaign in March 2014, and back on target too. Eight goals in the first five games of the season included a hat trick against Portland, as the Sounders effortlessly set the early pace; and his heroics continued in Brazil at the World Cup. Western Conference Champions and Supporters Shield winners, US Open Cup victors and Cascadia Cup finalists, the Sounders just missed out on a berth in the MLS final. But a noteworthy season regardless sets them up for thrilling times ahead.

Lincoln Red Imps—Giants in Waiting? 2014–

Sometimes, simply playing soccer is not enough. Sometimes, other factors regulate whether or not a nation, state, or territory can be recognized as a bona fide member of the sporting community. Factors like the long-simmering dispute between the United Kingdom and Spain over who should control Gibraltar, the strategically vital rock that sits on Spain's own shoreline, but has nevertheless been a British possession since 1704.

Gibraltar has possessed a Football Association since 1895, when the Gibraltar Civilian FA came into being, and a trophy, the Merchants Cup, was established for the handful of teams that then played on the rock. In 1901, the Gibraltar national team came into being; and in 1907, the Gibraltar League was launched. All of which took place under the approving eye of the English FA (with whom the GCFA affiliated in 1909) and the very disapproving gaze of Spain's Royal Spanish Football Federation.

This conflict flared into an international issue in 1997, when Gibraltar applied for membership of UEFA. For three years, the international body dallied; for three years, Spain ferociously lobbied against the rock being granted recognition. And finally the matter became an academic one when UEFA announced that membership of its august body was restricted only to countries that the United Nations already recognized as independent states.

Subject closed.

Or not. Gibraltar certainly were not taking the snub lying down, pursuing their case to the Court of Arbitration for Sport to point out, quite rightly, that even if UEFA's new law did make sense, the fact that Gibraltar's application had been made before it came into force dictated that they should not be bound by it. But in actuality, it didn't make sense, as the membership of the Faroe Islands, Northern Ireland, Wales, Scotland, and England all proved. In 2003, the CAS agreed that Gibraltar should be considered for UEFA membership; and when UEFA continued to vacillate, the court spoke up again. Finally, in 2006, Gibraltar was granted provisional acceptance and, seven years later, full membership was awarded.

At last . . . showtime!

The smallest UEFA member, behind even the picturesque pixies of San Marino, the Faroes, and Liechtenstein, Gibraltar immediately began preparing for her first European Championships campaign, all eyes focused on the 2016 competition and a qualifying group that pitted the rock against the might of Germany, Poland, Scotland, Georgia, and the Republic of Ireland. No worries there, then.

Before that tournament kicked off, however, Gibraltar first took her bow in the European Champions League with the competition debut of the Lincoln Red Imps.

Named for the impish visage that haunts the cathedral in the English city of Lincoln (and which is responsible for that team's nickname too), the Lincoln Red Imps formed in 1976. The team's core was initially built around the Gibraltar Under-15 side that, several years earlier, had undertaken a surprisingly successful US tour, bolstered by teenage players released by sundry other local sides—Glacis United, St Jago's, and the Blue Batons police youth team.

The Red Imps started their league life in Gibraltar's fourth division, and only slowly rose to the GFA Premier League. Promotion in 1983–1984, however, presaged an era of almost unparalleled success. For the past two decades, Gibraltar's soccer scene had been dominated by Glacis United. Now, however, a new giant was in town. The two teams shared the league championship in 1984–1985, but the Red Imps were only just beginning their reign.

Under the managerial eye of Charlie Head, a squad that starred Frank Barton, Mick McElwee, Francis Caruana, Terence Polson, Stephen Head, and Derek Alman would take the title six times more over the decade to come; the Rock Cup five times; and the Gibraltar League Senior Cup seven times in succession. Hardly surprisingly, the Red Imps also provided the backbone to a Gibraltar national side that was growing in strength, even outside of the UEFA family.

The 1993–1994 title was the Red Imps' last for a time; an aging team was being rebuilt, and the new generation was slow to find its feet. But the last championship season of the twentieth century saw the Red Imps serve notice of their intentions with a gallant championship win; and since regaining the title in 2002–2003, their stranglehold on first place has remained unbroken.

In 2011, the Red Imps finally smashed Glacis United's seemingly eternal record of nine championships in a row, racked up back in the 1970s, while their grip on the two Cup tournaments has been almost equally monotonous. Trebles of League, Rock Cup, and Senior Cup were scored in 2004, 2005, 2006, 2007, 2008, 2011, and 2014; League and Rock Cup doubles in 2009 and 2010. All building up to 2014–2015, and their triumphant entry into Europe.

The draw for the first qualifying round, fought out while the rest of the world was still in Brazil for the World Cup, pitched the Lincoln Red Imps against the Faroese champions, HB Tórshavn at the beginning of July 2014. And just eighteen minutes into the first leg, at home in Gibraltar, Joseph Luis Chipolina sent the entire stadium crazy when he scored the first-ever UEFA-recognized goal in his homeland's history.

For more than fifty minutes, the Red Imps protected their lead. But the Faroes team had experience on their side, strength and stamina. On seventy-one minutes, Levi Hanssen sent in the equalizer that Tórshavn had been threatening for so long, and when the two sides met in the second leg the following week, it was Hanssen who opened the scoring as assuredly as he had closed it in the first leg.

A goal up after eleven minutes, 3–0 ahead at the break, Tórshavn had a nasty shock when the Red Imps (in an almost all-white strip) came roaring out into the second half and, against all the odds, moved to within an ace of leveling the score. Goals from George Cabrera and John-Paul Duarte pulled the visitors back to 3–2, and the knowledge that one more Gibraltan goal would send them through to the next round on the away goals rule.

It was not to be. With Tórshavn digging deep for that extra gallon of gas, Levi Hanssen scored their fourth and, with just two minutes left on the clock, Frodi Benjaminsen put the result beyond all doubt. But still the Red Imps returned home in triumph. They had already accomplished more than any other Gibraltan side had ever managed, and accomplished more than anyone could have demanded of them, too.

The future is theirs.

9

Simply the (George) Best

Who Are the Finest Players?

P lace two soccer fans in a room together, and you will hear at least four different recitations of who the greatest players in the world are. At the very least.

One will comprise the stout-hearted, dour souls who performed week in, week out, for a comparative pittance in years and decades long gone by. Another will be populated by whichever loquaciously over-sponsored underperformers have most recently had their sneering visages plastered across the tabloid press, accompanying whatever litany of self-regarding fluff has been cooked up by their publicist this week. A third will argue that greatness is a quality that cannot be measured; it must be earned in the annals of the game as a whole, and not just within the narrow confines of its weekly TV coverage. A fourth will be dictated by however much money a player cost in his last transfer; because $140 million can't be wrong. And one more will argue that simply being elected Footballer of the Year by a coterie of unbiased and certainly incorruptible journalists is all the evidence you could possibly need for a player to ascend to the realms of immortality.

All of these, in some ways, are true. But they are also distorted. Certainly, neither a player's earning power nor his media profile, nor even his celebrity lover, can truly be considered when allotting the epithet of greatness to a soccer player. Those luridly colored boots might catch the eye on television, but it's what's inside the boots that really counts, and the sad fact is, the brighter a player's statement of individuality, the drabber his skills tend to be.

Pelé wore the same color boots as the rest of his teammates. So did George Best, so did Ferenc Puskás, so did Ladislao Mazurkiewicz. And who would dare argue against their immortality?

The more a player feels the need to call attention to himself, in word, in deed, in tattoo, hairstyle, or supermodel, the less likely it is that he actually merits the same notice on the field. Which in turn translates to the sad fact that assigning anything more than a modicum of genuine footballing prowess to the vast majority of today's absurdly coiffed prima donnas is like agreeing to let someone rewire your home, simply because you like their body piercings.

The strange thing about this blanket condemnation, of course, is the knowledge that every past generation of supporter has felt exactly the same pain, *not* through some rose-tinted recollection of a mythic era in which every single soccer player was either Steve Bloomer, Alfredo Di Stéfano, or Vasily Rats, but because every successive generation of player has essentially comprised 90 percent chaff and 10 percent genuine wheaty goodness. The only real difference is the extent to which the chaff will go to disguise its innate dullness.

Of course, "golden ages" are not hard to find and they are not, necessarily, buried deep in the recesses of the past either. The speed with which the nature of the game is consistently changing has already made it apparent that, for example, the days when Manchester United could win the English Premier League with a bunch of lads fresh out of the academy, as they did as recently as 1995–1996, are already long departed.

Indeed, if we are honest, they had already departed even then, as English television commentator Alan Hansen made clear following the so-called Fergie's Fledglings' first Premier League game together, a 3–1 defeat at Aston Villa on the opening day of the season. "You don't win things with kids," Hansen told a watching world. Nine months later, those same kids led Manchester United into the history books as the first club ever to claim both the Premier League and the FA Cup in a single season.

Close to twenty years on, however, would they get the same chance, at the same level? Probably not. But not because the standard of kids has declined (even if, as sundry doomsayers like to say, it probably has). They will not get the chance because, from the boardroom all the way down, the clubs that employ them thrive on newspaper headlines, hyperbole, and heffalumps.

Which means big money transfers, high-earning superstars, and replica shirt sales that recoup from day one. And the kids just sit on the sidelines, cooling their heels while their elders, but not necessarily their betters, get on with the serious business of getting their name onto the next high-profile One Hundred Greatest Players list to circulate the offices of potential sponsors and would-be club presidents.

So here's another list, but this time, one that attempts not only to consider the facets and factors that place a player, for example, on FIFA's Top 100 of the twentieth century, and the annual Player of the Year competitions of the world; but also those that appeal to a purer sense of soccer as an art

Everton's Brian Labone, dominant through the late 1960s and early 1970s.

form, a vocation, and a gift. Not a career. Among those indicia that are not considered, therefore, transfer fees, wages, and sponsorships are perhaps the most notable.

No attempt has been made to list players in any kind of "best of" order, although the first nineteen names on the list, noted without any biographical background or detail, are certainly those without whom no such list could

Lionel Messi celebrates his eighty-eighth-minute winning goal in the 2011 Super Cup Final. *Natursports/Shutterstock.com*

exist. No matter how tremendously refreshing it would be to read (let alone compile) a list of the Greatest Footballers of All Time–type poll that did not include . . .

Gordon Banks (England, b. 1937)
Franz Beckenbauer (Germany, b. 1945)
David Beckham (England, b. 1975)
George Best (Northern Ireland, 1946–2005)
Eric Cantona (France, b. 1966)
Johan Cruyff (Netherlands, b. 1947)
Dixie Dean (England, 1907–1980)
Duncan Edwards (England, 1936–1958)
Eusebio (Portugal, 1942–2014)
Garrincha (Brazil, 1933–1983)
Ryan Giggs (Wales, b. 1973)
Denis Law (Scotland, b. 1940)
Diego Maradona (Argentina, b. 1960)
Stanley Matthews (England, 1915–2000)
Lionel Messi (Argentina, b. 1987)
Pelé (Brazil, b. 1940)
Ferenc Puskás (Hungary, 1927–2006)
Ronaldo (Brazil, b. 1976)
Zico (Brazil, b. 1953)

Sadly, this is neither the time nor the place to do so.

Again, no effort is being made to actually rank the players on this list. Pelé may, as we are frequently informed, have been the greatest soccer player who ever lived. But we should qualify that. He was the greatest soccer player

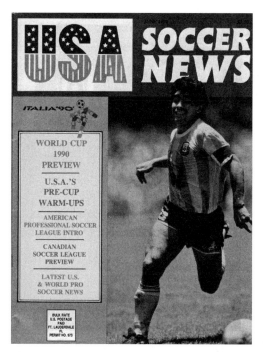

SOCCER NEWS

ITALIA'90

WORLD CUP
1990
PREVIEW

U.S.A.'S
PRE-CUP
WARM-UPS

AMERICAN
PROFESSIONAL SOCCER
LEAGUE INTRO

CANADIAN
SOCCER LEAGUE
PREVIEW

LATEST U.S.
& WORLD PRO
SOCCER NEWS

BULK RATE
U.S. POSTAGE
PAID
FT. LAUDERDALE
FL
PERMIT NO. 573

The much-missed *USA Soccer News* magazine recalls the Hand of God with the ball at his feet.

who played in his position, during his era. Was he a better player than Gordon Banks? Who knows. Pelé scored a lot more goals than Banks, but so he should have. He was employed as a striker. Banks was employed as a goalkeeper. One who made a lot more first-class saves than Pelé, including one from Pelé himself, at the 1970 World Cup, that the Brazilian still talks about today.

Like can only ever be compared with like, and for the same reason that one's favorite singer is rarely a mute bass player, and one's favorite actor is seldom a reclusive director; one's favorite predatory Argentinean *pibe* is seldom a chunky Bavarian clogger.

In terms of pure soccer-playing skill, the names on this list all touched greatness; all, at some point in their career, gazed down from a pinnacle that few others had ever reached. In other areas of their lives, maybe some of them let us down—Maradona and drugs, Best and alcohol, and so on.

But was one of them better than all of the others? Did Pelé outplay Platini? Is Messi mightier than Maradona? Was Best the best, or Beckenbauer? Is Gerd Müller the greatest, or is it really Ted MacDougall?

It really doesn't matter.

Or maybe it does. Who knows?

Carlos Alberto—Brazil (born 1944)

One of the 125 Greatest Living Footballers that Brazilian teammate Pelé selected as part of FIFA's centennial celebrations in 2004, Carlos Alberto began his career at Fluminense in 1963, but enjoyed his greatest years alongside Pelé at Santos, where he made 445 appearances between 1966–1974. He then returned to Fluminense, but played out his career in the NASL, appearing for the New York Cosmos and the California Surf. His fifty-three national team appearances include captaining the Brazil side that won the 1970 World Cup.

Amancio—Spain (born 1939)

"El Brujo," the wizard, spent four years at Deportivo de La Coruña before he joined Real Madrid in 1962, becoming a constant presence for the next fourteen years, a period that encompassed nine league titles, three Spanish Cups, and a European Cup (1965–1966). He made a total of 344 appearances in the white of Real, scoring 119 goals. His forty-two Spanish caps include the 1964 European Championship winning side.

Enrique Ballestrero—Uruguay (1905–1969)

Goalkeeper with Rampla Juniors, one of the early powerhouses of Uruguayan soccer, Ballestrero was an ever-present throughout the 1927 Championship winning season (that remains the side's greatest ever achievement), and the national team's 1930 World Cup squad.

He appeared in all four of Uruguay's games, conceding just three goals (one in the 6–1 semifinal destruction of Yugoslavia; two in the final against Argentina), and in the process became the first-ever recipient of FIFA's Golden Glove award. Yet he was, in fact, Uruguay's second-choice goalkeeper. The first, two-time Olympic gold winner Andrés Mazali, was dropped from the squad after being caught sneaking out of the team's hotel for a "conjugal visit."

Marco van Basten—Netherlands (born 1964)

One of the all-time great Dutch strikers, prolific with both Ajax Amsterdam, for whom he made 133 appearances between 1981–1987, and Inter, with whom he remained until injury curtailed his career at just twenty-eight. A Sky Sport poll in 2007 ranked Van Basten first on a list of the greatest athletes whose careers were ended by injury. Even so, his trophy cabinet includes three Dutch and three Italian league championships, a Cup Winners Cup with Ajax and two European Cups with Inter, together with the Netherlands' sensational 1988 Euros victory—with Van Basten's volleyed goal in the final still ranked among the greatest international strikes of all time.

Cliff Bastin—England (1912–1991)

Discovered playing third-division soccer with Exeter City, Bastin became an early, crucial component within Herbert Chapman's all-conquering Arsenal side of the 1930s. He joined the Gunners in 1929, and the tally of 150 league goals he scored for the side over the next eighteen years was to remain unsurpassed until 2006, when it was finally overtaken by Thierry Henry.

DaMarcus Beasley—United States (born 1982)

One of the new generation of US players to distinguish themselves so gallantly at the 1999 Under-17s World Cup, Indiana-born Beasley joined the MLS that March and was initially drafted to the Galaxy before being traded to the Fire, for whom he made ninety-eight appearances, and scored fourteen goals.

In 2004, he moved to PSV Eindhoven as the replacement for the Chelsea-bound Arjen Robben, helping the side to the Eredivisie title that same season. The following year, Beasley's equalizer set PSV up to win the Dutch Cup on penalties against Feyenoord, and in 2006 he was the first American to play in a Champions League semifinal (PSV lost on away goals to AC Milan).

After he left PSV, a brief stint in England was marred by injury; in 2007, Beasley then joined Glasgow Rangers. Since then he has also played for Hannoverscher Sportverein von 1896 in the Bundesliga, and Puebla FC in the Mexican Primera Division; while also retaining his place (albeit with mixed results) in the US national squad for four successive World Cups—2002, 2006, 2010, and 2014.

Igor Belanov—Ukraine (born 1960)

The 1986 European Footballer of the Year was the heartbeat of the majestic Dynamo Kyiv side that dominated the last years of Soviet soccer. Two league championships and a European Cup Winners Cup reflected the club's league prowess; internationally, Kyiv was responsible for most of the Soviet national team of the age—no fewer than thirteen players were featured in the USSR's 1986 World Cup squad, so unfortunate to travel no further than the last sixteen; and wretchedly unlucky too in the 1988 Euros, where they powered through to the final, only for a resolute Dutch side, and Belanov's missed penalty, to deprive them of the crown.

The fall of the Soviet Union opened the door for many of the country's most gifted players to ply their trade abroad. Belanov moved to Borussia Mönchengladbach in 1989, but made little impression there; nor did his fortunes improve when he dropped down a level and joined little Eintracht Braunschweig. In 1995, he returned to his Ukrainian homeland.

Orvar Bergmark—Sweden (1930–2004)

Swedish defender Bergmark tends to be best remembered today as manager of Sweden's 1970s national team. However, he was also a solid presence on both the club and international scene, making ninety-four appearances for Sweden between 1951and 1965, while his club career, though centered on Örebro SK, also included a short spell with AS Roma in Italy.

József Bozsik—Hungary (1925–1978)

One of the finest playmakers in European soccer history, Bozsik was the irrepressible right half for the Mighty Magyars who taught England a footballing lesson in 1953, whipping them 7–1 in Budapest and then 6–3 in London (the first continental side ever to beat the hosts at home). On either side of that, he and his team mates won an Olympic gold in Helsinki in 1952, and were runners-up at the 1954 World Cup.

A twenty year career spent with Budapest Honvéd (aka Kispesti AC) saw him make a total 477 appearances; internationally, he turned out for Hungary 101 times.

Andreas Brehme—Germany (born 1960)

The man who won the 1990 World Cup, when he converted the eighty-fifth-minute penalty that finally broke the stultifying deadlock that had hitherto engrossed West Germany and Argentina, Brehme was never a prolific scorer. But a career that took him from Saarbrücken in 1981, to Bundesliga giants 1. FC Kaiserslautern (1981–1986) and FC Bayern München (1986–1988), thence to Inter (1988–1992), Real Zaragoza (1992–1993) and back to Kaiserslautern (1993–1998) established him as one of the most gifted crossers the game has ever seen. He won eighty-six international caps between 1984 and 1994.

Billy Bremner—Scotland (1942–1997)

The diminutive Bremner was the combative epicenter of the Leeds United side of the 1960s and early 1970, an outfit whose notoriety is as great as their legend, and whose reputation for taking no prisoners established them among the most feared sides of the era.

Bremner made his club debut in 1960, with the team still in the English second tier. Their first season in the top division, 1964–1965, served notice of their intentions, however—they were runners-up in both the Football League and FA Cup.

The following year, manager Don Revie gave the captaincy to the man whom one English newspaper had already described as "[140 pounds] of barbed wire," and Leeds embarked into a period of glorious ascendancy. The League championship, the League Cup, and the UEFA Cup all wound up at Elland Road in the late 1960s, although dreams of a League, Cup, and European Cup treble in 1970 were shattered as the side wound up with nothing whatsoever.

Indeed, the Leeds of the 1970s were very much "always the bridesmaid, never the bride." Five times the League title seemed theirs for the taking, but they won it just once more, in 1974. Four times they reached the FA Cup final, three times they lost it. Final appearances in both the European Cup and European Cup Winners Cup ended in defeat, and while they did win a second UEFA Cup, it was small reward for all those years of dominance.

Likewise, Bremner's international career; he was capped fifty-four times for Scotland, but honors historically eluded the side, while his career ended in the ignominy of a lifetime ban after he and four other players were ejected from a nightclub in 1975. The ban was rescinded the following year, but Bremner never again played for his country.

Bremner left Leeds in 1976, after 587 appearances. He played on for a further four years with Hull City and Doncaster Rovers, before taking over the management of the latter. He would also return to Leeds, by now a second-tier side, in a similar capacity, but he was sacked in 1988 and returned to Doncaster. He resigned in 1991.

Charlie Buchan—England (1891–1960)

A revelation on the pitch, Charlie Buchan also became a legend off it, after he gave his name (and editorial prowess) to one of the most fondly remembered British soccer magazines of all time, the pioneering *Charlie Buchan's Football Monthly*.

Beginning his playing career with Woolwich Arsenal, Northfleet United, and Leyton Orient, Buchan moved to Sunderland in 1911 to become one of the most feared marksmen of the age. His tally of 209 goals in 370 appearances for the Wearsiders (still a club record) was sufficient for Arsenal to lure him back to London as manager Herbert Chapman set about bringing glory to the previously trophy-less Gunners. In fact, Buchan retired before that dream came to pass, earning just an FA Cup runners-up medal in 1927. But his tactical vision played a major part in fermenting Chapman's own, with Buchan the inspiration behind the WM formation with which Arsenal so baffled opponents in the years to come.

Buchan moved into journalism following his retirement; he also wrote one of the game's first coaching manuals. In 1947, he formed the Football Writers Association; and beginning in 1951, his *Football Monthly* ensured his name remained familiar to another twenty-three years' worth of young soccer fans (the magazine ceased publication in 1974, fourteen years after its namesake's death.)

Cha Bum-kun—South Korea (born 1953)

Having already proven himself by becoming (at nineteen) the youngest player ever to represent South Korea at international level, Cha Bum-kun came to international attention as the first of his countrymen to figure in the German Bundesliga.

In 1978, fresh out of the South Korean military (he played for the air force soccer team), he joined SV Darmstadt 98; and a season later he was transferred to Eintracht Frankfurt. He made an immediate impact, scoring in each of his first three games as Eintracht powered to a UEFA Cup triumph that same season.

Scoring forty-six goals in 122 appearances, Cha was at one point ranked among the most formidable marksmen in the Bundesliga, not to mention one of the three highest-earning players. Remarkably, not one of his goals was scored from the penalty spot; equally notably, his disciplinary record was all but flawless—in a decade in the Bundesliga, he received just one yellow card.

He won his second UEFA Cup in 1988, following a switch to Bayer 04 Leverkeusen—it was Cha who scored the late equalizer that sent the game (vs. RCD Espanyol) into extra time and then penalties.

In an international career that lasted into the mid-1980s, Cha led his country to four Merdeka Cups, one Asian Games title, and the 1986 World Cup; retiring from playing in 1989, he then managed the national team to the 1998 World Cup finals.

Claudio Caniggia—Argentina (born 1967)

A former sprinter who sacrificed none of his speed when he took up professional soccer, Caniggia's club career took him from Argentina's River Plate (1985–1988), through a decade of Italian success, and onto an impressive sunset in Scotland in the early 2000s.

News headlines, too, followed him, not least of all when he received a thirteen-month ban for taking cocaine in 1992–1993; or when his refusal to get a haircut saw him dropped from Argentina's 1998 World Cup squad. But, with the possible exception of Diego Maradona, no player better captured the magic of the Argentine national team of the early 1990s.

In Italy in 1990, it was Caniggia's goals that powered the side to the World Cup final; in 1994, his goals against Nigeria overshadowed the game's status as Maradona's last for Argentina. His own final appearance in an Argentine shirt, meanwhile, saw Caniggia receive a red card without ever setting foot on the pitch; he received it for swearing at the referee from the subs bench.

Yet sixteen goals in fifty appearances for the national team remind us that Caniggia was never a natural striker. He was, however, an astonishing play-maker, and at the age of forty-five, he proved he was still capable of his old tricks when he turned out for non-league Wembley FC in the opening Extra Preliminary Round of the 2012–13 English FA Cup, and scored the first goal in a 3–2 victory over Langford.

Amadeo Carrizo—Argentina (born 1926)

One of the founding fathers of modern goalkeeping (and the first of his breed to wear gloves!), the singularly named Amadeo made his debut for Argentinean giants River Plate in 1945, and remained with them until 1968, racking up 513 appearances that included the side's golden age of five championships in seven years (1952–1957). He later turned out for Club Alianza Lima of Peru, and the Colombian side Millonarios.

His international career was more modest, a mere twenty appearances that included a 6–1 drubbing at the hands of Czechoslovakia at the 1958 World Cup, but neither statistic detracts from his weekly brilliance at club level.

Bobby Charlton—England (born 1937)

MANCHESTER UNITED

Bobby Charlton

CENTRE FORWARD

Gentleman Bobby, a World Cup winner with England, and almost everything else with Manchester United.

Billy Wright was the first England player to pass one hundred international caps, Bobby Charlton was the second. Billy Wright was the star of one of the English 1950s' greatest sides, Bobby Charlton was *a* star within the other.

Charlton made his Manchester United debut in 1956, and finally bowed out in 1972, having played through both the peak years of the Busby Babes (Charlton miraculously survived the air crash that killed eight of his teammates in 1958), and the glory years that followed. As one third of the genius triumvirate of Charlton, Best, and Law that conquered first England, then Europe, through the mid-1960s, Charlton was—and remains—universally regarded as one of soccer's good guys, a man whose sense of sportsmanship and good behavior was so pronounced that his off-field relationship with the playboy Best could at most be described as lukewarm. On the field, however, and again with Law alongside them, they had no peer.

Charlton's greatest day with United came with their capture of the 1968 European Cup, following League championship triumphs in 1965–1966 and 1967–1968; with England, it was victory in the 1966 World Cup. Indeed, such was Charlton's influence on the pitch that many observers remain convinced that it was England manager Ramsey's decision to substitute Charlton twenty minutes from the end of England's 1970 World Cup quarterfinal that allowed the West Germans to turn a deserved reverse into a glorious victory. Had Charlton remained on the field, even the Germans admitted they might never have gotten back into the game.

Charlton retired at the end of the 1972–1973 season, having scored 199 goals in 606 appearances (a prodigious marksman, he was also on target for England forty-nine times). He moved briefly but unsuccessfully into management with Preston North End, followed by a directorship at Wigan Athletic. In 1984 he became a director at Manchester United, and is generally regarded as the calm head that insisted Alex Ferguson be allowed to stay on as manager during the Scot's first few fallow seasons.

Giorgio Chinaglia—Italy (1947–2012)

Born in Tuscany, but raised in Wales after his family emigrated when he was seven, Chinaglia joined Swansea Town in 1962, and remained on their books for four years (but just half a dozen League appearances), until military service recalled him to Italy. Three seasons at Serie C sides SSD Massese and L'Internapoli followed—Serie A's ban on foreign players at that time also included anyone who had played professionally overseas. In 1969, however, he was cleared to step up and he joined SS Lazio, just in time for their relegation to Serie B in 1971.

A nonplaying squad member at the 1970 World Cup, Chinaglia was one of the first Serie B players ever to be picked for the Italian national side, although Lazio's exile from the top flight proved fleeting. With Chinaglia now averaging almost a goal every other game, they won promotion the following season, and became Serie A Champions in 1973–1974.

In 1976, Chinaglia made headlines when, still at the peak of his playing powers, he left Lazio for the unknown pleasures of the New York Cosmos and the NASL. In a league otherwise dominated by inexperienced youth or one-final-payday legends (and Pelé), Chinaglia established himself as American soccer's first true superstar, a player who won respect and honors via what he was capable of doing *now*, as opposed to what he had accomplished in another land, in the distant past.

Seven years with the Cosmos, both outdoors and in, saw Chinaglia score 435 goals in 413 matches; naturally, he was the team's top scorer every year (an honor, incidentally, that he had also monopolized at Lazio). Twice, against the Roughnecks in a 1980 play-off, and the Sting indoors in 1981, Chinaglia scored seven goals in a single game, and his 1980 tally of fifty NASL goals (thirty-two in the regular season, eighteen in the play-offs) was never to be surpassed. Neither was his career total of 243 NASL goals.

Igor Chislenko—USSR (1939–1994)

A distinctive figure in the Soviet World Cup squads of 1962 and 1966, and the Euros of 1964 and 1968, Chislenko was also the brilliant power behind the Dynamo Moscow team that finally thrust city rivals Spartak and Torpedo aside in the late 1950s. Just eighteen when he made his debut in 1957, Chislenko had a 229-game career that included dramatic league-title wins in 1959 and 1963, and a Cup triumph in 1967.

Surprisingly absent from the national side's triumphant 1960 Euros squad, Chislenko was onboard throughout the 1964 competition, where the USSR finished runners-up; and in 1968, when they bowed out of the semifinal on the toss of a coin (their match with Italy ended in a draw, and UEFA had yet to decide upon a more sporting alternative to pure chance).

Alessandro Costacurta—Italy (born 1966)

"Billy" was one of the great defenders of AC Milan's great 1990s/2000s side, a seven-time winner of the Scudetto and four times a European champion. He won fifty-nine international caps, starring at the 1994 and 1998 World Cups, and the 1996 Euros.

Alessandro Del Piero—Italy (born 1974)

One of the most lethal goal scorers ever to grace the Scudetto, Juventus mainstay Del Piero netted 342 times in a career that stretched between 1993 and 2012; his ninety-one international appearances brought another twenty-seven goals, establishing him as the national side's joint fourth highest scorer. Following his retirement from Italian soccer, Del Piero moved to Australia to captain Sydney FC.

Alfredo Di Stéfano—Spain (1926–2014)

"His head was up all the time," Alex Ferguson once said of Di Stéfano. "He was such a fantastic footballer."

Argentinean born, but best remembered as a Spanish international (thirty-one appearances between 1957–1961), Di Stéfano had made sixty-six appearances for River Plate, 1945–1951, before he joined the exile of players moving to Colombia, following a players strike in his homeland. He remained there until 1953, during which time his performance in a 4–2 win over Real Madrid alerted the Spanish side to his brilliance.

However, he was also due to sign with Barcelona, precipitating a controversy that the Spanish FA eventually resolved by insisting he should play for them both, alternating seasons for the next four years. Under circumstances that have never truly been explained (at least to the satisfaction of the Barca faithful), the Catalans eventually backed down, albeit unhappily (the saga is still remembered within the two Spanish giants' catalog of grievances) and Di Stéfano stayed at Real for the next eleven years, an era that included their virtual ownership of the first five European Cups (1955–1960) and eight league championships. He played out his career (1964–1966) with RCD Espanyol, then moved into management, including stints with both River Plate (1981–1982) and Real Madrid (1982–1984, 1990–1991).

His death, days before the 2014 World Cup semifinals, brought tributes from across the soccer world, all of them echoing Bobby Charlton's heartfelt tribute to the BBC: "The footballing world has lost a great player and a great man."

Landon Donovan— United States (born 1982)

One of the most successful and decorated players in US soccer history, the all-time leading scorer (fifty-seven goals) and most capped international (156), Donovan came to most people's attention as the Golden Ball winner at the 1999 FIFA U-17 World Championship, following which he was signed, an all-but unknown, to Bayer 04 Leverkeusen.

The United States's Landon Donovan bows out of the international arena vs. Ecuador in an October 2014 friendly. *Miro Vrlik Photography/Shutterstock.com*

Failing to settle well in Germany, he was loaned to the San José Earthquakes in 2001, and promptly led them to the MLS Cup championships of 2001 and 2003. At the World Cup in 2002, he was voted Best Young Player; and in 2004, he was elected US Soccer Athlete of the Year for an unprecedented third year in succession.

The following year he rejoined Bayer 04 Leverkeusen, but again he struggled and he returned to the US, this time with the Galaxy—with whom he won his third MLS Cup. The arrival in 2007 of English superstar David Beckham spurred him to even greater heights. Beckham, for all the ballyhoo (and despite being given the captaincy that Donovan had hitherto held), did not really add that much to the Galaxy, and after a disappointing 2007, with the side failing even to make the play-offs, Donovan came good in 2008, scoring twenty goals that season. (He also enjoyed a short loan period with FC Bayern München.)

The following year, with the Galaxy beaten finalists in the MLS Cup, Donovan was league MVP and in 2010, he won the Supporter's Shield, while also becoming one of that select band of US internationals to represent the country at three World Cups.

Donovan and the Galaxy finally achieved all that their potential had threatened by taking the 2011 and 2012 MLS Cups. Donovan also made the first of two very popular loan spells with the English side Everton, being elected Player of the Month for January 2010.

Late 2012 saw Donovan take a highly publicized break from soccer, citing mental and physical exhaustion. He returned in March 2013 and, a year later, he scored the goals that established him the deadliest striker in MLS history. His omission from the 2014 World Cup squad was seen by many, both before and after the tournament, as one of the few decisive weak spots in coach Klinsmann's strategy.

Donovan retired, aged thirty-two, at the conclusion of that same season. With fairy-tale inevitability, the Galaxy won the MLS Cup in his final game.

Didier Drogba—Ivory Coast (born 1978)

His national team's all-time top scorer, Drogba is one of the most feared, and effective, strikers of the twenty-first century. A senior career that began with the French side Le Mans in 1998 has since taken him to fellow French clubs Guingamp and Marseille, Chelsea in England (where he became their all-time foreign-born top scorer), Shanghai Shenhua in China, the Turkish side Galatasaray, and back to Chelsea again.

At each one, his gift for goals brought honors, including Ligue 1 Goal, Team and Player of the Year gongs during his time at Marseille, two African Footballer of the Year and three Ivory Coast Player of the Year awards; three English Premier League titles and four FA Cups at Chelsea, before winning the Champions League in the final game of his first stint with the club; and both the Süper Lig and Süper Kupa at Galatasaray.

Captain of the Ivory Coast national team since 2006, he led them to three successive World Cups, and to the African Cup of Nations finals in both 2006 and 2012.

Dragan Džajić—Yugoslavia (born 1946)

Throughout the 1960s, and for most of the 1970s as well, mention the name of Red Star Belgrade, and you invoked the Yugoslav club's greatest player. Dragan Džajić spent all but two years of his long career with Red Star (a short stint at SC Bastia between 1975–1977 was the sole interruption), during which five Yugoslav league championships, four Yugoslav Cups, and the 1968 Mitropa Cup topped the list of honors he earned.

To that can be added his place in the great Yugoslav side that came so close to winning the 1968 European Championships, and his own achievements at that same tournament—UEFA Player of the Tournament, Top Scorer, and a third-place finish in FIFA's Balloon d'Or, behind the Manchester United pairing of George Best and Bobby Charlton.

The political upheavals of the late 1980s ensure that Džajić's record of eighty-five Yugoslavian international caps will never be eclipsed. Neither, however, will his place in Red Star's history—at the time of writing, he is serving his third stint as club president, while a 2013 poll confirmed him as the greatest Yugoslav player of all time.

Arsenio Erico—Paraguay (1915–1977)

Seventy years on, Paraguayan powerhouse Erico remains the all-time highest scorer in Argentinean soccer, 293 goals scored in a thirteen-year career spent with Independiente, after he was spotted playing for a Paraguayan Red Cross team, raising funds for victims of the Chaco War in 1933.

In fact, so vast was his impact that the Argentinean authorities offered him a small fortune to become a citizen in time for the 1938 World Cup. Erico refused, and his stock among the Argentinean people rose accordingly. Footballers who were perceived as being motivated by something other than money and glory were at a premium back then as well.

Following his time in Argentina, Erico wrapped up his playing days at the Paraguayan club where his career began in 1930, Nacional.

Elías Figueroa (born 1946)

Often described as Chile's finest player ever, Figueroa is distinguished by having played for probably the leading club in three South American nations—Peñarol of Uruguay (1967–1972), Internacional of Brazil (1972–1976), and Club Deportivo Palestino of Chile (1977–1980).

All three topped their respective leagues during his years in the side—two Uruguayan Primera Division titles in 1967 and 1968 were followed by the Intercontinental trophy in 1969 during his time with Peñarol; Internacional won the Campeonato Gaúcho five years in succession (1972–1976) and the Campeonato Brasileiro Série A in 1975 and 1976; Palestinos took the Chilean Cup in 1977 and the league championship in 1978.

Figueroa routinely racked up Player of the Year awards . . . in Uruguay in 1967 and 1968, in Brazil in 1972 and 1976, in Chile in 1977 and 1978, and across the continent annually between 1974 and 1976. He also figured for the Fort Lauderdale Strikers in 1981, before ending his playing days with Colo-Colo during 1981 to 1982.

Capped forty-seven times by Chile, Figueroa featured in three World Cups (1966, 1974, and 1982). He would briefly manage Palestino in the mid-1990s.

Alfredo Foni—Italy (1911–1985)

Having made his name as a sixteen-year-old at Udinese, before moving to Lazio in 1929 and Padova in 1931, stolid defender Foni joined Juventus in 1934. A star of both the 1936 Summer Olympics and the 1938 World Cup, he earned twenty-three caps in an international career cut short by World War Two.

Following his retirement from playing, Foni enjoyed a successful career in management, leading Inter to the 1953 and 1954 Scudettos, and coaching Switzerland's 1966 World Cup side.

Just Fontaine—France (born 1933)

Born in Morocco but a legend in the blue of France, Just Fontaine may have spent the first half of his playing career in the relatively unfashionable shadows of Casablanca (forty-eight appearances between 1950–1953) and Nice (sixty-nine, 1953–1956), but with Stade de Reims, whom he joined in 1956, he was a vital component in one of the all-time great French sides. Perhaps *the* vital component, particularly after teammate Raymond Kopa moved to Real Madrid in 1958.

A staggering 122 goals in 131 appearances for Reims is unlikely ever to be eclipsed; 165 goals in 200 Ligue 1 games likewise. But it is Fontaine's World Cup record that ensures his immortality outside of France—his record-breaking thirteen goals in a single World Cup, six games in 1958, has often been challenged, but has yet to be eclipsed, with no fewer than four of those strikes coming in one match, the third-place play-off against defending champions West Germany.

And all this in a career that injury ended at the age of just twenty-eight, in 1962.

Arthur Friedenreich—Brazil (1892–1969)

One of the pioneers of Brazilian soccer as it broke away from the essentially conservative guidelines of its British beginnings, the Afro-German Friedenreich was also the country's first-ever black professional player, at a time when segregation was rife in the land.

His playing career began with SC Germania in 1909, a side set up by (and for) German immigrants. By 1914, however, he had been selected for the national team for the first time, while playing regularly for Ypiranga. He moved then to Paulistano, where he was invariably the side's top scorer throughout the 1920s, before joining São Paulo in 1930. By the time he retired, he is said to have scored no fewer than 1,329 goals in 1,239 games—a total that exceeds even Pelé's tally. However, the scattershot nature of record keeping at the time, coupled with the confusion and disputes with which Brazilian soccer of the 1920s and 1930s was rife, make it equally possible that he scored 1,239 goals in 1,329 matches, placing him forty-two strikes behind Pelé.

Friedenreich was capped twenty-three times by Brazil, his starring roles including two Copa America triumphs (1919 and 1922) and a 1925 European tour during which he was feted as "the King of Football." However, internecine disputes within the Brazilian FA excluded him from the 1930 World Cup, with players from the Rio de Janeiro leagues alone being selected.

C. B. Fry—England (1872–1956)

One of the gentleman all-rounders at whose production the Victorian era excelled, Charles Burgess Fry was, at different times, a politician, a diplomat, an academic, the prospective king of Albania, an author, a publisher, an acrobat, a first-class cricketer, an England International soccer player, and an FA Cup finalist.

In the same season that he played fullback for England vs. Ireland, the superbly bearded Fry was an ever-present member of the non-league Southampton side that reached the 1901–1902 final, only to lose to Sheffield United. He also played for Corinthians, during their reign as the greatest English amateur side of the late 1890s, and later turned out for Southampton's south coast rivals Portsmouth.

Claudio Gentile—Italy (born 1953)

Libyan born Gentile was a crucial element in the all-but-impenetrable Juventus defense of the 1970s, joining the team in 1973 following single seasons at Arona and Varese, and remaining with the Old Lady for eleven years, and 283 appearances. It was an era that saw Juventus, and Gentile, win six Serie A championships, two Coppa Italias, a UEFA Cup, and a Cup Winners Cup, while he was also a star of Italy's 1982 World Cup triumph. There, he all but marked Maradona out of the game, then compounded the little Argentinean's discomfort by remarking, "Football is not for ballerinas."

Gheorghe Hagi—Romania (born 1965)

"The Maradona of the Carpathians," Romanian-born Hagi never seemed to stay in one place for long, but wherever he played, he left an indelible mark. A career that took him from little Farul Constanta in 1982, to the giants of Steau Bucharest, Real Madrid, Brescia, Barcelona, and finally Galatasaray at the turn of the century, established him among Europe's most prolific goal-getters.

He is certainly the greatest player Romania has yet possessed—as he proved by leading his country to three World Cups, in 1990, 1994, and 1998, and three Euros, too (1986, 1996, and 2000). He ultimately made a record 125 appearances for his national team, scoring thirty-five goals in the process.

Zlatan Ibrahimović—Sweden (born 1981)

Messi, Ronaldo, Neymar, Van Persie, Balitelli, Suarez . . . a few days in the company of the accompanying media left most people convinced that the 2014 World Cup was positively littered with "the greatest players in history," and maybe it was, even if none of them felt like proving it. Even so, their preeminence was possible only because the one player who has habitually put them all to shame, season after season since the late 1990s, was not there.

To paraphrase the title of his brilliant autobiography, He is Zlatan. *Herbert Kratky/Shutterstock.com*

Swedish-born to Bosnian parents, Zlatan Ibrahimović launched his career at Malmö FC but it was clear, very early on, that the domestic scene was never going to hold him. There again, neither has any other—over the next decade or so, Zlatan turned out for Ajax in the Netherlands, Juventus, Inter and AC Milan in Italy, Barcelona in Spain, and Paris St. Germain in France, winning almost every trophy it was possible to reach for, and still critics and admirers alike insist that he has never yet shown his true majesty.

The most complete player of his generation has also become one of the most controversial, with a string of on- and off-field incidents ensuring that he is seldom far from a tabloid headline. Unlike so many of the modern game's other self- (or otherwise) styled *enfant terribles*, however, Zlatan's brilliance has played him out of trouble every time. Yes, it is true that he was unfortunate not to grace the World Cup finals. But not as unfortunate as the finals were, not to be graced by him.

Andrés Iniesta—Spain (born 1984)

Barcelona midfielder Iniesta made his debut for the side in 2002 and, by 2004, was a first-team regular. A considerably better-balanced performer than many of his teammates, notable for maintaining his work rate throughout a game, and not just popping up for a single moment of brilliance in an otherwise messy sea of gray anonymity, Iniesta has remained at the forefront of selection ever since, while his international career likewise reflected the glories that consumed Spanish soccer through the 2000s.

Milutin Ivkovic—Yugoslavia (1906–1943)

One of the great inter-war stars of the Yugoslav scene, first with SK Jugoslavija, and then BASK Belgrade, Ivokovic also shone in the national team as it marched to fourth place in the 1930 World Cup.

A solid defender, Ivkovic made his league debut for SK in November 1922, aged just sixteen, and within two years had established himself as a permanent fixture within the state championship–winning side of 1924 and 1925. His international debut followed in October 1925, against Czechoslovakia; Ivkovic would go on to make thirty-nine appearances over the next nine years for the national side, including nineteen as captain. He scored two goals during this period—and balanced them out with two own goals.

A qualified medical professional, Ivkovic continued to play soccer until 1938, when the death of his wife, Ella, forced him to abandon sport in order to bring up the couple's two daughters. He died in May 1943, murdered by the Nazis as a political activist.

Jairzinho—Brazil (born 1944)

"The Hurricane" is one of just two players in World Cup history to have scored in every round of the tournament, including the final—the other is Uruguay's 1950 World Cup winner Alcides Ghiggia. Brazil's 1970 World Cup triumph is, naturally, regarded as the summit of Jairzinho's international success. At club level, however, he was equally prodigious.

Over four hundred appearances for Botafago between 1959 and 1974 saw the rangy winger collect almost every national and regional trophy on offer, including two state championships. Ironically, however, it was not until the last days of his career, playing now for Cruzeiro, that he got his hands on the Copa Libertadores, in 1976.

By that time, Jairzinho had also tasted European soccer, via a short stint with Olympique de Marseille (1974–1975); later, in 1977, he would move abroad again, to join Venezuela's Portuguesa—at that time, the most potent club in the country, with three successive championships already under their belt. Jairzinho helped them to a fourth, before returning to Brazil to play out a few final seasons with small local sides. He retired in 1982, at which time the Brazilian FA recalled him to the national side for the first time in some eight years, for a farewell cap in a friendly with Czechoslovakia.

Alex James—Scotland (1901–1953)

Scotsman James was twenty-one when he made his debut for Raith Rovers, remaining with the Kirkcaldy kings for three years before moving to English side Preston North End in 1925. It was his transfer to Arsenal in 1929 that established him as a legend, however, a combative inside forward who developed one of the most perfect passing rates in the history of the game, within one of the most powerful sides the game has ever seen.

Cliff Jones—Wales (born 1935)

One of that tiny community of world-class Welsh soccer players who have actually been permitted to grace the World Cup with their talents, Cliff Jones was still playing with Swansea Town when he was called up for international duty at the 1958 tournament—his home country's first and, to date, last appearance on the biggest stage on earth.

He played in all five games as the Welsh marched into the quarterfinals (eclipsing both England and Scotland in the process) and upon his return to the UK, Tottenham Hotspur manager Bill Nicholson took him to London, an early ingredient in what would become the double-winning Spurs team of 1960–1961, the FA Cup–winning side of 1961–1962, and the European Cup Winners Cup holders of 1962–1963.

Mario Kempes—Argentina (born 1954)

"El Toro" was the only foreign-based player on the roster as Argentina got ready to host and win the 1978 World Cup; two seasons in Spain, at Valencia, had seen Kempes pick up precisely where he left off in Argentina (where he'd played with Rosario Central), by becoming top scorer in La Liga. Now he was to do the same at the World Cup, collecting both the Golden Ball and the Golden Boot as best player and highest goal scorer at the tournament.

After five seasons in Spain, Kempes returned to Argentina in 1981, to join River Plate. But he soon went back to Spain, rejoining Valencia for the 1982–1983 season. Thereafter he became something of a drifter, playing for the Spanish side Hercules, before moving on to teams in Austria, Chile, and Indonesia, where he played his final season, 1995–1996, alongside Roger Milla, Jules Onana, and sundry other pre-retirement legends, at Pelita Jaya FC.

Raymond Kopa—France (born 1931)

Di Stéfano and Puskás might have grabbed the headlines as Real Madrid dominated European soccer in the late 1950s, but it was Kopa, the French inside right, who opened so many of the doors for their magic.

Launching his career at Angers at the end of the 1940s, Kopa moved to Stade de Reims in 1951. A side already dignified by Just Fontaine promptly swept to a position of absolute dominance, winning the French league in 1953 and 1954, before marching to the inaugural European Cup final in 1956. There their progress was halted by Real Madrid, but not before the Spaniards noticed Kopa.

They signed him the following season and, over the next three years (until his return to Stade de Reims), Kopa collected three European Cups and two Spanish league titles, while also starring in the French side that finished third at the 1958 World Cup.

Back in France, he then picked up two more championships with Reims before bringing his playing career to a close in 1967.

Brian Laudrup—Denmark (born 1969)

Injury cruelly shortened Laudrup's career, while restlessness prevented him from ever making the impact that his talents demanded. Having remained at his first club, Brondby, from 1986–1989, he spent the next decade on the move, with stints at SC Bayer 05 Uerdingen, FC Bayern München, ACF Fiorentina, AC Milan, Glasgow Rangers, Chelsea, FC København (the club fomed in 1992 from the amalgamation of veteran powers KB København and B1903 København) and Ajax Amsterdam, with only Rangers hanging on to his mercurial talents for more than a season or two. He made 116 appearances for the Ibrox side, scoring thirty-three goals and giving Scotland a taste of the brilliance he otherwise seemed to reserve for the international scene.

Between 1987 and 1998, Laudrup appeared eighty-two times in the colors of his country, scoring twenty-two goals and peaking, perhaps, in that tremendous 1992 European Championships triumph—famously, Denmark had not even qualified for the tournament; they were called in at the last minute after Yugoslavia were disqualified.

With no preparation (several of the players were recalled from vacation), Denmark went all the way, and that despite a slow start in the group stage seeing them qualify in second place behind Sweden, with one win, one loss, and one draw.

In the semifinals, another draw, 2–2 with the much fancied Dutch, was resolved on penalties. But the final could scarcely have been more decisive, as Denmark dismantled the Germans 2–0, and opened the way for a virtual diaspora of Danish players (including Brian's brother Michael, and goalkeeper Peter Schmeichel) to the rich and powerful teams of Europe.

Three years later, Laudrup won the Golden Ball for best player at the 1995 Confederations Cup; his solo goal against Saudi Arabia often ranked among the finest ever scored in that competition, and well worth seeking out on YouTube. He was also a distinguished presence at the 1998 World Cup, scoring in the Danes's 4–1 win over Nigeria. Denmark's quarterfinal exit to Brazil marked Laudrup's final international.

Michael Laudrup—Denmark (born 1964)

In 1999, Danish-born midfielder Laudrup was voted the greatest foreign player to grace Spanish soccer in a quarter of a century, an indication of just how brilliant, and how influential, a footballer he was.

In a career that saw him turn out for both Barcelona (1989–1994) and Real Madrid (1994–1996), plus KB and Brondby in the early eighties at home, Lazio and Juventus during a six-year spell in Italy (1983–1989), and Ajax at the end of his career (1997–1998), Laudrup (alongside brother Brian) was also at the heart of the magnificent Danish national team of the 1984 Euros and 1986 World Cup . . . and the somewhat less than magnificent one that flopped so badly at the 1988 Euros.

Less memorably, he retired from international soccer on the eve of Denmark's greatest triumph, following disagreements with the coach. Thus he missed his country's last-minute invitation into the 1992 Euros, and its against-all-odds run to the final and to victory. Laudrup would return to the side thereafter, but their moment had gone.

Billy Liddell—Scotland (1922–2001)

With a career spent wholly in the red of Liverpool, and his record of appearances and goals both high in the club's hall of fame, Scotsman Liddell is rightly regarded among the greatest players ever to call Anfield home. And that despite World War Two devouring many of his best years.

Liddell joined Liverpool in July 1938, signing professional terms early the following year, and seeming set to graduate from the youth team in time for the 1939–1940 season. War saw that campaign cancelled, however, and while Liddell would turn out for Liverpool in the regional league competition that ran throughout the conflict, it was 1945–1946 before he made his official team debut.

The following season saw Liverpool win their first League championship; 1949–1950 took them to the FA Cup final. It would be another two decades before Liverpool became the all-conquering behemoth of today's hoary legend, but it was not through lack of effort on Liddell's part. Indeed, so often did he appear to be carrying his teammates that the side became popularly known as "Liddellpool."

The war also delayed the launch of Liddell's international career. However, his twenty-nine caps (plus eight wartime appearances) included scoring against England on his debut, and victory in the 1951 Home International championships. Incredibly, he was not included in Scotland's 1954 World Cup squad.

Roque Máspoli—Uruguay (1917–2004)

Long-serving goalkeeper for the Uruguayan giants of Nacional (1933–1939) and Club Atlético Peñarol (1940–1955), Máspoli was also his nation's goalkeeper throughout the triumphant 1950 World Cup campaign. His performance in the final, the 2–1 victory that stunned Brazil and much of the watching world, is still reckoned among the finest displays of goalkeeping in Uruguayan soccer history.

The depth of Máspoli's knowledge, and the respect with which he was regarded, saw him launch a very successful coaching career following his retirement from playing. At Club Atlético Peñarol, the five national championships he won as manager made a perfect addition to the six he won as a player; while he would also become the oldest man ever to manage a major national side, when he took control of Uruguay (for the second time) at age eighty.

Ladislao Mazurkiewicz—Uruguay (1945–2013)

One of the all-time legends of Latin American goalkeeping, Mazurkiewicz was born in Uruguay to a Spanish mother and Polish father. A twenty-year career seldom took him far from Montevideo, with his years of greatest impact certainly those that he spent with Club Atlético Peñarol, 1964–1971. Although he would also enjoy some success with the Brazilian side Atlético Mineiro, and América de Cali of Colombia, it is for his exploits in the gold and black of the Sunflowers that he lives on in the collective memory.

That, and his heroics at the 1970 World Cup, marshaling his home nation from the back and seeing them through to the semifinal where, finally, Brazil halted their progress. In an international career that stretched between 1965 and 1974, Mazurkieicz won thirty-six Uruguayan caps.

Billy Meredith—Wales (1874–1958)

Already an established international, and two years past his thirtieth birthday too, the Welsh wizard was a familiar figure on the playing fields of Cottonopolis when he joined Manchester United in 1906; familiar and controversial.

Not content with constantly agitating for the creation of a players' union, much to the distaste of the English soccer authorities, Meredith was also serving a season-long ban at the time, after being accused of attempting to bribe an opposition player—on the orders, he insisted, of his manager.

He swiftly placed the unpleasantness behind him, however, leading United to their first FA Cup and League championship triumphs, in 1908–1909 and 1910–1911 respectively, the latter their first season at their newly opened show-piece stadium Old Trafford. Although his career, like everybody else's, was interrupted by the Great War, Meredith remained at United until 1921. Having established himself as the oldest player ever to turn out for the side (at 46 years, 281 days), he moved on.

Photographs offer us just a glimpse of Meredith in his pomp, a wiry, fierce-looking man with a mad gleam in his eye and a matchstick in his mouth, and that is when he is simply posing for the camera. What he must have looked like bearing down on goal, leaving defenders and even his own teammates in his wake, can only be imagined. But a league career total of 169 goals in 681 games tells its own story, while forty-eight appearances for Wales in an age when only England, Scotland, and Ireland offered them any regular opposition, is further testament to his longevity. A quarter of a century divided Meredith's first international from his last.

Roger Milla—Cameroon (born 1952)

The oldest goal scorer in World Cup history, Milla had already retired from international soccer (in 1987), when he was called up (by the country's prime minister!) for Cameroon's 1990 World Cup campaign. He led them to the quarterfinals, the first African nation to advance so far, and in the twilight of his career, Milla became an international superstar.

He had been an African legend for years beforehand, however, a star of the Léopards Douala side that won three successive league championships between 1972 and 1974, before moving to Tonnerre and inspiring them to the African Cup Winners Cup.

In 1977, Milla moved to France with Valenciennes, later moving to AS Monaco. Neither club seemed to know what to do with him; it took until 1980 before he became a team regular, first at Bastia (113 appearances, 1980–1984), and then AS Saint-Étienne (fifty-nine appearances, 1984–1986) and Montpellier HSC (ninety-five appearances, 1986–1989). Milla retired from French soccer in 1990, joining Montpellier's coaching staff.

Italia 1990 brought him back into action, and Milla ultimately continued playing for his country for another four years, while his club career continued on, Milla finally bowing out in 1996 following a stint with Putra Samarinda Football Club of Indonesia.

Bobby Moore—England (1941–1993)

Billy Wright was the first England player to pass one hundred international caps, Bobby Charlton was the second, and Bobby Moore was the third. Captain of England that eventful afternoon in 1966 when the World Cup was won, Moore also led West Ham United through the period when they were rightfully regarded as the Academy of Soccer, a skillful side who might not have won as many trophies as other teams, but who played according to a set of standards that others could only aspire to.

Three members of that World Cup winning team were Hammers, as Moore was joined by Geoff Hurst and Martin Peters. And it escaped nobody's attention that the latter pair were also England's goal scorers in the 4–2 win.

At club level, Moore collected winner's medals in the International Soccer League (1963), FA Cup (1963–1964) and the European Cup Winners Cup the following season; he was the Football Writer Association's player of the year in 1964 and in 1970, runner-up for the European Player of the Year.

Despite all this, he left West Ham in 1974, after 544 appearances, and enjoyed a second summer with Fulham, whom he led to the 1975 FA Cup final (where, ironically, they lost to West Ham). He also played several seasons in the United States, with San Antonio Thunder in 1976 and the Seattle Sounders in 1978. That same year, he joined the Danish side Herning Fremad, his recruitment part of a campaign promoting the national league's transition to professionalism.

Short-lived spells as manager of the Hong Kong side Eastern AA and, back home, Southend United marked the end of Moore's active involvement in soccer. Following his death from colon cancer in 1993, rumor and report alike castigated both West Ham and the English FA for their virtual shunning of Moore following his retirement, and it is true that were Moore to have retired from playing today, he would not be able to move for proffered ambassadorial and spokesperson roles. Back then, he was simply left to his own devices and, sadly, they weren't enough.

Alan Morton—Scotland (1893–1971)

The diminutive Morton launched his career with Queen's Park before joining Glasgow Rangers in 1920, as newly appointed manager Bill Struth set about creating the team that would take the Scottish championship nine times across the next decade. (Morton was, in fact, Struth's first signing.) He was also an international regular, his thirty-one Scottish caps including a starring role in the 5–1 demolition of England in 1928, which earned him the nickname "the Wembley Wizard."

Gerd Müller (born 1945)

The most prolific goal scorer ever to grace the Bundesliga, with 365 goals in 427 games, Müller holds a similar record in European club soccer (sixty-six in seventy-four games). He scored ten goals in the 1970 World Cup, and it was June 2014 before his tally of sixty-eight goals for the national side was overtaken by Miroslav Klose, albeit after more than twice as many games. Müller reached his total in sixty-two games, Klose in a staggering 133. As a well-respected England player once remarked after one of his personal records was broken, "anyone can hit a barn door if they're given enough free throws at it."

Small wonder that Müller's countrymen referred to him as "der Bomber"—at least when they weren't echoing the words of his first-ever coach, and affectionately referring to him as *kleines und dickes* . . . "short and fat." Because even in his pomp, Müller never really looked like a classic goal scorer. Maybe that was why he was so dangerous.

Müller was just sixteen when FC Bayern München first sighted him playing for TSV 1861 Norlingen, where he was averaging almost two goals a game; he joined the big city club in 1963 and remained there until the end of the 1970s brought him a golden retirement with the Fort Lauderdale Strikers.

In between times, both Bayern and the West German national side won everything worth winning, including the 1972 Euros and 1974 World Cup, and a hat trick of European Cups between 1974 and 1976. To which can be added four Bundesliga titles and a European Cup Winners Cup, while Müller personally received two German Footballer of the Year awards and the 1970 European Player of the Year. And he was still topping the Bundesliga's scoring lists at the end of his career, in 1978.

Alessandro Nesta—Italy (born 1976)

Four-time Serie A Defender of the Year, Nesta first came to attention as a teenager with Lazio in 1993. He remained there until 2002 when the club's financial problems forced his transfer to AC Milan. He also made seventy-eight international appearances between 1996 and 2006. Following his departure from Milan, he joined MLS side Montreal Impact.

Branko Oblak—Yugoslavia (born 1947)

Midfield maestro Oblak made his debut for NK Olimpija Ljubljana in 1966, scoring twice in a 2–1 win over Partizan Belgrade, and setting the stage for a dazzling career; 181 games with Olimpija preceded two years at Hajduk Split, 1973–1975, both distinguished by league and Cup doubles. Hajduk retained the Cup for the two following seasons, but Oblak moved on, joining West German side Schalke 04 in 1975 and FC Bayern München in 1977. There he won another national title, in 1979.

Oblak made forty-six appearances for the Yugoslavian national side, including the 1974 World Cup.

Antonín Panenka—Czechoslovakia (born 1948)

A member of the Czech side that so impressively won the 1976 European Championships, and finished third in the 1980 tournament, Panenka is one of the few men to have a style of penalty named after him, the soft chip straight down the middle that proved so decisive against West Germany in the 1976 final.

The bulk of Panenka's playing career was spent with just two clubs, Bohemians of Prague (1967–1981) and the Austrian outfit Rapid Wien (1981–1985).

Daniel Passarella—Argentina (born 1953)

Until Dutchman Ronald Koeman finally broke the record, Argentinean Passarella was the highest-scoring defender in soccer history, a center back who was a vital component in, and captain of, his homeland's 1978 World Cup winning side. A stalwart both at home (two stints with River Plate, in the seventies and late eighties) and in Italy, where he enjoyed spells with Fiorentina and Inter, Passarella was a logical inclusion within FIFA's Top 125 Living Players poll in 2004.

Adolfo Pedernera—Argentina (1918–1995)

Having made his first team debut at the age of sixteen, in 1935, "El Maestro" was a member of the near invincible River Plate side of the late 1930s, Argentinean champions five times in a decade, and two-times Copa America winners, too. World War Two kept Pedernera from truly shining on the international stage, but he continued playing into his thirties, including a stint as player-manager of the high-rolling Millonarios of Colombia.

Michel Platini—France (born 1955)

The current President of UEFA, a three-times winner of the FIFA Ballon d'Or, and one of the most lethal free-kick specialists that French soccer ever hatched, Platini spent the majority of his playing career at Nancy, the unfashionable French side with whom he suffered both the joys and pains of a career in soccer—relegation in 1974, a French Cup win in 1978. He was never a lucky player, though; frequently dogged by injury, he was also scapegoated by French supporters following the national team's less-than-brilliant performance at the 1978 World Cup.

In 1979, Platini moved to Saint-Étienne, with whom he won the league but lost two Cup finals; it was only after he moved to Italy, to Juventus in 1982, that the world can be said to have seen the true Platini. Three years in succession, his goals established him as the top scorer in Serie A; three times, too, he was European Footballer of the Year. He captained France at the 1984 Euros, and while many observers found it tough to say exactly what Platini's greatest talent was, what made him such an influential and exciting player, few would argue with Pelé when he said, "I liked how he was the brain organizing things on the pitch.

"He was a player who used his head in the broader sense. The way he shone with France and Juventus, and his capacity for taking free-kicks, made him *the* European footballer of the 1980s."

Tab Ramos—United States (born 1966)

Uruguayan-born Ramos grew up in New Jersey (his family relocated to the US when he was eleven); as a teen he played alongside John Harkes in the youth club side Thistle FC. He was also a two-time high school All-America and, in 1983, playing for New Jersey state champions St. Benedict, he became *Parade* magazine's National High School Player of the Year. The following year, he was drafted by the New York Cosmos, in the final year of the NASL, but elected to attend college instead.

A US citizen since 1982, Ramos was on the US Olympic soccer team in 1988; that same season he joined ASL side New Jersey Eagles. The following season he spent at the Miami Sharks, before becoming one of several players who agreed to place club soccer on hold and sign directly to the USSF, in the run-up to the 1990 World Cup.

Returning home following the tournament, Ramos joined the Spanish side UE Figueres on loan, before signing directly in 1991. He also played for Real Betis during his time in Spain.

A fractured skull sustained during the last-sixteen game with Brazil at the 1994 World Cup slowed Ramos's career somewhat; however, he played two mid-nineties seasons with Mexico's Tigres, including their championship-winning 1995–1996 campaign. He also joined the newly founded Metrostars in time for the first season of MLS action, and would remain with the New Jersey franchise for seven seasons, earning All Star honors in 1996, 1998, and 1999.

In 1998, Ramos became one of the first US players ever to appear at three World Cups, and he remained an international regular until 2000, collecting his eighty-first and final cap in the 4–0 win over Barbados that November. He retired from club soccer in 2002, and moved into coaching; he was US coach Jurgen Klinsmann's assistant at the 2014 World Cup.

Vasily Rats—Ukraine (born 1961)

In a career that amassed forty-seven caps for the USSR between 1986 and 1990, Vasyl "Vasily" Rats is probably best remembered for one piece of absolute magic, a 1986 World Cup goal hit on the volley from some twenty-seven meters out, straight into the top left-hand corner of the French goal, while the keeper (named, with such poetic irony, Bats) simply watched in astonishment. Bookmark it on YouTube; you'll want to watch it again and again.

A lethal goal scorer for both the USSR and club side Dynamo Kyiv, Rats was a three- time league champion with the Ukrainian giants; a three-time Soviet Cup winner; and a 1986 Cup Winners Cup champion too. In 1989, however, he joined the exodus of Kyiv teammates who moved to Europe following the collapse of Communism, breaking up a side that many believed had still to reach its peak. Rats joined Spain's RCD Espanyol, but a short, unhappy stay saw him make just ten appearances before returning to the Ukraine, and then wrapping up his playing days with the Hungarian side Ferencvárosi.

Antonio Rattin—Argentina (born 1937)

It is unfortunate that, to most English-speaking fans, Argentinean Rattin is best remembered for sparking a near riot during his country's 1966 World Cup quarterfinal match with England.

Sent off for allegedly swearing at the referee (despite Rattin speaking no German, and the ref speaking no Spanish), Rattin refused to leave the field to protest what he saw as an unfair bias against his side. He was finally escorted from the field by two policemen, leaving England manager Alf Ramsey to condemn the Argentineans as "animals."

The controversy completely overshadowed (again, in English-speaking lands) a magnificent career. The archetypal one-club player, and the archetypal number five too, Rattin remained with Boca Juniors his entire playing career, 1956–1970, making 352 appearances before moving into coaching, again at Boca. His international career saw him collect thirty-four caps (and score one goal), but again it is the events of 1966 that saw Rattin make his greatest mark on the game.

After witnessing the confusion surrounding Rattin's dismissal, referee Ken Aston had the brainwave that resulted in the introduction of yellow and red cards.

Bryan Robson—England (born 1957)

But for an appalling record of injuries, England's Captain Marvel might claim a place among the greatest players of his generation; but for an accident of timing, he might rate among the most decorated. A distinctive forward at his first club, West Bromwich Albion, Robson followed manager Ron Atkinson to Manchester United in 1981, where he became the longest-serving captain in the club's history. Atkinson's reign, however, was distinguished by just two FA Cup wins, in 1982–1983 and 1984–1985; and the incoming Alex Ferguson required some three years before he discovered the winning touch, by which time age and injury were both against Robson.

Nevertheless, he collected a third FA Cup (1989–1990), the Cup Winners Cup (1990–1991), UEFA Super Cup (1991), and League Cup (1991–1992), together with United's first two Premier League titles (1992–1993, 1993–1994), before he moved into management at Middlesbrough. Still, many observers have wondered just how much higher Robson might have flown had Ferguson's alchemy only matured a few years sooner.

Robson's talismanic effect was never in doubt; United began the 1985–1986 season with ten successive wins and the title surely in their sights—then Robson was injured, and they fell to fourth. Injury also forced him out of the 1986 World Cup after just two games, depriving manager Bobby Robson of the player he considered the best in England. Indeed, but for his regular visits to the treatment room, Robson would certainly have joined Billy Wright and the Bobbys Charlton and Moore among the select handful of players to have earned (and deserved) one hundred or more English caps; in the event, he stalled, in 1991, at ninety.

Cristiano Ronaldo—Portugal (born 1985)

Ronaldo's name and reputation were already on everyone's lips as an upcoming legend when he was taken to Manchester United in 2003, a precocious teenager whose earliest performances were marked (some say marred) by his insistence on showing off his remarkable ball control skills, often for no apparent reason but to humiliate a less gifted opponent.

Overcoming that tendency, he became a crucial member of the United side of the mid-late 2000s, and in 2007 Ronaldo became the first player in England to win all four Professional Footballers Association and Football Writers Association awards, for youth and adult players, in the same season. The following year, he won FIFA's FIFA Ballon d'Or for the first time, while his overall club honors at Old Trafford included three Premier League titles, two Football League Cups, one FA Cup, and the 2007–2008 Champions League.

Ronaldo joined Real Madrid in 2009 for a then-record £80 million ($135,022,800). Since then the honors have only continued accumulating; at the time of writing, he has collected two Copa del Reys, one La Liga, one Spanish Super Cup, and one Champions League. In addition, and despite a less-than-stellar 2014 World Cup, there are many observers for whom only Zlatan Ibrahimović and Lionel Messi rival Ronaldo for the title of the today's most gifted soccer player.

Nestor Rossi—Argentina (1925–2007)

One of *the* great Argentinean midfielders, Rossi's career with River Plate at home, and Millonarios of Columbia, saw him become one of the most decorated players of the 1940s and 1950s, long before the 1958 World Cup finally and so belatedly introduced him to European observers.

Five Argentine and six Colombian league championships join two Copa Americas and, wryly, the Little World Cup on Rossi's trophy cabinet, the latter an earlier forebear of the Intercontinental Cup, featuring four sides apiece from Europe and Latin America.

Hugo Sánchez—Mexico (born 1958)

A 1976 soccer Olympian, Sánchez was the undisputed star of Mexican champions UNAM throughout the late 1970s and early 1980s; a brilliant presence, too, on the NASL scene as he turned out for San Diego Sockers in the 1979 and 1980 seasons, and banged home twenty-six goals in just thirty-two games.

Atlético Madrid was the first major European side to move for him, taking Sánchez to Spain in 1981. He remained with Atlético for five years, and in Madrid for seven more, as he moved to Real in 1985. The team won five successive La Ligas; the goal-hungry Sánchez alone won four consecutive Pichichi trophies, and the European Golden Boot in 1989–1990. He returned to Mexico in 1992 and promptly led Club América to the CONCACAF Champions Cup.

Anton Schall—Austria (1907–1947)

One of the legends of Austrian soccer, "Toni" Schall was a devastatingly effective winger for both his club side, Admira Wacker, and for the national team, for whom he appeared in twenty-eight matches.

Schall was a member of the 1934 World Cup squad, but his international career was hampered by his homeland's absorption into Germany in 1938, precluding Austrian participation in the 1938 World Cup. Following his retirement from playing, Schall became manager of the Swiss side FC Basel, where he died aged just forty.

Salvatore Schillaci—Italy (born 1964)

Having spent most of the 1980s at Messina, a generally mid-table team in Serie A, "Totò" Schillaci was among the earliest recruits to Juventus following the installation of Dino Zoff as manager.

A well-regarded but scarcely headline-grabbing player, with a goal average of one every three-or-so games, his inclusion in Italy's 1990 World Cup squad likewise passed many observers by. It was his first international call-up, and he would not, in truth, enjoy a long international career—by the time of the 1992 Euros, he had again fallen out of favor.

But, from the moment he was substituted onto the field during Italy's first World Cup game against Austria, and scored the goal that broke a dreadful deadlock, Schillaci became a hero . . . a folk hero . . . and not only for his countrymen. Recipient of the Golden Boot as the 1990 World Cup's highest goal scorer (albeit with just six), he also received the Golden Ball, for the best player. But he was also the face of the games, his so-distinctive wild eyes and manic grin outranking even Paul Gascoigne's tears in terms of tournament iconography.

It is an honor he still celebrates. "The eyes, the eyes. Every time I meet people they always want me to do the 'wild eyes,'" Schillaci told the BBC in 2014. "It was an instinctive gesture that has stuck in people's minds, and I have done it many, many times." But goal scoring, too, was instinctive and he did that many times as well—although arguably, his best days were already behind him by the time the world caught up with him. One more season at Juventus was followed by an injury-plagued spell at Inter, and Totò wound up his career in the J-League in Japan.

Albert Shesternyov—USSR (1941–1994)

"Ivan the Terrible" was the all-but-unpassable obstacle at the heart of the defense for both CSKA Moscow and the USSR national side during the 1960s. Earning ninety international caps, many of them as team captain, Shesternyov starred at three World Cups and two European Championships, but honors were thin on the ground; he retired immediately after leading CSKA to their first league championship (and collecting the Soviet Footballer of the Year award) in 1970.

Andriy Shevchenko—Ukraine (born 1976)

One of the leading goal scorers in Champions League history, Ukrainian Shevchenko was a youth player at Dynamo Kyiv before graduating to the first team in 1994. A natural goal scorer, his sixty strikes in 117 games (and Kyiv's run of five successive championships) led to his move to AC Milan in 1999, where he remained deadly—127 goals in 208 appearances.

An ill-starred move to Chelsea dampened his prowess somewhat, as did an unsuccessful loan spell back at Milan. He had not lost his predatory instincts, however, as he proved upon his return to Dynamo Kyiv in 2009. In fifty-five appearances, he scored twenty-three times.

Shevchenko was similarly lethal in the international scene (111 appearances, forty-eight goals), while six Ukrainian Player of the Year awards, one Serie A

Foreign Footballer of the Year title, and the 2004 FIFA Ballon d'Or further testify to his impact.

Allan Simonsen—Denmark (born 1952)

Honors came early to Simonsen, a star in the Vejle BK youth setup through the 1960s, before moving up to the first team in time for their 1971 Danish championship–winning season. The following year, VB won the domestic double, but it was Simonsen's performance at the 1972 Olympics that took him to Borussia Mönchengladbach, with whom he won the Bundesliga and UEFA Cup in 1974–1975 and the Bundesliga again in 1975–1976 and 1976–1977. He also scored his side's only goal in their 3–1 defeat to Liverpool in the European Cup final, and the winning goal in the 1978–1979 UEFA Cup final.

European Footballer of the Year in 1977, Simonsen moved to Barcelona in 1979; then briefly, English second-tier side Charlton Athletic in 1982, the latter in protest at Spanish league regulations that restricted teams to playing just two non-Spanish players per game; Simonsen was competing with Diego Maradona for his place.

Charlton's financial problems, however, saw him return to Denmark after just sixteen appearances (and nine goals), where he rejoined VB for the last six years of his playing career. He later became the club's manager (1991–1994) before taking charge of the Faroe Islands (1994–2001) and Luxembourg (2001–2004) national teams.

A member of the fabulous Danish international side of the early 1980s, Simonsen scored twenty goals in fifty-five appearances.

Alberto Spencer—Uruguay (1937–2006)

Ecuadorian-born son of a Jamaican father, Spencer spent the bulk of his career in Uruguay, a star of the great Club Atlético Peñarol team of the 1960s, with whom he won the Copa Liberatadores three times. His record of fifty-four goals in that tournament has still to be beaten, while Spencer is also notable for having played internationally for both Ecuador and Uruguay, scoring goals for both.

Hristo Stoichkov—Bulgaria (born 1966)

At CSKA Sofia, in his native Bulgaria, he was known as "the dagger." At Barcelona, where he moved in 1990, he became "the gunslinger." Not bad for a player who, back in 1985, received a lifetime ban from soccer after getting into a fight at the Bulgarian Cup final. The suspension was ultimately scaled back to a mere month, and Stoichkov was on his way to immortality.

CSKA won three league titles and four Bulgarian Cups under his leadership; Barcelona won five La Ligas, including their fabled four in a row, between 1990 and 1993, together with three Spanish Super Cups, one European Cup, and a Cup Winners Cup. And Bulgaria, hitherto regarded as one of the lesser lights of international soccer, took fourth place at the 1994 World Cup, with Stoichkov emerging the tournament's joint top scorer.

Stoichkov returned to CSKA following his Barcelona years, then moved into retirement via spells with clubs in Saudi Arabia, Japan, and the US (the Chicago Fire and DC United). He then shifted into management and today, once again, he leads CSKA.

Davor Šuker—Croatia (born 1968)

Newly signed from his first club, and hometown side Osijek, Šuker had just begun making his mark on the great Dinamo Zagreb side of the late 1980s and early 1990s when war shattered his homeland.

A fringe player with the Yugoslavian squad as a teen, Šuker then lined up for Croatia at their first-ever international, an unofficial friendly against Romania in December 1990, while also winning two Yugoslav caps in 1991.

After two seasons during which his strike rate of thirty-four goals in sixty games brought him attention from across Europe, he signed with the Spanish club Sevilla in 1991, rapidly establishing himself among the most prolific marksmen around, both domestically and internationally. As Croatia marched into the 1996 Euros, Šuker scored a record-breaking twelve goals in ten qualifying matches, followed by three more in the final competition itself.

He moved to Real Madrid in 1996, where his free-scoring escapades saw him ranked the league's third highest scorer, while helping power his club to the championship. The Champions League followed, while the 1998 World Cup saw the Šuker-powered Croatia upset all predictions by coming within inches of an appearance in the final. They ultimately finished third, with Šuker scoring the winning goal in the decisive play-off with the Netherlands.

Following one further season in Spain, Šuker moved to England, first to Arsenal, and then West Ham. He wound down his playing career in Germany with two seasons (2000–2002) at TSV 1860 München. Today, he is President of the Croatian FA.

Alberto Tarantini—Argentina (born 1955)

Fiery Argentinean Tarantini was one of the first South American players to be transferred to the UK, when he joined Birmingham City following the 1978 World Cup.

His career there was dogged by ill discipline, but on either side of the adventure, he starred with Boca Juniors (for whom he played 179 times), River Plate, and, back in Europe, Toulouse. He made sixty-one international appearances, including the 1982 World Cup.

Carlos Valderrama—Columbia (born 1961)

His crazy blond afro was probably most people's first impression of *El Pibe*, the whirlwind of dramatic flamboyance at the heart of Columbia's 1994 World Cup side. By that time, however, Valderrama had already made his mark on both Colombian soccer (stints with Millonarios and Deportivo Cali) and the French scene—he played for Montpelier between 1988 and 1991, before returning to Colombia and guiding Atlético Junior to the championship in both 1993 and 1995.

He then relocated to the US, for spells with the Tampa Bay Rowdies, Miami Fusion, and Colorado Rapids. He retired from playing in 2004, and moved into management.

Berti Vogts—Germany (born 1946)

The future coach of both West and unified Germany, Kuwait, Scotland, Nigeria, and Azebaijan, a World Cup winner in 1990 and special advisor to the United States side for the 2014 World Cup, Bertie Vogts is often regarded today as a manager who used to be a player.

In fact, the opposite is just as accurate. Across a fourteen-year career spent wholly with Borussia Mönchengladbach, for whom he made 419 appearances, Vogts had defensive instincts that were at the heart of his side's magnificence throughout the 1970s—five-time Bundesliga champions, twice UEFA Cup winners, one-time German Cup holders, and 1977 European Cup finalists. His ninety-six international appearances include the 1974 World Cup victory.

Billy Wright—England (1924–1994)

Billy Wright was British soccer's first modern superstar, even as he upheld the increasingly unfashionable tradition of devoting his entire career to one club, at a time when that club was, at worst, the second best in the country—only the Busby Babes up in Manchester could rival Wright's Wolverhampton Wanderers.

But whereas United was still a glorious work in progress, Wolves was the finished article, league champions thrice in six years, FA Cup winners in 1949, and all of it accomplished under the imperious gaze of club captain Wright.

His qualities of discipline, skill, and gentlemanly behavior spread to the England side as well, as befits the first player ever to represent the country one hundred times. And there was glamor, too, as he married Joy Beverley, a member of the singing sensations the Beverley Sisters. At a time when the worlds of sport and entertainment could scarcely have existed further apart, their union was headline news, even as Wright refused to allow the razzmatazz to distract him from his career.

In 1954, shortly after Hungary taught England a footballing lesson both home and away, the Magnificent Magyars' top team, Honvéd, played Wolves in one of a series of games designed to inaugurate the English team's newly acquired floodlights.

With a brilliance that absolutely befits a nation that calls soccer "labdarúgás," Honvéd raced into what might have been an unassailable 2–0 lead . . . only to wind up losing 3–2 and seething quietly as Wolves manager Cullis dubbed his captain, and his team, the true "champions of the world." It was a boast that so enraged sundry Europeans that it was almost directly responsible for the birth of the European Cup.

Hanging up his boots in 1959, having made 490 appearances, Wright moved into management, taking care of the England Youth Team until 1962, when he was appointed manager of Arsenal. There he fashioned a side in his own swash-buckling image, a fabulously flowing creation built around some of the most breathtaking players of the age, wingers Alan Skirton and Geordie Armstrong, inside forwards George Eastham and Geoff Strong, and the magnificently marauding Joe Baker.

It was not a good match, however. So fluent in attack, Wright's Arsenal was considerably less convincing at the rear. Having steered the side into Europe for the first time during his maiden season, Wright was unable to improve on that initial showing and was sacked in 1966. He moved into television, but retained his ties with Wolves, joining the board of directors. Following his death, his ashes were scattered on the pitch, and visitors to Molineux Stadium today are greeted with a statue of Wright.

Eric Wynalda—United States (born 1969)

Fullerton-born Wynalda initially impressed in local, California youth soccer—as a striker with the Westlake Wolves, one season saw him score more goals (fifty-eight in sixteen games) than every other player in the league combined. He continued playing through high school and college, a star with the San Diego State University's Aztecs side through the late 1980s, and he signed professional terms with the USSF in 1990, shortly before becoming one of the (admittedly under-stated) stars of the United States' World Cup campaign. He won his first cap against Costa Rica in February that year; his World Cup, however, was marred by his receiving a red card during the opening game with Czechoslovakia.

In 1992, Wynalda joined the German side FC Saarbrücken, initially on loan before the 2. Bundesliga side purchased him outright for $405,000. Voted Best Newcomer of the Year in 1992–1993, and Player of the Year the season after, Wynalda also played for VfL Bochum before returning to the US in 1996 and leading the San José Clash into the first season of MLS soccer. Indeed, Wynalda scored the first-ever MLS goal, and ended the season as the US Soccer Athlete of the Year.

He shone at the 1994 and 1998 World Cups, becoming one of just three US players (alongside Tab Ramos and Marcelo Balboa) to appear at three World Cups; until 2007, Wynalda was the US national side's all-time leading scorer, with thirty-four goals in 106 appearances.

The last years of Wynalda's career were marred by injury, and he retired in 2002, to move very successfully into sports broadcasting.

Lev Yashin—USSR (1929–1990)

The Black Spider is the father of modern goalkeeping—the first custodian to truly take control of the game; to shout orders to his teammates; and to marshall his defense, he was also the first to realize there was nothing in the rules to prevent him from leaving his goal mouth to close down attacks wherever they might materialize. The 1958 World Cup, the first to be widely broadcast on television, created many heroes. In Yashin, it created a revolutionary.

His approach was no surprise to his native Soviets, of course; they had been enjoying Yashin's approach, and antics, since he first appeared on the domestic scene in 1950 with Dynamo Moscow. His international debut followed in 1954, and he remained a regular for both sides until his retirement in 1970.

The first goalkeeper ever to receive the FIFA Ballon d'Or and the European Footballer of the Year award (in 1963), Yashin was the USSR Goalkeeper of the Year in 1960, 1963, and 1966, while his most impressive statistics include over 150 penalty saves, and a record of keeping a clean sheet in approximately one-third of the games he played.

It is only fitting that, since 1994, the best goalkeeper at the World Cup finals should be awarded the Lev Yashin Trophy.

Ricardo Zamora—Spain (1901–1978)

Honored today by the goalkeeping trophy that bears his name, Ricardo Zamora—el Divino—was one of the most distinctive custodians ever to wear the white of Real Madrid, a three-packs-of-cigarettes-a-day man who disdained his club's regulation gear for a white polo neck and a cloth cap; and who once played on in an international (Spain vs. England in 1929) despite having broken his sternum.

Born in Barcelona, the young Zamora built his reputation for skill, daring, and a certain foolhardiness at RCD Espanyol, the dominant force in the regional Campionat de Catalunya championships. An argument with a club director saw him defect to Barcelona, but 1922 took him back to RCD Espanyol, where he remained until the end of the decade. He also became a regular in the newly founded Spanish national team, appearing in its first-ever international in 1920, and still onboard at the 1934 World Cup. He also represented the unofficial Catalan XI at a number of matches during the 1920s.

Zamora joined Real in 1930, the second season of the newly launched La Liga national championship; the Spanish Civil War, however, saw him arrested and imprisoned by the Republicans (and, on several occasions, reported dead) and only the intercession of the Argentine embassy won his release. Zamora fled to France and played for some time with OGC Nice. He returned to Spain in 1938 and moved into coaching and management.

Branko Zebec—Yugoslavia (1929–1988)

A superstar at home, where his club side, Partizan Belgrade, won the Yugoslavian Cup in his first full season, 1951–1952, then followed through with similar triumphs in 1954 and 1957; a hero, too, for his exploits with Red Star Belgrade, whom he joined for their 1960 championship-winning season; Zebec's greatest impact was nevertheless on the international scene.

Ultimately reaching the quarterfinals, Yugoslavia were a devastatingly attractive side at the 1954 World Cup, with Zebec earning international plaudits with a stunning goal against Brazil in the group stage. Four years later, with Zebec now the team captain, Yugoslavia were again unlucky to meet the Germans in the final eight. Zebec ultimately represented his country on sixty-five occasions.

Mustapha Zitouni—France (1928–2014)

Di Stéfano described him as one of the finest defenders he ever faced, and when Zitouni turned out for the French national side—which he did on four occasions in the run-up to the 1958 World Cup—he was odds on to make the squad for the big event. Instead, the Algerian-born Olympique de Marseille (and, before that, Stade Français FC and AS Cannes) star retired from French soccer, to form an unofficial side to represent his homeland's political aspirations.

A French colony at the time, Algeria was moving only slowly (and painfully) toward independence. Zitouni's National Liberation Front side played games around the world to draw attention and publicity for the cause; and five years later, with independence achieved, Zitouni remained in Algeria, playing for the club side RC Kouba, and winning seven caps for the newborn national side.

Dino Zoff—Italy (born 1942)

The first goalkeeper ever to captain a World Cup–winning side (Italy in 1982), and the oldest player ever to appear in one as well, Zoff is ranked behind Gordon Banks and Lev Yashin alone in any reasonable poll of the world's greatest custodians, and in statistical terms he might even eclipse them. Between 1972 and 1974, at the very peak of his playing powers, Zoff went 1,142 minutes without conceding a goal, a record that still stands today.

Zoff's earliest experiences of the professional game were dispiriting; both Inter and Juventus rejected him for being too short. Of course he is in good company there—Lionel Messi suffered a similar fate. But whereas Messi's growth was encouraged with hormone injections into the feet, Zoff allowed nature to take its course, sprouting thirteen inches in five years and making his Serie A debut for Udinese in 1961.

From there, he moved to Mantova, remaining there until 1967; Napoli until 1972 and finally to Juventus, where he was to play out the remainder of his career. By the time Zoff retired in 1983, he had made 642 appearances in Serie A, with 330 of them for the Old Lady—to whom he would return in 1988, as manager.

10

The Unfathomable Joy of Being the Underdog

Does Everybody Really Love a Winner?

ccording to statistics delivered in 2013 by the German company Sport+Markt, Manchester United are the best-supported club in the world.

Juventus boast 20 million fans; FC Bayern München have 24 million; Inter Milan 49 million; Liverpool 71 million; AC Milan 99 million; Arsenal 113 million; Chelsea 135 million; Real Madrid 174 million; and Barcelona 270 million. But United are streets ahead of them all, with an eye-watering 354 million people who claim . . . well, they probably don't *all* have "Red Til I'm Dead" tattooed on their hearts. But a few probably do. Or would like to, anyway.

The thing is, while all of this is very impressive, it tells only half of the story. For, no matter how many people claim to actively wave their arms and chant "ra-ra-ra" whenever Manchester United (or any of the other teams on the list) are mentioned . . . there are a lot more who don't.

It may not be an active hatred, although a lot of supporters, when asked about their hopes for a forthcoming trophy, will reply with a heartfelt "Anyone But [whoever]." It may not even be a conscious dislike. But nothing breeds ennui so quickly as seeing the same team take the honors every season, and when a new season kicks off and we pledge our allegiance afresh to our team, there are far many more millions who do *not* swear an oath to Bayern, Real, AC, Juve, or United, than do. Many, many more.

There are as many reasons for disliking or dismissing another team as there are for having your own favorites to begin with, and all of them are equally personal. Some might be so longstanding that one cannot even remember where the ambivalence began (if you even have the energy to care); others might be predicated wholly on the fortunes of your own team in any given week. "If Rovers win and United draw and City are crushed 8–0 before being eaten by bears on their way home, then [insert your team here] might possibly have a chance of reaching the play-offs." And some are so random that simply the wrong combination of letters in their name, or a never-forgotten glimpse of a mid-seventies

Manchester United moved into stately Old Trafford less than a decade after changing their name from Newton Heath. This photo dates from 1981, but it's still recognizably the Theatre of Dreams. *Photo by Dave Thompson*

striker's haircut, can be sufficient to induce a lifetime of loathing.

Needless to say, the bigger the team, the easier it is to hate them.

The Joys of Local Rivalry

Random hatred, such as that, is very distinct from a local rivalry. Very different indeed. Two teams sharing a similar geographical location, and eternally locked in loathing, care little for one another's status, success, or style. Their mere existence is sufficient to induce a lifetime of dislike.

In Glasgow, supporters of the two so-called Old Firm teams remained implacably opposed to one another even after one of their number, Glasgow Rangers, were condemned to the lowest tier of the national league in 2012–2013, while the other, Glasgow Celtic, remained a big fish in the top pond.

In Istanbul, Galatasaray supporters have nursed a bitter hatred of their Beşiktaş counterparts ever since that afternoon in August 1924 when Beşiktaş beat them 2–0. Although they'd have felt the same way even if the scores had been reversed, because results have nothing to do with rivalries, either. With the exception of such "battles of the biggest" as Spain's El Classico between Real Madrid and Barcelona, and the English tussles between Manchester United and Liverpool, where it's historical records as opposed to geographical location that are the bone of contention, proximity is all that matters.

Rivalries, then, have sound historical and cultural foundations, and entire books have been written about the most grueling of such contests. Roma vs. Lazio in the Italian capital, Boca vs. River Plate in Buenos Aires, Club América vs. Chivas in Mexico, Flamengo vs. Fluminense in Brazil, Real Madrid vs. Barcelona in Spain, Al Ahly vs. Zamalek in Cairo, Egypt.

Private vendettas, on the other hand, cannot be quantified, cannot be reasoned out, cannot be analyzed. They have nothing to do with zip codes, and nothing, either, in common with anybody else's reasons for disliking a certain team. There is, however, one circumstance in which they can be shared; and a time, too, when the aforementioned counting up of the "big teams'" supporters is truly revealed for the self-immolative facade that it is. It is the day that David meets Goliath.

The Triumph of the Tiniest

We all know the story, because we read a little about it back in chapter six. The plucky little local hero sent into battle against the biggest, meanest, strongest, nastiest giant that the enemy has at its disposal, and dispatching him with one well-aimed rock to the skull. Or, in footballing terms, the days on which one of the sport's sperm whales sets out on the routine destruction of some unfancied minnow from far beneath its attention . . . and is roundly and soundly beaten. And an entire nation, sick and tired of the slain heroes' monopoly on success, rises up to acclaim their tiny conquerors.

The rewards for such feats can be grand. In 1972, English non-leagu-ers Hereford United beat mighty Newcastle United in the FA Cup and so grasped the footballing imagination that they were non-league no longer. Elected into the Football League at the end of the season, by 1976, the Bulls were playing in the competition's second tier. They have since returned to whence they came, but that one long-ago night of glory lives on in the memory of everyone who witnessed it.

Hereford's 1972 Cup run ended at West Ham in the next round of the tournament. Other minnows, however, have proven more resilient.

The 2014 Dutch Cup final saw PEC Zwolle rip both the form book and

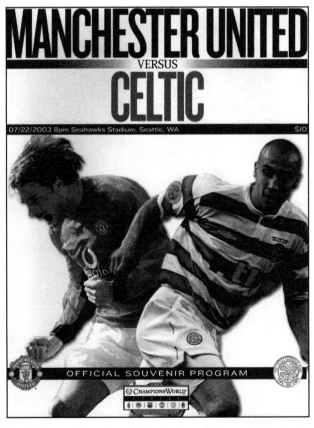

World beaters Manchester United take on Glasgow Celtic in the glamorous confines of Seattle, summer 2003.

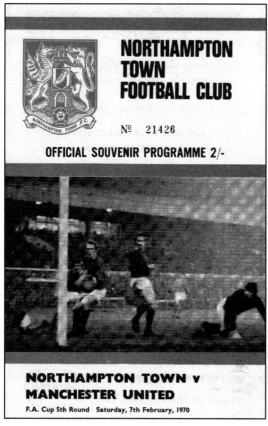

NORTHAMPTON TOWN FOOTBALL CLUB

№ 21426

OFFICIAL SOUVENIR PROGRAMME 2/-

NORTHAMPTON TOWN v MANCHESTER UNITED

F.A. Cup 5th Round   Saturday, 7th February, 1970

A potential upset in the 1970 FA Cup. But Manchester United's George Best had just returned from suspension, and he was in a goal-hungry mood. Six of United's eight goals were Bestie specials.

a century of tradition apart when they tore Ajax Amsterdam to shreds. Ajax, one of the biggest names in European, let alone Dutch, soccer, were on the verge of their fourth successive Eredivisie championship. Zwolle had only been promoted to the division two seasons earlier. Ajax had eighteen past Dutch Cup victories to their name; Zwolle had lost the only two finals they appeared in, in 1928 and 1977. And three minutes into this latest game, it looked like everything was going to play out as expected, as Ajax took an early 1–0 lead.

It was the only goal they were to score. Despite the game being disrupted (and even halted) by firework-hurling crowd trouble, Zwolle hit five goals without further reply, while their supporters merrily chanted for ten. In terms of shocking the Dutch system, not even the national team's destruction of Spain (by the same score, coincidentally enough) at the World Cup a few weeks later caused quite so many double takes as that result.

Such victories are not common; and that is one of the reasons why they are so satisfying. We like an underdog. No, we *love* the underdog. Yes, it's fun to support a constantly winning team, because success is pleasant, and constant success is addictive. But it is also boring. Can you even imagine how stultifying it must feel, living in one of those lands where the same tiny handful of clubs seem to win everything every year? Where even the kindest-hearted supporters of the giants can do no more than smile patronizingly down on those tiny teams whose entire existence is predicated around scrambling for mid-table respectability.

That is why, when the teenies meet the monsters, the joy that they feel when they snatch a victory is matched only by the humiliation of their better-heeled opponents, and the bigger the occasion (the Dutch Cup final, for example), the louder those emotions are amplified.

In France, where giant-killing excellence is annually recognized with the awarding of the Petit Poucet trophy to the best-performing amateur side in the Coupe de France, Fourth Division US Quevilly only narrowly missed out on a Cup final appearance in 2010, going down by 1–0 to eventual winners Paris St. Germain in the semifinal, but winning the hearts of the nation on the way. Two years later, they did make the final, before falling to Olympique Lyonnais.

The greatest of all French giant-killers, however, are Le Calais Racing Union football club, an amateur amalgam of schoolteachers, office workers, and dockers who rose from the obscurity of regional competition (the equivalent to English non-league, or the lower reaches of the US pyramid) to themselves reach the French Cup final in 2000. Sadly the fairy tale ended in a 2–1 defeat to Nantes, but the team's exploits aren't simply a reminder that, on the day, *anything* can happen in the game, but also an inspiration for every "little" team in the world.

Little teams like Inverness Caledonian Thistle, lowly denizens of the Scottish league underbelly who, on February 8, 2000, rolled up in Glasgow for what all agreed would be a ritual thrashing by the leviathan Celtic. Instead they won 3–1, and in the process inspired the London-based *The Sun* newspaper to what remains one of the most inventively brilliant headlines of all time (at least if you know your *Mary Poppins*): "Super Caley Go Ballistic, Celtic Are Atrocious."

Little teams like Kaiserslautern, Second Division conquerors of Bayer 04 Leverkeusen and Hertha Berlin in the 2014 German Cup, en route to a semifinal meet with FC Bayern München (where they came back to earth with a 5–1 drubbing).

Like CD Mirandés, plying their trade in the Spanish Third Division, but reaching the last four of the 2012 Copa del Rey with wins over RCD Espanyol, Villarreal CF, and Real Racing Club.

Giant-Killing on a Giant Stage

Giant-killers, one and all. But giant-killing is not confined to Cup, or even club competition. The international arena, too, has seen its fair share of such momentous occasions. Of these, perhaps the most remarkable was the United States's heart-stopping demolition of the myth of English superiority in 1950. But it is by no means the only serious shock to the system that international soccer has suffered.

In 1966, at the World Cup in England, unknown and unfancied North Korea made a similar impact when they defeated Italy 1–0. The Koreans returned home heroes; the Italian players, on the other hand, were pelted with rotten fruit when they got back. In 1990, Cameroon showed defending world champions Argentina not one iota of respect when they set about beating them in the group stage, and in 2002, Senegal did the same to France, at a time when Les Bleus were themselves the champions of the world.

In many ways, however, it is unfair to describe these latter-day victories as acts of genuine giant-killing. The shock of the final score owes more to the reputation and renown of the defeated sides, than to any genuine obscurity on the part of the victors, particularly now that many African, Asian, and North American sides are largely comprised of players well established as household names in Europe.

In the eyes of the media, and many supporters, too, teams from these continents are minnows by default, and to judge from the shock that accompanied Costa Rica's progress through the 2014 World Cup, they will probably remain so for some time to come. All the while, however, they will just keep on narrowing the gap, closing in on the ultimate prize until the day when not even the most blinkered Europhile can deny that his continent's hegemony has finally been shattered.

The true dwarves of today's international scene, then, are those nations that represent soccer's genuine grassroots, the tiny islands, states, and kingdoms that many people would be hard pressed to even assign to a continent, let alone find on a map. Montserrat and Macao. Anguilla and Andorra. Vanuatu, Gibraltar, Curaçao, and the Faroe Islands.

The Faroe Islands—Nobody Underestimates Them Now

Back in 1990, the Faroe Islands—an autonomous region of Denmark anchored in the northern Atlantic Ocean—had only just been accepted into the international football community. For the past sixty years (since 1930, when their national team was formed) the islands' soccer players had been arranging, and usually losing, friendly matches against the likes of neighbors the Shetland Islands, the Orkney Islands, Iceland, and Greenland. Other islands that many people felt were as obscure as they were. The Faroes didn't even meet their own mother country, Denmark, until 1982 when their under-21s battled out a credible 1–1 draw.

The standard of play was never especially high. It took the Faroes a full eighteen years before they won their first game, a 1–0 victory against the Shetlands in 1948, and in the years since then, they were victorious in just twenty-one more.

But they had experienced their moments of glory. An undefeated run all the way through the soccer competition at the 1989 Island Games (staged that year in the Faroes themselves) was nothing to sniff at, while there was also the small matter of a 1–0 victory over Canada's 1986 World Cup side. Small beans by other nations' standards, perhaps. But Canada was the biggest nation (both geographically and sportingly) that the Faroes had ever played. And they won.

Now they were entering an even wider world. Accepted into UEFA and FIFA, there was just blot on the Faroean landscape. The extreme weather to which the islands are subject prompted the local soccer authorities, Fótbóltssamband Føroya, to lay Astroturf in the national Gundadular Stadium in the capital, Thorshavn. Sadly, what made perfect sense to the Faroese ran contrary to current FIFA regulations, which forbade soccer to be played on artificial surfaces. The islands' competitive (as opposed to friendly) home matches, therefore, would all be played in Sweden.

It was a serious disadvantage, but the Faroes were growing accustomed to them. "The Faroes team is about the same standard of the Danish Second Division," said former Danish coach Sepp Piontek when he was asked his opinion of the latest additions to soccer's international community. "Which is not going to frighten international teams."

There are many players who can claim to have won everything they've played for. Roy of the Rovers has won everything there is and a bunch more as well. Such a shame he exists only in comic book form.

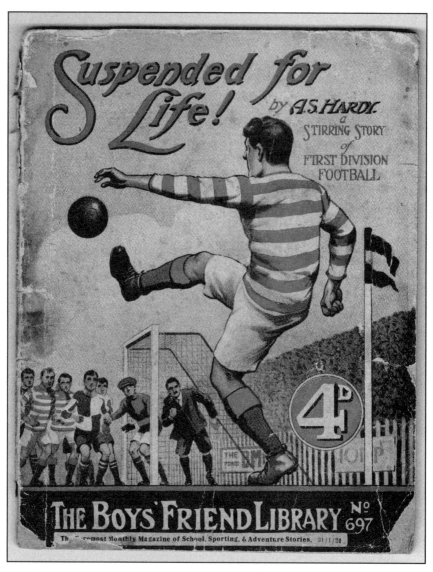

A thrilling tale of the ultimate sporting sanction—1920s-style.

It certainly didn't frighten Austria, as they arrived in Lanskrona, Sweden, on September 12, 1990, to play their part in the Faroes' first-ever competitive match, opening the qualifying competition for the 1992 European Championships.

What did frighten them was the prospect of arriving home again, where they'd be expected to explain how a solitary goal from a twenty-six-year-old clerk named Torkil Nielsen had sent the entire Faroes Islands into paroxysms of delight; and launched Austrian soccer into a process of self-examination that was all the more intense for the sheer disbelief that the scoreline ignited across the continent.

"Unsere Fussballprofis von 'Hobbykickern' blamiert," screamed the headline of the *Kurier* newspaper. *Our professionals were disgraced by a bunch of hobby kickers.* "0–1: Gegen Inselteam Unsere Fussballer das Gespott Europas!" *We are the laughingstock of European soccer.* Seventy-two hours later, coach Josef Hickersberger, the man who had only just steered Austria to their first World Cup in sixteen years, and who had just seen his contract renewed until 1993, was sacked.

Torkil Nielsen—whose wife gave birth to a baby daughter while the team was away in Sweden—described the goal as "one of the greatest moments of my life." It came in the sixty-third minute. Nielsen swooped down on goal from deep in the midfield and, with no less verve than one would expect from a Pelé, Best, or Maradona, crashed through the Austrian defense and unleashed a shot that left keeper Michael Konsel sprawling.

"These are boys who live on barren islands in the middle of the Atlantic," coach Pall Gudlaugsson told the world's press after the game. "They're used to hard work and they have to fight for their living. That approach led us to victory tonight." Before the match, he admitted, he'd been hoping that in five, maybe seven years, "We will be as good as, say, Luxembourg, Finland, or Norway." If the Austria result saw him bring that schedule forward a little, nobody would fault him.

Torleif Sigurðsson, president of Fotboltssamband Foroya, was equally defiant. Some people, he said when the Faroes' challenge was first announced, "think we don't have a chance and should leave it alone." He might have been thinking of the article in the British *World Soccer* magazine, which prophesied "the strangest soccer outpost in the continent could decide the fate of the 1992 European Championships . . . [by] the number of goals they concede."

But, "the only way for us to get on is to leave the islands and play other teams," Sigurdsson continued. And now that they had? "I cannot believe that we won!"

As with so many other fairy tales, the Faroes' triumph did not prove long-lasting. Their next game saw them beaten 4–1 by Denmark, although the British *The Guardian* newspaper insisted "all the praise went to the Faroese. They played with all the courage and tenacity you could wish for." And manager Gudlaugsson said, "Given the number of [Denmark's] chances, it was a moral victory for us."

A creditable draw with Northern Ireland was followed by a string of results that conformed stubbornly to the form book—0–7 vs. Yugoslavia, 0–5 in the return match with Northern Ireland, 0–4 against the Danes, and 0–3 when they came face to face again with the Austrians. The Faroes finished their qualifying campaign rock bottom of their group, with just three points to their name, one win and one draw. But there was no disgrace in that. Austria only had three points as well.

Twenty-Nine, Thirty, Thirty-One . . .

Sometimes, of course, you don't need to whip an established giant to make your mark in the history books. You just need to beat somebody. *Anybody.* As American

Samoa discovered in November 2011. That was when, for the first time in history, a soccer team representing the American protectorate in a FIFA-recognized competition won a game.

Not only that, but it perhaps also went some way toward erasing the stain of what remains the only other match they played that anybody remembers: the 2001 World Cup qualifier in which Australia scored no fewer than thirty-one goals against them.

Thirty-one. It works out to more than one every three minutes. It is more than the total number of goals conceded by Sporting Kansas City throughout the entire 2013 season. It is five fewer than the thirty-six that a Scottish village side called Bon Accord conceded against Arbroath in a Scottish Cup game in 1885, but it is five more than the twenty-six that Preston North End pushed by Hyde in the English Cup two years later.

It is a lot.

It is certainly the highest score ever registered in a full international match, and the highest ever seen in the World Cup, with Socceroo Archie Thompson's thirteen goals in that game the most ever scored by a single player at that level.

Statistics are not necessarily the most accurate guide to the game, of course. Behind the scenes, passport problems derailed almost all American Samoa's pregame preparations; when it came time to leave for Australia, only goalkeeper Nicky Salapu was able to make the journey. "I was the only experienced player," he recalled in the documentary *Next Goal Wins*. "It was a bunch of schoolkids playing against the Australian professional team." Literally schoolkids. "Most of them go to high school," Salapu explained. "Two elementary school—eighth-grade—kids were playing in that team."

Unfortunately, American Samoa's international luck would not improve even with their full team. True, no subsequent opponent ever came close to matching the Socceroos' rout. But not only were American Samoa rooted to the foot of FIFA's international standings for the next ten years, the two goals that they registered in that historic first win against Samoa in 2011 actually *doubled* their tally for the past decade!

Small wonder, then, said a watching BBC, that when the referee blew time on the game, both the players and their newly appointed coach, Dutchman Thomas Rongen, "celebrated as if they had won a major championship"; nor that Rongen expected no contradiction whatsoever when he described the victory as "part of soccer history," and possibly even a portent for a brighter future. "Maybe we have a chance to do something special here beyond this one game."

American Samoa first appeared on the international stage in 1983. Not yet a member of FIFA, the side entered that year's South Pacific Games, and after stumbling to defeat in their first two games, vs. Samoa (1–3) and Tonga (2–3), American Samoa racked up their first-ever victory by defeating the Wallis and Futuna Islands by 3–0.

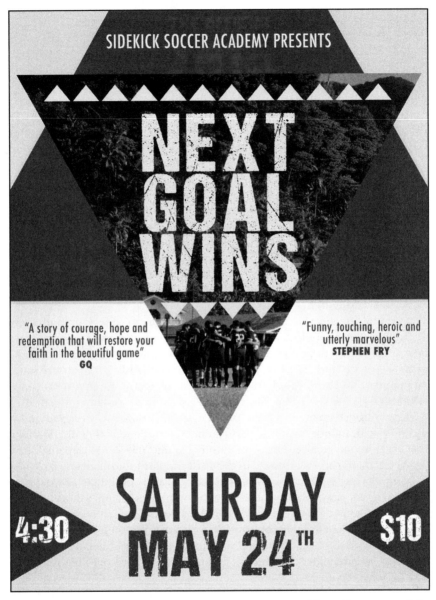

SIDEKICK SOCCER ACADEMY PRESENTS

NEXT GOAL WINS

"A story of courage, hope and redemption that will restore your faith in the beautiful game"
GQ

"Funny, touching, heroic and utterly marvelous"
STEPHEN FRY

SATURDAY MAY 24TH

4:30

$10

It was a false dawn. The 1987 competition saw American Samoa concede no fewer than twenty-two goals in their first three games (New Caledonia 0–10, Vanuatu 0–7, and Wallis and Futuna 1–5), and then all but double that deficit when they succumbed 0–20 to Papua New Guinea.

The gallant story of the American Samoans. How to come back from 31–0.

American Samoa faded from view after that. In 2002, however, newly accepted into FIFA, they set out on the long qualifying road to the World Cup, grouped with Fiji (a 0–13 defeat), Samoa (0–8), Tonga (0–5) . . . and the merciless Australians. They saw some improvement in 2006 as Samoa were held to a mere 0–4, and while Papua New Guinea (0–10) and Fiji (0–11) restored what onlookers might have described as normal disservice, American Samoa did at least finally register their first-ever Word Cup goal, a single strike in the 9–1 defeat by Vanuatu.

And so it goes on. The qualifiers for the 2010 World Cup (which doubled as the soccer tournament in the 2007 South Pacific Games) brought another goal, from future Bay Olympic (New Zealand) striker Ramin "the Machine" Ott, in the 12–1 defeat by the Solomon Islands. Vanuatu ran out 15–0 victors, though, and things did not improve. The 2011 SPGs brought five defeats, no goals, and two successive 8–0 defeats, to New Caledonia and Vanuatu.

But there were signs of progress, too. Tuvalu and the Solomon Islands netted just four apiece against American Samoa in their games, while a 2–0 defeat to Guam represented the closest American Samoa had come to victory since 1983.

Enter Thomas Rongen, once of Ajax Amsterdam, but more famously a member of that great Los Angeles Aztecs side of the late 1970s, playing alongside George Best and Johan Cruyff. Under his coaching tutelage, American Samoa learned to fight.

Goals by Ott and Shalom Luani (better known as an American footballer) dispatched Tonga, and Luani was on target again in the next game, as that first victory was followed by a hard fought, but very well-deserved 1–1 draw with the Cook Islands. "I knew," Rongen informed the BBC, "there were some intangibles that I could work with to turn this team around in a short space of time."

One of these intangibles, at least if media attention is anything to go by, is center back Johnny Saelua, a performing arts student at Hawaii University who made his international debut against Fiji in the 2006 World Cup qualifiers, before becoming an ever-present in the 2010 and 2014 tournaments.

He plays for the local side Black Roses . . . and is the first *fa'afafine*, or transgendered, player ever to compete in the men's World Cup. Samoan culture accepts and respects what it regards as a third gender; has done so since long before Westernizing influences moved in with their own prejudices and biases. Saelua's friends, his teammates, and viewers of the television documentary *Next Goal Wins*, incidentally, know him as Jaiyah. It's only stuffy old FIFA who stick with his birth name.

"She's an amazing person," goalkeeper Salapu said. "For her to be transgender is not a big deal for us . . . we feel like we have a sister in the team. But when she plays on the field, she doesn't play like a sister, she plays like a real man."

American Samoa may not be seen as a team around whose exploits the future of soccer will revolve. But at a time when sexual identities and gender politics are taking an ever greater role in the game, and a time when homophobia has finally been seen as great a crime as racism, American Samoan's soccer and, indeed, the islands' entire culture, offer the rest of the world a shining path that we can only hope will be followed by all.

Pressing the Self-Destruct Button

Sometimes, though, a giant doesn't need to be killed. Sometimes it does the job itself.

Soccer is an ever-changing universe of success and failure. A club that is on the top of the world this year might be at the bottom of the pile in the very near future. A side whose triumph seems an inviolate right today might turn around tomorrow to find failure a far more fitting companion.

Nobody who celebrated Liverpool's eighteenth English league championship in 1990 could ever have dreamed that they would still be awaiting the nineteenth a decade and a half later.

Nobody marking Barcelona's apparent conquest of the universe in 2009, the first team ever to win six major trophies in a single season (the European Champions League, La Liga, Copa del Rey, the Spanish Super Cup, the UEFA Super Cup, and the FIFA Club World Cup), could have foreseen a season in which they'd win nothing at all.

Footballing fortune turns on a dime, and sometimes you cannot even see where things went wrong. At Liverpool, superstition dates the side's decline to manager Graeme Souness's reign, and the decision to demolish "the boot room," the behind-the-scenes cubbyhole from which several generations of past supremos had schemed the club's dominance, but whose intimate confines, it was now decided, would be better put to use within the footprint of a shiny new media center.

Apparently they couldn't.

Other teams fall victim to the demons of finance, and the sheer economic unsustainability of big-city ambitions at a small-town club. In 1983, Waterschei SC THOR of Ghent, in Belgium, were just ninety minutes away from an appearance in the European Cup Winners Cup final. A semifinal defeat at the hands of Aberdeen (managed at the time by a young Alex Ferguson) ended that dream, and as their fans made the journey home that evening, they probably described the game as the most disappointing night they had ever endured. In fact, those were halcyon days. Within five years, their team had disappeared off the map, and there was a new power in the land, KV Mechelen. A new power, destined for a similar fall.

With a sugar daddy tycoon pumping unprecedented sums of money into the side, Mechelen seemed unstoppable. They took the Belgian Cup in 1986–1987, the Cup Winners Cup in 1987–1988, the league title in 1988–1989. They made the last eight of the European Cup . . . and then the wheels fell off their chairman's business interests and the soccer club suffered accordingly. By the early 2000s, KV Mechelen were in the third division.

An even harsher example. In 1981, FC Wageningen were battling Ajax and Feyenoord in the Dutch Eredivisie. Eleven years later, in May 1992, the eighty-one-year-old two-time winners of the Dutch Cup played their final game, against NAC Breda, and then collapsed into bankrupt oblivion.

There were some close calls, too. In England in the late 1980s, one of the original founders of the Football League, Burnley, came within ninety minutes of crashing out of the competition altogether. In France in 2011, eight-time league champions Nantes only narrowly avoided plunging into the third division, just a decade after claiming the league championship; in Germany in 2014, once mighty Hamburger SV, founder members of the Bundesliga, came within a single game of being relegated for the first time ever. And in Scotland in 2012, one of the biggest names in European sporting history suddenly found itself lining up to play its soccer against some of the teensy-tiniest.

The Fall and Fall of Glasgow Rangers

For over a century, the city of Glasgow has been divided between the blue of Rangers and the green-and-white of Celtic, and the Scottish game's honors have been almost equally split. When Rangers won the Scottish League in 2011, it was their fifty-fourth triumph. They had collected the Scottish Cup thirty-three times, the Scottish League Cup twenty-seven times, and all three at once on seven occasions.

None of which mattered a jot when the club plunged into insolvency and liquidation, and was forced to reinvent itself as a new company, and a new club. Rangers's lifelong membership of the Scottish league's top division was terminated; many people considered them fortunate to even be allowed to rejoin the competition at its lowest tier (fourth) in time for the next season. Any other club in similar straits, it was murmured darkly, would probably have been consigned to the non-league universe.

Not that anybody expected them to remain even there for very long. With the club retaining many of its players, its ground, its staff, and its command structure, successive promotions have, at the time of writing, left Rangers just one further season away from what supporters regard as their rightful place.

While it lasted, however, it really was . . . is *pleasant* too strong a word? Refreshing, maybe? Different? . . . to see somebody else have a crack at finishing second behind Celtic. In the same way that it was refreshing to see a club traditionally regarded among the world's most untouchable being held up as a salutary lesson to owners the world over, how not to run a club. Because usually, the kind of miscreants responsible for such a precipitous fall are simply allowed to get away with it.

Rangers are very much an example of just how a club's name and reputation can soar, regardless of its humble origins and background. Just once, in 1972, have Rangers won a major European trophy, when they picked up the European Cup Winners Cup (they were beaten finalists in 1961 and 1967, and were runners-up in the UEFA Cup in 2008). Their true sphere of influence is confined wholly to a northern nation with a population of just five million people—or roughly two-thirds of either New York or London; and even that dominance is split, as aforementioned, with Celtic.

Yet there can be few soccer fans anywhere in the world who are not aware of the two Glasgow giants, the Old Firm as they are locally known, the sheer enormity of their historical reputation far outweighing their own lack of global credentials, while the ferocity of their rivalry with Celtic outshouts almost any other derby. Rangers are Rangers (and Celtic are Celtic), and their preeminence needs no further qualification.

Rangers were founded in 1872, initially taking the field as Glasgow Argyle. It would be another sixteen years before Celtic got underway; and three years more before the Scottish League commenced. For now, Rangers were simply one of a handful of Scottish sides, all vying

Happier, more simple times for fallen giants Glasgow Rangers.

for supremacy, but generally kowtowing to the true giants of the era, Queen's Park (winners of the first three Scottish Cups) and Vale of Leven (winners of the next three).

Occasionally Rangers would raise their heads above the parapet long enough to seriously challenge the latter; in fact, their encounter in the 1876–1877 Scottish Cup final required three matches before Vale finally prevailed by the odd goal in five.

Two years later, battle was rejoined at the same stage of the tournament, and again honors were declared even following the first game. At least by Vale and their supporters. Rangers, on the other hand, were so incensed by the disallowing of what they considered to be a perfectly legitimate goal that they refused to even countenance a replay. Vale was awarded the Cup by default, and more or less vanished from contention thereafter. Founder members of the Scottish League in 1890, they played just two seasons before withdrawing for the joys of either non-league football, or friendlies and exhibition matches alone. They would return to the league on a couple of occasions thereafter, but never came close to recapturing their earliest glories.

Rangers, on the other hand, placed two Cup final disappointments behind them; paused in their history-making until the newly formed Celtic, too, had lost a brace of finals, and then battle was joined. The 1893–1894 Scottish Cup climaxed with the first-ever Rangers vs. Celtic final, and effectively they've been attempting to stage reruns ever since.

The Scottish League, too, became a two-horse race. Between 1890, when the top spot was shared between Rangers and Dumbarton, and 1950–1951, no team outside of the "big two" ever managed to defend a championship once wrested from the Glasgow giants. Hibernian's brace of titles at the dawn of the 1950s then went unrepeated until Aberdeen knocked both Rangers and Celtic off their perches in 1983–1984, and 1984–1985.

The giants learned their lesson, though. Since that time, they have not allowed anybody else to even sniff first place, a ruthless duopoly that is sometimes scaled back even further; Rangers' nine-in-a-row championship run between 1988–1989 and 1995–1996 equaling a similar Celtic achievement between 1965–1966 and 1973–1974.

There is, however, more to the Old Firm rivalry than simply the close encounters of two sporting powerhouses. Traditionally, the pair draw their support from very different quarters—Rangers aligned with the city's Protestant community, Celtic with its Catholic, with the ensuing sectarian mix frequently adding even greater tension to what is already a powder keg mentality.

Catherine Price's book *101 Places Not To See Before You Die* insists: "On Old Firm weekends, admission rates for local hospitals increase ninefold, and the cumulative total for arrests at Old Firm games is the highest in the world." And while much of the violence can be blamed upon situations that have nothing to do with soccer itself, beyond the Old Firm offering a convenient battleground for the two sides, still that battleground has often come very close to home. Such as the day in 1989 when Rangers abandoned a supposedly long-standing (but, in reality, long since shattered) prohibition on signing Catholic players.

Mo Johnstone arrived from the French club Nantes, but numbered Celtic among his other former clubs, a shift in loyalties that outraged fans of both sides of the divide—Rangers, because of his religion, Celtic because they had believed he would be returning to their side following his French sojourn. Scarves were burned, season tickets returned, posters defaced by outraged Rangers supporters, while it is said that Rangers' own kit man was so incensed that he even refused to give the player his halftime bar of chocolate!

Johnstone would eventually win over the Rangers' support when he scored an injury time winner against Celtic in November 1989, and by the time he moved on to Everton in 1991, little of the animosity that greeted him survived. Today, it would not even be an issue. Although sectarianism is still rife among sectors of Rangers' and Celtic's support, it is largely confined to chanting and songs. In a global soccer economy, where even the most parochial soccer club trawls in players from all over the world, the matter of a man's religion has retreated toward the very bottom of the average supporter's list of concerns. Indeed, in 1999, the Italian Lorenzo Amoruso became Rangers' first-ever Catholic captain, and while his six years at the club would be marked by some controversy, it was not because of his Catholicism.

So there they were, an institution. A name known around the world, a legend, a giant. And then along came the succession of financial misdeeds, mistakes, and miscalculations that led, in February 2012, to Rangers Football Club PLC entering administration over the alleged nonpayment of £9 million/$15 million (or approximately one-ninth of Gareth Bale) to the taxman. Which in turn triggered a chain of events that, while having absolutely nothing to do with anything that actually transpired on the pitch . . . the rules and playing of the game . . . saw Rangers enter the liquidation process.

A fresh club was formed around the sale of the old side's "assets, business, and history" for £5.5 million ($9,282,817), but hopes that the new outfit would simply pick up where its predecessor left off, in playing terms at least, were soon dashed.

In the weeks running up to a formal vote on Rangers' request to remain in the Scottish Premier League, the general consensus seemed to be that the authorities would simply rubber-stamp the application and put the entire unpleasant business behind them.

They reckoned without fan power. Supporters across Scotland were united against the proposal. In legal terms, the Glasgow Rangers of today were a wholly different organization to the Glasgow Rangers of old. A new organization, a new club. And, therefore, subject to the same rules and restrictions as any other new club.

Boycotts were threatened against any club owners who supported Rangers's attempts to short-circuit the system. Season ticket sales were threatened, cutting off the lifeblood of the myriad clubs who do not have television riches and multinational sponsors pouring cash into their coffers. On June 18, 2012, the SPL voted 10–1 against allowing the new team into the fold.

Stunned, but not exactly surprised, Rangers applied next for a place in the Scottish Football League. Preferably, they said, in the First Division. Again, early murmurs suggested they might be granted their wish; again, the fans made their feelings known. Out of thirty clubs involved in the vote, just five went along with Rangers's desires. The remaining twenty-five opted to make them start from the very bottom.

And so it was, on July 29, 2012, the fifty-four-time winners of the Scottish League Championship, thirty-three-time holders of the Scottish Cup, and twenty-seven-time victors of the Scottish League Cup kicked off their new life at the lowest level of the Scottish League, by traveling to Brechin City for the first round of the Ramsden Cup, a lower-leagues trophy they had never competed for in the past, and were probably scarcely aware even existed.

Neither did their former status help them. Though they pushed their way into the Cup quarterfinal, Rangers' progress was ultimately ended by Queen of the South, in a result that in any past season would have been regarded as a major act of giant-killing. This year, though, not so much. Queen of the South played one division higher than Rangers. *They* were the ones at risk of a giant-killing!

On August 7, Rangers kicked off their Scottish League Cup campaign, and again, they came unstuck in the quarterfinals. And on August 11, they ignited their league season, traveling north to Peterhead—and returning home with a 2–2 draw. Ultimately, Rangers would win the Third Division title, twenty-four points ahead of second-place Peterhead, but their procession was not without its moments of (for outsiders, at least) glorious schadenfreude.

On March 9, 2013, Rangers welcomed to Ibrox Park Annan Athletic, a club that has only played in the Scottish League since 2008 and had never finished higher than fourth in Division Three. Earlier in the season, in their first-ever match with Rangers, Annan battled to a creditable 0–0 draw. Today, they won 2–1. The lowest point in Rangers's long history had just found a new depth to sink to, and Annan's history had arrived at a brand-new high point.

Of course, and as already alluded to, Rangers's demise intrigues beyond its financial peculiarities. It fascinates because it undermines what had hitherto seemed one of the cardinal rules of world soccer: the big boys always get all the breaks.

Maybe that's why, when a big name *does* stumble, we all gather around to watch. Unless, of course, we're supporters. In which case, we just stick our heads in the sand and look around for someone to blame.

In fact, here comes a scapegoat right now!

The Buck Stops Here

Who's the Boss?

When Sir Alex Ferguson retired as coach of Manchester United at the end of the 2012–2013 season, he brought down the curtain on one of the most successful managerial careers of all time (if not *the* most successful).

In 1988, some of the most fearsome, and successful, managers in English soccer history gathered together to cut a record. Bobby Robson, Lawrie McMenemy, Alex Ferguson, Brian Clough, Terry Venables, and more were among the guilty men, and for further details, see chapter 12.

Chelsea boss Jose Mourinho during his side's August 2014 tussle with the Hungarians of Ferencvárosi. *Laszlo Szirtesi/Shutterstock.com*

He also set the stage for what Red Devils supporters would claim was one of the least successful. The paint was scarcely dry on new man David Moyes's parking space and already the team was on course for a record-breaking season. Assuming one wants to remember the kind of records he accumulated.

The side's lowest points tally since the dawn of the Premiership, and its lowest league position, too.

United's first home and away defeat to Everton (ironically, Moyes's former employers) since 1969–1970; and the first time that both the blue and red sides of Liverpool had taken maximum points from United.

The first home defeat to Newcastle in forty-two years, the first to Stoke in thirty years, the first to West Bromwich Albion since 1978, and the first to Swansea ever. And so on, until Moyes was sacked after fifty-one games in charge, to become the second shortest-lived boss in the Old Trafford club's history, ahead only of Lal Hilditch, the player-manager who lasted just thirty-three between October 1926 and April 1927. United ended Moyes's season having lost more home games in a single season than in any year since 1973–74—when they were relegated.

And if you think it was grueling reading through all of that, imagine living with it. Imagine getting up every morning and going into work, knowing that whatever you do during the day is only one half of the equation. In the eyes of everyone around you, standards that were set before you took the job—and sometimes, before you were even born—are just as vital as anything you might accomplish in the future; and maybe even more so, because the past is the yardstick against which your performance is truly being measured. As Moyes's successor, Louis van Gaal, discovered when his first game as United manager ended with a first-ever win at Old Trafford for Swansea, and a first opening-day home defeat for United since 1972.

The Coach That Drove Itself to Madness

It is said that soccer is a results-driven performance, and that is true. Only it's not just this season's results that a manager needs to keep an eye on. It's the corresponding fixture from forty-three (or whatever) years ago, as well.

It has been estimated that the average lifespan of a coach in the English Premier League is one year and two months. It is not much better in Germany, Italy, Spain—or anyplace else, for that matter. The age of the long-serving club boss eked out its final years through the stubborn resilience of Sir Alex Ferguson at Manchester United (twenty-six years until his retirement in 2013), Arsene Wenger at Arsenal (eighteen years and counting), and Thomas Schaff at Werder Bremen (fourteen years, until his departure in 2013).

Even at the highest level, most coaches count themselves fortunate if they survive a couple of seasons, while some clubs apparently consider themselves stable if they don't go through more than a couple in a year. Nantes, fighting relegation to the third tier of French soccer, got through three. So did Fulham, relegated from the Premier League in 2014. Chelsea, who finished third that same season, have gone through ten in a decade, and so exhaustively did they scour the profession for fresh blood that they are now back where they started in 2004, with José Mourinho.

As a point of comparison, the ten coaches who preceded Mourinho's first appointment between them survived a total twenty-three years (back to John Neal, in 1981), prior to which the club had only had fourteen coaches since its inception in 1905. As another point of comparison, however, Chelsea have been far more successful during the past decade of supposed managerial turmoil than they ever were in the ninety-nine years of calm that preceded it.

Critics of the merry-go-round, and there are many, rightly claim that the constant chopping and changing destroys the continuity that a club requires if it is to be successful. Chelsea and Real Madrid (likewise, ten coaches since 2004) could easily argue that the opposite is true. They would be in the minority in doing so, but they are also among the most successful teams of the era, perhaps even *the* most successful. They must be doing something right.

Once, the critics tell us, the coach was as much a part of a club's sense of continuity and tradition as its stadium or its nickname. Today, he is scarcely more permanent than the work experience kid selling programs in the parking lot. Although he does earn somewhat more money. As Massimo Cellino, the latest (2014) owner of much-troubled Leeds United put it, succinctly if less than reassuringly, "Coaches are like watermelons, you only know [how good it is] when you open it." And he should know. As owner of the Italian side Calgiari, he dismissed thirty-six coaches in twenty-two years.

The coach's job description has changed with his job security. For many years, from perhaps the late 1920s among the game's most advanced proponents, until as late as the 1990s, he was known as "the manager," and was the point at which every other aspect of the club converged.

He bought players and he sold them. It was the manager who met with the schoolboy prospect's parents and assured them their son was destined for greatness; it was the manager who met with the veteran legend's widow and assured her that the club would never forget.

It was the manager who answered the fan mail, and the manager who dealt with the press. He oversaw training, and he arranged the team's travel. He kept the board happy with his promises of great days ahead, and the players happy by fighting their corner when contracts were up for renewal. He could even be called upon (or, at least, so mercurial genius Brian Clough believed) to administer a sound smack around the head to any supporter foolish enough to run onto the pitch.

In short, the manager did everything outside of replacing burned out lightbulbs and cleaning the dressing-room bath, and there were many who did that as well.

Today, the coach (see? It even sounds less impressive) still has responsibilities. But he also has a staff, sometimes numbering in dozens, to handle any of the tasks that were once part and parcel of managing a team. Including recruiting new players and disposing of old, and actually selecting the matchday eleven. Once, a manager was responsible for building a team both on-field and off, and ensuring that every aspect of it worked as smoothly as possible. Today, a coach is simply one more cog within a machine and, in many ways, the most dispensable one of all.

Perhaps that is why it is so difficult to quantify the factors that make a great manager.

But we know the factors that don't and, in fact, the 2014 World Cup brought home to everyone just how little impact the world's most handsomely remunerated managers actually have on the game.

Fabio Capello, the much-traveled super-boss who so spectacularly did *not* lead Russia to glory at the 2014 World Cup, was on $9.5 million a year. Ghana, who only narrowly missed out on a berth in the last sixteen, were paying top man Kwasi Appiah $240,000 a year.

Jorge Luis Pinto, who oversaw Costa Rica's run to the quarterfinals, was on $380,000 per annum. Brazil's Luiz Felipe Scolari, perhaps the only man in first-class soccer in 2014 to receive an even sounder whipping from statistics than David Moyes, was on $3,973,730.

A coach's paycheck does not reflect his brilliance, then. How about the trophy room? Surely, a man who wins, for example, three league championships and four national cups, all within a nine-year span, should automatically be judged a superior coach to one who collects a single domestic cup and a handful of losers' medals across a similar period of time?

Maybe. But would admirers of Arsene Wenger agree with that? Bisect his first eighteen years at Arsenal, and his career has followed precisely that pattern.

Of course, the parameters for success have also changed immeasurably in the last twenty-or-so years. In Europe, where entry to the Champions League is often seen as the be-all and end-all of every club's endeavor, particularly in those countries that supply more than a single bona fide champion to each season's tournament, "success" can mean finishing the season as low as *fourth* in your domestic league. And it is amazing how easily a manager, a club, and, indeed, an entire culture's standards can slip if that is the best they have to aim for.

Certainly there are few less edifying sights than a stadium full of supporters joyously celebrating an achievement that any other field of competitive endeavor, from the Olympic Games to the pop charts, from Formula One racing to the shortlist for a job flipping burgers, would regard as a failure. Try speaking the words out loud. "Hey, well done! You finished fourth." And people wonder why so many fans scoff at the concept of the Europa League, a tournament apparently devoted to discovering which is the best *fifth*-best team around.

Of course, nobody reading (or, for that matter, writing) this is naive enough not to know that it is money that lies at the heart of this mad rush for just-above-averageness. For the playing and coaching staff of a club, Europe offers exactly the same thing as it always has, the chance to pit their wits and skills against the best (and fifth best) of the continent. But the rewards have ballooned out of all proportion, and the media's fixation on those rewards has, sadly, made bean-counters of us all.

Including the coaches.

Nevertheless, ranking the world's greatest coaches by their trophy hauls is generally regarded as the sharpest method of determining the great and the good, in which case a top fifteen could certainly be drawn from a list that looks something like this.

Carlos Bianchi—Argentina (born 1949)

Managerial career: Stade de Reims 1985–1988; Nice 1989–1990; Paris FC 1990–1991; Club Atlético Vélez Sarsfield 1993–1996; AS Roma 1996; Boca Juniors 1998–2001, 2003–2004; Atlético Madrid 2005–2006. Trophies: four Copa Libertadores; seven domestic titles

Brian Clough—England (1935–2004)

Managerial career: Hartlepools United 1965–1967; Derby County 1967–1973; Brighton and Hove Albion 1973–1974; Nottingham Forest 1975–1993. Trophies: two European Cups; two domestic titles; four domestic cups

Sir Alex Ferguson—Scotland (born 1941)

Managerial career: East Stirlingshire 1974; St. Mirren 1974–1978; Aberdeen 1978–1986; Scotland 1985–1986; Manchester United 1986–2013. Trophies: two Champions Leagues; two Cup Winners Cups; sixteen domestic titles; fourteen domestic cups

Béla Guttman—Hungary (1899–1981)

Managerial career: SC Hakoah Wien; Enschede 1935–1937; Hakoah Wien 1937–1938; Újpest Dózsa 1938–1939; Vasas SC 1945; Ciocanul Bucure ti, 1946; Újpest Dózsa 1947; Honvéd FC 1947–1948; Calcio Padova 1949–1950; Triestina 1950–1951; Quilmes 1953; APOEL 1953; AC Milan 1953–1955; Lanerossi Vicenza 1955–1956; Honvéd FC 1956–1957; São Paulo 1957–1958; FC Porto 1958–1959; SL Benfica 1959–1962; Club Atlético Peñarol 1962; Austria 1964; SL Benfica 1965–1966; Servette 1966–1967; Panathinaikos 1967; FK Austria Wien 1973; FC Porto 1973. Trophies: two European Cups; five domestic leagues; one Brazilian state championship; one domestic cup

Ernst Happel—Austria (1925–1992)

Managerial career: ADO Den Haag 1962–1968; Feyenoord 1968–1973; Sevilla 1973–1975; Club Brugge 1975–1978; Holland 1978; KRC Harelbeke 1979; Standard de Liège 1979–1981; Hamburger SV 1981–1987; FC Swarovski Tirol 1987–1991; Austria 1991–1992. Trophies: two European Cups; eight domestic titles; six domestic cups

Helenio Herrera—Argentina (1910–1997)

Managerial career: CSM Puteaux 1944–1945; Stade Français 1945–1948; Real Valladolid 1948–1949; Atlético Madrid 1949–1952; Málaga CF 1952; Deportivo La Coruña 1953; Sevilla FC 1953–1956; CF Os Belenenses 1956–1958; Barcelona 1958–1960; Inter 1960–1968; AS Roma 1968–1970; Inter 1973–1974; AC Rimini 1978–1979; Barcelona 1979–1981. Trophies: two European Cups; one Fairs Cup; seven domestic titles; three domestic cups

Ottmar Hitzfeld—Germany (born 1949)

Managerial career: SC Zug 1983–1984; FC Aarau 1984–1988; Grasshopper Club Zürich 1988–1991; Borussia Dortmund 1991–1997; FC Bayern München 1998–2004, 2007–2008; Switzerland 2008–date. Trophies: two Champions Leagues; nine domestic titles; eight domestic cups

Ştefan Kovács—Romania (1920–1995)

Managerial career: FC Universitatea Cluj 1953–1962; Steaua Bucharest 1967–1971; Ajax 1971–1973; France 1973–1975; Romania 1976–1980; Panathinaikos 1981–1983; AS Monaco 1986–1987. Trophies: two European Cups; three domestic titles; four domestic cups

Valeri Lobanovskiy—Russia (1939–2002)

Managerial career: Dnipro Dnipropetrovsk 1969–1973; Dynamo Kyiv 1974–1990; USSR 1975–76, 1982–1983, 1986–1990; UAE 1990–1993; Kuwait 1994–1996; Dynamo Kyiv 1997–2002; Ukraine 2000–2001. Trophies: two Cup Winners Cups; thirteen domestic titles; nine domestic cups

Miguel Muñoz—Spain (1922–1990)

Managerial career: Real Madrid 1959; CD Plus Ultra 1959–1960; Real Madrid 1960–1974; Spain 1969; Granada CF 1975–1976; Unión Deportiva Las Palmas 1977–1979; Sevilla 1979–1982; Spain 1982–1988. Trophies: two European Cups; nine domestic titles; three domestic cups

José Mourinho—Portugal (born 1963)

Managerial career: SL Benfica 2000; União de Leiria 2001–2002; FC Porto 2002–2004; Chelsea 2004–2007; Inter 2008–2010; Real Madrid 2010–2013; Chelsea 2013—date. Trophies: two Champions Leagues; one Uefa Cup; seven domestic titles; six domestic cups

Bob Paisley—England (1919–1986)

Managerial career: Liverpool 1974–1983. Trophies: three European Cups; one Uefa Cup; six domestic titles; three domestic cups

Nereo Rocco—Italy (1912–1979)

Managerial career: Triestina 1947–1950; FC Treviso 1950–1953; Triestina 1953–1954; Calcio Padova 1954–1961; AC Milan 1961–1963; Torino 1963–1967; AC Milan 1967–1973; ACF Fiorentina 1974–1975; AC Milan 1977. Trophies: two European Cups; two Cup Winners Cups; two domestic titles; three domestic cups

Jock Stein—Scotland (1922–1985)

Managerial career: Dunfermline 1960–1964; Hibernian 1964–1965; Scotland 1965; Celtic 1965–1978; Leeds United 1978; Scotland 1978–1985. Trophies: one European Cup; ten domestic titles; fifteen domestic cups

Giovanni Trapattoni—Italy (born 1939)

Managerial career: AC Milan 1974, 1976; Juventus 1976–1986; Inter 1986–1991; Juventus 1991–1994; FC Bayern München 1994–1995; Cagliari 1995–1996; FC Bayern München 1996–1998; ACF Fiorentina 1998–2000; Italy 2000–2004; SL Benfica 2004–2005; Stuttgart 2005–2006; Red Bull Salzburg 2006–2008; Ireland 2008–2013; Vatican City 2013–date. Trophies: one European Cup; three Uefa Cups; one Cup Winners Cup; ten domestic titles; three domestic cups

It's an impressive-looking roster, at the same time as it illustrates just how grotesquely skewed our vision of success in the game now is. Prior to 1955, after all, there was no European competition for managers to excel in. And prior to, let's say 1995, there were few bottomless troughs of money for them to play Monopoly with.

As the doyen of modern soccer writers, Simon Kuper, puts it in his book *Soccer Men*, "usually . . . the club with the biggest salaries finishes at the top of the league and the club that pays the least finishes at the bottom." Not *always*, but usually. Meaning, it doesn't really matter who is playing "coach" that season, not only because they'll probably be someplace else next year, but also because they don't write the checks.

Kuper continues: "[O]nly a few outstanding managers, like José Mourinho and Alex Ferguson, have much of an effect on results." Which is why a simple litany of who won what with whom is no guide at all, because it doesn't, *cannot*, take into consideration those managers whose accomplishments will not be so readily quantified.

Liverpool's Bill Shankly (1913–1981), whose tally of one UEFA Cup, three domestic titles, one FA Cup, and one English Second Division title looks pathetic when compared to some of today's heavy hitters, but who could outmanage most of them with one hand behind his back.

Manchester United's Sir Matt Busby (1909–1994), with his meager collection of one European Cup, five English titles, and two FA Cups; or Arsenal's Herbert Chapman (1878–1934), managing in an era when winning the league and/or cup was as good as it got. Four domestic titles and two FA Cups was all the reward he received statistically. But like Shankly at Anfield and Busby at Old Trafford, Chapman did not simply win things. He built things, too, and the modern Arsenal remains firmly in his shadow.

Willie Maley (1868–1958), who inaugurated the eternal dynasty of Glasgow Celtic; Bill Struth (1876–1956), whose thirty-four year tenure as Glasgow

Rangers boss saw him pick up (deep breath) eighteen domestic titles, twelve domestic cups, seven wartime championships, and thirty-six local, Glasgow trophies. But men like these were not measured by how many shelves the club carpenter had to erect.

They knew then, as (deep down inside) we know today, that in pure soccer-playing terms, material and financial performance are probably the most narrow-minded criteria by which managerial success should be judged.

A lower league boss who keeps his otherwise impoverished club afloat by nurturing youngsters and then selling them on, while rewarding the faithful with the occasional cup run or a flirtation with promotion, is arguably doing just as good a job as the Serie A supremo who is handed

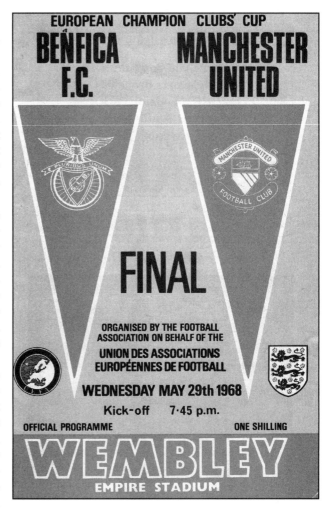

Sir Matt Busby's finest hour and a half (plus extra time). Manchester United's 4–1 victory in the 1968 European Cup Final.

the keys to the vault and told to win the league. Better, in fact, because without the lower league guy's efforts, spotting talent and bringing it to the fore, the big boys would have nobody to buy.

Throughout the twenty-four years (1983–2007) that Dario Gradi was the manager of Crewe Alexandra, the archetypal "lower league" English club, his discoveries included future England captain David Platt, Crystal Palace and England star Geoff Thomas, Liverpool's treble winner Danny Murphy and Welsh international Rob Jones, the incomparable Robbie Savage and future Glasgow Celtic captain and manager Neil Lennon.

Crewe never hit the big time throughout this spell (or any other, for that matter), but they never hit rock bottom, either. They just meandered happily

LIVERPOOL F.C.
Hail To The Kop
We Are Liverpool

The team that Bob Paisley built. Under his management, Liverpool ruled Europe like Charlemagne in shorts.

and healthily along, a well-run club with a well-designed setup, living comfortably within their means.

Compare that to those sides, and coaches, who pour fortunes into one season's success, then come horribly unstuck the following year—usually because the man who was able to put that money to the best use has either been sacked, or moved on to even greater challenges.

In 2008, with coach Harry Redknapp into his third year in the hot seat, Portsmouth won the English FA Cup, finished in the top half of the Premier League, and qualified for European competition. Then Redknapp departed for Tottenham Hotspur, and six years, two administrations, and *eight* managers later, once-proud Pompey were fighting for survival in the fourth tier.

Which is not to say that the men who replaced Redknapp were lesser coaches than he. But relationships change, circumstances too, and a situation that one boss might have been able to defuse with ease can leave another one haplessly floundering. It is not enough for an incoming coach to inherit a great team. He also needs the assurance that it is *his* team.

Of course, this can lead to its own problems. Countless promising appointments have been undone because the new man is so intent on surrounding himself with players and back-room staff that he has worked with in the past, that he fails to see what made the old squad tick so exquisitely. A truly great coach, after all, is not simply building a team. He is building a dynasty, and he is also building a universe, a world-within-a-world wherein his word is law, and his vision is paramount. But unless his successors share that vision, it is all ultimately destined for disaster.

Five successive managers of Liverpool, for example, emerged from the setup created by Bill Shankly following his appointment to what was then a mediocre second-tier side in 1959. Bob Paisley (Shankly's immediate successor, 1974–1983), Joe Fagan (1983–1985), Kenny Dalglish (1985–1991), and caretaker manager Ronnie Moran (1991) were all graduates of Shankly's legendary boot room—literally, the room where the players' boots were stored, but which Shankly co-opted as the place to talk tactics with his lieutenants. And whereas other clubs and, indeed, supporters might expect such crucial conversations to take place in airy gymnasiums or leather-seated offices, the boot room never lost its original boot-fulness.

In his private diary, discovered and disseminated to the media in 2011, Joe Fagan explained, "In time it would become furnished with luxuries like a rickety old table and a couple of plastic chairs, a tatty piece of carpet on the floor and a calendar on a wall that would later be adorned with photographs, ripped from newspapers, of topless models." But he was adamant. "There was little evidence to suggest this room was even part of a football club."

Nevertheless, it was from within the confines of the boot room that Liverpool's long-awaited promotion out of the second tier, in 1961–1962, was planned; and all that was to follow, as well: thirteen league championships, four FA Cups, four league Cups, two UEFA Cups, and four European Cups, all won within one glorious quarter-century span. And no sooner was one success safely installed upon the trophy room shelf, than its architects would be back in the boot room, scheming their next assault.

The day the Liverpool hierarchy decided that the club's needs would be better served by a shiny new media center than a poorly lit back room was probably the day that the all-conquering, all-powerful Liverpool that Shankly created went back to being just another club, scrapping for the trophies they had once all but owned, and yes, actually feeling proud of finishing fourth.

There is one other key to great management, however, that even the greatest manager cannot control.

His employers.

Is That a Checkbook in Your Pocket, or Are You Just After My Job?

In 1956, shortly before injury forced his retirement from playing, the mighty Len Shackleton—a star with both Newcastle United and their deadly rivals Sunderland—published an autobiography, *The Clown Prince of Soccer*, in which one chapter was titled "The Average Director's Knowledge of Football." The rest of the page was blank.

It caused a storm at the time and, were a modern player to include a similar chapter in a similar book, it would doubtless cause one today. But that does not change the fact that it is essentially true. Few of the men or women who own soccer clubs today know, or even care, anything more about the game than its earning power and its publicity value. And neither did those who ran clubs in the

Once among the world's most visible players, now its best-loved club owner, Miami mastermind David Beckham. *ESPN/Photofest*

past. They were, and they remain, businessmen pure and simple, and a soccer club is simply one more aspect of their business.

You cannot fault them for this. After all, if they knew about the game, they wouldn't need to employ others to do the job. And they probably wouldn't have made multimillions in whichever profession it was that enabled them to buy a soccer club in the first place. David Beckham's percolating Miami MLS franchise notwithstanding, can you name *one* successful top-flight soccer club that is actually owned by a soccer player? No, players play and businessmen wear suits, nod and say "a-ha" a lot.

Where their involvement with soccer breaks down is when they put their ignorance (which, we repeat, is *not* a bad thing) to one side and begin interfering in matters that have already been delegated to other employees. Team selection, for instance. Or transfer policy.

The annals of the game are littered with the stories of "the one that got away," but few resonate so loudly as the tale of how Sheffield United manager Harry Haslam was so impressed by the sixteen-year-old Diego Maradona that he agreed to a deal to bring the boy to England without even phoning his bosses to tell them.

Of course, the deal fell through—no way were the Sheffield United directors going to drop £200,000 (around £800,000/$1,350,000 today) on an unproven kid, simply because their manager thought he had potential. In fact, they wouldn't have flashed the cash even if Haslam had sat them down and, with tarot deck and TARDIS, proved to them that Maradona was destined to become one of the greatest soccer players the world had ever seen.

They weren't completely thoughtless, though. Haslam obviously had his heart set on buying an Argentinean, so they bought him one. Alex Sabella cost £40,000 (£160,000/$270,000) less than Maradona would have, and when the time came to sell him a couple of years later, they no doubt congratulated themselves on their business acumen. Leeds paid £400,000 (£1,199,241/$2,024,060) for the player. The following year, Maradona moved to Boca Juniors for a £1 million (£2,680,000/$4,523,263).

Of course, boardroom caution is scarcely an affliction confined to English administrators alone. In 2000, the Turkish side Gaziantepspor found themselves mulling the virtues of an eighteen-year-old spotted playing youth football in São Paulo, Brazil. They made inquiries and were

Kaka. Gaziantepspor could have had him for $2.5 million; they balked, and he finally sold for six times that amount. *Maxisport/Shutterstock* quoted the eye-watering sum of $2.5 million. Too much. The Falcons pulled out of the deal, and three years later, Kaka moved to Italy instead, for $15 million.

Hindsight is twenty-twenty, though. We hear a great deal about the bargains that the board passes over because they don't share the manager's faith in the latest genius to be unearthed; a lot less about the disasters that are averted for the same reasons. Where the conflict lies is within the very nature of the relationship between board and manager. Give an ambitious coach a blank checkbook and the next stop could be the bankruptcy court. (It has happened.) Question his judgment often enough, though, and he'll be moving on to more accommodating surroundings.

Changing the Playing Field

What do we learn from all this?

That being a coach is probably one of the most thankless jobs in soccer. When the team plays well, it's the players who get the credit. When the team plays badly, it's the coach who gets the sack.

In fact, the only thing worse than being the coach is being the supporter who watches each game with growing dismay, convinced that he (or she) could do a far better job. And he (or she) might well be correct, which is why the day is fast approaching when they may be able to do more than dream. Around the world, a growing number of clubs are now owned and operated by fans, a business model that may not yet have threatened the dominance of the game's wealthiest denizens, but which, some say, one day will.

In Germany, it is already illegal for any single individual or entity to own a Bundesliga club, a policy that allows supporters what, in the eyes of observers elsewhere, is an unprecedented level of involvement in the club's operations. It's not foolproof, but it is better than what happens in a lot of other countries.

In Spain, Barcelona, Real Madrid, and Atlético Madrid are among the clubs owned not by shareholders but by members.

In the English Premier League, the supporters' trust is the third largest shareholder in Swansea City, while the aforementioned Portsmouth are now wholly, but happily, controlled by the Pompey Supporters Trust.

There is a downside to all of this, the fact that the vast majority of fan-owned sides were forged in adversity; in response to, and even retaliation against, events unfolding in the boardrooms of already existing teams.

In 2005, Manchester United supporters were so outraged by their club's purchase by the American Glazer family they they even formed their own breakaway club, FC United of Manchester, and they have fared well in non-league climes ever since.

Other sides have risen phoenix-like from the ashes of clubs that one past owner too many had managed to batter into bankruptcy and extinction. In Poland, Hutnik Nowa Huta rose from the financial chaos that devoured Hutnik Kraków. In Japan, Yokohama FC was born after two local sides, the Flugels and the Marinos, were merged under the latter's name, leaving Flugels fans with no official option but to start supporting the team that had hitherto been their fiercest rivals. So they took an unofficial option instead. In Austria, SV Austria Salzburg was birthed among fans distanced from the original SV Salzburg when its new owners, the makers of the Red Bull drink, changed the team's name to that of their product. In England, AFC Wimbledon arose among supporters alienated by, again, the original team of that name being sold and transported to a different part of the country altogether.

Not every supporter-owned team has flourished, and not all of them will survive. The business models to which they adhere are still new, and unfamiliar enough for the current era to still be a learning curve. But business barriers are tumbling all the same, just as those that were once erected around race, religion, and even gender have been breached.

Once, it would have seemed impossible for a woman ever to officiate at a man's game, but female referees and assistants are now commonplace. Likewise, it was once unimaginable that a woman could take control of a man's team. But in 1999, Carolina Morace took charge of Italian Serie C1 team Viterbese for two matches; and in June 2014, Corinne Diacre was appointed manager of the second-tier French side Clemont Foot.

Both a former player and assistant coach with the French women's international side, Diacre admitted, during a press conference early on in her new career, that she was "trying to maintain my focus as much as possible, and to stay as much in the shadows as possible, because what interests me is that my players take the limelight, not me."

Weeks later, former Arsenal Ladies boss Shelley Kerr took over at Stirling University, of Scotland's Lowland League, in the fourth tier of that country's male pyramid structure. She too asked publicly to be judged on results, explaining, "I'm confident enough and completely focused on helping the guys develop as players. It shouldn't be about gender, it should be about your ability as a coach."

Of course there were elements of the media that would not permit things to be that simple. Nevertheless, the appointments of Diacre and Kerr were more than a simple "first" for the game's record keepers to note down. They might, and should, also mark a memorable "last" as well. The last time that such an appointment was regarded as something novel or unusual.

12

Soccer Songs

What *Are* They Singing in the Background There?

S occer is more than a sport. It is a lifestyle and, if that sounds at all hyperbolic, take a look around you, the next time you visit the mall. No, not just at the FIFA-branded soda bottles (although they're certainly a part of it), or the commemorative World Cup wall charts that were abandoned half-completed once your own team went home.

Look closer. Look at the soccer ball lamps and soccer field bedspreads. The soccer-themed books and soccer kit outfits. The T-shirts, the tea cups, the club-colored glow-in-the-dark carillion clocks, with eleven little players to pop out on the hour to tell you how many goals left till bedtime.

Look at the sheer wealth and welter of soccer-themed nicknacks with which it's not merely possible to decorate your home, you'd need a second home just to store the overflow in. And a second mortgage to pay for it all.

Soccer has inspired art. One of Britain's most beloved artists, the painter L. S. Lowry, gave us *Going to the Match* in 1928, and no other single image better conveys the ritual of winding your way to the stadium than that. (At least for those of us who can still remember when it was possible to walk to a neighborhood ground, as opposed to driving to a theme park on the outskirts of some distant industrial estate.)

Soccer has inspired fiction, novels with titles like Anthony Clavane's *Promised Land: A Northern Love Story*, Will Buckley's *The Man Who Hated Football* and J. L. Carr's *How Steeple Sinderby Wanderers Won the FA Cup*. And especially, let us not forget Simon Cheetham's *Gladys Protheroe, Football Genius*, itself a work of footballing genius.

It has forged movies, full-length Hollywood (and elsewhere) productions that range from the regrettably trite (has anyone ever sat through *Soccer Dog* in its entirety?) to the impeccably glorious (Ken Loach's *Looking for Cantona*); from the absurd (*Escape to Victory* (US title *Victory* alone) —Sylvester Stallone and Pelé combine as teammates in a Nazi POW camp) to the dynamic (*The Damned United*, based on David Peace's fictionalized account of Brian Clough's brief management of Leeds); and from the hilarious (*Gregory's Girl*) to the inspirational (*Bend It Like Beckham*).

Board games endorsed by the heroes of past eras. The ubiquitous Subbuteo, a "flick to kick" recreation of the full matchday experience, with accessories that over the decades have included 1/72nd scale grandstands, floodlights, mounted police, Her Majesty the Queen (to present the Cup), supporters, hooligans, ambulance-men and more or less every professional soccer team you could ever want a replica of.

Type "soccer memorabilia" into eBay and stand back as your eyes are assaulted by everything from politically incorrect gollywog footballers, given away by an English jelly company back in the 1960s, to bobble-headed plastic replicas of every Premier League star of the 1990s.

European GI Joes (Action Man to their English owners) kitted out for soccer-shaped heroism; board games and Beanie Babies; pre-owned Pelé neckties; postage stamps and costume jewelry, cell-phone cases and soccer-playing garden gnomes. Soccer Mom erotica. There is even a niche for soccer hooligan memorabilia, belts and boots, suspenders and knuckle-dusters, and a small rain-forest's worth of memoirs which *should* be titled *Oi, Wot You Lookin' At?*, whether they are or not.

And buried deep within the game's cultural and commercial psyche, the darkest and most dangerous secret of all: the soccer song.

Earwig Oh, Earwig Oh, Earwig Oh

Let's get one thing straight from the outset. We are not discussing the sometimes witty, oft-times mindless, and frequently so-obscene-that-the-television-really-ought-to-bleep-them-out songs and chants with which a live soccer audience will amuse itself during games; that vast repository of folk memories that can range from a casual "here we go, here we go, here we go," when the teams come out and the mood is good, to an ironic "it's just like watching Brazil," when it's really more like watching the grass grow; and on to the classic gallows humor of "we're going to win 6–5" when your team is down 5–0.

Named for a bird, Subbuteo quickly took flight—and today even enjoys its own world championship. Olympic status surely can't be far away.

The odes that could make an Anglo-Saxon lexicographer blush, and those that could put the average hospital ER on lockdown. It is amazing how many things a few thousand pissed-up soccer supporters can find to rhyme with "you're going home in a wheelchair" when they want to.

There are the songs that make sense solely to the initiated. In 2009, *The Guardian*'s Tom Lamont immortalized a chant, overheard at a Manchester United game, that managed to champion the side's South Korean striker Park Ji-Sung, discuss his native land's cuisine, and insult the entire population of Liverpool, and all that in just a few lines of melody borrowed from *Riverdance*:

> "Park, Park, wherever you may be,
> You eat dogs in your home country,
> Could be worse, could be Scouse,
> Eating rats in your council house."

And there are the songs that one recalls hearing about in the distant (mid-1980s) past, and which we still fervently hope are not mere apocrypha. The chant of Zenit Leningrad's most loyal support, for example:

> "Moscow boys sometimes have erections,
> Kiev boys often have erections
> But Leningrad boys *always* have erections."

All sung in Russian, naturally.

These are the songs of the people, the true folk music of an age that thinks it has grown too sophisticated for such simple pleasures, and which refuses to acknowledge that anything could be considered worth preserving if it doesn't come with a price tag and a barcode on it.

But they are not, in the context we are discussing here, soccer songs.

One day, all soccer records will be this awful. Or maybe they already are.

Soccer songs *do* have price tags and barcodes. They have writers, who crafted them with pen and paper. They have performers, who recorded them in professional studios; and they have retailers, genuine international record companies, who place them on sale in real stores and download outlets, in the knowledge that you, the discerning fan of [fill in the blank] will be utterly unable to resist paying money for them.

Or, at least, that's the general idea. The World Cup opening ceremony doubtless opened all of our eyes to the fact that "We Are One (Ole Ola)," performed by Pitbull featuring Jennifer Lopez and Claudia Leitte, was the official song of the 2014 World Cup.

But did you know that "Dar um Jeito (We Will Find A Way)," harnessing the abilities of Carlos Santana, Wyclef and Avicci and Alexandre Pires, was the official anthem of the games? That "Tatu Bom de Bola," by Arlindo Cruz, was the official song of the tournament's mascot?

That, for the past six World Cup tournaments, there has been an official World Cup CD; and that, in an historical hall of terpsichorean infamy that reaches as far back as 1962, the likes of Daryl Hall, Youssou N'Dour, Ricky Martin, Vangelis, Jean Michel Jarre, R. Kelly, Shakira, the Buenos Aires Municipal Symphony, and Placido Domingo have all been prevailed upon to sing a song of soccer by the powers that be?

And those are only the official FIFA-sanctioned selections, designed to commemorate the World Cup. Expand your ears out to the other three years and eleven months that yawn between tournaments, and reach way back in time as well, and you will discover that people have been writing and recording songs about soccer for almost a century now. And people have been buying them, too.

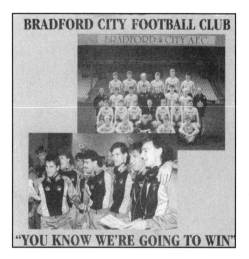

"YOU KNOW WE'RE GOING TO WIN"

Records such as this often sold the most copies locally—leaving supporters elsewhere scrambling for copies.

Jack Charlton took Irish hearts to the World Cup. Liam Harrison took Irish ears to purgatory.

Blaming Britain for Everything

As with so many other of the game's innovations, good and bad, the soccer song appears to be a British invention, dating back to the 1930s when music hall songbird Gracie Fields recorded the first one, immortalizing her hometown team of Rochdale.

A few fellow performers followed suit, but it was just a trickle at first; a handful of records over a handful of decades, but it was clearly a popular notion because, by the end of the 1950, the soccer song had crossed the English Channel and was gnawing at French ears, too. In 1958, just weeks after Pelé and Brazil enthralled the world at the World Cup final, Silvio Silveira Et Ses Rythmes Brésiliens struck vinyl gold.

Reggae producer Clement Bushay celebrates the 1972 season in its entirety.

Giorgio Moroder was the synth genius behind Donna Summer's "I Feel Love," Sparks's "The Number One Song in Heaven," David Bowie's "Cat People" . . . and this.

Recorded, sung, and released in France alone, the oddly tempo'd, and even more peculiarly intoned "Le Roi Pelé" celebrated the emergence of the latest monarch to bestride the Brazilian scene, and choice lyrics include the observation that he is "black like coffee." Presumably a useful factoid for those fans who experienced the tournament on radio that year.

The next tournament, the 1962 games in Chile, were likewise marked with the release of just one record, Los Ramblers' Spanish language classic "El Rock del Mundial." And four years later, English skiffle star Lonnie Donegan introduced us to "World Cup Willie," a genuinely contagious song about a genuinely likable mascot.

But the golden age of restraint and calm was about to come to an end. You could count in the tracks of a lone LP the number of soccer songs released around the world to this point. Maybe a double LP if you really dig deep. Now, a veritable industry was about to be born.

Blue Is the Color. Red's a Color Too. So Is Green.

In 1970, the England World Cup squad was dragged into a studio (none too willingly, judging by period footage) to record "Back Home," a plaintive ditty demanding that their home fans support them while they were away in Mexico, doing their bit. And they did! England went out in the quarterfinals, but "Back Home" went to number one, and in so doing, it finally ignited the blue-touch paper. Soccer songs were here to stay.

In England through the 1970s, a team only had to catch the faintest whiff of a Cup final to be trooping gamely into the studio to sing a song about it, and it didn't matter that the musicians who equally gamely accompanied them generally shuddered at the very thought of the gig (10cc's Kevin Godley, a sessioneer at Strawberry Studios in Stockport, grimly recalls this part of his career as "terrible").

Still, one could stuff a jukebox to bursting point with the anguished bellowing of so many sportsmen extolling the virtues of their club and its colors, its supporters and its stadium. Chelsea's "Blue is the Colour," Arsenal's "Good Old Arsenal," Tottenham Hotspur's "Nice One, Cyril," West Ham United's "I'm Forever Blowing Bubbles." There are more. Many, many more.

Neither were the players alone involved in such shenanigans. Musicians, too, eyed the hitherto barely tilled common ground that is shared by pop music and soccer, and gathered their inspiration accordingly.

In 1972, ace Jamaican producer Clement Bushay delivered "Football Reggae," a celebration of Derby County's league championship win that was rendered more inclusive with almost hilariously offhand mentions of at least a dozen other sides ("West Ham are another team . . ."). By the end of the record, one really cannot believe Bushay even knew *what* he was singing about, let alone who. It is brilliant.

Rod Stewart served up no such conundrum. In 1974, Scotland's Greatest Living Englishman contributed to *Scotland Scotland*, a full-length album celebrating that nation's qualification for the latest World Cup. Not only that, but Stewart even teamed up with playing legend Denis Law for a partial duet through Jimi Hendrix's "Angel."

"Tell you something, Rod," Law quips as the performance gets underway, "this will never sell a million," and he was correct. Not even with the Bay City Rollers, Junior Campbell, Middle of the Road, and Gallagher & Lyle likewise throwing

their tartan tam o'shanters into the ring; not even with squad veteran Billy Bremner solemnly assuring the people of Scotland that "we'll do our damnedest" to win the World Cup because "youse deserve it more than any nation has ever deserved it." *Scotland Scotland* did not sell a million.

Stewart was not discouraged, however. Four years later, he was back to cut a new single, "Ole Ola," and this time, all his backing singers were drawn from Scotland's World Cup squad. With all the consequent musical majesty with which that concept can be imbibed.

It is a magnificent song, a fabulous performance. Verses

Even Fatboy Slim couldn't resist!

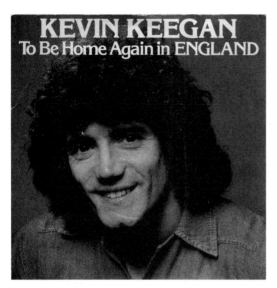

KEVIN KEEGAN
To Be Home Again in ENGLAND

Supporters of Scunthorpe, Liverpool, Hamburg, and Southampton all enjoyed the footballing skills of Superkegs. Fans of Newcastle, Fulham, and England cherished his management abilities. And some people enjoyed his singing, too. Apparently.

that namecheck every member of the Scottish squad; a chorus that rhymes "ole ola, ole ola" with "we're gonna bring that World Cup back from over thaaaar"; you didn't need a single drop of Hibernian blood in your veins to feel the adrenaline pumping when the song came on the radio. All of which leaves us utterly baffled as to why "Ole Ola" has since been absent from every "greatest hits" album Rod has ever released. In reaching number four on the British chart, it remains one of the twelve most successful singles he has ever released.

Other names followed Stewart's lead, artistically if not in terms of wild success. "Billy Don't Be a Hero" hit-makers Paper Lace paired with their local side, Nottingham Forest, for a song or two; new romantic refugees Heaven 17 became the Hillsboro Crew for an Artists Against Apartheid single with Sheffield Wednesday; and then all boundaries blurred altogether when, not content with making pop records, soccer players started eyeing up their chances of becoming pop *stars* as well.

In 1987, the Tottenham Hotspur striking partnership of Glenn Hoddle and Chris Waddle hit the giddy heights of #12 in the UK with a song called "Diamond Lights," a feat rendered all the more remarkable when one considers that beyond its gratuitous catalog number of KICK 1, the song had no sporting content whatsoever.

Pairing one of the country's top soccer idols with a pop song was not, of course, a new idea even then. A decade before Hoddle and Waddle (or Hobble and Wobble as it was oddly amusing to rename them), Kevin Keegan stormed the Top 10 with both a hit single, "Head Over Heels in Love," and a permed hairstyle that placed him on the very cutting edge of contemporary youth culture. Well, kind of. And a decade before that, George Best was so well known a player that he didn't even need to make records. Other people (Don Fardon) did it for him, scoring with the elegiac "Belfast Boy" and leaving Best to let his feet do the singing—which is generally the most sensible option for any of these people.

Sadly, they don't listen. In 1990, Paul Gascoigne linked with the might of a real pop group, Lindisfarne, to rerecord a boozy version of their "Fog on the Tyne" anthem, and the pairing almost made #1. Goalkeepers Peter Shilton and Ray Clemence recorded "Side by Side" which, in titular terms, amusingly mocked the England manager's insistence on playing them in alternate games, but musically was the sound of the clumsiest own goal ever conceded; and there were many more.

In each of these instances, success was fleeting. "Diamond Lights" was Hoddle and Waddle's one and only hit and, within a couple of years, the pair were playing their soccer in France. Coincidence? Maybe . . . maybe not. Asked, in 1997, to mark the tenth anniversary of their hit with a few words on the subject, both men merely mumbled something along the lines of "it was fun." In voices that suggested that it wasn't. Not really.

Even England's manager could not decide who was the best goalkeeper at his disposal—so he alternated them between games. Peter Shilton and Ray Clemence responded by making a record.

The Kicker Conspiracy

By the end of the eighties, English soccer had probably sunk as low as it could possibly go. It was an era scarred by the disasters at Heysel, Bradford (both 1985), and Hillsborough (1989); shattered by English soccer's ban from European competition; and presided over by a government that regarded soccer as a disease, and its supporters as less than animals.

An age when the game's sole cheerleaders seemed to be the fanzine editors who fought to give the ordinary fan a louder voice than either the hooligans or politicians; an age when an ambitious politician would rather die than admit to a liking for soccer; a time when conventional celebrities distanced themselves from even the game's greatest names.

Which was when, and possibly why, maverick dub producer Adrian Sherwood gathered together a crop of like-minded musical friends and created the Barmy Army, an anarchic electro-punk dance monster that was cast firmly within the mutant rave culture of the age, and still shakes the walls today. The Army's one and only album, *The English Disease*, employed throbbing rhythms, scything guitars, raucous chants, and sampled crowd and commentary to paint the most dramatic aural portrait possible of the state of the game in the UK at the end of the eighties.

The album's very artwork is a child of its time. Instantly recognizable cartoons of coaches Bobby Robson, Jack Charlton, and Brian Clough are gathered around a table football game, but the players all have the heads of asses

SINGALONGA FULCHESTER UNITED

Fulchester United's half-man, half-fish goalkeeping stalwart. Follow his adventures monthly in *Viz* magazine. You won't believe your fins.

(or, perhaps, Anubian jackals), and rising above them, Margaret Thatcher resplendent in full Freddy Krueger drag, one hand jerking the strings of her then–sports minister puppet, the other impaling soccer players on her outsized razor-sharp fingernails.

Against this, the Barmy Army is a storm of sound, a roar of protest, a wall of sonic modernity, but one that is shot through with moments of stirring tradition and glory, a tapestry of chorus and quotation designed to illustrate just how deeply embedded in national life the game really was. If any single record can take credit for the fact that, over the next few years, the quality of British soccer songs would (at least fleetingly) improve, then the Barmy Army is it.

Coincidentally, however, it was not the only move in a genuinely likable musical direction being undertaken at the time. Also in 1989, dour Mancunian dance band New Order was commissioned to record the theme tune to a new television show, pairing the outrageous chatter of George Best and Rodney Marsh aboard the prosaically titled "Best & Marsh."

In eschewing any of the traditional gimmickry associated with a soccer song—namely, herds of male voices raised in buffalo-like lowing, while simulated crowd noises roared them through every chorus—the theme caught the ear of the English Football Association as well, as it pondered the once-every-four-years (if they're lucky) dilemma of selecting the song with which the country would sing England into the World Cup.

It was a traditionally fraught undertaking. In 1972, still flush from the success of "Back Home," England recorded their 1974 World Cup song before they had actually qualified for the tournament, which meant it sounded pretty silly when they fell at the final post. Or it would have, had it ever been heard of again.

In 1982, England swore "This Time We'll Get It Right," and proceeded to get it very, very wrong. In 1986, they declared "We've Got the Whole World at Our Feet," and were knocked out by Diego Maradona's hand. But still, the invitation for New Order to make the record was sent out and, though few would ever have predicted it, the band agreed. Indeed, singer Bernard Sumner later admitted, "We recorded 'World in Motion' because it was such an unexpected thing for us to be doing. But we wanted to bring some respectability to a disgraced musical genre."

They may or may not have succeeded in that aim, but "World in Motion" did indeed become the most successful football record since "Back Home," topping the British chart for a month that summer, and faltering only when England's time in the tournament ended with defeat to the Germans in the semifinal.

Cowritten with comedian Keith Allen, the Stephen Hague–produced single also paired New Order with a clutch of the 1990 England World Cup squad—Peter Beardsley, Paul Gascoigne, Steve McMahon, Chris Waddle, Des Walker, Craig Johnston, and a hyper-actively rapping John Barnes among them. But not every participant was as enthusiastic as the Liverpool star, as Manchester United's Brian McClair let on when his autobiography recalled a conversation he had with England captain Bryan Robson.

Robson: "We've just made a record for the England World Cup Squad with some blokes called New Order."

McClair: "You'll have a number one there, no problem."

Robson: "Never, no way! There's no way that rubbish is going to get to number one."

Which, no doubt, is the reason why soccer players make lousy clairvoyants, and have to leave that kind of thing to octopi.

You'll Never Win Anything with Squid

Six years later, on the eve of the 1996 European Championships (staged that year in England), another band, the Lightning Seeds, linked with the home team to record another number one hit. Stirring once again, "Three Lions" is probably best remembered for its insistence that football was "coming home." Which it was. But it didn't stay.

Nor, although we have spared their blushes so far, has the United States steered clear of the scene. Indeed, no sooner had they qualified for the 1990 tournament than Team USA was coaxed into a recording studio to tape a World Cup rap record with Def Jef and DJ Eric Vaughn.

Sadly, the end result, "Victory," was so appalling that even the USSF allegedly disowned it. It was screened once on the cable sports channel Prime Sports Network, at halftime during one of the team's pre-tournament friendlies, and probably showed up in a few other unsuspecting forums, too. But not only was it never given a full release, it didn't even get a full airing on PSN. Halfway through, the song faded out and the program went to commercial. And the commercial was preferable.

And yet . . .

And yet, it is not simply fashionable to laugh at soccer songs, it is almost impossible not to. With just a few po-faced exceptions, they are not made to be taken seriously, and some get the laughs in before even the critics and fans have had the chance. In 1988, as part of the Sport Aid charity drive, British coaches including Alex Ferguson, Brian Clough, Terry Venables, George Graham, and Bobby Robson combined as the Boss Squad to record a number composed by

SCARBOROUGH
FOOTBALL CLUB

WE PLAY FOR
SCARBOROUGH
THE 1ST TEAM SQUAD

Stating the obvious, Scarborough-style.

the writers of television's *Red Dwarf*, Rob Grant and Doug Naylor, and produced by the brains behind *Spitting Image*'s musical interludes, Phil Pope. In fact, the only thing wrong with "The Worst Song Ever" was its title. It was actually one of the best. "Red is the color," sang the massed ranks of dressing room disciplinarians, "white's a color too, another color's green . . ."

All of which is not only true, it also illustrates a crucial truism. Love them or hate them, there is something deliciously reassuring about soccer songs, a reminder that people should not take the game as seriously as they sometimes do, and that occasionally it's okay to simply let your hair down and do a really stupid dance, while yowling discordantly along with a record made by people who sing even worse than you do.

It is true, perhaps, that the Village People's contribution to Germany's 1994 World Cup song, "Far Away in America," scarcely hit the heights of their golden oldies "Go West" and "YMCA." But the accompanying video is probably the one and only occasion upon which you will see both Lothar Matthäus and Jurgen Klinsmann smiling at the same time, in the same room.

It is true, too, that misty-eyed memories of the fabulous Danish side of the early-mid- 1980s are horribly undone by exposure to "Re-sepp-ten," the 1986 World Cup squad's collaboration with the immortally named Dodo and the Dodos. Fulham fans might prefer a second successive relegation to prolonged exposure to "Vive El Fulham," Tony Rees and the Cottagers' brutal mid-seventies subpoenaing of "Y Viva Espana" ("this year we're gonna win the Cup, Y Viva el Fulham").

Music-loving Italians may or may not have thanked the artist known as Negramano for updating Guido Ferilli's old mid-1970s chestbeater "Un Amore Così Grande" for the 2014 World Cup, and there are doubtless certain sensitive ears that have still to rid themselves of the sonic whine that was *the* all-pervading sound of the 2010 tournament . . . no, not the vuvuzelas that transformed every stadium into a concrete bowl filled with very playful wasps, but Shakira and Freshlyground's ruthlessly keening "Waka Waka (This Time for Africa)."

And there were surely kinder ways of recalling (in 1978) Uruguay's 1950 World Cup triumph than by unleashing the light orchestral disco of Victor Hugo Morales and Los Campeones across what would otherwise have been a gloriously atmospheric collection of excerpts from the games themselves. Somehow, it feels almost anticlimactic to slip from the impassioned commentary of that unforgettable Uruguay vs. Brazil final, into something so mundane as a song.

Almost, but not quite. There are few moments more moving in live soccer than the sound of a packed FA Cup final crowd united in singing "Abide with Me," the hymn that has been an integral part of the day's ritual since 1927, and that despite its composer, Henry Francis Lyte, having written it (in 1847) to comfort himself as he lay dying from tuberculosis.

Nor can any but the stoniest heart fail to be melted by the sound of Liverpool's Kop when it launches into the anthemic "You'll Never Walk Alone," a piece of theater so profound that even the mighty Pink Floyd employed a recording of it on their 1971 LP *Meddle*.

And one can even get a little misty-eyed watching black-and-white television reruns of some rainswept seventies grudge match, and listening as the supporters while away the frigid hours with a jolly little sing-song.

Such as the one that legendary disc jockey John Peel encountered when he went to see Scottish side Meadowbank Thistle, and was thrillingly bemused as the crowd (or the handful—the game's attendance was barely three hundred) amused itself with a chant:

> "Give us an F!
> Give us an I!
> Give us an S!
> Give us a U!
> Give us an L!
> What's that spell?"

Well, it spells "fisul," of course. As in "Meadowbank Fisul."

Sometimes, a game, or the memory of a game, is so profound, and so bound up in myriad emotions, that music is the only suitable accompaniment to it. An observation that still may not excuse, or even explain, "The Fulham Stomp." But at least we tried.

Soccer Songs in Surprising Places—the First XI

A smattering of soccer songs that escape the scorn of the genre's foes.

Morrissey—"We'll Let You Know" (1992)

Or, the hooligan's lament, highlighting Morrissey's third album, *Your Arsenal*, with a rare and beautifully understated attempt to see soccer violence from the other side of the barbed-wire fence.

The Undertones—"My Perfect Cousin" (1980)

Canned nostalgia for the sixties generation, highlighted by the pitiful cry, "he flicked to kick and I didn't know"—a reference to the once all-consuming juvenile love of the table soccer game Subbuteo, which was also featured on the single's picture sleeve.

The Fall—"Kicker Conspiracy" (1983)

It was an age, Fall frontman Mark E. Smith reflected to the *New Musical Express*, "when no bugger wanted to know about soccer songs." The game was in turmoil, beset by violence, haunted by tumbling attendances, crippled by underachievement, and assailed on all sides by hordes of the so-called Casual hooligans, designer-label devotees who swaggered round in matching shirts and knuckledusters. More than that, though, it was a period when soccer itself was uncool, uncouth, un-everything that a right-minded mid-eightiess pop star should be thinking about. How could the Fall resist?

Half Man Half Biscuit—"All I Want for Christmas Is a Dukla Prague Away Kit" (1985)

Another ode to Subbuteo, and the phenomenal range of options that the game's catalog seemed to offer.

The Decemberists—"The Sporting Life" (2009)

Titled for an early sixties movie about rugby but, according to frontman Colin Meloy, written about his days playing youth soccer for the YMCA in St. Helena, Montana.

Herman's Hermits—"It's Nice to Be Out in the Morning" (1968)

Songwriter Graham Gouldman's gorgeous paean to hometown Manchester kicked off the Hermits' *Mrs. Brown, You've Got a Lovely Daughter* movie soundtrack with a visit to "United's ground where the champions score/A hundred goals to the Reds fans' roar." Which, considering the Hermits were far bigger in the US than in England, could not have made a lot of sense to the teenyboppers.

Ashley Hutchings & Ernesto de Pascale—"The Lion of Highbury" (2008)

From the Anglo-Italian duo's *My Land Is Your Land* CD, a beautifully phrased recounting of the legendary England vs. Italy game in 1934, a closely fought and fiery 3–2 victory for the English that history still recalls as "the Battle of Highbury." "The English had the victory but Italy had our hearts."

Die Toten Hosen—"Bayern" (2000)

German punk veterans whose name translates as the Dead Trousers, Toten Hosen are notoriously dedicated supporters of Fortuna Düsseldorf. Which does not bode well for a song dedicated to Bayern München . . .

Kirsty MacColl—"England 2, Colombia 0" (1999)

Or, how a casual meeting in a bar while the World Cup's on the television can turn to despair and pain.

The Hitchers—"Strachan" (1997)

"She waited for the match to start to start a fight with me." And so the Irish punkers encapsulate a moment that so many men can identify with, before hitting back with the riposte that they all wish they had thought of. "It's a program about art . . . and the greatest midfield artist of them all walked out onto the park." Former Manchester United and Scotland ace Wee Gordy, of course!

The Waterboys—"Burlington Bertie And Accrington Stanley" (1993)

Glorious nonsense imbibed with that breathy portentousness that only the Waterboys ever pulled off with such conviction, "Burlington Bertie" was wacky wordplay, deranged doggerel, and the maniacal invocation of the English league side that plunged into oblivion in 1962 (but has since returned in ruder health than ever—good on ya!).

[substitute] Alexi Lalas—"Kickin' Balls" (1994)

Stop laughing at the back. A lot of Lalas's musical admirers didn't even know he played soccer. And, presumably, vice versa.

13

What Did He Just Say?

A Collection of Soccer Quotations

"[David] Seaman is a handsome young man but he spends too much time looking in his mirror, rather than at the ball. You can't keep goal with hair like that."

Brian Clough (manager, Nottingham Forest)
discussing the Arsenal goalkeeper of the day

"Of course I didn't take my wife to see Rochdale as an anniversary present. It was her birthday. Would I have got married in the football season? Anyway, it was Rochdale reserves."

Bill Shankly (manager, Liverpool)

"Five days shalt thou labour, as the Bible says. The seventh day is the Lord thy God's. The sixth day is for football."

Anthony Burgess (novelist)

Many a true word, apparently, is spoken in jest.

Luis Suarez scores against England at the 2014 World Cup—his final full game before his mouth landed him in some serious trouble. *AGIF/Shutterstock.com*

"At United we strive for perfection, if we fail we might just have to settle for excellence."

Sir Matt Busby (manager, Manchester United)

"Whoever invented soccer should be worshipped as god."

Hugo Sánchez (player)

"I spent a lot of money on booze, birds, and fast cars. The rest I just squandered."

George Best (player)

"When I think of the Middle Ages I think of castles, Catholicism, and taking your kids to soccer practice."

Jarod Kintz (author)

"Curses cannot touch me: I wear my underwear inside out."

Adrian Mutu (player)

"These are just things that happen out on the pitch. It was just the two of us inside the area and he bumped into me with his shoulder."

Luis Suarez (player) after biting World Cup opponent

"We accept people here, imperfections and all. I am sure Luis Suarez will be someone positive for us in the future."

Andoni Zubizarreta (Barcelona director of sport)
after signing Luis Suarez after biting World Cup opponent

"I'm seeing some good things. I think in preseason you see some bad things as well and those are the things you try to correct."

Peter Taylor (manager, Gillingham FC)

"Whenever I hear young footballers of today grumbling about their lot, I can't help but tell them they should count their lucky stars they are not having to work down the mines."

Jock Stein (manager, Glasgow Celtic)

"Sometimes in soccer you have to score goals."

Thierry Henry (player)

"As you know, I'm no soccer fan. I didn't see a single match, not even the [World Cup final]."

Argentine President Cristina Fernandez de Kirchner,
welcoming her nation's soccer team home from the World Cup

"Football is regarded as a given disability that has to be worked around. If I were wheelchair-bound, nobody close to me would organize anything in a top-floor flat, so why would they plan anything for a winter Saturday afternoon?"

Nick Hornby (author)

Cristiano Ronaldo. He says he's not a perfectionist, but imagine how he'd play if he was!
AGIF/Shutterstock.com

"Football is a simple game; twenty-two men chase a ball for ninety minutes and at the end, the Germans win on penalties."

Gary Linekar (player)

"We must have had ninety-nine percent of the game. It was the other three percent that cost us the match."

Ruud Gullit (manager, LA Galaxy etc)

"If a chairman sacks the manager he initially appointed, he should go as well."

Brian Clough

"A football team is like a beautiful woman. When you do not tell her, she forgets she is beautiful."

Arsene Wenger (manager, Arsenal)

"It is better to win ten times 1–0 than to win once 10–0."

Vahid "Vaha" Halilhodži (player)

"Every disadvantage has its advantage."

Johan Cruyff (manager, Barcelona, etc.)

"Success is no accident. It is hard work, perseverance, learning, studying, sacrifice, and most of all, love of what you are doing or learning to do."

Pelé (player)

"Players lose you games, not tactics. There's so much crap talked about tactics by people who barely know how to win at dominoes."

Brian Clough

"My father used to say, 'If you want to know the artist, look at the art.' He was usually talking about Stanley Matthews or Don Bradman when he said it."

David Peace (author)

"The first ninety minutes are the most important."

Bobby Robson (manager, England, etc.)

"Soccer is an art more central to our culture than anything the Arts Council deigns to recognize."

Germaine Greer (author)

"The rules of soccer are very simple, basically it is this: if it moves, kick it. If it doesn't move, kick it until it does."

Phil Woosnam (NASL chief)

Roy Keane. One of the twenty-first century's greatest players, and one of the game's most controversial spokesmen, too. *Eoghan McNally/Shutterstock.com*

"The trouble with referees is that they know the rules, but they do not know the game."

Bill Shankly

"If God had wanted man to play soccer, he wouldn't have given us arms."

Mike Ditka (American footballer)

"Rome wasn't built in a day. But I wasn't on that particular job."

Brian Clough

"To say that these men paid their shillings to watch twenty-two hirelings kick a ball ismerely to say that a violin is wood and catgut, and that Hamlet is so much paper and ink."

J. B. Priestley (author)

"Complaining about boring football is a little like complaining about the sad ending of *King Lear*: it misses the point somehow."

Nick Hornby (author)

"I was a soccer cheerleader. It doesn't get nerdier than that. I was fired from the soccer cheerleading squad after one year, which I believe to this day is unprecedented. You have to understand, no one went to the soccer games. In fact, I believe part of my duties as a cheerleader was to bake brownies for the team."

Kathy Griffin (actress)

"How could you have a soccer team if all were goalkeepers? How would it be an orchestra if all were French horns?"

Desmond Tutu (Archbishop)

"I wouldn't say I was the best manager in the business. But I was in the top one."

Brian Clough

"I am not a perfectionist, but I like to feel that things are done well."

Cristiano Ronaldo (player)

"Some people tell me that we professional players are soccer slaves. Well, if this is slavery, give me a life sentence."

Bobby Charlton (player)

"For a player to be good enough to play for Liverpool, he must be prepared to run through a brick wall for me, then come out fighting on the other side."

Bill Shankly

"International football is the continuation of war by other means."

George Orwell (author)

"Some people believe football is a matter of life and death, I am very disappointed with that attitude. I can assure you it is much, much more important than that."

Bill Shankly

"If you're in the penalty area and don't know what to do with the ball, put it in the net and we'll discuss the options later."

Bob Paisley (manager, Liverpool)

"I don't believe skill was, or ever will be, the result of coaches. It is a result of a love affair between the child and the ball."

Roy Keane (player)

"Every kid around the world who plays soccer wants to be Pelé. I have a great responsibility to show them not just how to be like a soccer player, but how to be like a man."

Pelé (player)

"The goalkeeper is the jewel in the crown and getting at him should be almost impossible. It's the biggest sin in football to make him do any work."

George Graham (manager, Arsenal, etc.)

"I know more about soccer than about politics."

Harold Wilson (British prime minster)

"Soccer matches should be something special, something people eagerly look forward to, something that brightens life."

P. J. O'Rourke (author)

"I want kids. I want a soccer team, and I want a husband."

Lady Gaga (singer)

"A penalty is a cowardly way to score."

Pelé

"Everything I know about morality and the obligations of men, I owe it to football."

Albert Camus

"I believe that a bad Super Bowl halftime show is still better than a soccer game."

Ron White (comedian)

"The thing about football—the important thing about football—is that it is not just about football."

Terry Pratchett (author)

"I never comment on referees and I'm not going to break the habit of a lifetime for that prat."

Ron Atkinson (manager, Manchester United, etc.)

"Football is the ballet of the masses."

Dmitri Shostakovich (composer)

"Contrary to popular belief, I don't spend a whole lot of time following soccer. But as I have traveled around the world to better understand global development and health, I've learned that soccer is truly universal. No matter where I go, that's what kids are playing. That's what people are talking about."

Bill Gates (computer guy)

"Behind the windows of Manchester, there is an insane love of football, of celebration and of music."

Eric Cantona (player)

"In a world haunted by the hydrogen and napalm bomb, the football field is a place where sanity and hope are still left unmolested."

Stanley Rous (FIFA president)

There's no in between—you're either good or bad. We were in between."

Gary Linekar

"In all modesty, my summing up of 1955–6 and 1956–7 must be that no club in the country could live with Manchester United."

Matt Busby

"If you are first you are first. If you are second, you are nothing."

Bill Shankly

"I loathed the game, and since I could see no pleasure or usefulness in it, it was very difficult for me to show courage at it. Football, it seemed to me, is not really played for the pleasure of kicking a ball about, but is a species of fighting."

George Orwell

"Without being too harsh on David Beckham, he cost us the match."

Ian Wright (player)

"I think football would become an even better game if someone could invent a ball that kicks back."

Eric Morecambe (comedian)

"Football is all very well a good game for rough girls, but not for delicate boys."

Oscar Wilde (author)

"That lad must have been born offside."

Sir Alex Ferguson (manager)

"Fergie said I was a Manchester United player in the wrong shirt—I said he was an Arsenal manager in the wrong blazer."

Tony Adams (player)

"The ball is like a woman, she loves to be caressed."

Eric Cantona

"I don't believe there is such a thing as a 'born' soccer player. Perhaps you are born with certain skills and talents, but quite frankly it seems impossible to me that one is actually born to be an ace soccer player."

Pelé

"If a player is not interfering with play or seeking to gain an advantage, then he should be."

Bill Shankly

"When Manchester United are at their best I am close to orgasm."

Gianluca Vialli (player)

"You have to allow yourself to lose control from time to time."

Eric Cantona

"We didn't underestimate them. They were a lot better than we thought."

Bobby Robson

"We lost because we didn't win."

Ronaldo (player)

"As long as no one scored, it was always going to be close."

Arsene Wenger

"Alex Ferguson is the best manager I've ever had at this level. Well, he's the only manager I've actually had at this level. But he's the best manager I've ever had."

David Beckham (player)

"At a football club, there's a holy trinity: the players, the manager, and the supporters. Directors don't come into it. They are only there to sign the checks."

Bill Shankly

"I used to go missing a lot . . . Miss Canada, Miss United Kingdom, Miss World."

George Best

14

Continental Competitions

When Is a League Not a League?

F irst things first. Any reference to the Champions League, here or elsewhere, should be accompanied by pointing out that it is not, in fact,
actually a league, at least under the criteria by which other competitions
are devised and described. Rather, it simply apes the qualifying stage and early
rounds of the World Cup and sundry other championships, in which competitors are placed into groups of between three and six, so that each can play the
others twice. None of which have ever referred to the process as a league. It is
a pedantic point, of course, but one that has given rise to some confusion as
newcomers to the game wonder why the World Cup is a cup and the Champions
League is a league, when both adhere to exactly the same format for deciding
their eventual champions. Thankfully, few people search for logic in the world
of corporate branding, and so we move on.

Champions of Europe—Chelsea take the 2012 Champions League title.
Laszlo Szirtesi/Shutterstock.com

Great Game, Shame About the Theme Music

They are, the marketing men inform us, the most prestigious club competitions in the world. They are certainly the most widely televised and loudly promoted. The cash rewards that they offer can make even the richest team richer; and chasing those rewards can have the opposite effect, and reduce millionaires to slumdogs overnight. But victory transforms princes into kings, legends into epics, and champions into Champions of Champions.

Maybe that's why they call (most of) them the Champions Leagues.

In the same way that the domestic cups of the world are organized by their national football associations, and the World Cup is the preserve of the planet's governing body, FIFA, so the continental championships are run by the continental federations: Europe's is overseen by UEFA (the Union of European Football Asociations), South America's by CONMEBOL (the Confederación Sudamericana de Fútbol), North America's by CONCACAF (the Confederation of North, Central American, and Caribbean Association Football), Asia's by the AFC (Asian Football Confederation), Africa's by the CAF (Confederation of African Football), and Oceania's by the OFC (the Oceania Football Confederation).

These bodies are responsible for every aspect of the tournament, from choosing the host and establishing the qualification process, to handling television and sponsorship rights and, of course, to "maintaining the brand"—no matter how hideous, and utterly devoid of sporting romanticism that term might sound. Indeed, it is branding that has ensured the comparative uniformity of the competition's titles, regardless of their very diffuse historical roots.

In Europe, the UEFA Champions League grew out of the plain old European Cup, a one nation/one club tournament that first enthralled the continent during the 1955–1956 season, and continued to do so until 1992–1993 brought about both a revised format (the aforementioned World Cup style mini-leagues, in place of the original home-and-away knock-out contest) and opened up admission to second-, third-, and eventually even fourth-placed sides, as well as the actual champions. The European Champions League is the richest and, according to the marketing men, the most avidly followed and widely watched, of all the trophies.

In North and Central America, the CONCACAF Champions Cup has been bringing continental glory to the champions (and otherwise) of North and Central America and the Caribbean since it was launched in 1962.

In Asia, the AFC Champions League (originally the Asian Champion Club Tournament, and variations thereof, until its renaming in 2002) has certainly had its ups and downs, including a fourteen-year spell during which it wasn't even competed for, so little interest did it arouse. Today, however, it is now firmly established as the continent's key event.

In Africa, the African Cup of Champions morphed into the CAF Champions League in 1997, and over the years, it has had to contend with war, revolution, famine, and more. Yet still it routinely delivers up potential world-beaters.

In Oceania, the OFC's Oceania Champions League started life as a one-off play-off between the Australian and New Zealand champions in 1987, before being reborn as a federation-wide event in 1999. It became what the locals call the O-League in 2007, and while it struggles beneath the smallest membership of any of the game's regional governing bodies (a mere seven; CONMEBOL has but ten, but what a ten they are; CONCACAF boasts forty-one, Asia has forty-six, Europe fifty-four, and Africa fifty-six), it grows stronger every year.

Only Latin America has (so far) resisted the temptation for titular history to be sidelined in favor of global streamlining. The Copa Libertadores that was born in 1960, and became the training ground for so many of the world's all-time greatest players, remains the Copa Libertadores today (although commercialism has got a foot in the door. Since 2012, the competition's official title has been the Copa Bridgestone Libertadores, after its Japanese tire-manufacturing sponsor.)

The competitions have something else in common, though. Once it has been won, each then dispatches its winner to an annual world championship. There to battle to discover who was the greatest soccer team on the planet.

Which is all people wanted to find out in the first place.

Sir Thomas Lipton's Tea Cup

The taste for pan-continental competition is not new. In 1909, teams from Italy, Germany, Switzerland, and England were invited to compete for the Sir Thomas Lipton trophy in a competition being staged in Turin, Italy. The three continental powers duly sent their most powerful representatives: Stuttgarter Sportfreunde, FC Winterthur, and a composite Juventus/Torino XI.

Not for the last time, however, the English FA declined to compete in a foreign-run tournament, so the trophy's benefactor, tea magnate Lipton, instead extended the invite to West Auckland FC, a non-league amateur club from northern England. Not for the sake of making up numbers but because, at that point in history, England's amateur soccer scene was at least the equal of its professional frontier, and West Auckland were one of the mightiest sides in the country. As they proved by not merely winning the trophy on this first occasion, but also by successfully defending it two years later, by demolishing Juventus 6–1 in the final.

Many histories have subsequently described the Sir Thomas Lipton trophy as the first World Cup; indeed, in 1982 a television dramatization of the 1909 competition, *The World Cup: A Captain's Tale*, was screened in the UK. But it was not, in truth, the first event of its kind in Europe, or even in Turin. In 1908, the Torneo Internazionale Stampa Sportiva brought sides from Italy, France, Germany, and Switzerland together in pan-European combat, with the Swiss side Servette running out eventual victors.

And a full decade before that, in 1897, central Europe thrilled to a knock-out style Challenge Cup opened up to teams from throughout the Austro-Hungarian Empire—at that time, a vast entity that comprised modern Austria,

Czechoslovakia, Hungary, Croatia, Slavonia, Bosnia and Herzegovina, adding up to a tract of land that reached all the way to the borders of the Ottoman Empire.

In the event, the difficulties of travel ensured that very few clubs entered beyond those based in the administrative centers of Vienna, Prague, and Budapest, with Vienna utterly dominating the tournament. But the opportunity, at least, was there.

The first three finals, in 1898, 1899, and 1900, were fought by exclusively Viennese teams; the next five, while more cosmopolitan, were won by them. Not until 1908–1909, when the contest returned after a three-year break, did the Challenge Cup find itself carried beyond the Vienna city limits, when the Hungarian side Ferencvárosi TC defeated the Wiener Sport-Club 2–1. But honors were reversed when next the trophy was competed, in 1910–1911, and that was the end of the Challenge Cup.

The Cup was forgotten, but the idea did not disappear. In 1927, the now independent nations of Austria, Hungary, Czechoslovakia, and Yugoslavia inaugurated the Mitropa Cup, the brainchild of Austrian FA chief Hugo Meisl.

It was an exclusive competition. Entry was restricted to domestic league titleholders, and either the Cup winners or the league runners-up, a true tournament of champions that was won in this inaugural year by Czechoslovakia's Sparta Prague, but in truth, any of the clubs involved could have taken the title; and so they did.

Ferencvárosi TC in 1928, and Újpest Dózsai in 1929 (in which year, Italian sides replaced the Yugoslavs) established a brief period of Hungarian dominance; four of the next seven finals then went to Austrian sides, with the Italians of Bologna (twice) and Sparta Prague interrupting the sequence.

The very constitution of the trophy was awe-inspiring. The 1930s, the first decade of the World Cup, were dominated by these same nations—Italy won the World Cup in 1934 and 1948, defeating Czechoslovakia and Hungary respectively. Yugoslavia were semifinalists in 1930, Austria in 1934. In geographical terms, the Mitropa Cup was being fought for in the very heart of world soccer supremacy, as its prime contenders were soon to demonstrate.

Other nations were invited to participate. In 1936, with entrance now open to four clubs per nation, Switzerland made its Mitropa bow; in 1937, Yugoslavia returned to the fray, alongside Romania. But storm clouds were gathering. In 1938, Austria effectively ceased to exist following its absorption into Hitler's Greater Germany, and the following year, just eight teams entered the tournament, two apiece from Czechoslovakia, Italy, and Hungary (including eventual victors Újpest Dózsai) and one each from Yugoslavia and Romania.

With war now tearing across Europe, the 1940 tournament was contested by an even smaller field of nations, with just Hungary, Yugoslavia, and Romania taking part, and all was going well for a time. Only when Ferencvárosi TC and Romania's Rapid Bucaresti won through to the final did the turbulent politics of the age finally get in the way. Miles away from any soccer stadium, a long-disputed territory in northern Transylvania, a Romanian holding since

1919, was being ceded back to Hungary. Ill feeling was rife on both sides; so much so that the game simply could not go on. Instead, the tournament was abandoned, incomplete.

The Mitropa Trophy lay unclaimed and uncontested for the next decade. But it reemerged (initially as the Zentropa Cup) in 1951, and—albeit with certain modifications—it would continue until 1992. By that time, however, other truly Europe-wide competitions had long since pushed the Mitropa Cup into obscurity, if not irrelevance, and its final decade was devoted not to champions' football, but to the winners of the competing nations' second divisions. The final tournament was won by FK Borac Banja Luka of Bosnia and Herzegovina.

Meanwhile, a second international contest had got underway in western Europe. Beginning in 1949, the Latin Cup brought together the champions of France, Italy, Portugal, and Spain—respectively, in that inaugural season, Stade de Reims, Torino (opening the season that would end with the tragedy of the Superga air disaster), Sporting Lisbon, and eventual winners Barcelona. Subsequent victors would include SL Benfica (1950), AC Milan (1951), Barcelona again (1952), and Stade de Reims (1953). But though it would ultimately continue on until 1957, 1955 saw the same nail driven into the Latin Cup's coffin as would ultimately see off the Mitropa Cup. In 1955, the newly formed UEFA sent out invitations to the clubs that would contest the first continent-wide European Cup, a champions-only contest that would put an end, at last, to all the spurious claims that clubs and media had been making about themselves for so long.

We Are the Champions of the Universe

No matter how dominant their respective regions were, the Latin and Mitropa Cups were purely regional affairs. The quest to find a true "world champion," then, tended to be a somewhat more freelance operation, clubs embarking upon tours of other lands, arranging as many games as they could in the time allowed, and then drawing their own conclusions from the results.

The nature of these outings was officially friendly, but the sense of competition that they aroused was often anything but. In September 1945, with European soccer still struggling to get back on its feet following World War Two, the Soviet champions Dynamo Moscow visited the UK for a series of games against Chelsea (a 3–3 draw), Cardiff City (a 10–1 Muscovite mauling), Arsenal (bad-tempered and fog-bound, but again a Soviet victory, 4–3), and Glasgow Rangers (2–2).

As a spectacle, it offered British sports fans some of the most exciting soccer they had seen in years. But neither host nor visitors appeared especially impressed by one other, with author George Orwell possibly delivering the most succinct summary of the entire affair:

"Now that the brief visit of the Dynamo team has come to an end, it is possible to say publicly what many thinking people were saying privately before the Dynamos ever arrived. That is, that sport is an unfailing cause of good will, and

In 1991, the European Cup Winners Cup was nearing the end of its life, but Manchester United celebrated England's return to European soccer by winning it regardless.

that if such a visit as this had any effect at all on Anglo-Soviet relations, it could only be to make them worse."

Not all visits proved as volatile as the Soviet sojourn, of course. Over the next decade, foreign tours became a major preoccupation for clubs all over Europe, and with them, certain bragging rights. Indeed, it was when Wolverhampton Wanderers declared themselves champions of Europe after beating the visiting Hungarians of Honvéd that certain figures in authority agreed something needed to be done. Claiming such titles was all very well. But proving them required something more than a string of random friendlies.

The European Cup Is Born

A new tournament was conceived, and sixteen clubs were invited to participate, representing the cream of Austria (Rapid Wien), Belgium (Anderlecht), Denmark (BK Frem København), England (Chelsea), France (Stade de Reims), Hungary (Honvéd—despite the Wolves result, one of the most vocal claimants of that unofficial "best in Europe" title), Italy (AC Milan), the Netherlands (Holland Sport), Portugal (Sporting CP), the short-lived nation of Saarland (Saarbrücken), Scotland (Hibernian), Spain (Real Madrid), Sweden (Djurgården), Switzerland (Servette), West Germany (Rot-Weiss Essen), and Yugoslavia (Partizan Belgrade).

The acceptances came in, but so did the refusals. The champions of Holland, Hungary, and Denmark all declined the opportunity to compete for a variety of reasons, and they were replaced by the teams that ran them closest for the title: PSV Eindhoven, Vörös Lobogó, and AGF Aarhus.

England posed a sterner challenge, however, as the FA outright refused to allow Chelsea, or any other English club, to participate. No amount of persuasion or argument could change the authorities' mind, but rather than go it alone and deliberately flout the FA's authority (which is what Manchester United would do the following season), finally, Chelsea obediently stepped aside to be replaced by the Polish champions Gwardia Warszawa—who promptly fell at the first hurdle.

With no true precedent to judge by, few observers had any idea how the tournament would pan out. In an age when sports coverage, even in the soccer-craziest lands, was restricted almost exclusively to domestic happenings, the most powerful foreign teams were just that. Foreign.

Gleaning clues from international squads was possible, but that too was unreliable. When England traveled to Spain for a friendly in May 1955, the home side fielded just three of the Real Madrid players who would sweep all before them as the European Cup progressed: Francisco Gento, Hector Rial, and José María Zarraga. And when the return match was played in November, there was not one.

The uncertainties, and indeed the inequalities of European competition were swiftly revealed, however. In the first round, Scotland's Hibernian crushed the West German representatives 4–0 in one leg, 5–1 on aggregate. Rapid Wien put six past PSV, while Vörös Lobogó's two-legged 10–4 thrashing of Anderlecht was made up of a 6–3 victory in the first leg, 4–1 in the second.

Other scores were just crazy. Reputations be damned; Saarbrücken, relishing their homeland's first and only taste of European club competition, caused a major shock when they defeated AC Milan by the odd goal in seven (before being stomped 4–1 in the return); while Partizan's 5–2 second-leg slaughter of Sporting CP utterly belied the tense 3–3 draw they played out a couple of weeks earlier.

With only sixteen competing teams, the second round was also the quarterfinal, but the goal-getting did not slow down. Hibernian progressed on a 4–1 aggregate over Djurgården; the French and Hungarian sides fought out a fourteen-goal aggregate thriller; Real Madrid sneaked past Partizan by virtue of a 4–0 win at home, which was almost overhauled by a 3–0 defeat in Belgrade; and AC Milan went positively crazy in Vienna, a dour 1–1 draw being followed by a triumphant 7–1 thrashing.

Real continued living on the edge in the semifinal, a 5–4 aggregate victory over AC Milan blotting out the memory of the 2–1 defeat they suffered in Italy. But Stade powered past Hibernian to set up a pulsating final match.

At first, it was all the Frenchmen, Stade racing into a two-goal lead within ten minutes of the kickoff. Inevitably, however, Real fought back. Alfredo Di Stéfano, Madrid's mercurial genius, pulled one goal back in the fourteenth minute; Rial got the equalizer on the half-hour mark.

The French regained the lead on the hour; Marquitos pulled Madrid back to level pegging seven minutes later. And finally, with little more than ten minutes to go, Rial scored his second and, with Madrid ahead for the first time all game, that is how the match ended. Real Madrid were the first-ever champions of Europe; and, for the next five years, they were its only champions.

Much was made, in 2013–2014, of Real Madrid landing their tenth European Cup Champions League title, their 4–1 victory over neighbors Atlético Madrid looking a lot more impressive on paper than it did throughout the match itself—the game was deep into five minutes of second-half stoppage time before Real finally neutralized the 1–0 lead that Atlético had held for much of the match.

Yet Real's tenth title, the legendary La Decima, is perhaps less impressive when one considers how long it took them to make it to ten—forty-four years—compared with the mere five it took to get them to reach five. In 1956–1957, Fiorentina fell 2–0 in the final. In 1957–1958, with Di Stéfano emerging the tournament's top scorer, AC Milan were dispatched 3–2 following a 2–2 draw; the following season saw a replay of the first-ever final end with a 2–0 Spanish victory, while 1959–1960 brought what, for many people, remains the greatest European Cup final of all time, as Real took on the German champions, Eintracht Frankfurt.

The tournament had grown. No fewer than twenty-six nations now competed, from both Western Europe and the Communist Eastern Bloc. From the two Irelands (Northern and the Republic) in the west to Turkey in the east, from tiny Luxembourg to debutantes Greece, the European Cup was truly all-encompassing, and it could be enthrallingly one-sided.

There was no such thing as seeding in those days. Teams' names went into the bag and they were pulled out again, one by one. So Real put twelve goals past Luxembourg's Jeunesse Esch, Barcelona slammed eight past CDNA Sofia of Bulgaria, and seven past AC Milan. IFK Göteburg left Northern Irish eyes crying with a 7–3 aggregate; and Belgium's Anderlecht might have been undisputed serial champions of their homeland, but they were well established as the whipping boys of the European Cup.

Following on from their 10–4 mauling in the first tournament, 1956–1957 then saw them crushed 12–0 by Manchester United. No matter that Belgium's entry to the 1957–1958 event, Royal Antwerp, fared no better (Real flattened them by 8–1); 1958–1959 saw Standard de Liège undo all past damage by demolishing Heart of Midlothian in the first round, Sporting Clube de Portugal in the second, and only narrowly succumbing to Stade Reims in the quarterfinals.

The pride was back on the face of Belgian soccer; and then Anderlecht returned for 1959–1960 and were steamrollered by Glasgow Rangers. In much the same way as Wolverhampton Wanderers, whose intemperate boasting back in 1954 had set the European Cup ball rolling in the first place, were steamrollered by Barcelona in the quarterfinal. Four unanswered goals put the Spanish champions ahead in the first leg; a staggering 5–2 win in Wolverhampton confirmed the Basques' semifinal berth.

There they would meet Real Madrid, in the tournament's first-ever single-city derby.

El Classico was already well established in the Spanish calendar, with all of its footballing and political rivalries already in place; Barcelona standing proud as the unspoken representatives of Spain's downtrodden left wing, Real bold and brilliant as the all-but-state-sponsored face of the fascist dictator General Franco; Barcelona as the sporting soul of Catalonia's independent aspirations, Real as the firm grip of government.

Real clearly appreciated the significance of the ensuing battle, and they made no mistakes. At home, the ever-reliable Di Stéfano opened the scoring; the Hungarian mastermind Puskás scored a second, and Di Stéfano netted the third in a 3–1 win. Away, Real engineered the exact same score, this time with Puskás opening and closing the goal tally, and Gento hitting the middle one.

With Eintracht doing unto Rangers what they had done unto Anderlecht, only more so . . . Rangers stopped at a 7–2 aggregate, Eintracht hit them for twelve, six in each leg . . . the final, to be staged, ironically, in Glasgow, promised to be an absolute humdinger. But none could have predicted how much of one. Ten goals rained in, with Eintracht even taking the lead through Richard Kreß before the combined forces of Di Stéfano and Puskás set about tearing them to shreds.

Di Stéfano hit the equalizer, then put Madrid ahead, and when the teams went in at half time, 2–1 was a reasonable reflection on the nature of the game. Or so most onlookers felt. Puskás, however, believed different. The game had barely restarted than he scored his first. Ten minutes later, he sank a penalty. On the hour, he completed his hat trick, and in the seventy-first minute he appeared to put the game out of reach. Twenty minutes to go, and the score was 6–1; and now, the Germans woke up.

A minute on from the restart, Stein made it 6–2. Di Stéfano retaliated immediately. 7–2. Stein raced to the other end and hit back. Four goals in five minutes, and suddenly it was 7–3. A Hampden Park record crowd of 127,000 was breathless. The watching TV audience was spellbound. In years to come, generations of players and managers from around the world would describe the 1960 European Cup final in general, and Di Stéfano's role in particular, as the greatest they ever witnessed; as the impetus, even, behind their own dreams of soccer greatness.

In 2014, following Di Stéfano's death, Alex Ferguson recalled for the BBC. "In the semifinal, Eintracht Frankfurt beat Rangers and we looked upon Eintracht Frankfurt as almost certain to win the Cup—but of course Real Madrid were a special team. I had the pleasure as a young man of being influenced by the great Real Madrid and Di Stéfano."

That was the climax of Real's European adventure. The following season, drawn again against Barcelona, they tumbled out in the first round, 4–3 on aggregate, and opened the way for Portugal's SL Benfica to finally shatter the

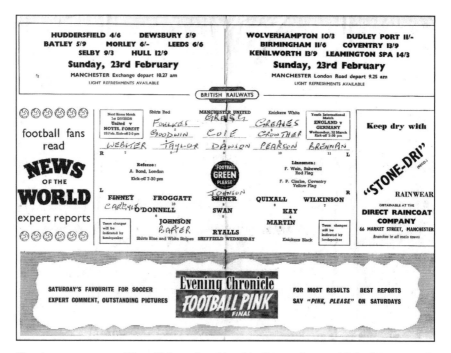

The show must go on. The still heart-breaking blank teamsheet published for United's next game, following the disaster.

team boarded the first of the flights that would take them home. They would be changing planes in Munich, but they expected to be home by dinnertime.

Instead. . . . Twice, the appalling conditions at the airport had caused the team's plane to abort takeoff; the third time, the old Elizabethan airliner just kept going and going, until it hit first a perimeter fence, and then a house on the other side of it.

News of the disaster was painfully slow in filtering through to England. By nightfall, however, there was barely a family in the country unaware of, or unmoved by, what had happened. So absolutely had United dominated the game that their players were household names. And every time another of those names was added to the roll call of the dead, so a fresh shockwave swept across the land. Roger Byrne . . . Geoffrey Bent . . . Eddie Colman . . . Mark Jones . . . David Pegg . . . Tommy Taylor . . . Liam Whelan.

Fifteen other names—sports journalists, club officials, crew, and passengers—followed. Club secretary Walter Crickmer, trainer Tom Curry, chief coach Bert Whalley, the journalists Alf Clarke, Donny Davies, Frank Swift, Eric Thompson, Henry Rose, Archie Ledbrooke, George Follows, and Tom Jackson. Travel agent Bela Miklos, and one of manager Busby's closest friends, Willie Satinoff. Cabin steward Tom Cable.

With the news of the dead, of course there came tales of survival. Bobby Charlton, flung clear of the wreckage, was uninjured, but would be out of the game for some weeks. Matt Busby was fighting for his life in an oxygen tent in Munich's Rechts der Isar Hospital. Billy Foulkes, Harry Gregg, Kenny Morgan, Denis Viollet, Albert Scanlon, Johnny Berry, Jackie Blanchflower. And Duncan Edwards, too, had survived, although he lay in a coma, so badly injured that even if he did live, he might never play again.

In the event, he never recovered consciousness and, two weeks after the crash, on February 21, he too passed away. It had been said in the past, as the Busby Babes had grown in stature, that if God liked soccer, then he must have loved United. Now it was said that He had loved them too much.

A little battered by the passing years, a rosette produced to mark Chelsea's 1971 Cup Winners Cup triumph.

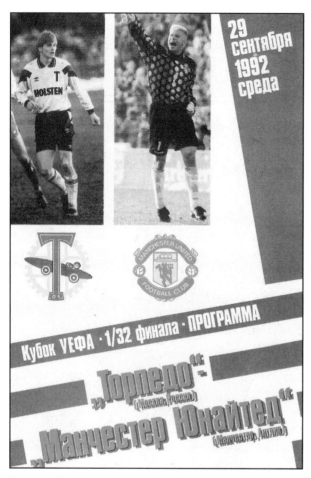

Europe offered even the continent's most traveled sides and supporters a chance to see fresh cities. Manchester United travel to Moscow in 1992.

Somehow United survived. The Football League gracefully postponed their next scheduled league match, and not until February 19 could the country pour out to pay tribute to the shattered team. An incredible 66,123 crammed Old Trafford to watch United take on Sheffield Wednesday in the fifth round of the Cup, and as they surveyed the team sheet in the matchday program, there was scarcely a dry eye in the house. The team sheet was blank.

With a patchwork team, United powered three goals past an opposing eleven who, as overcome as any in the stadium, must have wished they could have been anywhere else, doing anything else. Emotion, as much as talent, swept United to Wembley that year, there to see the fairy tale cruelly curtailed by two goals from Bolton Wanderers' Nat Lofthouse.

But the phoenix was to continue to rise all the same. In 1963, United won the FA Cup; in 1965 and 1967 the League Championship; and in 1968, they became the first English club to lift the European Cup. But of all the players who swept them to victory, ten years and three months after Munich, only one truly understood the depths of emotions that manager Busby was feeling; Bobby Charlton, the last of the original Busby Babes.

Almost six decades have elapsed since Munich, but still, to thousands of people—many of whom were not even born at the time—it takes only the slightest jolt to bring the emotions flooding in, including the deaths of those who survived. Jimmy Murphy, United's assistant manager at the time of Munich, missed the trip because it clashed with his duties with the Welsh national side. But it was he to whose care the entire team was entrusted while Busby struggled for life in a German hospital. Murphy passed away in 1989. Since then, Berry (1994), Blanchflower (1998), Violett (1999), Wood (2002), Scanlon (2009), Morgans (2012), and Foulkes (2013) have also left us, and, of course, Busby himself, also in 1994.

Tributes to the dead continue to be paid every year at United's Old Trafford home, where the great clock outside remains halted at the exact time of the air crash. Articles, books, even songs have mourned the tragedy.

There has even been a movie made around the disaster. David Tennant's *United* may not add much to the sum of already-existing knowledge and folklore that surrounds both team and tragedy, but its focus on the human side, on the lives and laughter of the players themselves, raises them higher than even the most exquisitely written printed description. Chilling, on the other hand, are those scenes set in the offices of the game's administrators, bringing home to us just how avoidable the disaster actually was; how official intractability was as much a part of the ultimate tragedy as any amount of snow and ice. Any soccer traditionalist mourning, today, the fact that so much power is now concentrated in the hands of the clubs would do well to watch *United*, to remind themselves of how things were when the authorities called all the shots.

Besides, the movie's very existence illuminates the greatest tribute of them all: the fact that close to sixty years after the disaster, the dead remain household names.

Manchester United's 1968 European Cup triumph remains inextricably linked to the memory of the Babes, and Busby's driving ambition to complete the job they began. Three decades later, the club's 1999 Champions League victory was the culmination of Alex Ferguson's equally relentless drive to place himself alongside Busby in the pantheon of Britain's greatest club managers.

That his side left it until the last possible opportunity before securing victory only added further flavor to the proceedings. With just a few minutes of stoppage time to go, FC Bayern München were such nailed-on winners that their colored ribbons had already been affixed to the trophy, and their supporters were already singing songs of triumph and joy. At which point, Manchester United popped up with two goals in as many minutes and snatched the glory away from them.

"Football. Bloody hell," remarked Alex Ferguson when he was asked to explain the comeback afterward, and a more cogent definition of the game's unreliability would be hard to conceive. Not until 2014, and Real Madrid's equally last-minute smash-and-grab equalizer against Atlético, can the outcome of a European Cup final be said to have deceived so many onlookers, but still they required thirty minutes overtime in which to complete the job. The United team of 1999 didn't even need that.

Into Battle in Latin America

The European Cup was just five years old when UEFA's South American counterpart, CONMEBOL, established the Copa Libertadores. The oldest continental federation of them all, founded in 1916 (UEFA did not come into being until 1954), CONMEBOL had already been operating an international tournament, the Copa América, since 1916, but previous attempts to launch a similar contest for club sides had crashed against the twin demons of travel and finance.

As recently as 1948, the city of Santiago, Chile, tried hosting a continent-wide challenge cup, but the sheer weight of costs and losses ensured that nobody was in the mood to repeat the exercise, not even the winners, Brazil's Vasco da Gama.

The success of the European Cup, however, encouraged all concerned to try again and in April 1960, the new tournament got underway. It proved an instant success, too, while confirming the hegemony that continues to dominate regional soccer today. Uruguay's Club Atlético Peñarol were winners of the first two competitions, Brazil's Santos, with Pelé in full flight, the next pair; Argentina's Independiente the two after that.

Initially open to national champions only, playing in a straight knockout competition, the Copa's constitution saw its first major change in 1962, when entrants were placed into three groups of three, World Cup–style, with the winners of each going into the semifinals alongside the previous year's winner. By 1968, however, every nation had two teams in the tournament, with the league system expanded accordingly, and each nation permitted to sort out its own means of qualification as well.

Argentinean sides absolutely dominated the late sixties and early seventies. Between 1967, when Racing Club defeated Nacional (of Uruguay) in a play-off, and 1979 when Paraguay's Olimpia defeated Boca Juniors 2–0 over the two-legged final, the trophy left the country—indeed, the capital, Buenos Aires—just once, in 1976, when it enjoyed a quick vacation in Brazil. Every other competition ended in an Argentinean victory, and with it a whole new level of controversy as the South American victors lined up to meet, and invariably savage, their European counterparts in the Intercontinental Cup—perhaps the most violent, bad-tempered and ill-starred international competition ever devised.

Tensions between European and South American footballing nations had always simmered beneath the surface, with occasional World Cup conflicts marking their escalation. It was the 1966 World Cup that acted as the decisive spark, however, the world watching in disbelief as foul play and fouler refereeing decisions saw Brazil more or less physically bundled out of the contest before the group stage was even complete.

Shocked and outraged, Brazil effectively withdrew from international competition of all description for the next four years, with Santos (whose star player Pelé had come in for some especially brutal treatment) the first club to follow suit, when they declined their spot in the 1967 Copa Libertadores.

Other nations, however, decided to make their feelings felt somewhat less politically. Argentina, too, had suffered from some very questionable refereeing at the World Cup, most notably in their quarterfinal game with England—or, as Argentineans prefer to refer to it, *el robo del siglo*, the theft of the century.

There, captain Anton Rattin was sent off for no truly just reason that any neutral onlooker could see, and in the game's aftermath, England manager Alf Ramsey branded the Argentineans "animals." It was a reputation that their countrymen would now set about living up to with a vengeance.

Five players, two of them Argentinean, were sent off across the 1967 Intercontinental Cup meetings between Racing Club and Glasgow Celtic. The following year, Estudiantes' two-legged tie with Manchester United was little more than a war of attrition, and in 1969 all hell broke loose as Estudiantes met AC Milan in the second leg, trailing the Italians by 3–0 from the first game.

Estudiantes' players booted balls at the Milan team as they warmed up, while their fans poured hot coffee on the Italians as they emerged from the tunnel before kickoff. Elbows flew, boots, too; later, rumor insisted that the Argentineans had even carried needles onto the field with them, to prick their opponents.

Milan's Pierino Prati was knocked unconscious; Gianni Rivera was on the receiving end of a punch from goalkeeper Alberto Poletti, but the worst was reserved for Argentinean-born Nestor Combin, a French citizen who was by no means the first South American to ply his trade in Europe, but probably was the first ever to be accused of treachery by his countrymen.

Battered on the field, with one Argentinean elbow breaking both his nose and his cheekbone, Combin was knocked unconscious and, while he lay insensible, he was arrested for draft dodging—he had never registered for national service in Argentina. Of course he hadn't, he lived (and had served) in France. But he was kept in a cell overnight while that was sorted out, and there was just one consolation to the entire affair. Estudiantes may have won the leg, but AC Milan took the Cup on aggregate.

Nor were Estudiantes to escape unpunished. Even at home, opinion was outraged by their behavior on the field. One newspaper headlined its report "The English Were Right," while three players received swingeing punishments: Poletti was banned from the sport for life (he was later pardoned), Suarez was banned for thirty games, and Eduardo Manera for twenty. Poletti and Manera also received short prison sentences.

Today, the modern successor to the Intercontinental Cup is a decidedly less dramatic affair; and the Copa Libertadores, too, has lost much of its earlier reputation for bloodletting, instead becoming the showcase for some of the most dazzling soccer skills of the age. Flamenco, winning for Brazil in 1981, lined up with Zico, Leander, Nunes, Carpegiani, and more, a veritable golden generation.

The Colombians America de Cali captivated the world with three successive finals appearances, between 1985 and 1987, even if sympathy was all they ultimately had to show for their efforts—they lost all three matches. But a

Colombian side, Atlético Nacional, would win the tournament in 1989, the first representatives of their nation ever to take the title, and they did so under the most dramatic of circumstances. Tied 2–2 after two legs, Nacional and their opponents, the Paraguayan Olimpia, required no fewer than *four* rounds of penalties before a winner was finally decided, with even Nacional's goalkeeper, the great René Higuita, numbered among the scorers.

The same two sides would meet again at the semifinal stage in both 1990 and 1991, but this time it was the Paraguayans who won through, to defeat Barcelona of Ecuador in the 1990 final, then fall to Colo-Colo of Chile in 1991. A sequence of finals, incidentally, that is also notable for the absence of any team from the continent's "big three"—Argentina, Uruguay, and Brazil.

Normal service would be resumed in 1992 as Brazil's São Paulo won the first of two titles in succession, then reached a third where they went down to Argentina's Vélez Sarsfield. But the Copa of the nineties, for the most part, would remain in Brazilian hands, and while the first decade of the twenty-first century saw the balance of power shift, 2010 saw Brazilian sides reclaim their stranglehold, with successive victories for SC International, Santos, Corinthians, and Atlético Mineiro.

Brazilian sides are still some way away from ever catching up with Argentina's record of tournament triumphs—Independiente have seven titles, Boca have six, Estudiantes have four. No Brazilian side has more than three. But the conflict itself is certain to remain continental club soccer's most glorious, and competitive.

15

The Biggest Stage of All

Club? Or Country?

While the World Cup is unquestionably the premier international tournament in the world, it was neither the first, nor—in those regions where qualification for the FIFA showpiece was restricted to just one or two nations—the most important.

As recently as 1990, North/Central America, Africa, and Asia received just two automatic spots apiece (at 2014, they accounted for thirteen of the thirty-two available places), while Oceania's single champion is still forced to qualify through a two-legged play-off with CONCACAF's *fourth*-best nation. It's a state of affairs that leaves vast tracts of the planet scrapping for a very minor piece of the action and one that has, accordingly, encouraged the rise of some remarkable local or regional tournaments.

In Asia—a landmass, lest we forget, that extends from the Middle Eastern shores of Europe, all the way to Japan—the oldest international soccer tournament is the Merdeka Cup. Established by Malaya in 1957, to help commemorate the country's newly won independence, staged annually until 1988, and sporadically since then, the tournament was initially open only to teams from Southeast and Eastern Asia. India, Pakistan, Singapore, Thailand, Japan, Hong Kong, Taiwan, and South Korea were the most reliable entrants, with Singapore and South Korea in particular establishing themselves as regional powerhouses.

The growth of soccer's popularity in the Middle East, however, saw that area move into Merdeka contention during the 1970s, with several African nations also accepting invitations, Libya, Ghana, and Senegal among them. Representative sides from Latin America and Europe were also featuring in the last years before the competition lapsed into semi-obscurity, and in so doing, brought a taste of true international soccer to a region which, for all FIFA's claims to be benefitting the worldwide game, had hitherto been regarded very much as a poor relation of the superpowers.

It is not alone. Today, Asian ambitions are assuaged by the AFC Challenge Cup, established for the benefit of "emerging countries," and in 2014 won, against more challenging odds than most nations could even contemplate encountering, by Palestine. Victory, sealed by a fifty-ninth-minute goal by Ashraf Nu'man, also guaranteed them a first-ever berth in the Asian Cup, at least in

Scorer of a record thirteen goals at the 1958 World Cup, France's Just Fontaine receives the Adidas Platinum Boot award from UEFA President Michel Platini during the Opening Ceremony of the sixty-fourth FIFA Congress in Brazil in 2014.

as much as anything in Palestine's destiny can be described as "guaranteed." Again, anybody thinking their country has had a hard time of things should spend some time with the DVD *Goal Dreams* (also known as *World Cup Inshallah*), a documentary tracing Palestine's quest to qualify for the 2006 World Cup.

In and around Oceania, the South Pacific Games bring the hope of glory and, more importantly, the benefits of experience, to islands that many people would be hard pressed to ever locate on a map. Throughout the world, competitions abound whose entrants might never taste World Cup glory, whose pursuit of the statue begins and ends with a single qualifying match or two some four years before the tournament is actually held. When they raise their voices, as they periodically do, to demand a more equitable share of the World Cup bounty, it really is difficult to fault them.

There again, when Jules Rimet, a French lawyer and honorary President of FIFA, put forward his plan for all the nations on earth to compete for a title of Champions of the World, it is unlikely that he ever realized precisely what he was setting in motion. More so even than the Olympic Games, the World Cup is the planet's number-one sporting event. The 1990 tournament, the fourteenth, saw 116 nations enter the competition. Fourteen years later, for the 2014 competition, 203 nations entered, including first-timers Curacao and Aruba.

The mind-boggling reach of the Internet often prompts people to complain that the world is growing smaller. FIFA's expanding membership suggests quite the opposite.

1930—We'll Swap Balls at Halftime

Jules Rimet first forwarded his idea at FIFA's 1920 Antwerp Conference. Eight years later, the FIFA World Congress announced that the first World Cup would kick off in just two years time, and would continue to be played every four years, with the eastern and western hemispheres alternately hosting the competition.

Inevitably, the competition was born in controversy. Anxious to draw Latin America closer into its organization, FIFA elected to stage the inaugural competition in Uruguay, immediately alienating the European nations who, as the largest bloc of countries in FIFA, believed that they should have the first bite at the cherry.

Italy, whose own bid to host the first-ever games had been shut down very early on, withdrew altogether. Other nations, mindful of the sheer expense of traveling to Uruguay, likewise backed out. And those that did make it were witness to some of the most farcical situations that any major tournament can ever be said to have hosted.

A Romanian side that was present only because their country's king threatened to close down the factory where the bulk of the players worked, unless they were given time off for the tournament.

A French team that was on the verge of equalizing against Argentina when the referee blew for full time . . . six minutes *before* the ninety was up.

The semifinal that was held up after the US coach, rushing onto the field to treat an injured player, tripped and was rendered instantly unconscious by the bottle of chloroform that shattered in his bag. Or the other semi, in which Uruguay's third goal was almost certainly scored as a result of one of the perimeter policemen kicking the ball back into play.

The competing teams were divided into four groups, one comprising four nations, the others three, each to play its groupmates once. And swiftly, a pattern emerged that would remain an immutable law of the World Cup for the next eight decades until that afternoon in Brazil, exactly eighty-four years after the first-ever World Cup game was played in 1930, when Germany finally swept away the notion European nations could not succeed in South America. Because, until then, they hadn't.

Just one European nation, the rugged Yuogoslavs, survived the opening rounds to reach a semifinal date with Uruguay, while the United States was paired with Argentina in the other. Then, in one of those statistical quirks that world soccer so enjoys producing, both matches concluded with 6–1 score lines. The US and the Slavs took early baths; Uruguay and Argentina, fierce footballing rivals since the first ball was ever kicked over the River Plate, would meet in the final.

An astonishing 90,000 spectators witnessed the first-ever World Cup final, and by halftime, few would have bet against the visitors sweeping to victory. Argentina led 2–1, having run the Uruguayans ragged in the process.

But they did so with the help of a very special weapon. Prior to the game, it was realized that the two nations were accustomed to playing with two very differently designed and weighted balls, and neither was willing to play a full match with the wrong one.

A compromise was reached; they would play one half with each ball. That way nobody could claim to have been at an unfair disadvantage. And so, with the Argentineans kicking the ball they preferred, they marched to that very handy halftime lead.

But they reckoned without the properties of the Uruguayans' chosen ball. For in the second half, three goals sent the host nation (whose preparations for the competition included two months of high-pressure training) soaring to victory. The next day, July 31, was declared a national holiday throughout Uruguay. The World Cup had produced its first World Champions—and, perhaps, fore-shadowed the debates over the nature of the official World Cup ball that have grown shriller, it seems, every year, but culminated in 2010 with the controversy surrounding the Adidas Jabulani. That's the one condemned by Robinho with the words, "for sure the guy who designed this ball never played football."

1934—All That Way for One Lousy Game

Preparations for the 1934 tournament, awarded to Italy, commenced amidst fresh dispute. The Uruguayans, still disappointed by Europe's lack of interest in the first competition, announced that they would not be defending their title, and while the number of nations entering the competition more than doubled to twenty-nine, this time it was Europe who dominated the listings.

Indeed, of the sixteen nations who survived the short knockout competition that commenced a few days before the main event, just three hailed from the Americas—Argentina, Brazil, and the US, who whipped Mexico 4–2 to stamp their passport to the first round. There they were pitched against the host nation, and seven goals to one later, they commenced their journey home.

Believing that it would heighten excitement, the World Cup on this occasion was conducted as a knockout competition. However, it also proved a grossly unsatisfactory arrangement, particularly for the eight teams who had come all that way simply to play ninety minutes of soccer under the Italian sun. Brazil and Argentina, beaten by Spain and Sweden respectively, followed the US and Mexico home, and Europe prepared for the remainder of the tournament to be battled out in exclusively European terms, heedless of the fact that it made an absolute mockery of the competition's title.

Nevertheless, Italy's final victory remains one of the most dramatic in World Cup history. With just twenty minutes remaining in an unbearably tense match, Czechoslovakia grabbed a one-goal lead, and it took what most observers described as a genuinely freak equalizer from the brilliant Orsi to even keep Italy in the game.

Overtime was called for and, early into the first period, Schiavio rammed home what would become the Cup-winning goal for Italy—while setting team-mate Luis Monti up for a unique place in the record books. Four years earlier, this Uruguayan born of an Italian father was playing in the side that won the first World Cup. In an age before FIFA tightened the rules surrounding such things, he was now winning another, with a different team.

1938—Mussolini Muscles in Another One

France was selected as the venue for the third World Cup, in 1938, and once again, the number of entrants (twenty-five) outweighed the number of first-round matches which could be staged—and that despite both Uruguay and Argentina being absent. (Uruguay was wracked by political problems; Argentina were, quite justifiably, angered by FIFA's decision to give the tournament to a European nation for the second successive time.) Ultimately, the western hemisphere was represented by just two countries, Brazil and Cuba, but if anybody thought they were there simply to make up the numbers, they were in for a major surprise.

Once again, the competition was to be decided on a knockout basis, and after battling Romania to a 3–3 tie, the plucky Cubans went on to win the replay 2–1. The Brazilians, too, were level at the end of the first ninety minutes' play against Poland, before dispatching their opponents during the extra thirty minutes of such fiercely contested overtime that it would be another seventy-six years before Brazil would again concede five goals in a World Cup match. Unfortunately, on that occasion—the 2014 semifinal against Germany—they did not have a half dozen of their own to reply with.

Cuban dreams of glory evaporated in the second round with an 8–0 rout at the hands of Sweden, while Brazil made heavy but ultimately victorious going of beating the Czechs, eventually winning 2–1 at the second attempt. Elsewhere, the host nation was mortified to be on the wrong end of a 3–1 scoreline against Italy, while the much-fancied Swiss team was beaten by Hungary—whose first round opponents, the Dutch East Indies, remain the only representatives of that area ever to make the World Cup finals tournament. They lost, 6–0.

England arrive back in London, still shell-shocked by their so-unexpectedly early exit from a 1950 World Cup tournament that most people thought they would walk.

The semifinals loomed and, while Italy beat Brazil by 2–1, the Hungarians punished Sweden with five brilliantly hit goals to one, to set the stage for a memorable final. But though the Hungarians were most people's favorites to lift the trophy, it was not to be. The Italians, managed once again by Vittorio Pozzo, swept to a 4–2 victory, even more impressive than that of four years previous. The World Cup returned to Rome . . . where it was to remain for another twelve years, tucked safely beneath the bed of the head of the Italian FA.

1950—The Loudest Silence in History

The World Cup ground to a halt throughout the Second World War, its name kept alive instead, by impromptu tournaments arranged, of all places, in prisoner of war camps on every continent. Almost as soon as hostilities were over, however, FIFA began preparing for the competition's revival, an event that was guaranteed extra spice by arrival in the FIFA fold of the four British nations in 1946.

It is no secret that it was the World Cup that finally persuaded England, Scotland, Ireland, and Wales to rejoin FIFA. But if they thought—as England undoubtedly did—that, as inventors of the game, the world championship was theirs for the taking, they were in for a nasty surprise.

England at this time had scarcely tasted defeat. Excluding their annual domestic squabbles with Scotland, Ireland, and Wales, the Home Championships, England had lost but nine games, all on foreign soil, since their first foreign international in 1908. And against the countries competing alongside them in the final stages of the 1950 tournament, to be staged for the first time in Brazil, England's record was incredible.

They had never played Bolivia, Brazil, Chile, Mexico, Paraguay, Uruguay, or the US. But World Champions Italy had lost four successive games against the English. Switzerland had been punished 6–0 two years previously, and Spain by 7–1 in 1931. Only Sweden, who had finally beaten England at the *fifth* attempt in 1949, and Yugoslavia, who won the teams' only meeting in 1939, could claim English scalps. But, in Brazil in 1950, the myth of English invincibility was to be crushed forever.

The tournament had reverted to the grouping system preferred at the 1930 event, and which has remained in use ever since. The thirteen qualifying nations (an odd number arrived at following a slew of withdrawals) were divided into four groups, two of four teams, one of three and one of two—joint favorites Uruguay, and little Bolivia. The winners of each group were then placed into a final pool of four, again to be decided on a league basis. Brazil, Uruguay, Sweden, and England were universally regarded as the likeliest competitors.

Three out of four isn't bad.

The awkward balance of Uruguay's group ended predictably, with an 8–0 victory. Elsewhere, Brazil and Sweden both snatched victory from very tight competition, the Swedes putting together an admirable display to beat the still formidable World Champions of Italy, while Brazil kicked off as they intended to proceed, by crushing Mexico in the opening game in the newly constructed Maracanã in São Paulo. Brazil won 4–0 with two goals from Ademir and one each for Jair and Baltazar.

And England? England beat Chile, but lost to Spain. Chile thrashed the US, but they lost to Spain as well. And the US lost to Spain and lost to Chile, but, in a match that is replayed whenever American soccer pride is at stake, they beat England by one goal to nil on a sunny afternoon in Bela Horizonte. It is said that when news of the result first came over the wire, post people, and many newspaper editors, read it as a misprint. Surely it should have said 10–0?

Thus it was that Spain replaced the prophesied England in the final pool, although they—like Sweden—seemed to be there simply to give the Brazilians someone to humiliate. Uruguay made hard work of their matches; they beat Sweden by the odd goal in five, and could only tie 2–2 with Spain. Brazil hammered seven past the Scandinavians, another six past the Spaniards, and marched into the final—and deciding—tie against Uruguay with every reason to expect victory.

In the event, they were to be disappointed. In front of a world-record attendance of 200,000, Uruguay won by 2–1 to take the trophy—such shock to the Brazilian footballing system that the final whistle was greeted by what has since been called the loudest silence in history. It was a national shame that would not, *could* not, be repeated until, with ghastly irony, the next time the World Cup arrived in their home country, in 2014.

1954—German Superiority Starts Here

The 1950 tournament was the last in which nations were "invited" to compete. From hereon in, a qualifying competition was to be held to weed out a final sixteen countries from the growing number of competitors. Uruguay, as holders, And Switzerland, as hosts of the upcoming 1954 event, were granted automatic entry to the next competition; the remaining nations had to fight their way out of the geographically arranged ranks for one of the final fourteen spots.

There were few surprises. Brazil, Yugoslavia, France, Hungary, West Germany, Austria, Italy, Belgium, Czechoslovakia, England, and Scotland all won through as expected; they were joined by Turkey, Mexico, and South Korea, representing the weaker corners of the globe. Then, all sixteen were placed into groups of four, from each of which, two nations would qualify.

Following their humiliation of four years previous, all eyes were again on England. No longer regarded as the game's masters—that position had been usurped by the magical Hungarians who had even snatched away England's unbeaten home record the previous year—they were still expected to at least make the last four. Instead they fell at the quarterfinal stage, eliminated by Uruguay.

It was a high-scoring tournament. In their group matches, Hungary dismissed South Korea by 9–0, and a supposedly weak West German side by 8–3. There again, those same Germans hit Turkey for four and South Korea for seven, then met Turkey in a play-off and won by 7–2.

In Group One, Brazil smashed five past Mexico; in Group Three, Uruguay slammed seven past Scotland, and Austria blasted five into the Czech net. Even England battled to a magnificent 4–4 tie with Belgium.

The predilection for goals continued on into the quarter- and semifinals. Austria and Switzerland competed in a twelve-goal thriller that was finally won by the Austrians 7–5. The South Americans were both involved in six-goal games; Uruguay beating England by 4–2, Brazil falling to Hungary by that same margin in a brutally vicious match that, even today, is remembered as the Battle of Beme.

The semis saw Hungary put another four past Uruguay, while West Germany massacred neighboring Austria by 6–1, and the watching world took a deep breath in anticipation of what, if the two nations' group encounter was anything to go by, would prove one of the most one-sided in World Cup history: Hungary vs. West Germany.

That the Hungarians lost, their first defeat in five years, is now a matter of record.

At one stage, they led by 2–0. But against all odds, goals from Morlock and Rahn (two) pulled the Germans back into the game, and for the first (but not the last) time, the World Cup went to Germany.

1958—A Boy Called Pelé

West Germany remained amongst the favorites for the 1958 tournament, to be held in Sweden. However, they were not to remain so for long. While Italy and Uruguay had both fallen in the qualifying competition, the much-admired Russians were competing for the first time, while Brazil—quietly rebuilding the side that had fallen so ignominiously in 1954—were again a power to be reckoned with.

They swept to victory in their group matches; only England, who held them to a goalless tie (the first in World Cup history) seemed able even to compete with the skillful Brazilians. But English hopes of advancing to the quarterfinals were dampened first by the team's inability to do anything more than tie their other matches (with Russia and Austria), and then by their defeat in the second-place play-off with the Russians.

Indeed, of the four British nations who qualified for the final tournament (the only time this has ever happened), it was the unfancied tiddlers, Wales and Northern Ireland, who impressed. Both won second-place play-off games, both marched triumphantly into the last eight. There, their dreams came to an end, Northern Ireland falling to France, Wales to Brazil. But they perished with a pride that their supposedly better-known neighbors never experienced.

Into the semifinals, and with Brazil absolutely crushing the quietly confident French by 5–2, only the host nation Sweden seemed capable of snatching victory away from the magical South Americans. They beat Russia in the quarterfinals and West Germany in the semis. Facing off in Stockholm, with the home crowd firmly behind them, they seemed certain to at least give the Brazilians something to think about.

They failed. Dismally. Having scored the first goal of the game, Sweden then collapsed as their opponents, their attack masterminded by a brilliant seventeen-year-old named Pelé, first equalized, and then began piling in the goals. The final score, 5–2, tells only part of the story. Pelé and Vava each scored twice, and the watching Swedes could only look on in dismay as their national team was literally run into the ground. And given the youthful nature of the Brazilian side, it was a display that many people expected to witness many times again in the future.

1962—Brazil Once Again

The next World Cup, in 1962, was to be held in Chile. No European side had ever truly impressed in South America, and with that brilliant Brazil side still to reach maturity, it was unlikely that dismal record would be broken this time around.

Again there were few surprises in the qualifying rounds, although the failure of Sweden and France to qualify did raise a few eyebrows. And in the final competition, the early elimination of Uruguay, Colombia, and Argentina was also to upset the balance somewhat. Brazil and hosts Chile did make it through, however—the former despite losing Pelé to injury during the early stages—and their semifinal meeting was, for many people, as good as any final.

Brazil won, 4–2. In the other semi, the Czechs beat Yugoslavia by 3–1 to reach their second-ever final. But the result was never in doubt. Brazil lifted the trophy for the second successive time, and joined Italy and Uruguay in needing to win the competition just one more time for the World Cup to become their personal property.

Any team capable of becoming World Champions three times, Jules Rimet had decreed, deserved to retain that title, and the attendant trophy, in perpetuity. However, there was very nearly not a World Cup for them to keep. Shortly after the 1966 competition got underway, in England, the World Cup was stolen.

1966—What the Linesman Saw

After eight years in Brazil, the World Cup arrived in England early in 1966, to be kept until the presentation ceremony at the end of the final. With four months to go, the English FA decided to place the trophy, alleged to comprise twelve pounds of solid gold (in fact, it was primarily silver), on display at the annual Stampex philatelic show in London. And, in the early hours of Sunday morning, March 20, it disappeared. Some $6 million worth of stamps were ignored.

It was not the first time the English had lost a valuable trophy. In 1895 the FA Cup had been stolen from the window of a Birmingham jewelers shortly after Aston Villa took possession of it. It was never recovered, and is believed to have been melted down. Would the same fate await the World Cup? That was unlikely: its intrinsic value was only around $3,000; if money had been the object, the stamps would have been a more likely target.

The description of a scar-faced man, seen around the hall on the morning of the theft, was circulated. Rewards totaling nearly $10,000 were posted. And then a mysterious parcel arrived at the home of FA Chairman Joe Mears. In true classic kidnap style, it contained a part of the missing trophy, and a note demanding $30,000 ransom. Otherwise the Cup was dead.

Mears contacted the police, the manhunt was stepped up, but all in vain. The World Cup was recovered, but not through the resources and resolve of Scotland Yard. It was the inquisitive nose of a mongrel dog named Pickles. Out walking with his master, South Londoner David Corbett, Pickles found a heavy, newspaper-wrapped package in a bush. Corbett picked it up, opened it—and there lay the trophy. Corbett immediately reported his find, and eventually received close to $9,000 in reward money. Pickles received a number of bones and a special medal from the National Canine Defence League; and one Edward Betchley, a London dock laborer, was given two years in prison for his part in the theft.

After all that excitement, the actual competition might have proved an anticlimax, particularly for England. Certainly things started badly, with a goalless tie with Uruguay in the opening game. Victories over Mexico and France followed, but if any impartial headlines were to be written, they concerned West Germany and Portugal, winners of Groups Two and Three, and North Korea, runners-up to Russia in Group Four and shock conquerors of Italy.

The Koreans beat the Italians 1–0, and at one point in their quarterfinal engagement with Portugal, they seemed set to repeat the feat when they roared into a 3–0 lead. But they lacked the tactical know-how to maintain their lead once the first burst of euphoria had worn off, and the Portuguese, led by the masterful Eusebio, ran out 5–3 victors.

England's uncertainty continued into their quarterfinal match with Argentina, that bad-tempered match that set the stage for so much future animosity between European and South American sides. Indeed, it will always be a matter of conjecture whether England could have beaten them had the Latins remained at full strength for the entire match. As it was, with Argentinean captain Rattin sent to an early bath, England beat ten men by 1–0, and moved into a semifinal game with Portugal.

Russia and West Germany made up the other semifinal, with the Germans booking their passage to the Wembley end game by 2–1. England defeated Portugal by the same margin the following day. The loser's goal, incidentally, was the first England conceded throughout the tournament, yet still the Portuguese people know this match as *Jogo das Lágrimas*—the Game of Tears. The great Eusebio, the most brilliant player his country has ever produced, was inconsolable in its aftermath.

And so to Wembley, and a capacity crowd that was utterly hushed as the Germans took the lead, through Haller. Geoff Hurst equalized for England, and with thirteen minutes remaining, Martin Peters made it 2–1 to the host nation. Wembley was still celebrating when, just seconds from the end of normal time, Weber equalized for the Germans.

Half an hour of extra time loomed, and suddenly England came good. Two goals from Hurst (or maybe just one—the other did look dodgy, even at the time), the second struck just moments before the final whistle, sent England into paroxysms of delight. Germans still complain about the linesman who gave England's third goal the thumbs-up; historians and experts begrudgingly acknowledge that they may have a point. But nothing, at the time, could dim England's glory.

Not even the afternoon, almost a year later, when Scotland—who had not even qualified for the 1966 World Cup—traveled down to London, beat the World Champions, and proclaimed themselves the best team in the world.

1970—The First Color TV World Cup

England entered the 1970 tournament staged this time in Mexico, looking back upon just four defeats in their last thirty-three matches. Both at home and abroad, they were the firm favorites to overcome not only the world, but also the heat that Mexico would bring to bear on the competitors. There was, it seemed certain, no way that they could lose.

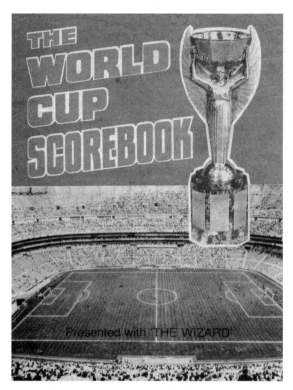

A souvenir of the imminent 1970 World Cup, given away free with the British comic *The Wizard*.

Sadly, for the English, not everybody believed what they heard. Certainly not a young West German striker named Gerd Müller. With England 2–0 ahead in their quarterfinal encounter, and just twenty minutes left to play, Müller ran himself ragged, an inspiration in every corner of the field. Gallantly the Germans hauled themselves back into the match, equalized, and dragged the tiring English into extra time.

Afterward, all manner of reasons for the English capitulation were floated; the loss, through food poisoning, of goalkeeper Gordon Banks, widely regarded as the greatest custodian in the world. (He had certainly proved as much against Brazil in the group stage.) His replacement, Peter Bonetti, was nervous, inexperienced, and underprepared.

It was his error, coupled with manager Alf Ramsey's inexplicable decision to substitute Bobby Charlton moments after Franz Beckenbauer scored Germany's first goal, that truly allowed the foe back into the game. That, and the quite audacious skills of German Uwe Seeler, whose equalizing goal was scored, deliberately, with the back of his head, echoing the Goal of the Tournament contender that Brazilian Leônidas da Silva unleashed at the 1938 World Cup.

The tournament had been waiting ever since for someone else to score a backward header, and the opportunity of dragging the defending World Cup champions into thirty minutes of stoppage time that they weren't in any fit shape to play was obviously a suitable incentive to deliver it. And while England were first to score in extra time, Geoff Hurst's murderous shot was mysteriously disallowed and it was left to Müller to deliver the deathblow. It would be another twelve years before England graced another World Cup.

But the Germans were tired as well; you could see their exhaustion even as they lined up to meet Italy in the semifinals. In the other game, the remaining South American sides, Brazil and Uruguay, were set to do battle. In the eyes of the neutrals watching, either match would have made an acceptable final, and the games lived up to that grand billing. Italy won their match by the odd goal in seven, Brazil by the more comfortable margin of 3–1.

But Brazil vs. Italy was a game that the entire world wanted to see: whoever won the Cup would, under the third-time-lucky ruling, keep the Cup. And it was Brazil who came out tops, bettering their semifinal tally to run out 4–1 victors, with Pelé—in his last major international appearance—scoring twice.

1974—New Cup, New Format

To replace the one that they would keep, a new trophy was generously handed over by the Brazilian FA, this time with the stipulation that it could never become the personal property of one nation again. But the old Cup was not to remain for long in Brazilian hands. In 1984 it was stolen for the second time in its life, but this time it was never recovered. The World Cup that holds pride of place at Brazil's soccer headquarters is a replica.

West Germany hosted the World Cup in 1974, and to mark the inauguration of the new trophy, a new system was created. The tournament was divided into three phases: the first involving the usual sixteen competitors in four groups of four, would be followed by a second round featuring the top two from each group, again in groups of four. The winners would then meet in the final.

It was an interesting lineup of nations that took their places in the draw. Russia was absent after refusing to meet Chile in a qualifying play-off; having tied the first of the two matches 0–0 in Moscow, Russia suddenly announced that in protest against the Chilean government's mistreatment of left-wing activists, they were no longer interested in competing. Their reservations were honorable, and indeed justified; the very stadium where the match was due to take place was simultaneously being utilized for mass executions. But when FIFA sent a delegation to Chile to investigate the accusations, they found no evidence whatsoever to support the Russian claims—no, not even a squeak from the estimated seven thousand people who were being held in the area beneath the stadium even as the dignitaries were feted on the field above.

The match went ahead without the Soviets, and lasted as long as it took the home team to dribble the ball up the field and bury it in an empty net.

Besides, the Soviets were scarcely the most noteworthy absentees. That dubious honor went to England, winners in 1966, quarterfinalists in 1970, and now mere onlookers in 1974. Sir Alf Ramsey, mastermind of the 1966 victory, was sacked as a consequence, but it really wasn't his fault. England would fail to qualify again in 1978.

Three wild-card nations—the minnows Australia, Zaire, and Haiti—did make it through to the final competition, drawing howls of protest from those more "advanced" soccer-playing nations who had not made it. Howls that may have been justified. Like El Salvador and Israel in 1970 (and unlike North Korea in 1966), not one of them was capable of producing any real shocks—their inclusion was simply geared toward justifying the World Cup's name. Australia alone managed to get a point, fighting a 0–0 tie with Chile. Zaire and Haiti both conceded fourteen goals as they fell to three successive defeats apiece, and into the second phase marched both East and West Germany—sides who, it was alleged, had already decided upon the ideal result before kicking off their historic first-ever World Cup meeting: Yugoslavia and Brazil, Holland and Sweden, Poland and Argentina.

Of the sides who did not make it through, the unluckiest were, without doubt, the Scots. Against Zaire, they should have scored a netful of goals—certainly they had the chance to. Instead they could manage but two and were eliminated from the competition on goal difference. Italy, too, suffered from their inability to crush Zaire, although whereas but one goal would have made all the difference to the Scots, the Italians would have needed at least three more to have overtaken Argentina in the final phase table.

Brazil, a mere shadow of their former selves, finished second, behind Holland, in their phase two matches, and—in the play-off for third place—fell by 1–0 to Poland on the day before the final. Poland, of course, closed as runners-up to the hosts, and on July 7, West Germany made up for all the disappointments of their recent defeats by defeating Holland by 2–1.

However, it was Holland who were to be remembered as the team of the tournament. Their club sides were already the dominant force on the European scene, and aided by players of the caliber of Cruyff, Rensenbrink, and Neeskens, the national side seemed certain to emulate them on the international scene.

In the event, the Dutch were never to take the World Cup home, although they again came close in 1978, reaching the final, only to be defeated again by the host country, Argentina.

1978—Never Mind the Repressive Military Government. Look at All the Ticker Tape.

This year's small fry were represented by Tunisia, Mexico, and Iran, the latter a surprise package qualifying from a continental competition that many Westerners had assumed would easily have been won by Malaysia.

Just two years before, after all, footballing brains the caliber of Billy Bingham (Everton), Gordon Milne (Coventry City), Dave Mackay (Derby County) and Dettmar Cramer (FC Bayern München) had sung the praises of Harimau Malaya, while mighty Arsenal had completely come unstuck at the Mayalsians' hands during a friendly tour in 1975. In Penang, the Gunners drew 1–1; in Kuala Lumpar, they lost 2–0, and manager Bertie Mee was adding his voice to the chorus convinced that Mayalan soccer was about to emerge from the obscurity of the region, and explode onto the world stage.

Undone in their quest to qualify for the 1974 World Cup (the first for which they entered), Malaya consoled themselves by winning the Merdeka Trophy later that same year. They won bronze in the Asian Games, and silver in the 1975 SEAP Games, only narrowly going down to gold medalists Thailand. They won a

second Merdeka Trophy in 1976, and in that year they also achieved a victory in the invitational King's Cup in Thailand.

True, they had yet to impress in the slightest in the premier regional trophy, the Asian Cup, but when the World Cup qualifiers kicked off in 1977, Malaysian hopes were high—especially after their opening qualifier, with Thailand, was transformed into a ten-goal bonanza, with Mayala scoring six of them. But a goalless draw with Indonesia put them on the back foot, and everything fell apart against Singapore, Malaya's traditional regional rivals.

It was not enough that they were up against the infamous Kallang Roar, the truly intimidating sound of a stadium packed with Singaporean supporters. They

Scottish hopes were sky-high before the 1978 World Cup, with manager Ally MacLeod even suggesting his side was good enough to win it. They weren't.

had to contend with a dubious penalty decision that ultimately gave Singapore a 1–0 victory, and a 1–1 draw with Hong Kong marked the end of the adventure.

But the controversy did not end there, as Hong Kong marched into the final qualifying round against Iran, South Korea, Australia, and Kuwait—and were soundly obliterated. All eight of their games ended in defeat, and the suggestion that it had been corruption, rather than footballing skills, that pushed them so far—or held Malaysia so far back, nobody ever seemed certain—proved a sour end to an era in which Malaya truly believed they could reach for the stars. They would win the 1977 SEA Games, and the 1979 tournament too. But their greatest moment had passed.

It was Iran, incidentally, who put an end to Scotland's hopes and assured their status as surely the most luckless World Cup contenders of the 1970s. While Holland hit three past the Iranians, and Peru four, Scotland could salvage but a scrappy 1–1 tie; and once again goal difference sent them crashing home, the suddenly vainglorious strains of Rod Stewart's World Cup single still ringing in their ears.

Meanwhile, Tunisia held a few surprises in store when they convincingly defeated Mexico, 3–0, and then held West Germany to a goalless tie. Maybe the midges did have some bite after all.

It was business as usual elsewhere, however, with Italy and Argentina qualifying from Group One, Poland and West Germany (Group Two), Austria and a surprisingly lackluster Brazil (Group Three), Peru and Holland (Group Four). The second phase, too, went according to the form book, with Brazil and Italy winning through to a repeat of the 1970 final in the play-off for third place, Argentina and Holland making it through to the final.

Argentina triumphed over all, with a 3–1 victory that at last showed the true brilliant nature of a side marshaled by Mario Kempes and featuring, too, such talents as Osvaldo Ardiles, Alberto Tarantini, Ricardo Villa, and the truly remarkable Américo Gallego. Capped seventy-three times by the national team, Gallego spent his entire playing career at just two clubs, Newell's Old Boys (1974–1980), where he made 262 appearances; and River Plate (1981–1988, 180 appearances).

Subsequent histories have allowed a lot of controversy to spill over the awarding of the 1978 World Cup to Argentina, and the ruling junta's actions once it arrived. But none could dispute the beauty and genius of that year's team. And now all eyes turned to Spain, where the 1982 tournament was to be held—and with it, an increased entry of twenty-four qualifying nations.

1982—More Nations, Same Winners

The value of the 1982 finals was diminished in many eyes by the absence of Holland, whose wizardry—although ultimately unrewarded—had established them as perhaps the most entertaining side on the international stage throughout the 1970s. Neighbors France and Belgium qualified in their stead, the former a vastly improved side to that which had not made the finals since 1966.

Another seemingly habitual absentee, England, also made it through, with El Salvador joining them in likewise booking their first finals berth since 1970.

The enlarged final format opened the door to more of soccer's developing nations, Algeria, Cameroon, Kuwait, and New Zealand. However, it also necessitated, for the first time, a conscious effort being made to "seed" combatants according to past—and present—merit.

It was a controversial decision, one that opened the tournament up to accusations of having already had its semifinalists at least, ordained long before the competition got underway. Each of the six groups of four contained one side of proven winning potential, one of lesser, but still exciting ability, a third weaker outfit, and a fourth drawn from the lowest ranks. And, on the whole, everybody conformed to expectations.

Only Northern Ireland, topping Group Five over hosts Spain and highly rated Yugoslavia, spoiled the party, and they were swiftly put back in their place by defeat at the hands of semifinalists France in the second phase. Algeria, on the other hand, *should* have marched on, but when the final game in their group left West Germany and Austria knowing precisely what they needed to do in order for them both to qualify, and send the Algerians home . . . well, nobody was surprised when they did it.

One of the most stultifying games in World Cup history duly played itself out, with even German and Austrian supporters in the crowd howling for the players to at least make the pretense of playing a soccer match. Afterward, FIFA looked into what the German media was already calling the *Nichtangriffspakt von Gijón*, or the "Non-aggression pact of Gijón," and declared itself satisfied that nothing untoward had taken place. But the modern practice of playing the final, and often decisive, group games simultaneously was introduced immediately after this tournament, to ensure that two teams could never again take their destinies so firmly in hand.

Austria fell in the second phase; it was left to the West Germans to join Poland, Italy, and France in the semis. Brazil and Argentina, the only non-Europeans to reach the second phase, finished second and third behind Italy.

The final most people were by now expecting, Italy vs. West Germany, thus materialized, and having sized one another up throughout a drab, goalless first half, the game erupted into life for the final forty-five minutes, Italy scoring three goals to their opponents' one. Twelve years too late for them to win a permanent keepsake of their superiority, Italy had won their third world title. Would they make it four?

1986—The Hand of God and the Morality of a Tomcat

For the 1986 tournament, the second to be staged in Mexico (the originally scheduled hosts, Colombia, withdrew in 1982), the second-phase competition reverted to the knockout basis abandoned after the 1970 games, although the potential for both predictable finalists and unpredictable upsets was again retained by the practice of seeding combatants.

The Scottish World Cup squad serenade their supporters once again.

Thus Italy, Bulgaria, and Argentina found themselves facing the unknowns of South Korea; Mexico, Belgium, and Paraguay were to be confronted and possibly confounded by Iraq; France, Hungary, and Russia by Canada; Brazil, Spain, and Northern Ireland by Algeria; Poland, Portugal, and England by Morocco. (Group Five comprised West Germany, Uruguay, Scotland, and Denmark, none of whom could truly be termed an unknown quantity.) And sure enough, there was a shock . . . and sure enough, it involved England.

Having already fallen 1–0 to Portugal, they went in against Morocco, who had tied with Poland, already weakened by a tournament-ending injury to skipper Bryan Robson. Indeed, England were a mere shadow of themselves, and only poor finishing on Morocco's part prevented a veritable rout. The dismissal of the influential Ray Wilkins further weakened England's grasp on the game, and when full time finally arrived, they considered themselves fortunate to have escaped with a goalless tie.

Morocco were no flash in the pan. They wiped Portugal out by 3–1 to take the Group F title; England, finally putting their game together, hit three against Poland to take second place, and against almost all the odds, the two entered the last sixteen.

The remainder of the first phase tournament had gone comparatively smoothly. Argentina and Italy, as expected, triumphed in Group A, Mexico and Paraguay emerged from Group B, Russia and France from Group C, Brazil and Spain from Group D. Only in the fifth grouping was controversy to return, when Scotland and Uruguay fought out a goalless tie so bad-tempered that soccer-playing relations between the two have yet to be restored. (The pair finished fourth and third respectively, behind Brazil and Denmark.)

The round of sixteen was most notable for the undeserved dispatch of the Soviets, 3–4 at the hands of Belgium; for Morocco's ferocious defense—and West Germany's intimidating attack—in the latter's barely warranted 1–0 victory; and for England's sudden discovery of a lethal new strike force, pairing Gary Lineker and Peter Beardsley.

Having hit a hat trick against Poland in the final First Phase match, Lineker scored another two goals, Beardsley one, to defeat Paraguay at the next stage. And Lineker established himself as the tournament's top scorer in the quarterfinal against Argentina, when he hit his sixth goal in a match that is otherwise best remembered for revealing to the world the true two faces of Diego Maradona.

On the one hand, we saw the little genius whose second goal against England is widely regarded among the most perfect strikes ever executed; and on the other, we met the shameless charlatan whose first goal was a blatant and deliberate handball.

It would have counted regardless of how Maradona referred to it afterward. The referee, incredibly, saw nothing wrong with the goal, and what the ref says stands. But the Argentinean's post-match (and, indeed, post-career) gloating over what he called "the hand of God" left a very sour taste in many people's mouths, one that seriously impacts upon Maradona's otherwise unimpeachable standing among the greatest players in world history. Great players, the argument goes, don't cheat. But if they do, they don't publicly celebrate and boast when they get away with it.

English protests notwithstanding, the tournament moved on. Hosts Mexico, conquerors of Bulgaria at the previous stage, finally bowed out after West Germany took them to penalties at the end of a fiercely contested 0–0 tie; Spain and Belgium, and Brazil and France, too, needed spot kicks to separate them, with the French triumph ranking among the entire tournament's most exciting moments.

After such action, the semifinals—France vs. West Germany, Belgium vs. Argentina—seemed somewhat anticlimactic. Neutrals were still mourning the dismissal, earlier in the tournament, of the ever-entertaining Danes and Soviets, but all four survivors fought gallantly until the Germans and Argentinians went through, both by the deceptive scoreline of 2–0.

Argentina won the final 3–2, and were widely anticipated to travel just as far the next time around, in Italy in 1990.

1990—Wake Me When It's Over

And so they did, albeit via some of the most horrendously boring play ever witnessed from a so-called major team, competing in a so-called major tournament. Even in the group stage, Argentina did just enough to qualify—one win (over the Soviets), one draw (with Romania) and one defeat (shockingly, to Cameroon) saw them finish *third* in Group B, to qualify for the next stage as one of the four highest-ranked losers.

Yet the Argentineans were scarcely alone in deploying negative tactics. The Republic of Ireland, making their first-ever appearance in the World Cup, were scarcely the masters of wide-open play either, while England topped their group by virtue of being the only team among the four (they were grouped with the Republic, Egypt, and the Netherlands) to actually win a game, 1–0 in their final tie with Egypt. Every other match in the group ended either 0–0 or 1–1, and this at a time when the American media, mindful of the next competition being staged in the US, was watching with the most cynical eye it could muster.

Qualifying for their first World Cup in forty years, the United States side itself scarcely got off to the best of starts, simply falling apart in their first game, to lose 5–1 to a Czech side that was hardly vintage quality. But they rallied after that, holding hosts Italy to a mere single-goal victory, and while they would lose again, to Austria, to book an early flight home, there was no shame in the 1–2 reverse, as Bruce Murray became the first American to score in the modern World Cup.

And so the round of sixteen, where Cameroon followed up the shocks they meted out to Argentina and Romania (a 2–1 win) in the group stage, by dumping out Colombia. Argentina scratched another single goal win to remove Brazil from contention; and the Republic overcame Romania on penalties after what felt, at the time, like an endless 0–0 draw.

A replay of the 1974 World Cup final saw West Germany (appearing for the last time as a divided nation) beat the Netherlands, England removed Belgium, Yugoslavia saw off Spain, and the hosts defeated Uruguay. Which left the tournament's other surviving minnows, Costa Rica (shock conquerors of both Scotland and Sweden) to be brought back to earth by the free-scoring Czechs—who would, in the quarterfinals, find their every goal-seeking instinct shut down in a dour competition with the Germans.

The negative play was contagious. The Irish adventure was throttled at the hands of a dourly workmanlike Italy, and the so-entertaining Yugoslavs were closed down by Argentina, then dispatched via penalties. It was sad to see them go; even Lothar Matthäus, not generally regarded as the most gracious connoisseur, described Germany's group match with Yugoslavia as the best international he ever played in.

It was left to England and the still-surprising Cameroon to provide the game of the round, if not the match of the tournament—a five-goal thriller that saw England take a twenty-fifth-minute lead through David Platt; before Cameroon struck back twice in five minutes, a Kundé penalty just past the hour mark,

RadioTimes

WORLD CUP

90

SPECIAL

**Enjoy the month-long
festival of football in Italy
with our eight-page
pull-out World Cup guide**

**Team talk with BBC
experts John Motson,
Barry Davies and
Denis Law**

**Fill-in chart of the
draw, plus details of the
BBC's coverage**

**Free: 50 videos
of the brilliant Brazilians**

followed by an Ekéké strike that still looks good on YouTube.

A special edition of Britain's *Radio Times* magazine setting viewers up for the 1990 tournament.

With eight minutes to go, England won a penalty and an inevitable Gary Lineker equalizer; then, in extra time, a second one. Cameroon were out, much to the horror of a worldwide audience that had absolutely adopted them as the smiling face

A philatelic souvenir of the USA's first appearance at the World Cup finals since 1950.

of an otherwise dismal tournament; and when both semifinals went to penalties following 1–1 draws, only the tear-stained visage of losing Englishman Paul Gascoigne stands out as a memory worth treasuring from either game. Well, that and the look of sheer horror on Chris Waddle's face as he hoofed his penalty into the stratosphere, and gifted the game to a West German side that had scarcely got out of second gear all tournament long.

How fitting, then, that the final, too, should be decided from the spot, an eighty-fifth-minute penalty that West Germany's Andreas Brehme made no mistake with, condemning Argentina not only to a well-deserved defeat, but also to the ignominious record of becoming the first side ever to fail to score in a World Cup final. The hosts, incidentally, finished in third place, beating England 2–1 in the battle of the losing semifinalists, the day before the main event. It would be too much to describe the game as another of the best games of the entire tournament. But it was certainly one of the least worst.

1994—America's Games

In stark contrast with the snore-bore of 1990, the 1994 tournament lives on in the memory as one of the most gripping of all recent contests, at least until 2002 sent the form book flying out of the window, and 2014 sent the window out after it.

Staged in the United States, the 1994 event saw Greece, Saudi Arabia, and a post–Soviet Union Russia make their finals debut; and the Germanies unified for the first time since 1938. Bolivia made their first finals appearance since 1950, Switzerland their first since 1966, and Africa offered up three qualifiers for the first time, FIFA's reward for Cameroon's gallantry in 1990. Nigeria joined Morocco and the Indomitable Lions.

The official gameday program issued for the 1994 World Cup.

Some familiar old names, however, would not be joining us. Yugoslavia was still serving the international suspension that was a part of the United Nations sanctions brought on by the war that was tearing the nation apart. (The modern competitors Serbia, Croatia, and Bosnia and Herzegovina would ultimately be born of Yugoslavia's final collapse.)

The nation of Czechoslovakia had already dissolved into two separate countries while World Cup qualifying was already underway, and completed its games as the Representation of Czechs and Slovaks (RCS). Ultimately, however, they failed to qualify.

Chile was serving out a suspension, while other regulars—Uruguay, Hungary, France, and Scotland all failed to qualify. So did England, despite their dramatic display in 1990 and so, sadly, did the defending European Champions, Denmark. And, finally, we bade farewell to Diego Maradona, the Hand of God clearly not being supplanted by the Bladder and Bloodstream of God. He was expelled early on in the tournament after failing a drug test.

Hoping to remedy the sheer defensive drudgery of the 1990 World Cup, FIFA introduced three points for a win, instead of two, in the group stage. It paid off, too; in fact, even the draws seemed more exciting this time around, particularly in Group One, where the hosting US got off to a reasonable start in a 1–1 with Switzerland, and then stunned all observers with a 2–1 victory over Colombia. How tragic that the memory of that win is so intertwined with its denouement, the murder of Colombian defender Andrés Escobar, shot to death outside a bar in a Medellín suburb ten days later, apparently in retaliation for the own goal that ended Colombia's World Cup.

The US themselves advanced to the second round as one of the best third-place sides; there they were removed by Brazil after a hard-fought game decided by a single goal. Surprises, however, there were plenty, as unfancied Saudi Arabia finished second in their group, after defeating both Morocco and Belgium; as the Republic of Ireland beat Italy at the group stage; and Nigeria *topped* their group with victories over Bulgaria and Greece. The same Bulgaria who, regrouping in the round of sixteen, then proceeded to defeat all comers en route for the semifinals. There they fell to the similarly revitalized Italy, while the other shock heroes, Sweden, went down 1–0 in a replay of the 1958 World Cup final against Brazil.

The first World Cup final ever to be decided on penalties followed, a turgid 0–0 draw played out by Brazil and Italy; in terms of excitement, the third-place decider that ended Sweden 4, Bulgaria 0, was far better value.

1998—The World Returns to France

The 1998 World Cup brought the competition back to its birthplace (or, at least, that of founder Jules Rimet) for the first time since 1938 and, appropriately, allowed the French to claim the trophy for the first time.

A expanded format saw thirty-two nations competing in the final, opening the possibility of qualification to ever more diverse corners of the planet—albeit, critics sighed, at the expense of the tournament's own claim to represent the pinnacle of soccer-playing skills.

That said, first-time representations from Croatia, Jamaica, Japan, and South Africa were not to disgrace themselves, with Spain proving the competition's first surprise flop, as they fell to Nigeria and only tied with Paraguay. They did rally to blast six goals into the Bulgarian net in the final match, but it was too little, too late. Spain took the short road home.

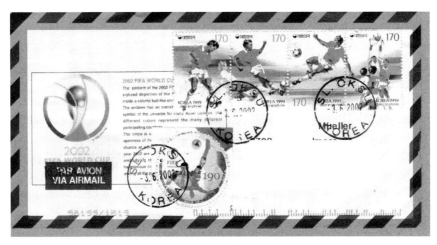

A spectacularly messy philatelic cover celebrating the 2002 finals in South Korea and Japan.

Shocking, too, were Scotland's defeat to Morocco and Brazil's to Norway, while the United States seem to thoroughly capitulate when the brave performances of 1990 and 1994 were followed by abject surrender to Germany, FR Yugoslavia, and—with all the cultural and political baggage that attended the tie—Iran.

Still, the last sixteen threw up some gripping ties, not least of all Brazil vs. Chile, Denmark vs. Nigeria (both ending in 4–1 wins for the first-named team), and England vs. Argentina, reopening wounds left to fester since the Hand of God game twelve years earlier. And if it was controversy you were hoping for, the game didn't disappoint as two penalties were awarded inside the first ten minutes; as Michael Owen, already one of the youngest players ever to compete in the World Cup, sweetly scooped one of the finest goals ever seen there; and Javier Zanetti grabbed a miracle equalizer on the very stroke of halftime.

There would be no further goals in the second half, but there was plenty of drama, as England's David Beckham was sent off for petulantly kicking out at Diego Simeone. But the ten men came close to clinching it, only for Sol Campbell's winning goal to be disallowed for a disputed foul on the goalkeeper, and when extra time ended goalless, penalties set the Argentineans through to the quarterfinals.

The quarterfinals saw further penalties decide France's game with Italy. But Brazil knocked out Denmark, the Netherlands defeated Argentina, and Croatia established themselves as every neutral's favorite when they sent Germany packing 3–0. They would ultimately finish third, defeating the Dutch in the play-off, while the French hosts lined up against Brazil in what was universally predicted to be one of *the* great games of the century.

The Brazilian side of the day was as golden as any past generation, but not for the first time, nor for the last, the impression of an all-powerful team was, in fact, the consequence of one single magician maintaining the illusion throughout the eleven.

In the 1970s, removing Pelé from the Brazilian team often revealed just how reliant his teammates were on his talismanic presence. At the 2014 World Cup, the extraction of Neymar would have disastrous consequences. In 1998, it was Ronaldo who was relied upon to shine, and when he had an off-day—as he certainly did this afternoon—the entire team had one with him.

Two goals up at halftime, with Zidane looking lethal every time he approached the Brazilian penalty box, France were perhaps merciful to add just one more in the second half. And not even the news that a Brazilian government inquiry was opened to try to discover what went wrong with their team could detract from the victor's triumph.

2002—Two Hosts and Lots of Winners

The first World Cup to be staged in Asia was also the first to be staged across two hosting nations, Japan and South Korea. And from the outset, it proved to be one of the most remarkable, and remarkably unpredictable, World Cups ever staged.

Where do you begin? With the group stage elimination of the reigning world champions, who finished bottom of their group after an opening day defeat to Senegal had already got things off to the unlikeliest start imaginable?

With the gallantry of Turkey, destined to ride all the way through to the third-place play-off, and that despite being confronted with some of the most farcical play-acting ever seen in a World Cup match, when they met Brazil in their opening match?

With Portugal, a star-studded side glittering with the majesty of Luis Figo and Rui Costa, going down to both cohosts South Korea and the resurgent United States? With Argentina following them to an early exit after a draw with Sweden and defeat to England?

There was drama aplenty, too, in the round of sixteen when South Korea put Italy to the sword, and their winning goal scorer, Ahn Jung-Hwan, found himself a figure of vitriolic hatred when he reported back at his day job . . . he played for Italian club side Perugia.

And there was controversy, in that same game, as Francesco Totti was dismissed for what the referee insisted was a deliberate dive, but which cameras and onlookers alike felt was anything but, and when the Italians also had a perfectly good goal ruled out . . . as would Spain, when they came up against the South Koreans in the quarterfinals. Twice, Spanish celebrations were cut short by the referee's whistle, and penalties pushed the cohosts into the semifinals.

There they encountered Germany, even as the competition's other surprise package, an astonishingly penetrative Turkish side, met Brazil, and there both dreams ended to set up, at last, an end to Ronaldo's nightmare of four years previous. He scored twice to give Brazil their fifth World Cup, and condemn Germany to a record fourth final defeat.

2006—But . . . But . . . Butt.

Perhaps, the Germans hoped they would do better next time, when the tournament returned to Germany itself?

No, they wouldn't. A semifinal defeat at the hands of a grippingly resurgent Italy saw the host nation content itself with third place, in a tournament that reestablished Europe's place as the dominant power in continental soccer politics (Portugal were the other beaten semifinalist; Argentina and Brazil alone took South American aspirations into the quarterfinal), while France's march to the runner's-up spot included a gripping win over Spain and a well-deserved 1–0 over Brazil.

True, the final itself was largely uninteresting, a 1–1 draw that saw both France and Italy cancel each other out, and whose most lingering memory is of Zinedine Zidane headbutting Marco Materazzi, and leaving the field in such disgrace.

Prior to all that, though, there were gripping performances from the Côte d'Ivoire, Angola, and Ghana; a moment of magic as tiny Trinidad and Tobago took Sweden to a 0–0 draw; and Australia proved themselves the comeback kings of the year, 1–0 down to Japan with just six minutes to go—and then Tim Cahill popped up with two goals in five minutes, before substitute John Aloisi hit a third during stoppage time.

At the same time, though . . .

At the same time, 2006 goes down in the history books as one of the least exciting World Cups ever . . . or, at least, of the television age. The usual names

At one of the most colorful World Cups ever, delighted Bafana Bafana supporters prepare to cheer on home side South Africa in the opening game vs. Mexico. *fstockfoto/Shutterstock.com*

dominated, the usual victims suffered, and goals were at such a premium that even the tournament's top scorer, Germany's Miroslav Klose, hit just five goals all competition long. Yet he was positively profligate when compared to his peers. No other player scored more than three, and Italy's top scorers were all tied on two.

Which is why people still remember the headbutt. It was the first time all tournament that something actually happened.

2010—What's That Sound?

It was Pelé who predicted that an African nation would win the World Cup before the end of the twentieth century, an indication of just how fervently he believed in the continent's growing strength on the soccer field.

History did not agree with him, but a mere ten years after Pelé's prophesied window closed, an African nation did *host* the tournament, as the world turned its attention to South Africa.

Who promptly became the first host nation not to progress beyond the group stage.

They were in good company, though. Both of the 2006 finalists, Italy and France, also went out at that stage, and so did New Zealand, despite being the only team not to lose a single game in the first round. Three draws, against Paraguay, Slovakia, and that shockingly inept Italian side were not, however, sufficient to power them into the round of sixteen.

South Korea, disappointing last time out, partially rebounded—they were unlucky to limp out of the group stage with a win, a draw, and a single defeat (to winners Argentina), although they were never likely to threaten a reprise of 2002. The United States, on the other hand, boldly topped their group over England, Slovenia, and Algeria, and it's only when you look at the statistics that you realize just what an underwhelming achievement that was—one win and two draws were sufficient for the US and England to claim the top two places, with the highest-scoring match in the entire group being the US's 2–2 draw with Slovenia. In fact, more goals were scored in that one game than in any three others played in what should have been, but wasn't, called the Group of Deathly Boredom.

Just two teams reached the round of sixteen with 100 percent records, Argentina and the Netherlands, and both burst through that barrier with little problem either. Other fancied sides, however, hiccuped. Ghana took out the United States, Germany overwhelmed England, Spain pushed out Portugal, Argentina defeated Mexico, and it was small consolation when FIFA supremo Sepp Blatter personally apologized to the English and Mexican FAs for the inexplicable, if not inexcusable, refereeing errors that very likely affected the entire outcome of their games.

Into the quarterfinals, and it was au revoir to Argentina and Brazil, but Paraguay chased Spain to the very end before accepting a 1–0 defeat, and we came within just one second of despicable gamesmanship from witnessing our first-ever African semifinalist. With Uruguay and Ghana tied at one apiece as the last moments of extra time loomed, a Ghanaian shot was incontrovertibly and unstoppably goal-bound. Until Luis Suarez, at that time merely at the outset of his love affair with on-field controversy (and dining), raised a hand and blatantly cleared it off the line.

Of course Suarez was sent off, but that did not matter to him, or to his team-mates. A certain goal was averted, and now the pressure was on Ghana to make the penalty count instead. With comic inevitability, it didn't, and so the match went into penalties—from which Uruguay emerged triumphant.

Thankfully they did not prosper. With Suarez banned from the semifinal, the Uruguayans went down by the odd goal in five to the Netherlands, while a single goal alone was sufficient to push Spain past Germany.

It was the Netherlands' third final, the Spaniards' first, and no less than last time out, the scale of the event was a lot more impressive than the match itself—a niggling, nasty little affair, with the Dutch seemingly abandoning all the brilliant hallmarks that had powered their 1970s predecessors to two successive World Cup finals, and relying upon brute strength and spitefulness to pinch and punch them to victory. The fourteen yellow cards that referee Howard Webb flashed as the game went on more than *doubled* the previous record of six in the 1986 final.

Goalless after ninety minutes, the deadlock was finally broken four minutes from the end of extra time, when Iniesta connected with a Fàbregas pass, and volleyed the ball into the net. It was the 145th goal of the tournament—the lowest final tally of all time.

And so another less-than-stellar World Cup rolled into the history books. Thankfuly, 2014 would more than remedy that.

2014—Victory Is the Only Language the Germans Understand (Although They Also Speak German Quite Well)

US preparations for the 2014 event saw the expectedly sticky passage through the qualifiers ultimately enacted with sufficient panache to seriously raise hopes for the main attraction. But the absence of Landon Donovan from coach Jurgen Klinnsman's final squad did much to put a damper on hopes.

Even as he neared the end of his career, Donovan remained a talismanic figure, a veteran of three previous campaigns whose experience, if not his energy, could have proved invaluable. As Bruce Arena said when the news broke, "If there are twenty-three better players than Landon, then we have a chance to win the World Cup."

Instead, Klinnsman opted for youth (and DaMarcus Beasley), although he did have the decency to sound suitably dismayed when his own son Jonathan, a goalkeeper on the US's Under-18 roster, responded to the news by tweeting "HAHAHAHAHAHAH DONOVAN HAHAHAHAA I DIDNT EVEN NOTICE UNTIL MY PHONE NOTIFIED ME" followed by four tearful emoticons and another "HAHA."

The elder Klinnsman rapidly went into damage-limitation mode, reveal-ing that his offspring was a huge Donovan fan, and even "has his jersey in his room." Which must have been reassuring for Donovan. Imagine if the boy had genuinely disliked him.

So, there was the hint of a nasty taste in the mouth even before the 2014 tournament got off to what now felt like its usual shoddy start. Or at least, that's what it looked like, as the Japanese referee shattered the opening game's stalemate between Brazil and a surprisingly resilient Croatia, by gifting the hosts with an utterly spurious penalty (and then disallowing a perfectly good equalizer), to ensure the feel-good factor at least made it through day one.

But a tournament that many outsiders believed had just the one preordained winner (even the draw favored Brazil's unstoppable progress) had more than its fair share of surprises in store.

Attacking play was the order of the day. Goals positively rained in—four in that traditionally dour opening game, four more when Croatia met Cameroon, and again when they played Mexico. Brazil shared five goals with Cameroon, the Netherlands put five past Spain, and once again the defending champions were lined up for an early flight home. France's tie with Switzerland saw seven goals, five of them scored by a magnificently fluid French side; and the World Cup was a record-breaking thirteen games old before the first draw was recorded, between Nigeria and Iran. The total of 136 goals scored during the group phase was, incredibly, only nine fewer than were hit throughout the *entire* 2010 tournament.

Thrilling too was what the pre-tournament writers termed this year's Group of Death: Germany, Ghana, the United States, and Portugal. Of course the two European sides were favorites to advance, and the Germans had no problem doing so. Poor Portugal, though. Crushed 4–0 by Germany in their first game, they were genuinely, and irrefutably, lucky to salvage a 2–2 draw from their game with the US, and genuinely unlucky that their 2–1 victory over Ghana was not enough to see them through.

But the US had triumphed over Ghana by the same score, while keeping their defeat to Germany down to just one goal. It was goal difference, then, that sent Portugal reeling back to Europe, while the US entered the round of sixteen, where their 2–1 defeat to Belgium became the most viewed soccer game in US television history.

Equally tight was Group D, the lineup of Uruguay, England, Italy, and Costa Rica defying all the pundits' attempts to predict who would be heading home with the Central Americans—especially after it became apparent that the Central Americans had no intention of leaving.

They swamped Uruguay by 3–1, beat Italy 1–0, and had so easily qualified for the round of sixteen that they could afford to take their foot off the pedal for the final match against England—a 0–0 draw that condemned England to a shockingly early bath, shared with the equally disappointing Italians.

Disappointing, but unforgettable. For it was against Italy that Uruguayan striker Luis Suarez—he of the Ghanian gamesmanship in 2010—delivered that single moment of madness that ensured this was one World Cup that would never be forgotten.

The calculated handball that sent Ghana home last time around was only the beginning of Suarez's appetite for unseemly headlines. Twice since that time, he had been censured for biting opposition players, once during his time with Ajax Amsterdam in Holland, and once following his transfer to Liverpool. He landed a seven-match suspension for the first snack, and a ten-game ban for his second. He sat out another eight games after racially abusing Manchester United's French defender Patrice Evra.

Seriously. This relatively slender, and very simple, publication proved *almost* as diverting as the tournament itself. Next time around, everyone should buy one.

In the 1920s, that was a lot of money. Today, it would scarcely buy a Premier League toenail.

A dynamite player he may have been, with a penchant for scoring goals as though they were going out of fashion. But his brilliance came with a barrel load of caveats, and on the greatest stage of them all, before probably the biggest television audience of his life, he let slip another one, biting down on Italian Giorgio Chiellini, and then collapsing to the ground, clutching his mouth, as though he'd just taken a shoulder to the jaw, and not vice versa.

Another ban swung into place, as FIFA ruled him out of Uruguay's next nine internationals, while also banning the player from any soccer-related activities for the next four months. Which didn't stop Barcelona from promptly making him the third most expensive player in history, when they bought him from Liverpool just short weeks later. But from Uruguay's point of view, it spelled disaster. Suarez was more than a useful player; he was the best they had, and replacing him was never going to be a matter of simply pulling someone else off the bench. Into the round of sixteen they went, still smarting with indignation, and out of the World Cup they tumbled, 2–0 to a Colombian side that had just introduced the world to its own secret weapon, AS Monaco striker James Rodriguez.

Destined both to pick up the Golden Boot for the tournament, and then join Real Madrid for the next season, Rodriguez scored both of Colombia's goals against Uruguay. Elsewhere at the same stage, Germany and Algeria met in what some commentators hoped would be a delayed grudge match, the North Africans finally afforded an opportunity to avenge themselves for the *Nichtangriffspakt von Gijón*—but wasn't.

Brazil, meanwhile, ran Lady Luck as close to the edge as they ever have, by taking Chile to penalties after a ferocious 1–1 draw; and they called upon her again in the quarterfinals, as they faced Colombia and the lethal Rodriguez.

Sure enough, he scored one against them. But Brazil had already scored twice, and while Rodriguez's penalty should have been the cue for his side to pull themselves back onto an even footing, luck remained on Brazil's side. At least for now. But then Neymar went down injured, and a nation held its breath. For as valuable as Suarez was to Uruguay, Neymar was priceless to Brazil.

Costa Rica bade farewell in the quarterfinals, run ragged by the Netherlands but still not bowing out until the penalty shoot-out ensured it was mathematically impossible for them to advance. Belgium, conquerors of the United States, fell to Argentina, Germany squeaked past France. It was time for the semifinals, and two games that, in any other year, could easily have been the final itself.

Argentina vs. Holland was awful, 120 minutes that felt like three times as long, and wound up with a penalty shoot-out that itself had a grueling inevitability to it, from the moment Vlaar missed the first Dutch kick. But perhaps no game could have lived up to any expectations that day, for twenty-four hours earlier, the world watched in stunned disbelief as Germany took on Brazil in the other semifinal—and put them to the sword.

Five goals up at halftime, the Germans played like an exhibition team. The Brazilians, on the other hand, didn't play at all. People knew, and predicted, they'd miss the injured Neymar. But nobody realized they'd miss him this much.

The records seemed to tumble with every passing minute.

The largest-ever margin of victory in a World Cup semifinal.

Brazil's first home defeat since 1975.

The first time Brazil had conceded five goals since they beat Poland 6–5 in the 1938 World Cup, and almost double their previous heaviest-ever defeat (3–0 to France in 1998). It was the first time they'd let in six since a 6–0 pounding by Uruguay in 1920.

Brazil's once unassailable record of the most goals scored in World Cup competition, a total of 221, was overtaken—the Germans had now scored 223. And even Ronaldo's record as the all-time greatest goal scorer in World Cup history fell to Miroslav Klos.

It was the worst defeat any host nation had ever suffered in World Cup history, more than doubling the previous record. Four German goals scored in six minutes marked the most rapid accumulation ever.

It was the first time occasion upon which a team has conceded five goals in one half of a World Cup semifinal, or seven in the full game. The back page headline of Britain's *Daily Star* newspaper probably summed the match up the best, the single word "Sambaargh," and *still* Brazil's humiliation was not complete. They lost the third-place play-off to the Netherlands, the first time they'd lost two home matches back-to-back since 1940.

Meanwhile, Germany had a record eighth World Cup final to play. And, duly, to win, scoring deep into extra time against an Argentine side that, once again, did just enough to keep themselves in the game, but never seemed interested in actually scoring a goal. In fact, if you could have dispensed with the first ninety, or even 120, minutes of every game they played, and just gone straight into penalties, they would probably have been a lot happier.

Certainly many eyebrows were raised when, at tournament's end, Argentinean striker Lionel Messi was awarded the Golden Ball as player of the tournament. Four goals in the group stages really marked the sum of his contributions, and vocal critics across the globe (including FIFA president Blatter) let it be known how surprised they were that he should take the glory. Messi has since made it fairly apparent that he feels the same way himself.

16

On Top of the World

But It's Not All About FIFA, Is It?

n June 2014, four days before FIFA's World Cup shindig kicked off in São
Paulo, ConIFA's was wrapping up in Sweden, with Countea de Nissa's 5–3
penalties victory over Ellan Vannin.

It had been a hard-fought battle, as tough as the eventual goalless final score
suggests, but a lot more exciting, too. Both sides pushed, both sides scrapped.
No overpaid superstar grandstanding here; no so-called genius sitting out the
bulk of the game, then stirring himself to a moment of match-winning brilliance
just when all looked lost; nobody, in fact, that you've probably ever even heard
of. Beginning with the combatants themselves.

The Countea de Nissa represents the separatist ideals of the County of
Nice in France, one of the original States of Savoy that were founded in the
fourteenth century, but which were controversially annexed by France in 1860.
Ellan Vannin represent the Isle of Man, one of the original six Celtic nations
and an independent Viking kingdom long before it was absorbed into England
in the fourteenth century. And ConIFA is the Confederation of Independent
Football Associations, an umbrella organization for all those people who have
never showed up at the FIFA World Cup, and likely never will.

They hail from across the globe. Zanzibar were forced to pull out of the
ConIFA World Football Cup when the players learned they could not get the nec-
essary visas. But fellow Africans Darfur made it, and so did Abkhazia, Kurdistan,
Nagorno-Karabakh, Tamil Eelam, and the eventual third- and fourth-placed sides
South Ossetia and Arameans Suryoye, all Asian members of the confederation.

From Europe, there came Aquitania and the Occitania, the historic land
that once encompassed southern France, northern Spain, and parts of Italy,
too, and which the Romans knew as the Seven Provinces. Padania, an aspiring
breakaway state in the Po Valley of northern Italy. Sápmi, the home nation of
the Sami people of Lapland and thereabouts.

The French-Canadians of Quebec entered, but then withdrew; and there
were apologies sent by Cilento (in Italy), Franconia (in Bavaria), the island
of Heliogoland, the principality of Monaco, the disputed Turkish enclave of
Northern Cyprus, and the organization's most recent member, the Romani
people. With or without them, however, the ConIFA World Football Cup
amounted to a gathering that proves, once and for all, that not everything in
world soccer is all about FIFA.

They may want you to think it is. There may be times when you even *believe* it is. But it isn't. Soccer existed long before that gaggle of worthy administrators first gathered in a room in Switzerland in 1904, it will exist long after they have vanished, and it exists today beyond, above, and even *in spite of* FIFA.

Welcome to What Author Steve Menary Calls the Lands That FIFA Forgot. Or Overlooked. Or Ignored. Or Didn't Even Know About in the First Place.

We mentioned earlier that there are many corners of the globe where the locals' soccer-playing aspirations are hampered by any number of factors, not least of all the fact that their individual confederation within FIFA has many more members than it will ever have places at the World Cup. There are even more, however, who are not even members of FIFA, and are unlikely ever to become one. Occasionally, one will break from the pack and make the leap. But the others just get on with things, building their own competitions within their own world.

They are not necessarily countries, although some of them are. Others are breakaway provinces and self-governing islands. Want-away territories and distinct linguistic communities. Autonomous regions and unrecognized states. Homeless cultures and landless societies. And when they gather together to play, and the ConIFA contest reaches its apex, the final is the culmination of eight days of soccer fought out between corners of the planet that many people aren't even aware exist; ethnic minorities, geographical flukes, traditional homelands that modern politics insist are simply a part of some larger body—but which, in the eyes of their actual inhabitants, are as separate as any "established" nation.

And why are they not members of FIFA?

How long is a piece of Fergie Time?

There is not, and never has been, any hard and fast ruling to determine who can become a FIFA member and who can't.

It certainly has nothing to do with being a "real" country, or having a seat at the United Nations, which is most people's interpretation of that designation. Seven full-fledged sovereign nations—the Federated States of Micronesia, Kiribati, Nauru, Palau, and Tuvalu in the Asian and Oceania regions, Monaco and the Vatican City in Europe—currently play their soccer outside of FIFA's jurisdiction.

Twenty-two nonsovereign entities, on the other hand, are members, the majority of them located among European holdings in and around the Caribbean: Anguilla, Aruba, Bermuda, British Virgin Islands, Cayman Islands, Curaçao (the former Dutch East Indies, World Cup heroes of the 1930s), Montserrat, Puerto Rico, Turks and Caicos Islands, and the US Virgin Islands. Guam, Hong Kong, Macau, the Faroe Islands, American Samoa, Cook Islands, New Caledonia, Tahiti, and the four countries that comprise the United Kingdom complete the list.

Sometimes, it is politics that get in the way of an application that, had it been filed by a different aspirant, would have sailed through without a hitch.

Until the courts made it difficult to resist any longer, Gibraltar was refused UEFA membership because of pressures exerted by Spain. Tibetan ambitions are undercut by China. Mayotte, a French territory off the coast of Africa, has had its membership blocked by the Comoros Islands, who claim the island for itself; the Falklands, in the south Atlantic, have likewise been historically stymied by Argentina. Kosovo continues to battle against Serbian objections, despite having seceded back in 2008.

Other places are halted by a lack of facilities. And others because, in a world that is largely defined by lines on a map, they don't really exist. Or they do, but only in the eyes of their inhabitants.

Whatever the reasoning, it has been estimated that, worldwide, there are close to six thousand ethnicities and regions that remain unrepresented in "official" soccer-playing circles, and periodically the various organizations that cater to their well-being will draw attention to that fact.

The Island Games and Other Pots

The most firmly established of the competitions catering to these outsiders is the Island Games Association, formed in 1985 to organize a biennial Olympic-style competition played out, as their name suggests, between islands from around the world, regardless of whether or not they have UN, FIFA, or any other form of recognition.

Twenty-seven islands are currently members, ranging from the Isle of Wight, a simple block of chalk moored off the southern English coast, to the full-fledged nation of Iceland; from the Welsh island of Ynys Môn, to the vast icy autonomy of Greenland; from Bermuda to Malta, from the Caymans to the Shetlands, from Prince Edward Isle to the Falklands.

Eighteen different sports are included in the Island Games, with every competitor selecting between twelve and fourteen to compete in each games. Soccer became part of the curriculum in 1989, with the hosting Faroe Islands, on the eve of their debut in UEFA's European Championships, taking the gold medal, Ynys Môn the silver, and the Åland Islands (an autonomous archipelago off the coast of Finland) the bronze.

Since that time, soccer has become one of the most popular attractions within the Island Games, with the roster of gold medalists speaking loudly both for the sheer scope of the games' membership, and for the fact that FIFA membership (enjoyed by several of the competitors) is not necessarily a guarantee of success.

The Faroes retained their title in 1991, as their FIFA status perhaps suggested they should. But the English Channel Island of Jersey (nonmembers) was triumphant in 1993, 1997, and 2009, the Isle of Wight (ditto) in 1995 and 2011, Ynys Môn (likewise) in 1999. Another of the Channel Islands, Guernsey, was victorious in 2001 and 2003, the Scottish Shetland Islands in 2005, Gibraltar in 2007, and Bermuda in 2013. That's three wins for FIFA and ten for the rest. Sweet.

Barcelona's Nou Camp—the spiritual heart of Catalonia's footballing aspirations.

The French FA's shortlived (2008–2012) Coupe de l'Outre-Mer likewise allowed some extraordinarily overlooked soccer outposts of the world (or, in this instance, the former French empire) to match their prowess against the great and the good.

The lineup for the tournament reads like a childhood stamp collection. Mayotte, an island off the coast of Mozambique, who defeated FIFA members Tahiti 3–1 in the opening round of the 2012 tournament. St. Pierre and Miquelon, members of the French FA, but recognized no further than that. French Guiana, Guadeloupe, Martinique, St. Martin, and Reunion, all of whom having continental recognition, but have not yet won FIFA's approval; and, at the top of the heap, Tahiti and New Caledonia, both of whom possess full FIFA membership. A status that has conferred absolutely zero benefit upon them, at least so far as this tournament was concerned.

All three Coupe de l'Outre-Mer finals competed between 2008 and 2012 were played between Reunion and Martinique, all three bronze medals went to Guadeloupe—all nations from within the second sphere, those that have continental affiliation but not full international recognition.

So much, then, for the suggestion that the FIFA World Cup recognizes only the cream of the world's game. Martinique, like the Shetlands, like Kiribati, like the County of Nice, might never actually qualify for the World Cup finals. But their triumphs in other tournaments prove that if soccer-playing ability were the only attribute upon which entry was predicated, they would not disgrace themselves.

Until that time, they will play on wherever they can. And other organizations will spring up to cater to other lands.

Even with the Island Games as a working example, attempts to organize the soccer-playing aspirations of the world's many and varied unaffiliated peoples were slow to take root. December 2003, however, saw the birth of the Nouvelle Fédération-Board, a soccer organization representing the teams of all nations, dependencies, regions, minorities, states, and stateless people that FIFA had chosen to overlook. Eighteen months later, in partnership with the Unrepresented Nations and Peoples Organization, the NF-Board launched the UNPO Cup, a four-team contest scheduled to coincide with UNPO's seventh General Assembly in the Hague, and climaxed by the UNPO Cup final between South Moluccas and Chechnya.

The following year the NF-Board alone inaugurated the VIVA World Cup, a three-nation contest that saw hosts Occitania joined by the gambling paradise of Monaco and the eventual victors, a team representing the northerners of Sápmi. Since that time, the VIVA World Cup has expanded to embrace some fifteen different nations, among them Padania, of northern Italy, Western Sahara, Darfur, Gozo, and the 2012 finalists, Iraqi Kurdistan and Northern Cyprus.

A Nation Without a Country

For perhaps obvious reasons, no records exist concerning the first unofficial nation to take to the soccer fields, although the northern Spanish land of Catalonia was certainly one of the earliest. An eleven representing Catalonia first played in 1904, initially taking on other Spanish club sides but moving into the international arena too. In February 1912, Catalonia played their first match against foreign opposition, losing 7–0 to France in Paris, but winning the return match, that December, by 1–0.

Drawing their squad from throughout the Spanish leagues, but primarily those clubs that fell within Catalonia's own boundaries (the giants of Barcelona included), the Catalans in the late 1910s and into the 1920s competed for the Copa Príncep d'Astúries, a tournament arranged between different Spanish regions, and running out cup winners on five occasions.

Friendly matches pitted them against the likes of Czechoslovakia, Spain, and the visiting Brazil, and while Franco's dictatorship certainly pushed down hard upon Catalan dreams of autonomy, the team itself survived, even playing Spain and, on one occasion, featuring the great Alfredo Di Stéfano within their ranks. More recently, Dutchman Johan Cruyff was Catalonia's coach between 2009 and 2013, while their current squad includes players the caliber of Gerard Pique, Jordi Alba, Cesc Fàbregas, and Victor Sánchez.

The continuing story of the Catalans ranks among the game's most romantic, at the same time as illustrating just how vital a tool soccer can be within the political aspirations of any emergent nation. A national soccer team is more than a sporting institution. It is also an ambassador, or at least an emissary, carrying the state's name far and wide.

In decades gone by, a worldwide stamp album was considered the best geography lesson a youngster could require, every page opening up a new and fascination nation to discovery. Philately has, sadly, declined as a young person's hobby today. International soccer fixtures, on the other hand, have never lost their fascination. That was what French international Mustapha Zitouni was banking on, when he retired from representing France on the official stage in 1958, in favor of playing in the colors of his Algerian homeland. At a time when Algeria itself did not exist as an independent nation.

Indeed, it was Zitouni who formed the team that would travel Europe raising awareness of the Algerian people's struggle to win independence from France. Of course that side never received FIFA recognition. But within eighteen months of the Algerian flag being raised over the newly freed nation for the first time, in July 1962, it was taking its place at FIFA headquarters, too.

The number of nations who have transitioned from FIFA outsiders to full-fledged and paid-up members remains tiny. Just as the number of people who really care about such things is, likewise, tiny. What, they ask, does it matter, whether a pinprick island in the South Pacific has a chance to play in the World Cup qualifiers? Their participation—indeed, their very existence—is not going to affect the final result, so why should it matter?

But it does matter. That is why, whenever another tournament comes along, pitting the unknown against the unloved for ninety minutes of sporting combat, ever-wider swathes of the soccer-watching world pay attention.

For they know, as we know, and as everybody who loves soccer for what it *is* (as opposed to what it can earn) knows, of all the qualities that the game represents, its fortitude, and its power to unify, are by far its greatest.

No power on earth, be it finance nor politics, law nor legislation, war nor disaster, has ever stopped the game in its tracks. Or even come close to doing so.

In 1914, the Great War turned the lamps out over Europe. But the troops played soccer in the trenches. In 1985, a major earthquake shook Mexico to its core. But the nation staged the next year's World Cup regardless. In 2010, another earthquake devastated Haiti. Among the myriad images that came out of the stricken island over the weeks that followed, one of the most arresting was a group of youngsters playing soccer in the rubble. They didn't even have a ball to play with. They had an old empty can.

Soccer survives where everything else is in chaos. Soccer lives where every-thing else feels hopeless. Billionaire oligarchs and self-serving administrators might kid themselves that they control the game, because they happen to hold a few of the purse strings. But soccer itself is not about money; it is not about glory; it is not about having a pair of fluorescent yellow boots and a girlfriend who is 40 percent silicone-gel. And slowly, the world is coming to see that.

Here Come the End-of-the-Book Predictions

No soccer fan knows the future. No soccer fan can take either success or failure, or even middle-of-the-table anonymity for granted. But that does not stop us from trying, albeit from a considerably better-informed perspective than might have been employed fifty years ago.

Back then, after all, the entire world believed that, by the dawn of the twenty-first century, we would all be flying around with personal jet packs, holidaying on distant planets, and pondering the outcome of the Many Worlds Cup, the Planet Earth (represented by a superbreed of genius robots) versus the multi-tentacled slime blobs of Alpha Centauri.

Instead . . .

The immediate future would appear to be firmly in hand. The 2018 World Cup is set to be staged in Russia, the 2022 in Qatar. Unless they aren't. At the time of writing, both decisions are being questioned from what seems an ever-increasing number of political, legal, ethical, and moral directions. Money has always talked when it comes to organizing a World Cup, but this time, for the first time, a lot of people seem to be questioning where it came from, where it went, and what it did.

FIFA will reform, willingly or otherwise. Forget the journalists and investigators who have warned for years that the organization is rotten from within. The headlines speak even louder.

In 2011, FIFA VP Mohamed bin Hammam was banned from soccer for offering bribes. Jack Warner, high up in CONCACAF, resigned while being investigated for bribery; CONCACAF chairman Chuck Blazer stood down amid allegations of corruption; Nigeria's Amos Adamu and Tahiti's Reynald Temarii were suspended after trying to sell World Cup votes; CONMEBOL president Nicolás Leoz resigned for "health and personal" reasons, a week before the publication of a FIFA ethics report that accused him of accepting bribes, and all of this *before* lawyer Michael Garcia finally delivered his own long-awaited report into the organization in September 2014. A report whose contents, FIFA promptly announced, would not be made public.

Another FIFA vice president and (until his death in July 2014) long-time Argentinean FA president Julio Grondona once admitted, "The clubs [who vote for him] know I'm the least bad option," and in August 2014, with the Qatar controversy truly swirling, England hero Gary Lineker snapped, "It makes you feel sick." He told *GQ* magazine, "The whole FIFA thing, the corruption at the top level is nauseating. Sepp Blatter has run it like a dictatorship for so long and he comes out with so much nonsense."

Yes, FIFA will reform.

Soccer songs will continue to be laughed at, and transfer fees will continue to soar. Team jerseys will grow more absurdly festooned with advertising slogans, and the day of the first sponsored tattoo cannot be far away. New colors will be invented to cater to some spoiled superstar's taste in boot design.

The "Financial Fair Play" (FFP) legislation that UEFA began introducing in 2011–2012 in a bid to control the game's out-of-control finances will see a whole new strata of administration develop, in the form of the lawyers and accountants hired exclusively to find ways around the laws.

The vast majority of the managers in charge of the top clubs today will be in charge of different top clubs before the end of the year; and the vast majority of players who kissed their team's badge at the end of last season will be swapping spit with a different one at the start of the next.

There is one looming development, however, that does not invite cynicism or mirth, and that is the continued slow decay of the old, established order. The giants of the game are approaching saturation point. Their growth, for so long dependent upon wholly artificial sustenance, will eventually reach a point of no return. In some countries, the process has already begun. In others, the clubs continue throwing PR at the problem in the hope it will go away. But one day, the money will run out.

As the traditional models die, others will rise to replace them. Those areas of the world that the "established" powers still like to refer to as "emergent" will continue to emerge, and we will certainly see at least one African, Asian, or North American World Cup winner at some point within the lifetime of some of this book's readers.

Nations that were once regarded as makeweights within FIFA's worldwide membership have already become at least passing powers within the game, and others will rise, both from within FIFA's ranks and without, to join them.

None can predict how the map of the world will be reshaped over the next fifty years, but if borders are redrawn with even half as much fervor as they have been in the past half-century, we should prepare to greet some remarkable new powerhouses.

The upsurge of interest in grassroots soccer, too, is set to change the face of the wider game.

Supporters, priced out of following their Superliga sides, are already shifting their spectating attention to smaller teams, local teams. Across Europe, non-league attendances, while still minuscule compared with the big boys, are on the rise; and, throughout all the continents, different peoples, different societies, are flexing sporting muscles they once never knew existed, and playing soccer because *they want to.*

And that's all it comes down to, really. The rich will continue getting richer, and the day is surely coming when the top teams in the world will have grown so fat and bloated, and absurdly self-important, that they won't even bother with playing soccer anymore. They'll just form a fat-cat coterie of mutual self-indulgence, and publish their bank balances in lieu of results.

Results that the rest of us will completely ignore, because we were priced out of their stratosphere long, long before, around the same time that we finally realized the shareholders were more important than the players, the club, or the history, and set out to find or form new teams. New heroes. New worlds. New cups.

Kurdistan's Aras Mustafa Mohammed in full flight against Tamil Eelam at the ConIFA World Football Cup on June 3, 2014.

And the words with which we began this book are also those with which we can also end it, for they remain as true here as they were back then.

For as long as man has had feet to kick with, he has kicked things. And that is really all we know about the future of soccer.

All we know, and all we need to know.

Football. Bloody hell.

Appendix 1
World Soccer Timeline

1857: In England, the world's oldest soccer club, Sheffield FC, is formed.

1860: Lausanne Football and Cricket Club forms in Switzerland. Turn- und Sportverein München von 1860, the sports club that fathered the German soccer club TSV Munich 1860, is launched, although soccer does not become a part of its activities until the 1890s.

1862: In England, the world's oldest surviving Football League club, Notts County, is founded.

1863: The English Football Association (FA) is founded.

1865: Buenos Aires FC forms in Argentina.

1867: The Youdan Cup, played between a dozen clubs in the English city of Sheffield, is the world's first soccer tournament. Named for a local theater owner, Thomas Youdan, it is won by Hallam FC. In Scotland, the country's oldest surviving club, Queen's Park, is founded.

1870: The first-ever game is played between English and Scottish representative sides.

1871: The English Football Association launches the FA Cup. The first tournament will be won (in 1872) by Wanderers. Wanderers will also chalk up victories in 1875, 1876, and 1877.

1872: The first official game between England and Scotland ends 0–0. Scottish side Queen's Park become their homeland's first side ever to appear in an official competition, when they enter the English FA Cup. The first Welsh club, Wrexham FC, forms.

1873: The Scottish Football Association is formed, alongside the inaugural Scottish FA Cup. The first winners are Queen's Park, who beat Clydesdale 2–0.

1875: The wooden crossbar replaces a length of tape strung between the goal posts. Soccer arrives in Germany courtesy of a touring Oxford University side.

1876: Scotland meet Wales for the first time and win 4–0. Canada's first soccer club is formed by the Carlton Cricket Club.

1877: Vale of Leven break Queen's Park's stranglehold on the Scottish FA Cup, by beating Glasgow Rangers 3–2 in the final.

1878: Wrexham win the first-ever Welsh Cup, defeating Druids 1–0. They will in turn lose the following year's final to Newtown White Stars before Druids win three successive finals (1880–1882).

1883: England, Scotland, Wales and Ireland launch the British Home Championship. The first tournament is won by Scotland.

1885: Professionalism is legalized by the English FA. Canada beat the United States 1–0 in the first international played outside Europe. In Scotland, Arbroath beat Bon Accord 36–0 in a Scottish FA Cup game.

1886: England's Blackburn Rovers complete the first-ever hat trick (three successive wins) of FA Cup victories. The US win their first international game, 3–2 vs. Canada in Newark, NJ. Scorers are Gray, Swarbuck, and McGurck.

1887: In Germany, Hamburger SV, and in Argentina, Gimnasia y Esgrima de La Plata, become their country's first clubs. In England, Preston's 26–0 victory over Hyde FC remains an FA Cup record; Preston also hold the record for the second highest victory in the Cup, 18–0 vs. Reading in 1893.

1888: The English Football League is formed with twelve members. (A second division follows in 1892.) The inaugural season (1888–1889) is won by Preston North End, who also win the FA Cup to claim the first-ever "double." A Football World Championship is staged between Scotland's Renton FC and England's West Bromwich Albion. It is won by the Scots, 4–1.

1889: Football Associations form in Denmark and the Netherlands.

1890: The Scottish Football League is formed. Goal nets are used for the first time.

1891: Penalty kicks and linesmen are introduced. Shrewsbury Town become the first English side to win the Welsh Cup.

1892: Glasgow Celtic win their first Scottish Cup. The following season they win their first Scottish League championship, and in 1894, cross-city rivals Glasgow Rangers win their first Cup. Henceforth, the two teams will dominate Scottish football.

1895: Sunderland become the first side ever to win the English League Championship three times. The Chilean FA is established.

1897: Aston Villa become the second side to claim the English League and Cup double.

1900: The Deutscher Fussball Bund is founded in Leipzig.

1901: The FA Cup is won by a non-league side, Tottenham Hotspur.

1902: Bankrupt and struggling, Newton Heath change their name to Manchester United. At Rangers' Ibrox Stadium in Glasgow, twenty-five supporters die when a stand collapses at the Scotland vs. England game.

1903: While Bury beat Derby County 6–0 to establish the record score for an English FA Cup final, Wrexham's 8–0 victory over Aberaman Athletic is the highest score ever recorded in a Welsh Cup final. Wrexham also hold the second and third highest margins (7–0, 6–0). VfB Leipzig win the first official German championship.

1904: FIFA forms with an initial membership of Belgium, Denmark, France, Germany, Netherlands, Sweden, Switzerland, and, pending the creation of a Spanish FA, Madrid.

1905: The first £1,000 transfer, Alf Common from Sunderland to Middlesbrough. Austria, Italy, and England join FIFA. Berwick Rangers, an English club founded some twenty years previous, joins the Scottish FA, becoming one of just a handful of clubs to compete in a national league different from what they might ordinarily have become members of—in Berwick's case, because of geographical concerns.

1906: Hungary and the Czechs join FIFA.

1908: Soccer debuts at the Olympics. The first victors are a combined United Kingdom team, 2–0 vs. Denmark. The Charity Shield, played between the winners of the English Football League and the Southern League, is inaugurated. Manchester United are the first winners. Finland and Norway join FIFA.

1910: Wales, Scotland, and Luxembourg join FIFA. Ireland join the following year. Argentina win the first Copa America; Uruguay and Chile finish second and third.

1911: Wrexham win their third successive Welsh Cup final.

1912: Cardiff City win their first Welsh Cup. Great Britain win the second Olympic soccer tournament, 4–2 vs. Denmark. Argentina, Chile, Canada, and Russia join FIFA.

1913: The United States join FIFA. The Lamar Hunt US Open Cup is launched as the National Challenge Cup; Brooklyn Field Club beat neighbors Brooklyn Celtic 2–1 in the final. Swansea Town win their first Welsh Cup.

1916: Despite World War One raging through much of Europe, the US national side undertakes a Scandinavian tour. Uruguay win the inaugural Copa America; Argentina and Brazil finish second and third.

1917: Uruguay retain the Copa America; with Argentina and Brazil again finishing second and third.

1918: World War One is still raging as Olympique de Pantin defeat FC Lyon 3–0 to claim the first-ever Coupe de France.

1919: The Inter-Allied Games celebrate the end of the war. The newly constituted nation of Yugoslavia joins FIFA. Brazil win the Copa America, defeating Uruguay 1–0 in a final play-off.

1920: England's Football League expands to include a Third Division, drawn from the Southern League. A northern division will follow in 1921. All four home nations (England, Scotland, Wales, and Ireland) withdraw from FIFA. At the Olympics, Belgium take gold with a 2–0 win vs. Czechoslovakia. Uruguay win the Copa America. In Chile, the formation of Club Deportivo Palestinos by Palestinian immigrants to Santiago establishes what remains the Middle Eastern state's most durable representative on the worldwide soccer scene. Two-time Chilean league champions Palestinos are formed; today the club plays in the traditional Palestinian national colors of red, back, and green; while club veterans include Palestinian international legend Roberto Bishara.

1921: Paraguay and Costa Rica join FIFA. Argentina take the Copa America.

1922: Brazil beat Paraguay 3–1 to claim the Copa America.

1923: The English FA Cup final is played at Wembley for the first time, and Bolton Wanderers beat West Ham United 2–0. Brazil, Uruguay, Egypt, Latvia, Lithuania, Poland, Estonia, Portugal, Turkey and the newly formed Republic of Ireland join FIFA. Uruguay win the first of two successive Copa Americas.

1924: The US conducts a short European tour prior to joining the Olympic Games in Paris. A 3–2 victory over Poland is followed by a 1–3 defeat vs. Ireland. The team advances to the second round of the Olympic competition. Uruguay ultimately take the gold, beating Switzerland 3–0. Bulgaria and Peru join FIFA; the Home Countries rejoin but will depart again in 1928.

1925: The US racks up its highest international score for almost seventy years, 6–1 vs. Canada; and repeats the feat the following year. (The current record, set in 2008, is 8–0 vs. Barbados.) Thailand becomes the fortieth member of FIFA. Argentina take the Copa America.

1926: Ecuador and Bolivia join FIFA. The Copa America goes to Uruguay.

1927: Welsh team Cardiff City become the first (and thus far only) non-English side to win the English FA Cup. Greece join FIFA. Argentina wins the first of two successive Copa Americas, this year and in 1929 (there is no competition in 1928).

1928: English sides Arsenal and Chelsea become the first teams to play in numbered shirts. At Wembley, Scotland crush England 5–1. In the Olympic Games in Amsterdam, Argentina rout the US 11–1 in the first round; the Argies ultimately take silver, behind Uruguay. The Philippines join FIFA, but Canada joins the Home Countries in leaving the organization.

1929: Playing outside the United Kingdom for the first time, Scotland defeats Norway 7–3. Surinam, Mexico, Japan, Iceland, and Palestine join FIFA.

1930: Thirteen nations enter the first-ever World Cup, in Uruguay: Romania (FIFA's newest member), Peru, Paraguay, Belgium, Argentina, the United States (who topped their group with a 100 percent record), Argentina, Chile, France, Mexico, Yugoslavia, Brazil, Bolivia, and the hosts. The top team from each of the four groups advances to the semifinals, where both the US and Yugoslavia succumb by 6–1 to the finalists Argentina and Uruguay respectively. Uruguay win the final 4–2.

1931: Aston Villa score an English record 129 goals in a season, yet finish runners-up to Arsenal. China join FIFA.

1932: Albania and the Netherland Antilles (Dutch East Indies) join FIFA.

1933: Haiti, Guatemala, and Cuba join FIFA.

1934: Uruguay opt not to participate in the second World Cup in Italy, to protest the lack of European participation in the 1930 event. Sixteen nations take part in a straight knockout tournament: Italy, who beat the US 7–1; Spain; Brazil; Austria; France; Hungary; Egypt; Czehsolsovakia; Romania; Switzerland; Netherlands; Germany; Belgium; Sweden; and Argentina. That first round of games sees all four non-Europeans eliminated, and the final is won by Italy, 2–1 vs. Czechoslovakia. Germany's 3–2 win over Austria gives them third place.

1935: Arsenal win their third successive English League championship. Lebanon joins FIFA. The Copa America resumes following a six-year hiatus and is won by Uruguay.

1936: At the Olympic Games in Berlin, the US are dispatched 1–0 in the first round by eventual gold medalists Italy. Austria take the silver. Colombia joins FIFA.

1937: The Scottish Cup final between Celtic and Aberdeen attracts 147,365 fans, a world record for a national cup final. A European international record is set when 149,415 attend Scotland vs. England at the same ground, Hampden Park in Glasgow. Syria joins FIFA. Argentina defeat Brazil 2–0 for the Copa America.

1938: Italy retain the World Cup, beating Hungary 4–2 in the final, after defeating the host nation, France, in the quarterfinals. Brazil beat Sweden for third place. Other competing nations in the straight knockout include Norway, Belgium, Poland, Czechoslovakia, Netherlands, the Dutch East Indies, Switzerland, Germany, Austria, Cuba, and Romania. El Salvador and Panama join FIFA.

1939: Peru win the Copa America for the first time. The outbreak of the Second World War sees league and cup soccer postponed across much of Europe.

1941: Argentina win the Copa America.

1942: Uruguay win the Copa America.

1943: With French soccer continuing on despite the Nazi occupation, Olympique de Marseille set a new record with a 4–0 victory over Girondins de Bordeaux in the replayed Coupe de France final. Remarkably, the following season sees the score equalled by Équipe fédérale Nancy-Lorraine, one of several Vichy-run "federal teams" launched during the wartime years. They defeated another federal team, representing Reims-Champagne.

1945: The end of World War Two sees soccer resume across Europe and elsewhere. Iran becomes FIFA's latest member; Canada and the Home Countries will rejoin in 1946. However, the war takes its toll on membership. Lithuania, Latvia, and Estonia, all now absorbed into the Soviet Union, lose their membership as the USSR takes Russia's place in the organization. Germany and Japan are temporarily outlawed—their membership will be restored in 1950. Argentina win the first of three successive Copa America titles.

1946: At Burnden Park, Bolton, thirty-three fans die when a wall collapses, and the crowd panics, during Bolton's English League match with Stoke City. Until 1971, it is the worst British sporting disaster ever. The table football game Subbuteo is launched by designer Peter Adolph; Subbuteo will grow to become the world's favorite soccer substitute, with its own leagues, trophies, and championships expertly aping the real thing.

1947: Glasgow Rangers win Scotland's first treble of the league championship, league cup, and FA Cup. The inaugural North American Championships see the US defeated 5–0 by Mexico and 5–2 by the hosts Cuba.

1948: A record Football League attendance is set by the crowd of 83,260 at Manchester United vs. Arsenal. At the Olympics, the US are thrashed 9–0 by Italy—Sweden are gold medalists, Yugoslavia silver. A European tour immediately after sees the US lose 11–0 to Norway and 5–0 to Northern Ireland. Afghanistan,

India, Pakistan, South Korea, South Vietnam, Sudan, Cyprus, and New Zealand become FIFA members.

1949: At the North American Championship in Mexico, the US are defeated 6–0 and 6–2 in two games with the hosts, but hold Cuba to a 1–1 draw before defeating them 5–2. Brazil win the Copa America, 7–0 vs. Paraguay. Colombian soccer turns professional but internecine fighting escalates and the nation is suspended from FIFA—at which point, the league's organizers, DIMAYOR, launch an aggressive campaign, titled "El Dorado," to attract the best players from around the world, and pay them some of the highest salaries in the game. Included are Alfredo Di Stéfano, Charlie Mitten of Manchester United, and Nestor Rossi of River Plate.

1950: The first World Cup since the Second World War is staged in Brazil, where the hosts are defeated in the final match by Uruguay. The war years have taken their toll on the notion of sport being above politics. Despite being readmitted to FIFA this year, neither Germany nor Japan were permitted to compete in the World Cup, while the Soviet bloc withdrew prior to the qualifying rounds.

Elsewhere, regional politics see Ecuador, Peru, Argentina, Burma, Indonesia, the Philippines, Belgium, and Austria all pull out during the qualification phase, while Scotland and Turkey withdraw after qualification. Nevertheless, a strong field sees Mexico, Switzerland, Yugoslavia, Chile, Spain, India, Paraguay, Sweden, Bolivia, France, Uruguay, England, and the US join the hosts and the defending champions Italy in Brazil, for a competition best remembered for the United States' shock 1–0 defeat of England.

Ceylon (modern Sri Lanka), Nicaragua, and Iraq join FIFA.

1951: Honduras join FIFA.

1952: Warming up for the Helsinki Olympics, the US are defeated 6–0 by Scotland in a friendly, before bowing out of the games, 8–0 vs. Italy. Hungary win gold, Yugoslavia silver. Indonesia, Laos, Singapore, South Africa, and Venezuela join FIFA.

1953: Hungary beat England 6–3, the first foreign side ever to win at Wembley. However, visiting New York, England avenge themselves for 1950 by defeating the US 6–3. Cambodia and Ethiopia join FIFA. Paraguay win the Copa America, defeating Brazil 3–2.

1954: Hungary are red-hot favorites to win the 1954 World Cup in Switzerland, only to lose 3–2 in the final to a West German team they had already defeated 8–3 in the group stage. Austria finish third, beating Uruguay, and also share a World Cup record for the most goals scored in a game, 7–5 vs. Switzerland. Other qualifiers include Yugoslavia, France, Mexico, Turkey, South Korea, Czechoslovakia, Scotland, England, Switzerland, Italy, and Belgium. Hong Kong and Taiwan join FIFA; Colombia is readmitted.

1955: Argentina win the Copa America. The Inter-Cities Fairs Cup is launched to promote European trade fairs, and was open only to cities holding such events. Unlike the other major European tournaments, it is not organized by UEFA. The first tournament, staged over a four-year period (1955–1958), is won by a Barcelona XI who defeat a representative London side 8–2 on aggregate.

1956: The inaugural European Cup, played between the champions of every UEFA member nation, is won by Real Madrid. At the Olympics, the US are eliminated at the qualifying stage by silver medalists Yugoslavia, 9–1. The USSR take gold. Malaysia and Morocco join FIFA. Uruguay win the Copa America.

1957: Argentina win the Copa America. Real Madrid win their second consecutive European Cup. As qualifying for the 1958 World Cup gets underway, the US are soundly defeated both home and away by Mexico (0–6, 2–7) and Canada (1–5, 2–3). Burma joins FIFA.

1958: Eight Manchester United players die in the Munich Air Disaster, while returning home from a European Cup game in Belgrade. A hastily rebuilt side still reach the FA Cup final. Real Madrid win the third European Cup, while Brazil win the World Cup, defeating hosts Sweden 5–2 in a final remembered for signaling the emergence on the world stage of the teenage Pelé. France beat West Germany 6–3 for third place. China resigns from FIFA, but new members North Korea, Ghana, Jordan, and the Dominican Republic lift membership to eighty-six.

1959: Uruguay win the last Copa America for four years. Billy Wright becomes the first player to represent England one hundred times. Real Madrid and France's Stade de Reims repeat the first European Cup final and, once again, the Spaniards win. In Los Angeles, the US are defeated 8–1 by England; at the Pan American Games in Chicago, however, victories over Haiti (7–2) Cuba (5–0), and Mexico (4–2) are topped by a 5–3 win over an admittedly second-string Brazil. Defeats to Costa Rica (2–3) and Argentina (1–4) bracket the triumph. Malta, Saudi Arabia, Nigeria, and Uganda join FIFA.

1960: Beating Eintracht Frankfurt 7–3 in the European Cup final gives Real Madrid their fifth successive victory. The second Inter-Cities Fairs Cup final is won again by Barcelona, who defeated Birmingham 4–1 on aggregate. Yugoslavia are the Olympic gold medalists, Denmark take silver. New FIFA members include the Ivory Coast, Kenya, Somalia, Tunisia, and Puerto Rico.

1961: Tottenham Hotspur win the English League/FA Cup double, the first side to do so in the twentieth century. SL Benfica (Portugal) break Real Madrid's monopoly on European Cup wins with a 3–2 defeat of Barcelona. Fiorentina (Italy) win the inaugural European Cup Winners' Cup. Roma win the Inter-Cities Fairs Cup. Guinea joins FIFA.

1962: SL Benfica confirm their preeminence by retaining the European Cup following a 5–3 defeat of Real Madrid. Atlético Madrid beat Fiorentina to win the European Cup Winners' Cup. Fellow Spaniards Valencia win the Inter-Cities Fairs Cup, beating Barcelona. In Chile, the seventh World Cup is won by Brazil, 3–1 vs. Czechoslovakia. The hosts beat Yugoslavia for third place, while also earning notoriety for their part in the so-called Battle of Santiago, an especially ill-tempered first-round match with Italy. The referee of the game, Englishman Ken Aston, is remembered as the subsequent inventor of yellow and red cards. In Germany, the Bundesliga is founded.

As independence sweeps the former British and French empires, FIFA membership leaps from ninety-six to 109. By the end of the decade, 136 nations will be members; by the end of the 1980s, 165.

Mexico's Guadalajara defeat Communicaciones (Guatemala) 6–0 on aggregate to claim the first CONCACAF Champions League title.

1963: Bolivia win the Copa America. Tottenham Hotspur become the first English side to win a European trophy, when they triumph in the Cup Winners' Cup. AC Milan are Italy's first European Cup winners. Valencia retain the Inter-Cities Fairs Cup. Brazil make amends for their last Pan-American debacle by thrashing the US 10–0 at the Games. Chile (2–10), Argentina (1–8), and Paraguay (0–2) also defeat the US.

Haitien of Haiti are CONCACAF Champions Cup winners. In Scotland, referee Jim Finney sets an example that a lot of other referees could learn from (but won't). Fifteen minutes from the end of a fractious Scotland vs. Austria game, with the visitors 4–1 down and hacking anything that moved, Finney sends off an Austrian player for spitting—"and while you're at it," he declares, "the rest of you can go off too." The entire team is dismissed and the match is abandoned.

1964: The first of two successive European Cup wins for Internazionale (Inter) Milan. Sporting Lisbon win the European Cup Winners' Cup. Valencia reach their third consecutive Inter-Cities Fairs Cup but lose to Real Zaragoza in the second successive all-Spanish final. England visit New York and win 10–0 against the hosts. Hungary are Olympic gold medalists, Czechoslovakia silver. The world's worst soccer disaster takes place in Lima, Peru—318 supporters killed during rioting precipitated by a disallowed goal during Peru's Olympics qualifier against Argentina. FC Koln take the first-ever Bundesliga title.

1965: West Ham United win the European Cup Winners' Cup. Ferencvárosi of Hungary win the Inter-Cities Fairs Cup. SV Werder Bremen win the Bundesliga.

1966: Real Madrid claim their sixth European Cup. Borussia Dortmund win the European Cup Winners' Cup. Another all-Spanish final sees Barcelona win the Inter-Cities Fairs Cup. In England, the host nation wins the eighth World Cup, beating Germany 4–2 with the help of one still-disputed goal (the third). The tournament overall is the best-attended in World Cup history and will remain so until the 1994 finals in the US. Portugal defeat the Soviet Union for third place.

1967: Alianza (El Salvador) defeat Jong Colombia of the Netherlands Antilles 4–2 on aggregate to take the third CONCACAF Champions League title. Uruguay win the last Copa America until the tournament is reborn in 1975. Manchester United collect their seventh English League Championship and their last for twenty-six years. Scotland defeat the World Cup–holding England 3–2, while Glasgow Celtic become the first British club to win the European Cup, 2–1 vs. Inter Milan. FC Bayern München become the second successive German side to win the European Cup Winners' Cup. Dinamo Zagreb win the Inter-Cities Fairs Cup. Welsh Cup winners in 1964 and 1965, Cardiff City now embark on a string of five successive Cup victories (1967–1971); to be followed by further victories in 1973, 1974, and 1976, and losing appearances in 1972, 1975, and 1977, a sequence of thirteen successive finals.

1968: Manchester United become the first English side to win the European Cup, 4–1 vs. SL Benfica of Portugal. Leeds United win the Inter-Cities Fairs Cup. Inter Milan win the European Cup Winners' Cup. Hungary are Olympic gold medalists, Bulgaria silver. In Kaysari, Turkey, forty-four are killed and six hundred injured during rioting between supporters of the home side and visitors Sivasspor. In Buenos Aires, Argentina, more than seventy are killed in a crush at the Boca vs. River Plate match. Mexico's Toluca take the CONCACAF Champions Cup.

1969: Cruz Azul of Mexico claim the third of three successive CONCACAF Champions Cup titles. Newcastle United win the newly renamed European (formerly the Inter-Cities) Fairs Cup. AC Milan beat the rising Ajax Amsterdam in the European Cup final. Slovan Bratislava win the European Cup Winners' Cup. Qualifying for the 1970 World Cup is marred by war breaking out between El Salvador and Honduras following an ill-tempered match in the qualifying rounds.

1970: The English FA Cup final goes to a replay for the first time since moving to Wembley, Chelsea eventually triumphing over Leeds United. Saint-Étienne set a new record score in the Coupe de France final, defeating Nantes 5-0. Feyenoord defeat 1967 winners Glasgow Celtic in the European Cup final. Arsenal win the European Fairs Cup. In Mexico, in a match often described as the greatest-ever World Cup final, Brazil beat Italy 4–1 to win their third World Cup. Defending champions England are defeated at the quarterfinal stage by West Germany, throwing away a 2–0 lead to lose 3–2. The victorious Brazilians win the existing Jules Rimet Trophy outright.

1971: Arsenal win the English League and Cup double. In Glasgow, sixty-six are killed when a stairway gives way during a game between Rangers and Celtic at Ibrox Park. Ajax Amsterdam win the first of three successive European Cup finals. Chelsea become the second successive English side to win the European Cup Winners' Cup; Leeds United win the final European Fairs Cup.

1972: Club Deportivo Olimpia of Honduras defeat Surinam's wonderfully named SV Robinhood 2–0 in the CONCACAF Champioins League final. Glasgow Rangers win the European Cup Winners' Cup. UEFA introduce a new tournament to replace the European Fairs Cup, the UEFA Cup. Tottenham Hotspur are the first winers, following an all-English final vs. Wolverhampton Wanderers. At the Olympics in Munich, the US are defeated 0–3 by Malaysia before holding Morocco 0–0. Poland are gold medalists, Hungary silver.

1973: Inter Milan win the European Cup Winners' Cup. New Zealand win the inaugural Oceania Nations Cup. Transvaal become the first-ever Surinamese winners of the CONCACAF Champions Cup, but will lose the following year's final to Guatemala's Municipal.

1974: East Germany's FC Magdeburg win the European Cup Winners' Cup; West Germany's FC Bayern München win the first of three successive European Cup finals; while West Germany also becomes only the fourth team ever to win the World Cup on home soil, defeating the Netherlands to collect a new trophy, the FIFA World Cup Trophy. Poland—who eliminated England in the qualifying stages—defeat Brazil for third place.

1975: The Scottish League creates the Premier Division from the old First Division. Dynamo Kyiv of the Soviet Union win the European Cup Winners' Cup. The reborn Copa America is won by Peru, 4–1 vs. Colombia. Transvaal reach their third successive CONCACAF Champions Cup final, but fall 3–1 on aggregate to Atlético Español of Mexico.

1976: Salvador's Aguilla defeat SV Robinhood by an aggregate 8–2 in the CONCACAF Champions Cup final. In England, rock star Eton John becomes chairman of Watford FC. Belgium's Anderlecht win the European Cup Winners' Cup; they will reclaim the title in 1978. At the Olympics, East Germany take gold, Poland silver.

1977: SV Robinhood's second successive COINCACAF Champions League final ends in defeat once again, 1–0 to America of Mexico. English side Liverpool win the first of two successive European Cups. Hamburger SV win the European Cup Winners' Cup. China's historic first visit to the US sees the two teams play out a 1–1 tie, before the US win two further games 1–0 and 2–1.

1978: The eleventh World Cup is hosted, and won, by Argentina, defeating the Netherlands. The tournament is largely overshadowed by the military junta that had taken control of the country two years earlier, and for whom the World Cup is regarded as an opportunity to show a happier face to the watching world than the news headlines normally allowed.

Administrative problems see the cancellation of the final round of games in the CONCACAF Champions Cup. Three victors are therefore recorded:

Universidad de Guadalajara, Communicaciones, and Defence Force of Trinidad and Tobago.

1979: Now staged every four years, the Copa America is won by Paraguay, 3–1 vs. Chile. England's Nottingham Forest, managed by Brian Clough, win the first of two successive European Cups. Barcelona win the European Cup Winners' Cup. A visiting Soviet Union side beat the US 1–3 and 1–4 at matches played in Seattle and San Francisco. Club Deportivo Futbolistas Associados Santanecos of Salvador defeat Jong Colombia in the CONCACAF Champions Cup, 8–2 on aggregate.

1980: Valencia retain Spain's grip on the European Cup Winners' Cup. Australia win the Oceania Nations Cup. At the Olympics, Czechoslovakia take gold, East Germany silver. Mexico's UNAM win the CONCACAF Champions Cup.

1981: The English FA launches a new system awarding three points for a League win instead of two. Ties continue to earn one point. Liverpool win their third European Cup. Dinamo Tbilisi win the European Cup Winners' Cup. Transvaal defeat Atlético Marte in the CONCACAF Champions Cup final.

1982: The CONCACAF Champions Cup goes to UNAM, conquerors of Robinhood. Aston Villa's European Cup victory confirms them as the sixth successive English side to win the continent's premier trophy. Barcelona reclaim the European Cup Winners' Cup. Spain host the World Cup, expanded from sixteen to twenty-four nations, and won by Italy, 3–1 vs. West Germany, who arrive in the final having won the tournament's first-ever penalty shootout in the semifinal vs. France. In Moscow, at least sixty-six supporters (unofficial reports state up to 340) are killed in a crush during the UEFA Cup match between Spartak Moscow and HFC Haarlem, after an injury time goal sees departing crowds rush back into the ground. Incredibly, the Soviet system is able to cover up the disaster so well that even the Haarlem players only learn about it seven years later. Colombia, scheduled hosts of the 1986 World Cup, withdraw; the games will take place in Mexico instead.

1983: Robinhood lose their second successive CONCACAF Champions Cup final, 6–1 on aggregate to Atlante of Mexico. Uruguay win the first of two successive Copa Americas, defeating Brazil 3–1 in the final. In 1987, they will defeat Chile 1–0. Alex Ferguson wins his first European trophy, managing Aberdeen to a 2–1 win over Real Madrid in the Cup Winners' Cup final. Hamburger SV win the European Cup.

1984: Liverpool become the first British club to win a treble of league championship, league cup, and European Cup. Juventus win the European Cup Winners' Cup. At the Olympics, France become the first non–Eastern Bloc nation to take the soccer gold since 1948; Brazil the first to take silver since 1960. Violette of Haiti win the CONCACAF Champions Cup.

1985: The Bradford fire disaster kills fifty-six spectators at the final league game of the season, Bradford City vs. Lincoln City; in Belgium, the Heysel Stadium disaster sees thirty-six Juventus fans killed before the European Cup final, when rioting Liverpool supporters cause a wall to collapse. Incredibly, the game is played in the aftermath; Juventus win 1–0. Everton win the European Cup Winners' Cup. At the CONCACAF Champions Cup, Defence Force defeat Olimpia 2–1 on aggregate to take the title.

1986: Costa Rican side Alajuelense defeat Transvaal 5–1 to claim their first ever CONCACAF Champions Cup title. With English clubs banned from European competition as a consequence of Heysel, Steau Bucharest of Romania become eastern Europe's first European Cup winners; Dynamo Kyiv win the European Cup Winners' Cup. The 1986 World Cup is won by Argentina, 3–2 vs. West Germany, and dominated by the mercurial Diego Maradona and his so-called "Hand of God"—the blatant handball with which he scored against England in the quarter inal.

1987: Porto (Portugal) win the European Cup; Ajax win the European Cup Winners' Cup. In England, Wimbledon win the FA Cup just a decade after joining the Football League. America (Mexico) defeat Defence Force 3–1 on aggregate to take the CONCACAF Champions Cup.

1988: Olimpia defeat the returning Defence Force 4–0 on aggregate to lift the CONCACAF Champions Cup. Dutch side PSV Eindhoven win the European Cup; Belgian underdogs Mechelin surprise Ajax to win the European Cup Winners' Cup. The USSR take gold at the Olympics, impressively defeating Brazil 2–1. In Kathmandu, Nepal, a violent hailstorm breaks out during an international match against Bangladesh. Supporters seeking shelter from the ice pellets stampede for exits that are found to be locked; ninety-three die in the ensuing panic.

1989: UNAM open a sequence of four successive Mexican victories in the CONCACAF Champions Cup, defeating Cuba's FC Pinar del Rio 4–2 on aggregate. Brazil win the Copa America, this year competed for in a league format. In England, the Hillsborough Stadium disaster sees ninety-four Liverpool supporters killed during the FA Cup semifinal game with Nottingham Forest. Twenty-five years later, an inquiry (ongoing at the time of writing) into the disaster makes it apparent that it was the police, and not the supporters, who both precipitated and worsened the situation. AC Milan win the first of two successive European Cups; Barcelona win the European Cup Winners' Cup.

1990: In the CONCACAF Champions Cup, America defeat last year's beaten finalists FC Pinar del Rio 8–2 on aggregate to take the title. Sampdoria win the European Cup Winners' Cup. Staged in Italy, the World Cup is won by West Germany, competing in their final international tournament before a unified German team is created; they defeat Argentina 1–0 in a final that is as drab as the remainder of the tournament—the meager goals-per-game average of 2.21 has yet to be surpassed.

1991: With the Copa America now being staged every two years, Argentina win the retained league format. The United States win the inaugural Gold Cup, defeating Honduras on penalties. English clubs are readmitted to European competition for the first time since the Heysel disaster, and FA Cup holders Manchester United win the European Cup Winners' Cup. Yugoslavia's Red Star Belgrade win the European Cup. In Orkney, South Africa, forty-two supporters die in a stampede at a Kaizer Chiefs vs. Orlando Pirates friendly. Puebla make it three Mexican titles in a row as they defeat Trinidad and Tobago's Police FC by 4–2 on aggregate to take the CONCACAF Champions Cup. The collapse of the Communist regimes of Eastern Europe, and the dismantling of the Soviet Union, sees FIFA membership swell from 165 in 1990 to 191 by 1994.

1992: The English Premier League is formed from the old Football League Division One. The inaugural championship will be won by Manchester United, who now launch into two decades of unparalleled domination of the English game. In France, eighteen fans are killed at the Stade Armand Césari in Bastia, Corsica, ahead of the Coupe de France semifinal between SC Bastia and Olympique de Marseille. Over 2,300 are injured. The remainder of the tournament is cancelled.

Barcelona bring the European Cup back to Spain (who also take gold at the Olympics). Werder Bremen win the European Cup Winners' Cup. America rack up Mexico's fourth successive CONCACAF Champions Cup with a 1–0 win over Alajuelense. The inaugural King Fahd Cup (aka the Confederations Winners Cup and the Intercontinental Championship) is contested in Saudi Arabia. Argentina beat the hosts 3–1 in the final; the United States defeat the Ivory Coast 5–2 to claim third place.

1993: Mexico claim the second Gold Cup, crushing the US 4–0 in the final. Argentina retain the Copa America, 2–1 vs. surprise package Mexico. Marseille become France's first European Cup winners, as the tournament is renamed the Champions League. Parma win the European Cup Winners' Cup. The CONCACAF Champions Cup is won by Costa Rica's Saprissa. Countrymen Cartagines will take the 1994 title; Saprissa will win in 1995, to complete a trilogy of back-to- back Costa Rican triumphs.

1994: AC Milan win the Champions League; Arsenal win the European Cup Winners' Cup. The fifteenth World Cup is staged in the United States, a controversial choice due to the game's lack of traction in the country at the time, but a successful one; the total attendance for the tournament remains the highest in World Cup history. Brazil win the tournament, defeating Italy in the first final ever to be decided on penalties. The United States themselves are eliminated by Brazil in the round of sixteen.

1995: For the first time, the Copa America goes to penalties, with Uruguay triumphant over Brazil. Ajax Amsterdam defeat the defending champions Inter in the Champions League final. Real Zaragoza win the European Cup Winners' Cup. Wrexham win the Welsh Cup for a record twenty-third time (they were beaten finalists on an equally record-breaking twenty-two occasions.) The second King Fahd Cup, staged again in Saudi, sees Denmark defeat Argentina 2–0. Mexico finish third, defeating Nigeria on penalties.

1996: Mexico claim their second Gold Cup, 2–0 vs. Brazil. DC United beat the LA Galaxy 3–2 to win the first MLS Cup. They will repeat the feat in 1997 (2–1 vs. Colorado Rapid) and 1999 (2–0 vs. the Galaxy) and finish second (to Chicago Fire) in between times. Australia win the Oceania Nations Cup. The World Cup's worst-ever disaster takes place in Guatemala, during a qualifying match between the home nation and Costa Rica—at least eighty die during a stampede before the game had even started. Cruz Azul win the first of two successive CONCACAF Champions Cup titles. Having already won their first league/FA Cup double in 1994, Manchester United become the first English side to win a second. Arsenal will become the second in 1998, only for Manchester United to win a third in 1999. Arsenal collect their third in 2002. Juventus defeat the defending champions Ajax in the Champions League final; Paris St. Germain win the European Cup Winners' Cup. The Welsh Cup undergoes a major change as UEFA decree that only teams playing in the Welsh League can compete, thus bidding farewell to Cardiff City (twenty-two wins), Swansea City (ten wins), Wrexham, and more. Llansantffraid are the first Cup winners under the new system. Nigeria win gold at the Olympics, ushering in a new age of newspaper headlines insisting that African soccer is on the verge of dominating the world.

1997: Brazil defeat Bolivia 3–1 to win the Copa America. Borussia Dortmund win the European Champions League. Barcelona beat defending champions PSG to win the European Cup Winners' Cup. The King Fahd Cup comes under FIFA's aegis and is renamed the Confederations Cup, to be competed for by eight teams representing the six continental confederations, the World Cup holders, and the host nation. Brazil defeat Australia 6–0 in the final; the Czech Republic, invited to participate after European Champions Germany decline, take third, defeating Uruguay 1–0. Cruz Azul defeat the LA Galaxy to win their second successive CONCACAF Champions Cup title.

1998: Mexico's third Gold Cup victory is assured with a 1–0 final victory over the US. The Scottish Premier League is formed. Real Madrid win the European Champions League; Chelsea win the penultimate European Cup Winners' Cup. Expanded to thirty-two nations, the World Cup is won by the host nation France, who defeat a strangely misfiring Brazil 3–0 in one of the most one-sided finals ever. New Zealand win the Oceania Nations Cup. DC United become the United States' first-ever victors in the CONCACAF Champions Cup.

1999: Brazil retain the Copa America, 3–0 vs. Uruguay. Manchester United add the Champions League to their domestic double. Lazio win the last-ever European Cup Winners' Cup. The host nation Mexico win the Confederations Cup, defeating Brazil—invited to participate after World Cup holders France decline their invitation. The United States defeat Saudi for third place. Mexican club side Necaxa win the CONCACAF Champions Cup.

2000: Canada win their first-ever Gold Cup, defeating Colombia 2–0. Kansas City Wizards win the fifth MLS Cup, defeating Chicago Fire 1–0. FIFA initiate the Club World Championship (now the Club World Cup), featuring the winners of the six continental championships. In the first final ever to be contested by two teams from the same country, Spain's Real Madrid beat Valencia to win the European Champions League. Barry Town win the first of three successive Welsh Cups. Australia win the Oceania Nations Cup. Cameroon's Olympic gold apparently confirms the high hopes of 1996. Bhutan becomes FIFA's 204th member. The LA Galaxy become the United States's second winners in the CONCACAF Champions Cup.

2001: Colombia win the Copa America, defeating Mexico 1–0. San José Earthquakes win their first MLS Cup, defeating the Galaxy 2–1. FC Bayern München win the European Champions League. Australia defeat American Samoa 31–0, a record win in international football. In Johannesburg, South Africa, forty-three die in a crowd stampede during a match between Kaizer Chiefs and Orlando Pirates—the same sides that played during the Orkney disaster ten years earlier. In Accra, Ghana, 126 die following a match between Hearts of Oak and Asante Kotoko, apparently when departing supporters found the exit gates locked and the police, misreading the situation as a riot, started lobbing tear gas into the tightly packed crowds. A dress rehearsal for the World Cup, the Confederations Cup is staged in South Korea and Japan. France emerge champions, defeating Japan. Australia beat Brazil for third place.

2002: The United States win only their second-ever Gold Cup, defeating Costa Rica 2–0. Three-time losing finalists the LA Galaxy finally get their hands on the MLS Cup, beating the New England Revolution 1–0. Real Madrid win the European Champions League for a record ninth time. The World Cup, staged in Japan and South Korea, is won by Brazil, 2–0 vs. Germany. South Korea finish fourth, behind Turkey, just two of many surprises littering the tournament—including the collapse of France, who finish last in their group; and the emergence of the United States as a major footballing power, as they progress to the quarterfinal. Pachuca of Mexico win the CONCACAF Champions Cup.

2003: Mexico win the Gold Cup, defeating Brazil 1–0 in a replay of the 1996 final. The Earthquakes whip the Fire 4–2 to take their second MLS Cup. Russian billionaire Roman Abramovich takes over Chelsea, ushering a new era of financial dominance into the English game. In the first-ever all-Italian final, AC Milan win the European Champions League. Host nation France retain the Confederations Cup, defeating Cameroon in the final. Turkey beat Colombia 2–1 to take third place. Mexican side Toluca win the CONCACAF Champions Cup.

2004: The Copa America is again decided on penalties, as Brazil pip Argentina. DC United win their fourth MLS Cup, beating the Wizards 3–2. Porto, under the management of José Mourinho, win the European Champions League. Argentina take gold at the Olympics, Paraguay silver. Alajuelense win the CONCACAF Champions Cup. In the German Cup, Kaiserslautern's Carsten Jancker sets a new scoring record with six second-half goals in his side's 15–0 win over fourth-tier Schonberg.

2005: Penalties again decide the Gold Cup, the US triumphing over Panama. The Galaxy take their second MLS Cup, 1–0 vs. the Revolution. Liverpool win the Champions League (for the fifth time) on penalties, having fought back from 3–0 down to draw 3–3 with AC Milan. The game is routinely regarded as the greatest Champions League final ever. Brazil win the Confederations Cup, defeating Argentina 4–1. Hosts Germany are third, with a 4–3 victory over Mexico. This is the final biennial tournament; future Confederations Cups will take place once every four years, beginning in 2009. Saprissa win the CONCACAF Champions Cup.

2006: For the first time, the MLS Cup goes to penalties, with Houston Dynamo winning out over the Revolution. Barcelona beat Arsenal to win the European Champions League. The World Cup, staged in Germany, is won by Italy, on penalties over France. The hosts finish third, while a record twenty-eight red cards and 345 yellow cards are handed out throughout the tournament —with four reds and sixteen yellows being brandished during just one match, a round of sixteen encounter between Portugal and the Netherlands. Mexico's America win the CONCACAF Champions Cup.

2007: The United States finally best Mexico in a Gold Cup final, running out 2–1 victors. The Copa America final repeats the 2003 meeting of Brazil and Argentina, with the Brazilians victorious 3–0. The Revolution reach their third MLS Cup final in a row, and are beaten for the third time, too, 2–1 in a replay of last year's encounter with the Dynamo. Inter Milan win the European Champions League for the seventh time. Pachuca win the first of two successive CONCACAF Champions Cup titles.

2008: The Columbus Crew win the MLS Cup, 3–1 vs. the New York Red Bulls. In the first all-English final, Manchester United beat Chelsea on penalties to win the European Champions League for the third time. Bangor City win the first of three successive Welsh Cups. Argentina retain gold at the Olympics, Nigeria take silver.

2009: Mexico avenge themselves for their 2007 Gold Cup final defeat, thrashing the US by a record 5–0. Real Salt Lake beat the Galaxy on penalties to take the MLS Cup. Barcelona beat Manchester United to win the European Champions League. In the Confederations Cup in South Africa, Brazil defeat the United States 3–2 to claim victory. Spain beat the hosts 3–2 for third place. The CONCACAF Champions Cup is rebranded as the Champions *League*, and climaxes with an all-Mexican final, CF Atlante defeating Cruz Azul 2–0 on aggregate.

2010: The MLS Cup goes to the Rapids for the first time, after a 2–1 victory over FC Dallas. Inter Milan win the European Champions League. The World Cup is staged in South Africa, the first African nation to host the event, and won by Spain, who defeat the Netherlands 1–0 in the final. For the first time ever, the host nation is eliminated in the first round, as are both the previous tournament's finalists. The second all-Mexican final in CONCACAF Champions League sees Pachuca defeating last year's beaten finalists Cruz Azul on away goals. Remarkably, both beaten semifinalists were also Mexican, Toluca and UNAM.

2011: Mexico's Monterrey defeat Real Salt Lake 3–2 on aggregate in the final of CONCACAF Champions League. The third successive US vs. Mexico Gold Cup final ends with the second successive Mexican triumph, 4–2. Uruguay defeat Paraguay 3–0 to win the Copa America. The Galaxy beat the Dynamo 1–0 to take the MLS Cup. In a repeat of the 2009 final, Barcelona beat Manchester United to win the European Champions League for the fourth time. South Sudan becomes the 209th member of FIFA.

2012: In a rerun of last season's decider, the Galaxy successfully defend their MLS Cup, beating the Dynamo 3–1. Financial misadministration sees Glasgow Rangers liquidated. A new club rises and begins life in the Scottish Third Division. Chelsea win the European Champions League. Wigan Athletic win the English FA Cup in the same season as they are relegated from the Premier League. FC Bayern München embark on what will become a German record fifty-three Bundesliga games without defeat (until April 2014). Egyptian player Ahmed Hassan makes a record 184th appearance for the national side. Mexico take gold at the Olympics, defeating Brazil, while Mexican club Monterrey win their second successive CONCACAF Champions League, defeating Club Santos Laguna 3–2 in the tournament's third one-nation final in four years. Incredibly, the same teams will compete next season's final as well, with Monterrey running out 4–2 victors. In Egypt on February 1, seventy-nine fans lose their lives during fighting at a game between Al Masry and Al-Ahly.

2013: The United States defeat Panama 1–0 to take the Gold Cup. Sporting Kansas City defeat Real Salt Lake on penalties to win the MLS Cup. The most successful manager in British soccer history, Sir Alex Ferguson, retires as manager of Manchester United. His successor, David Moyes, formerly managed Everton. In the first all-German final, FC Bayern München beat Borussia Dortmund to win the European Champions League for the fifth time. The first-ever woman is elected to the FIFA executive committee, Lydia Nsekera from Burundi. Brazil claim their third successive Confederations Cup, defeating Spain 3–0. Italy are third after a penalties victory over Uruguay. The CONCACAF Champions League ends with yet another all-Mexican final, as Cruz Azul defeat Toluca on away goals. Both beaten semifinalists were US sides, the Sounders and the Galaxy. New York City FC and Orlando City are announced as the MLS's twentieth and twenty-first franchises.

2014: Barcelona miss out on the Champions League semifinal for the first time in seven seasons, while defending champions FC Bayern München are dismissed at the semifinal stage by eventual winners Real Madrid. The Indian Super League launches with eight franchise cities competing the first season, based in Bengaluru, Delhi, Goa, Guwahati, Kochi, Kolkata, Mumbai, and Pune. Germany win the World Cup, defeating Argentina in the final, having already demolished hosts and favorites Brazil 7–1 in the semifinal. Louis van Gaal, manager of third-place Holland, takes over as manager of Manchester United immediately after the tournament. Western Sydney Wanderers become the first Australian side to win the Asian Champions League. Two games into Algeria's 2014–2015, all soccer is suspended indefinitely after JS Kabylie's Cameroonian player, Albert Ebosse, is struck and killed by an object thrown from the crowd. South African soccer goes into mourning after Orlando Pirates goalkeeper Senzo Meyiwa, captain of the national side, is killed in an apparent robbery at this home in October. In Morocco, Real Madrid defeat San Lorenzo of Argentina 2-0 to take the FIFA Club World Cup.

Appendix 2
Selected Glossary

Soccer terminology is a homogenous creature, loaning and borrowing words from language to language. The following concentrates on terms most common to the English language, in all its variants.

agent—Short for "a gentleman," as befits the universal honesty, honor, and most of all recognition of, and adherence to, the legal and moral prerogatives that are involved when acting as a player's business representative. Ha-ha-ha.

aggregate score—Applied in those competitions where two teams play each other twice, at home and away, with the winner determined by the combined score over both games, or "legs."

assist—The American language's premier contribution to the terminology of the game. An assist is accomplished by delivering the ball to the player who ultimately scores the goal. Prior to its arrival, this act was generally referred to as "making the goal."

away goals—In those competitions where teams advance to the next round after playing one another twice (usually home and away), away goals are counted as double to determine a winner when the aggregate score (qv) remains equal. It's not a perfect solution, but it's better than the old system of tossing a coin.

backpass rule—The 1992 amendment to the game's laws, forbidding goalkeepers from using their hands to collect a back pass from a teammate.

ball boy—Those children who hang round the side of the field, hastening to collect any ball that has strayed out of play, and hand it back to a player.

banter—A recent addition to the lexicon, exceeding its dictionary definition by becoming the standard soccer player's justification for absolutely any off-color comment. "Yes, I called the referee a swivel-eyed loon, but it was just banter."

bastard in black—A term of non-endearment historically deployed against the referee, rendered archaic by the rule change that allowed them to wear a multitude of other colors instead.

Beautiful Game, the—Whoever came up with this term to describe soccer (Pelé, author H. E. Bates, and English commentator Stuart Hall have all been credited with it), one hopes they are collecting royalties. Particularly as it is sometimes very difficult to understand what they meant by it.

bosman, do a . . .—Named for the Belgian Marc Bosman, who instituted a major change in the rules surrounding transfers by initiating the legal action that, in the view of the European Union in 1995, permitted players to move to a new club for free once their contract had expired.

bung, take a . . .—To accept an unofficial, and generally secret personal payment as part of an otherwise legal transaction, such as a transfer fee.

buying the title—Accusation thrown at clubs who, after spending large amounts of money on players, actually win something with them. However, this term only applies to opposition sides. Your own team never "buys the title." It "strengthens the squad."

bye—Process by which a club is allowed free passage through one (or more) rounds of a knockout tournament.

cap—Figurative (but sometimes literal) award made to players on every occasion that they represent their country in an international.

clean sheet—See "shut out."

cup tie—A single game in a cup competition. See "draw."

derby—A term applied to a game between two teams sharing a rivalry either in local terms or, in more recent times, success. But also a once-leading English club, and a horse-racing term too.

dive—The ability to earn a sizable portion of your salary either by feigning death or, equally dramatically, the sudden loss of one leg (or, at least, one's balance) in an attempt to win an advantage from the "bastard in black" (qv). An appallingly dishonest stunt when performed by an opposition player, it often becomes an act of startling skill and finesse when undertaken by your own team's star striker.

down to ten [men]—The fate of a side following the dismissal (see "red card") of a player.

draw—In English, a match where both sides end with the same number of goals. A tie, as Americans might put it. However, a "Cup Draw" refers to the process of pairing sides together in a cup tournament, with the resultant match also referred to a "Cup Tie," regardless of whether it actually was tied. Or drawn.

early doors—Term popularized by English manager Ron Atkinson for tactics employed during the opening phase of a match. "They parked the bus early doors."

eleven—Also XI; a full side of players on the field.

explaining the offside rule to your girlfriend—Complicated courting ritual involving two salt-and-pepper pots, the ketchup bottle, and the vinegar.

extra time—Thirty minutes added onto the regulation ninety to try to break a deadlock that would otherwise require a replay to determine the winner. If deadlock remains, the game then goes to "penalties" (qv).

fergie time—A popular media term for stoppage time awarded to Manchester United during Sir Alex Ferguson's tenure as manager.

four four two—Literally, four defenders, four midfielders, and two strikers; one of the most common of modern team formations as the teams take their places prior to a kickoff. Other popular formations include 4-3-3 and 2-3-2-3, but antique purists continue to pine for the days of 2-3-5.

fourth official—Someone who wanders up and down the side of the field, allegedly "assisting" the referee in making decisions. Television cameras do much the same job, but their evidence remains inadmissable.

game—A single encounter between two teams, or the wider sport. See "Beautiful Game, the."

goalkeeper—The man who keeps goal. Also known as the goalie, the keeper, the last man, the custodian, and more.

goal line technology—An electronic device that lets the match officials know when a goal is actually scored, on those not-so-rare occasions when four and sometimes even five of them managed to look the other way at the crucial moment.

golden goal—A seemingly discredited means of determining a winner in a drawn game, without taking it to penalties. Essentially, the players continue to play until one of them scores, at which point the match is over. Which is great if somebody scores . . .

handbags—Term applied to those moments when two or more opposing players go mano to mano, as though preparing to batter one another senseless, but without actually doing so. From the more general expression "handbags at dawn."

hat yrick—In 1858, cricketer H. H. Stephenson bowled out three opposing players from three successive bowls. His teammates purchased him a hat to celebrate the achievement, since when the term "hat trick" has become the standard term for any soccer player scoring three goals in a single game. See also "Perfect Hat Trick."

hit us on the counter—A term favored by sour (and usually defeated) managers to explain how the opposition, having spent most of the game "parking the bus," were then able to snatch a goal against the run of play.

injury time—Stoppage time; the period added on at the end of each forty-five-minute half to compensate for any stoppages during the game, and which is occasionally distorted into Fergie Time.

international—Game played between two sides each representing a different nation.

journeyman—A player who spends his entire career shifting between numerous clubs.

jumpers for goalposts—A term alluding to the misty-eyed recollection of soccer in those halcyon days before money, tattoos, unusual haircuts, and multihued boots sucked the innocence out of it. If no jumpers (or jackets) are available, cowpats, trees, and small children may also be employed.

kissing the badge—A display of unequivocal loyalty and love evinced by a star player, normally enacted shortly before he ups and moves to another, more successful, team.

leg—Beyond the obvious body part, a "leg" is the term defining one or other of the two games played in a competition that pits teams against one another both at home and away, i.e., first leg, second leg.

long ball—Also known as Kick and Rush and Route One, a style of play that involves getting the ball into the opponent's goal area as swiftly as possible. Which would seem a very effective way of playing, and usually proves thus. Opposing managers, however, disdain it because it isn't as pretty as fannying around passing it to one another in the hope of boring the opposition to death.

lost the dressing room—A term applied to a team manager who has lost the respect or support of, or even control over, his players.

magic sponge—Until the advent of sundry modern medical aids, the Magic Sponge was indeed a sponge, whose apparently unremarkable appearance masked its magical ability to rejuvenate the most appallingly injured player simply by being applied to the sore bits.

man on—An archaic term uttered a player wishing to indicate he is available for a pass. Most frequently deployed by British-born players hoping to demonstrate their superior tactical knowledge over non-British teammates. "The New York Cosmos were okay, but I shouted 'man on,' and that Pelé bloke didn't even look up."

managerial merry-go-round—Descriptive of the seemingly never-ending spectacle of managers being hired and fired in short succession by one team after another, all of whom are fated to repeat the process ad infinitum.

match—Interchangeable with "game."

normal time—Ninety minutes, regulation.

nutmeg—To cheekily poke the ball through the legs of an opposition player.

the odd goal in [three/five/seven]—To win or lose by a single goal (1–2, 2–3, 3–4, 11–12, etc.)

offside trap—Exploiting the offside rule to your own advantage, usually by having your entire team run in the opposite direction to the ball moments before an opposing player touches it.

offside trap (2)—Exploiting the offside rule to your own advantage by telling your girlfriend she clearly understands it, and that now you should go do something else.

onion bag—A term for the goal inexplicably favored by ESPN commentator Tommy Smith.

parking the bus—A term favored by sour (and usually defeated) managers to explain how the opposition prevented their team from scoring. See also "hit us on the counter."

penalty—A shot on goal taken from the penalty spot, following an infringement within the larger box around the goal. In the US, a "spot kick."

penalties—A series of shots on goal taken from the penalty spot following a deadlocked ninety minutes and extra time, the effect of which is to transform a tightly balanced battle between two titans of the game into an absolutely random lottery.

perfect hat trick—The art of scoring three goals in a single match, one with each foot and one with the head.

pitch—The field.

red card—Literally, a piece of card that is red, raised to an offending player to let him know he is being dismissed from the field of play. See also "yellow card."

referee's assistant—The two people who run up and down the sidelines, raising flags when they spot an infraction. Previously known as "linesmen," which actually makes more sense.

replay—The process by which a drawn game is played again in order that an outright winner might be determined.

scratch—Withdraw from a scheduled game, granting the other team a walkover.

selling a dummy—Two players conspiring to confuse an opposition player, by making him think one player has (or is about to receive) the ball when really, it's the other.

shut out—To prevent the opposition from scoring.

shut up shop—See "parking the bus."

squeaky bum time—Term popularized by Sir Alex Ferguson that neatly encapsulates those last few weeks of the season when all honors are still up for grabs.

stoppage time—See "injury time."

strengthen the squad—See "buying the title."

tapping up—The art of making an unofficial (and illegal) approach to another team's player or manager, with a view to persuading them to exchange loyalties at some point in the near future.

tie—In the US, a tie tends to mean a game that ends with honors and scores even (see "Draw"). In England, it is often also applied to a single game between two teams, particularly in a cup competition. See "cup tie."

tier—A division within a single league.

transfer window—Those dates in the calendar during which teams are permitted to buy and sell players, usually confined to the off-season months, and a shorter midseason period.

twelfth man—A loud and vociferous support.

walkover—Form of victory achieved when the scheduled opponents scratch.

yellow card—Cousin of the red card, raised to indicate that a player has committed an infraction worthy of censure, but not demanding dismissal. Two yellow cards in a single game do, however, equal one red, and off the offender trots.

Bibliography

Adolph, Mark. *Growing Up with Subbuteo: My Dad Invented the World's Greatest Football Game.* Cheltenham, UK: SportsBooks Ltd., 2006.

Agnew, Paddy. *Forzia Italia: A Journey in Search of Italy and Its Football.* London: Ebury Press, 2006.

Brown, Paul. *The Official Guide to the Unofficial Football World Championships, an Alternative Soccer History.* Blaydon-on-Tyne, UK: Tonto Press, 2006.

Burns, Jimmy. La Roja: *How Soccer Conquered Spain and How Spanish Soccer Conquered the World.* New York: Nation Books, 2012.

Campomar, Andreas. *Golazo!: The Beautiful Game from the Aztecs to the World Cup.* New York: Riverhead Books, 2014.

Connelly, Charlie. *Stamping Grounds: Liechtenstein's Quest for the World Cup.* New York: Little Brown, 2002.

Douglas, Geoffrey. *The Game of their Lives: the Untold Story of the World Cup's Biggest Upset.* New York: Perennial Currents, 1996.

Ferguson, Alex. *My Autobiography.* London: Hodder & Stoughton, 2013.

Foot, John. *Winning at All Costs: A Scandalous History of Italian Soccer.* New York: Nation Books, 2007.

Goldblatt, David. *The Ball is Round: A Global History of Soccer.* New York: Riverhead Books, 2006.

Green, Geoffrey. *The Official History of the FA Cup.* London: Heinemann, 1960.

Hesse-Lichtenberger, Ulrich. *Tor!: The Story of German Football.* London: WSC Books, 2003.

Hornby, Nick. *Fever Pitch.* New York: Riverhead, 1998.

Ibrahimović, Zlatan, *I Am Zlatan: My Story On and Off the Field.* New York: Random House, 2014.

Inglis, Simon (Ed). *The Best of Charles Buchan's Football Monthly.* Swindon, UK: English Heritage, 2006.

Inglis, Simon. *League Football and the Men Who Made It.* London: Willow Books, 1988.

Jennings, Andrew. *Foul!: The Secret World of FIFA: Bribes, Vote Rigging, and Ticket Scandals,* London: HarperSport, 2006.

Kuper, Simon and Szymanski, Stefan. *Soccernomics: Why England Loses, Why Spain, Germany, and Brazil Win, and Why the US, Japan, Australia—and Even Iraq—Are Destined to Become the Kings of the World's Most Popular Sport.* New York: Nation Books, 2009.

Kuper, Simon. *Soccer Men: Profiles of the Rogues, Geniuses, and Neurotics Who Dominate the World's Most Popular Sport.* New York: Nation Books, 2011.

Lowe, Sid. *Fear and Loathing in La Liga: Barcelona, Real Madrid, and the World's Greatest Sports Rivalry.* New York: Nation Books, 2014.

Lyons, Andy and Ronan, Barney (eds). *When Saturday Comes: The Half Decent Football Book.* London: Penguin Books, 2005.

Maximus, Lucius. *How Malaysia Never Reached the World Cup: Harimau Malay's 40-Year Chronicle of Failure.* Malaysia: Fixi Mono, 2014.

McGinnis, Joe. *The Miracle of Castel di Sangro: A Tale of Passion and Folly in the Heart of Italy.* New York: Broadway Books, 2009.

Menary, Steve. *Outcasts! The Lands That FIFA Forgot.* Studley, UK: Know the Score, 2007.

Montague, James. *Thirty One Nil: On the Road with Football's Outsiders: A World Cup Odyssey.* London: Bloomsbury, 2014.

Motson, John. *Motson's FA Cup Odyssey: The World's Greatest Knockout Competition.* London: Robeson Books, 2005.

Newsham, Gavin. *Once in a Lifetime: The Incredible Story of the New York Cosmos.* New York: Grove Press, 2006.

Peace, David, *The Damned Utd.* Brooklyn: Melville House, 2014.

Riches, Adam. *Football's Comic Book Heroes.* Edinburgh: Mainstream Publishing, 2009.

Rippon, Anton. *Gas Masks for Goalposts: Football in Britain During the Second World War.* Stroud, UK: The History Press, 2007.

Seddon, Peter. *The World Cup's Strangest Moments.* London: Portico, 2010.

Tatarsky, Daniel. *Flick to Kick: An Illustrated History of Subbuteo.* London: Orion, 2005.

Thompson, Dave. *Those We Have Loved: Volumes One/Two*, Hendon, UK, 1987/1988.

Thompson, Ian. *Summer of '67: Flower Power, Race Riots, Vietnam and the Greatest Soccer Final Played on American Soil.* Lexington, KY: CreateSpace, 2014.

Tossell, David. *Playing for Uncle Sam, the Brits Story of the North American Soccer League.* Edinburgh: Mainstream Publishing, 2003.

Wahl, Grant. *The Beckham Experiment: How the World's Most Famous Athlete Tried to Conquer America,* New York: Crown, 2009.

Wangerin, David. *Soccer in a Football World.* Philadelphia: Temple University Press, 2006.

Ward, Colin. *The Bootsy Egan Letters.* Edinburgh: Mainstream Sport, 1998.

Wilson, Jonathan. *Behind the Curtain: Travels in Eastern European Football,* London: Orion Books, 2006.

Wilson, Jonathan. *Inverting the Pyramid: The History of Soccer Tactics.* New York: Orion, 2009.

Index

THE FAQ SERIES

Soccer FAQ
796.334 THOMP   31057012136084

Thompson, Dave.
WEST GA REGIONAL LIBRARY SYS